IN NEAR
RUINS

IN NEAR RUINS

Cultural Theory at the End of the Century

Nicholas B. Dirks, Editor

UNIVERSITY OF MINNESOTA PRESS
Minneapolis
London

Every effort was made to obtain permission to reproduce the illustrations in this book. If any proper acknowledgment has not been made, we encourage copyright holders to notify us.

The University of Minnesota Press gratefully acknowledges permission to reprint the following. An earlier version of chapter 3 was published as "Looking for the 'Real' Nigga: Social Scientists Construct the Ghetto," in *Yo' Mama's Disfunktional! Fighting the Culture Wars in Urban America,* by Robin D. G. Kelley, published by Beacon Press, copyright 1997 by Robin D. G. Kelley, reprinted by permission of the author. Parts of chapter 5 are adapted from *Discourses of the Vanishing: Modernity, Phantasm, Japan,* by Marilyn Ivy, copyright 1995 by the University of Chicago Press, reprinted by permission of the publisher. Parts of chapter 6 are adapted from *On the Subject of "Java,"* by John Pemberton, copyright 1994 by Cornell University, used by permission of the publisher, Cornell University Press. "Aunt Helen," from *Collected Poems, 1909–1962,* by T. S. Eliot, appears in chapter 7 and is used by permission of Faber and Faber, Ltd., and Harcourt Brace & Company. Chapter 8 is reprinted from *Feminist Studies* 21, no. 2 (summer 1995): 379–404, by permission of the publisher, Feminist Studies, Inc., c/o Department of Women's Studies, University of Maryland, College Park, Maryland 20742.

Published by the University of Minnesota Press
111 Third Avenue South, Suite 290
Minneapolis, MN 55401-2520
http://www.upress.umn.edu

Library of Congress Cataloging-in-Publication Data

In near ruins : cultural theory at the end of the century / Nicholas
   B. Dirks, editor.
       p.   cm.
   Includes bibliographical references and index.
   ISBN 0-8166-3122-0 (hc : alk. paper). — ISBN 0-8166-3123-9 (pb :
alk. paper)
   1. Culture.   I. Dirks, Nicholas B., 1950–   .
HM101.I539   1998
306—dc21   98-27833

Printed in the United States of America on acid-free paper

Contents

Preface

Nicholas B. Dirks

Some years ago I was asked to convene an interdisciplinary conference at the University of Michigan around the question of culture: Why was the word *culture* used so frequently, so provocatively, and for so many different purposes. The conference itself was part of a triptych, addressing the resurgence of interest around three key terms in the human sciences: *history, power,* and *culture.*[1] When the original idea for this set of conferences was formulated in the late 1980s, we were preoccupied by disciplinary questions; how it was that words like *history, power,* and *culture* circulated well beyond their originary disciplinary locations without creating significant disciplinary confusions or realignment. Through seminars and workshops we confronted the real force of disciplinarity, the ways in which disciplinary languages, positions, and preoccupations shaped debate. Much of this was enhanced by the institutional context of a major research university, committed as it is to professionalization and the attendant reproduction of disciplinary identity/difference. We were utopian in spirit, and persisted against all odds in our belief that we could transform ourselves and our professional practices by detaching some core theoretical and methodological concerns from their disciplinary genealogies and moving into new spaces of argument and debate. Needless to say, the disciplines are still very much intact. However, much has changed in the intervening years, though not always in the directions many of our interlocutors desired, and obviously not because of the signal importance of our discussions, which were conducted in the much larger contexts of transformation that have shaped and reshaped academic practices in the United States and beyond. Certainly the rise in the prestige and influence of literary studies in wider debates about culture (and social theory more generally) has been reflected in the changing constituency of the Michigan discussion, as in the general movement toward the humanities on the part of swing disciplines such as history and anthropology. But we would like at the very least to think that the growing rapprochement between disciplines such as history and anthropology and the acceptance within certain quarters of those disciplines that critical theoretical questions of the sort raised in the essays of this volume are fundamental have had something to do with the kinds of discussions and programmatic initiatives that have taken place here in Ann Arbor over the last decade.

All three conferences were productive, sometimes explosive, expressing poignantly the ferment and the tensions of the times. In the first conference we learned that academics from a wide variety of disciplines were invoking history as the new panacea, despite wildly variant ideas of history, few of which would in any case be recognized or accepted by card-carrying historians. In the second conference we were told that power was everywhere, as elemental force, fundamental relation, and ultimate explainer, and yet discussions about power tended to dissolve into the familiar debates about the ideal and the real, the sublime and the ridiculous, the place of politics inside the academy, and the limits of theory. In the third conference we unintentionally learned that the politics of representation and culture began in the very forms of representation and publicity used to announce the conference itself, with impassioned protest against the ironic depiction of a Benetton advertisement providing the enframing energy and controversy of the academic event.

When I formulated the position paper for the third conference, I began with the premise that culture was leaking out of anthropology and high literary studies, leading to the curious collision of used ideas and new programs: from historical studies of popular culture to the new sociology of culture, from anthropological claims about cultural systems to exploding genres of film and media study, from the academy in general to new forms of cultural politics around ethnic, racial, and sexual identities. But as time went on, the term *culture* was used to name so many issues and predicaments, from what was then still a new field of "cultural studies" to new movements and theoretical convergences within and across disciplines or fields such as history, sociology, communications, gay and lesbian studies, media studies, and critical theory (not to mention such areas as identity politics, the advertising industry, and the changing art world, among so many other things), that it became difficult to know how to contain the original conference idea. Viewed in the purely disciplinary terms that had enclosed its origins, a conference on culture no longer seemed either manageable or interesting.

The papers that I assembled for the conference, which provided the basis for the volume that has now emerged out of it, do in fact reflect some of the original disciplinary intent. The authors collected here come from a representative mix of disciplines — three from history, four from anthropology, three from literary criticism, and one from a department of communications — and write with varying degrees of engagement in the wider fields of cultural studies, gender studies, and critical theory. But unlike those of previous conferences, these papers contain little explicit discussion of disciplinarity. Instead, they present a set of allied but different approaches to problems in cultural analysis that work to demonstrate, rather than explicitly advocate, an engaged, interdisciplinary, political, theoretically self-aware position on the state of culture. They also reflect the particular mix of historical, anthropological, and literary study that came to dominate certain discussions at Michigan and that might be seen as the ground for a new kind of historically and critically based cultural studies, one that seeks engagement not just with the contemporary West but with cultural forms and movements across the globe.

In my introductory essay, I attempt to excavate the terrain for any discussion of cultural theory in the waning years of the twentieth century. I take my text from the recent novel *The English Patient,* by Michael Ondaatje, which won the Booker Prize well before becoming the basis for the Academy Award–winning motion picture. I had long been aware of the power of Ondaatje's prose: his extraordinary evocations of exile, winter, and loss in *In the Skin of the Lion,* his lush memoir and account of return to Sri Lanka in *Running in the Family.* As soon as I began *The English Patient* I realized that Ondaatje was telling his own story of seduction and betrayal through the story of a man burned black beyond recognition in the last moments of World War II, at about the time Ondaatje was born. In those days it was still possible to believe that the universal values of the Enlightenment, combined with the transcendent aspirations of romanticism, were as yet undeterred by the tragic trajectories of modern history. And yet the war not only acquainted Europe with the horror at the heart of its own darkness in the Nazi holocaust, it also revealed the inequalities and limits that were fundamental to Europe's own sense of itself and the world. Europe and America readily accepted the justice of dropping the new lethal weapons of a post-atomic age on Asia, at the same time that Europe itself had to realize that the war was not just about Europe. When Britain declared war without consulting its newly elected government in India, the Congress government resigned and committed itself to working for immediate independence, disregarding the war, deliberately trespassing the boundaries between nationalist resistance and treason; indeed, the last straw for British imperial rule in India was the Red Fort trial, where lawyers such as Jawaharlal Nehru defended Indian military officers who, as prisoners of war in Southeast Asia, had joined with the Japanese in mounting an offensive on India across Burma in the last years of the war. As much as the Second World War was about the failure of Europe to maintain its own civility, the war was a signal that empire would not be able to last in a world of growing nationalist and anti-European sentiment.

Characteristically, Hollywood has transposed Ondaatje's elegy into a seemingly universal tale, where war and nationalism work to destroy the purity of passion, the singlemindedness of desire. The movie makes no mention of the bomb, gives no indication that the real reason Kip leaves Hana and the villa is because of the atrocity of Hiroshima rather than the death of his English friend and tutor. I had written my own essay on *The English Patient* long before I knew there would be a film, never thinking that such a meditative prose poem could be converted into a *Lawrence of Arabia* for the nineties. But the recent Hollywood production has reminded us forcefully that the very document that can be used so directly to exemplify Benjamin's claim that all civilization is based on barbarism can also be recuperated effortlessly for the universal aesthetics of a film that shows the horrors of war at the same time that it erases all talk of anticolonial nationalism. Indeed, it is the apparent historical referentiality of the film that legitimates the claim, once again, for the autonomy of aesthetics from history itself.

I use the novel to demonstrate both the ways in which history dramatically overtakes the claims for transcendence and universality embedded in the aspirations of the Hungarian cartographer/anthropologist/explorer/enlightenment man who becomes the unmarked (because so deeply marked) bearer of Europe's original sin and to suggest that Europe's capacity for self-recognition, as well as its ultimate fall, are deeply implicated in the history of colonialism (a claim I have made more directly elsewhere).[2] I take the novel to be an allegory of culture's conceit, a way of charting how we might confront culture as an object of study and a site of theory as we move rapidly, now a half century after that war, toward an altogether new century. This volume of essays conspicuously lacks any explicit example of what we now call postcolonial theory, and yet I begin with an essay that seeks to evoke the critical positionality of the best of this body of theory. Rather than cite again the brilliant polemics of Edward Said or consult the figures whose names stand so iconically for the postcolonial within the Western academy, I inaugurate the volume with a haunting note of discord taken from the words of a writer who sketches out an allegory of the postcolonial predicament from one very particular perspective. No critical consideration of "culture," or "cultural theory" more generally, should be allowed to proceed without questioning the location of culture in, or in respect to, Europe. No discussion of the tension between high/elite and low/popular culture should be engaged without critically engaging the way the former is also positioned in Europe and the latter in the anthropological gaze that leads so naturally to the colonial world. Despite the fact that much of the popular culture in this particular volume is located not just within the West but within the United States, it is with my own concern to challenge both the always already hidden assumptions of Western foundationalism and the ethnocentrism of most critical cultural studies (whatever the particular discipline) that I commence this volume.

Perhaps, in retrospect, the major problem with focusing on the disciplinary dimensions of theoretical and methodological work is thus not the intransigence of disciplines — the problematic of our original charter — but the tacit inattention to the hegemonic location of all the disciplines in the metropolitan West. In all the (inter)disciplinary discussion at the University of Michigan that led to this volume, we rarely (if ever) brought in interlocutors who challenged not so much the disciplinary order of things as the way in which the disciplines were always assumed to be naturally positioned in the universal knowledge fields of the Western academy. The first chapter in this volume, therefore, after my introductory essay, is on the problem of popular (and highly political) forms of history in India, by Gyanendra Pandey. When Pandey addresses the power of some forms of history being written outside the academy, he is not only repositioning our gaze beyond the normal corridors of historiographical production, he is interrogating an academy that is based in India itself, and that even when it fails to persuade larger audiences of its rhetorical truths, suggests for communities such as that collected for the conference on which this volume is based the need to look at the politics of writing history in "other" national, and institutional, locations. And when Pandey asks us about the stakes of writing other forms of history, he challenges us to think about history not just as a cultural form but as a cultural politics that must always be profoundly local. Pandey reviews different ways in which history has been rewritten by certain fundamentalist groups in India to mobilize political support for "Hindu" causes, and he reflects about whether academic historians might not learn from the success of these rhetorical strategies, both in their efforts to write more effective histories and in relation to their own considerations of the nature of historical truth.

The next essay is written by another historian of subaltern life and experience, Robin Kelley, who takes on the ways in which various social scientists have used forms of the "culture concept," frequently borrowing from anthropology and sociology (the particularly offensive version surrounding the notion of the culture of poverty), to understand the fundamental nature of black urban culture. Kelley expands on the observation of Greg Tate that "perhaps the supreme irony of black American existence is how broadly black people debate the question of cultural identity among themselves while getting branded as a cultural monolith by those who would deny us the complexity and the complexion of a community, let alone a nation." Kelley is critical in particular of the ways social scientific "cultural" analyses miss fundamental aspects of the cultural text and its larger social milieu, mistaking content for context, surface meaning for lived experience, homogeneous cultural essences for commonly shared but widely contested semiotic codes. The problems behind these misinterpretations are both epistemological and political. Kelley is concerned about the ways certain cultural texts are literalized rather than regarded as performative, generic, and socially lived. And he critiques the traditional anthropological premise that views those cultures as especially monolithic that have been socially, politically, and economically dominated.

If Kelley illustrates the danger in borrowing older anthropological concepts of culture when engaged in contemporary cultural study, the next essay by Valentine Daniel interrogates the idea of culture itself from within a striking, and horrific, moment of anthropological crisis. On his way to do fieldwork in Sri Lanka in 1983, ethnic violence flared, and horrible riots touched off massive unrest, ethnic genocide, terrorist action, state repression, and unspeakable acts performed by thousands of ordinary and ordinarily peace-loving citizens. Instead of collecting folklore from Tamil plantation women workers, Daniel found himself collecting narratives of murder, torture, persecution, and mayhem. Confronting the incapacity of cultural theory to account either for the eruption of such violence in these moments of ethnic terror or for the narratives that emerge, painfully and often unconsciously, from the victims and victimizers alike, Daniel finds himself caught between amnesia and aporia, between the incoherence and the banality of violence. He asks himself, and us, what kind of cultural theory could possibly be adequate for an anthropology overtaken by horror.

But culture is resilient. It survives in the preoccupations of the anthropological theorist, as in the anthropological recognition that culture emerges most powerfully when it appears to have been lost, when it is the object of nostalgia and mourning, memory and recuperation. Marilyn Ivy shows how this is so in fundamental ways in Japan, how the very notion of "Japanese culture" was itself produced within the history of the modern nation-state. Reading the place of ancestor worship and the invocations of dead spirits on Mt. Osore as the space of memory and of loss, Ivy shows how tradition itself, the primary subject of anthropological theorizing about culture, becomes a site in which the figuration of Japanese national-cultural identity takes place, a fetish yielding all the contradictions of desire and death, a symbol for utopian thinking that simultaneously, and necessarily, succumbs to the relentless operations of commoditization under late capitalism, a substitution for the anxiety around what is and what is not Japan.

Like Japan, "Java" too becomes a figure that achieves its power through the complex history of its own production in John Pemberton's marvelous tale of the ruins of culture, and the culture of ruins, in Indonesia. Pemberton provides us with a historical account of the emergence of "culture" in the modern sense, carefully unraveling the political forces that propelled an epistemological economy that appears to be the flip side of the phantasmatic economy described by Ivy. Modern constructions of "culture" and "tradition" literally have no analogue in precolonial Java — approached through the textual traces of an extraordinary archive housed in the palace of a kingdom that has carried the cultural and political burden of colonization — but instead were created within a concretely rendered colonial vortex. Not that colonialism "invented" either the categories or their contents; it rather prepared the way and incited the mechanisms of their realization, even within structures of refusal and resistance: "As this discursive figure of 'Java' was repeatedly reinvested with all that might *not* represent Dutch colonial presence, the contours of what much later would be readily identified as 'Javanese culture' began to emerge." Pemberton doubles back at the end to the ruined palace of old, rebuilt in ways that signaled "a point beyond even the strange comfort of ruins," illustrating thus the multiple ways in which the peculiar power of culture, in modern-day Indonesia and for recent generations of anthropologists alike, has become so compelling.

Such figurative spectres haunt more than the question of identity and tradition in places like Japan and Java, for they can take the form of a Victorian old lady in the context of debates over culture and gender in Britain, both in the nineteenth century and in academic debates of great moment in the last half of the twentieth century. For Adela Pinch, the Victorian old lady is a central figure for culture, both in modernism generally and in post-1970s cultural feminism in particular. Her attention to this figure takes her from arguments between E. P. Thompson and Raymond Williams back in time through Gaskell's novel *Cranford* and the fascination of some Victorian ladies for rubber bands, an object that links privatized desires and public commodity forms, that ties together Pinch's own fascination with the fetish as a meditation on the embarrassments around sexuality in women's writing and feminist criticism on the one hand, and the economic entailments of imperial appropriation and market capitalism on the other. This intricate essay explores the subtle circuits of exchange between persons and things that increasingly resemble the shape and capacity of the rubber band itself, reminding us that specific figurations of culture are both profoundly rooted in history and suggestive of sites where the private and the public, the personal and the political, become thoroughly commingled, ever threatened by the confusions of commodity fetishism on a global scale. Culture here is always gendered, even as gender is always produced in relation to histories that move us out of the domestic spaces of polite cultural texts and into fields of exploitation and embarrassment that undermine any easy attempt to recuperate the Victorian old lady.

The Victorian old lady, of course, is both a figure of sexual repression and of national culture. Moving from nineteenth-century Britain to late-twentieth-century America, less has changed than we might think. Lauren Berlant shows us how the construction of a domain of privacy mirrors the public commitments of the national project, now more than ever. Interrogating recent debates on pornography, from those involving Andrea Dworkin, Catharine MacKinnon, and Tipper Gore to the high-minded defenses of artistic autonomy by John Frohnmayer, Berlant demonstrates how appeals to the power of the state and the integrity of the nation collaborate around heterosexual bourgeois values and the peculiar constitution of the conditions of protected private and public "acts." In her devastating critique of the formation of a national consensus on behalf of certain forms of sexuality, Berlant aligns herself with the sex-radical tactic that seeks to "de-elect the state and other social formations that have patriarchalized and parentalized national culture." Cultural critique here undermines the conceit that the privacy of the home is somehow separated from either the state or the nation, and becomes the basis for a political commitment to risk and struggle on behalf of a very different kind of relationship between sexuality and nationality than that so far imagined either in Victorian Britain or contemporary America.

In a parallel argument, Laura Kipnis shows us how the national obsession with fat, in particular through the optic of pornographies that feature fatness, reveals the relationship between political repression and desire, between class privilege and the aesthetics of taste, and between national standards of normalization and the multiple circuits of pleasure, resistance, deviance, and embodied domination that "fat" in all its various genres represents. The essay demonstrates ways in which a cultural studies sensibility can yoke analyses of offbeat (even hard core) genres and critical sociological evaluation of mainstream values in order to show continuities and uniformities both in national imaginaries and private fantasies. Kipnis focuses our gaze on other forms of "live sex acts," showing us once again the profoundly public nature of the private and the relentlessly private effects of the public. In the midst of an ambivalent fascination with the workings of taboo, her analysis reveals the social and political recalcitrance accorded any well-meant effort to cordon off the domain of culture.

Michael Taussig returns our encounter with culture to the heart of anthropology's invention of itself through the encounter with the shaman and the workings of magic. By retracing the long relationship between Franz Boas, the founder of modern American anthropology, and George Hunt, a longtime "informant," collaborator, and shaman, Taussig shows us how the anthropological investment in alterity makes the fundamental mistake of assuming a world of mysterious magic and innocent faith out there in anthropologyland. Taussig uses these moments of ethnographic investment to display the extravagant workings of mimesis, of trickery and concealment, in shamanic practices, at the same time that anthropological "faith" in the "faith" of others misrecognizes the fundamental skepticism at the core of a magical world. While Taussig reveals to us the Nietzschean world of the shaman, where "untruth [appears] as a condition of life," he suggests ways in which the reliance of modernity's self-representations on other representations (of others and otherness) conceals/reveals its own fragile capacities to contain the enchantment of performance, conceit, and trickery itself. For Taussig, the truth of shamanism is only available in the confessional moments when skepticism and faith are shown to depend upon each other, and the mimetic character of the modern finds its own contradictions reflected in a theory of magic that refuses to accept the limits or to struggle against the desires of most anthropological conceptions of culture.

If all of the chapters convey new forms of cultural critique, the closing essay by Marjorie Levinson questions the possibility of critique itself, understood as a simultaneously materialist and reflexive project. Starting with Wittgenstein's and Derrida's comments on the self-containment of representation (including those language games that, like philosophy and critical theory, claim to move outside the circuits of language and culture), Levinson traces the overturning of ontology, from the epistemological hermeneutics of Kant and Hegel to the present, only to find critique lying, at the end of the century, on its death-bed. The essay analyzes the constitutive paradox of critique: namely, a commitment on the one hand, to the sociohistorical rewriting of our documents of civilization, and on the other, to what resists the identity principles of our own time and place as well as those that structure the study text. The essay is an attempt to confront both the founding contradiction of critique and the exhaustion of the available forms of critical writing. At the same time, the author holds faith with the social and intellectual values informing the project of critique, and tries to imagine and instantiate a practice of knowing geared to the special conditions of the present. The essay concludes with a list of examples and possibilities, a nontheorized array of critical procedures that might satisfy the Enlightenment's classical interest in freedom through knowledge and its no less venerable attachment to effects and logics that resist the tendential idealism of both pure and practical reason. Happily, Levinson's examples include the names of Michael Taussig and Valentine Daniel, in particular, an essay by the latter that appears in this volume. However, there seems little doubt that this volume itself, if only because its mode of circulation and therefore its consumption are inescapably pregiven, cannot satisfy the twin imperatives of a critique that takes seriously its provenance in both the Enlightenment and Romanticism.

On the other hand, it may be precisely by sketching the limits of this present critical intervention that we can signal its greatest power and most lasting significance. All of these essays convey both frustration and humility about the task of cultural critique at the same time that they oscillate between a sense that culture itself is the problem and the recognition that culture is a site—for inquiry as well as critique—that is impossible to escape. In other words, culture is both a predicament and a ruin, an object of critique and the means by which we attempt here to engage in critique.

Notes

1. The conferences were all organized by the Program in the Comparative Study of Social Transformations (CSST), which was founded in 1987 and continues to run regular seminars, conferences, and workshops at the University of Michigan. Beginning with the "core" disciplines of history, anthropology, and sociology, it has now become far more broad-based and interdisciplinary than it was at the start, reflecting the larger transformations that have taken place in theoretical, methodological, and even disciplinary domains over the last decade well beyond the University of Michigan. Terrence McDonald, Professor of History, convened the first conference around history (which led to the publication of T. McDonald, *The Historic Turn in the Human Sciences* [Ann Arbor: University of Michigan Press, 1996]); Geoff Eley, also Professor of History, convened the second conference on power during the winter of 1992 (plans for a volume fell through), and I convened the third conference in October 1993.

2. See my introduction to my edited volume, *Colonialism and Culture* (Ann Arbor: University of Michigan Press, 1993).

1

In Near Ruins: Cultural Theory at the End of the Century

Nicholas B. Dirks

The Villa San Girolamo, built to protect inhabitants from the flesh of the devil, had the look of a besieged fortress, the limbs of most of the statues blown off during the first days of shelling. There seemed little demarcation between house and landscape, between damaged building and the burned and shelled remnants of the earth . . . Between the kitchen and the destroyed chapel a door led into an oval-shaped library. The space inside seemed safe except for a large hole at portrait level in the far wall, caused by mortar-shell attack on the villa two months earlier. The rest of the room had adapted itself to this wound, accepting the habits of weather, evening stars, the sound of birds. There was a sofa, a piano covered in a grey sheet, the head of a stuffed bear and high walls of books. The shelves nearest the torn wall bowed with the rain, which had doubled the weight of the books. Lightning came into the room too, again and again, falling across the covered piano and carpet.

— *Michael Ondaatje,*
The English Patient

The English patient of Ondaatje's novel is a man burnt black beyond recognition, beyond identity. Cared for by a shell-shocked Canadian nurse, he lies in the Villa San Girolamo, a bombed-out ruin in the hills north of Florence, a structure that once housed a nunnery and then the Germans. They mined the place when they left, only to have it taken over by the Allies as a hospital and morgue. By the time the novel opens, the only patient left is a man who has forgotten his name and lost his history. His body, iconic in early passages of the body of Christ, reveals nothing in its charred flesh. His sense of self is

1

anchored only in the fragmentary narratives of his life in the desert and his marginal notes and diary entries inscribed on the margins and in the added pages of his one possession, a battered copy of *The Histories* by Herodotus. His stories fill the villa during the days just after the cessation of war in Europe, his life the vehicle for Ondaatje's extraordinary elegy on the decline and fall of Western civilization.

If Herodotus and Florence together signify the best of the West, the great moments of Western self-invention and achievement, the rise of history and art, the triumph of beauty and reason, the English patient is the ideal subject of the Enlightenment. He is also the exemplar of colonial knowledge and the epitome of colonial adventure. An expert on the desert, he knows the Bedouin as only colonial agents could:

> I am a man who can recognize an unnamed town by its skeletal shape on a map...So I knew their place before I crashed among them, knew when Alexander had traversed it in an earlier age for this cause or that greed. I knew the customs of nomads besotted by silk or wells. When I was lost among them, unsure of where I was, all I needed was the name of a small ridge, a local custom, a cell of this historical animal, and the map of the world would slide into place.[1]

There was no uncertainty, no resistance, no self-doubt; the cartography of colonial knowledge was total and absolute, no fragment less than the sign of the whole.

Colonial knowledge was also, so the claim went, disinterested. The English patient went to the desert, with other English friends, because of his love of untamed spaces: "We seemed to be interested only in things that could not be bought or sold, of no interest to the outside world."[2] But if knowledge was pure, if only in its originary enlightenment conceit, it was soon overtaken by war and the imperatives of nation-states. Madox, the patient's best friend through ten years of desert exploration, could not bear the onset of war, the way it divided him from his small circle of friends, the noise it brought to his quiet fantasy of the desert: "And Madox returned to the village of Marston Magna, Somerset, where he had been born, and a month later sat in the congregation of a church, heard the sermon in honour of the war, pulled out his revolver and shot himself....Yes, Madox was a man who died because of nations."[3] Clifton, who had joined the desert party on a lark after Oxford and marriage, turned out to be an intelligence officer for the British, his accumulated knowledge of the desert an added advantage once war was declared. And the English patient, well, he wasn't really English, after all. His story, first told in fragments that gave nothing away, was finally extracted during a long session of morphine, administered by Caravaggio the thief, who had used his skills for the counterintelligence efforts of the British and then, in the aftermath of war, followed his old family friend Hana, the nurse, to the villa. The English patient was in fact Hungarian, and had turned to help the Germans after the onset of war, guiding spies such as Rommel across the great North African desert. Caravaggio, with a thief's expertise in fragments, deduced his identity from the stories he first heard, having followed Almásy's case when he was posted in Cairo. But he could not have guessed the contingence of Almásy's betrayal.

Ondaatje's novel, at first seemingly seduced by the omniscience of colonial knowledge, traces its inexorable progression to the nuclear explosions over Hiroshima and Nagasaki. In the end, the novel—and this is where the true difference lies between fiction and history—is a romantic tale, writ small. Almásy had fallen in love with Clifton's wife when she seductively recited lines from Herodotus by a desert campfire. It was an ancient story of betrayal, first by a husband of his wife, and then in return by a wife who conspires with the man her husband had chosen to see her naked in order to appreciate the beauty of his wife. As Almásy said when he narrated this story of falling in love, "Words, Caravaggio. They have a power."[4] History turned into romance through the seduction of language. But desire folds back into history when the story continues, for Almásy chose to side with the Germans only because the English suspected him, refusing to help him when he crawled into a military camp from a ruined desert crying out for them to rescue Katharine, whom he names, wrongly, as his wife. Though her husband is now dead, victim of a suicide crash that sought to take his wife and her lover to the next world with him, Almásy is unable to speak the husband's name, a name resonant with English upper-class credentials and military significance. And so he cannot save the woman he adores, and in retreat joins the enemy. Madox and Clifton die from broken hearts, Katharine from the misrecognition of war, and Almásy fades away (his colonial knowledge of the desert the means of his escape), only to be burned black, beyond recognition. When Almásy finally tells his tale, he has moved beyond desire for either morphine or memory. Strangely, without memory all he can do is read the history of Herodotus. And he comes to his end, for his death is just a matter of time, a romantic who could not accept the inevitable appropriation of his knowledge and life:

> We die containing a richness of lovers and tribes, tastes we have swallowed, bodies we have plunged into and swum up as if rivers we have hidden in as if caves. I wish for all this to be marked on my body when I am dead. I believe in such cartography—to be marked by nature, not just to label ourselves on a map like the names of rich men

and women on buildings. We are communal histories, communal books. We are not owned or monogamous in our taste and experience. All I desired was to walk upon such an earth that had no maps.

He was, in the end, misguided. The condition of possibility of such romance was the colonial map that led directly to world war after world war, not to mention the daily oppressions of colonial rule. And in the final scene in the villa, the English patient has a gun directed at him by the Sikh sapper who had also taken refuge in the villa, a loyal soldier who had spent the war defusing unexploded bombs. He held his gun on the English patient after hearing about the explosion of the atomic bomb, a bomb he could never defuse. Holding the charred throat in the rifle's sight, he says, "My brother told me. Never turn your back on Europe. The deal makers. The contract makers. The map drawers. Never trust Europeans, he said. Never shake hands with them. But we, oh, we were easily impressed — by speeches and medals and your ceremonies. What have I been doing these last few years? Cutting away, defusing, limbs of evil. For what? For *this* to happen."[5] And when Caravaggio shouted out that the English patient was not English, it did not matter at all, though the sapper left him unharmed, returning home instead, though with his own troubling memories of Hana, his lover, to disturb the simple pleasures of his own national awakening.

The Florentine villa is still a ruin. The majestic mansion built by culture was hollowed out by the middle of the century, destroyed from within by the convulsions of world war, dismantled from without by the relentless historical logic of decolonization. Until the war it was still possible for many to believe the truth of Matthew Arnold's pronouncements on the relationship of culture and anarchy. For Arnold, culture was not just the irrelevant preoccupation of the pedant, of interest only to "a critic of new books or a professor of belles lettres."[6] Neither was culture of concern only to the upper classes. Culture was about the pursuit of perfection, about the contemplation of and devotion to sweetness and light: "It seeks to do away with classes; to make the best that has been thought and known in the world current everywhere; to make all men live in an atmosphere of sweetness and light, where they may use ideas, as it uses them itself, freely."[7] Culture was thus, for Arnold, a "social idea": "The men of culture are the true apostles of equality. The great men of culture are those who have had a passion for diffusing, for making prevail, for carrying from one end of society to the other, the best of knowledge, the best ideas of their time."[8] These men of culture must strip the discourse of culture of all jargon and cant, humanizing and diffusing the benefits of culture for all. But the more Arnold argues, the more it becomes clear how limited his notion of equality is: the masses should have culture disseminated to them by the "men" of culture in order to stem the inherent anarchy of the crowd. Culture, which is both animated by religious impulses and the modern substitute for religion, "is the most resolute enemy of anarchy."[9] And culture combats anarchy not just through its celebration of the sublime, but because it teaches us to nourish "great hopes and designs for the State."[10] If culture is religion, the state is the new citadel of the sacred: "Thus, in our eyes, the very framework and exterior order of the State, whoever may administer the State, is sacred."[11] And so the state and culture conspire to check the unruly and uplift the public, to forbid both "despondency and violence."

Culture in Arnold's Victorian view of the world has thus not only been tamed, but harnessed to the task of state control in the face of growing concern over the unruly mobs that threatened the pretensions and peace of a democratizing and secularizing England.[12] Arnold makes explicit the disciplining function of cultural value and the cultural elite; it is hardly surprising that Arnoldian phrases crop up time after time in the rhetoric of the conservative right in America (and Britain) today. William Bennett and Lynn Cheney both quoted Arnold in their recent attacks on the National Endowments for Art and Humanities, giving voice to the concerns of many on the right that culture is supposed to combat anarchy rather than promote it. But Arnold's gloss of culture—the best that has been thought and known—as "sweetness and light" in the service of the state and the "men of culture" seems not only to provide a target for the most reductionist materialist critique of the superstructure but to parody even the most benign celebrations of culture emerging out of enlightenment discourse itself. Edmund Burke, whose writings on the sublime were of critical importance in the foundation of enlightenment aesthetics, realized that the power of culture was more complicated; Burke privileged darkness over light, secrecy over clarity. He also saw terror as the true source of the sublime: "Whatever is fitted in any sort to excite the ideas of pain, and danger, that is to say, whatever is in any sort terrible, or is conversant about terrible objects, or operates in a manner analogous to terror, is a source of the sublime; that is, it is productive of the strongest emotion which the mind is capable of feeling."[13] For Burke, the sublime has much more to do with pain than with pleasure.

The sublime for Burke is not just about pain and terror but, anticipating Kant, about the incommensurability of experience, at least some kinds of experience, and reason. As Sara Suleri has written,

> Burke's famous catalog of the horrors of sublimity is thus strongly linked to a sense of temporal disarray, to a conviction that sequential derangement must necessarily attend the spectator's implication in the sublime.

> If a discourse of difficulty is the only idiom that will suffice to repre-
> sent such derangement, then it demands to be recognized as clarity on
> its own territory, and resists a translation into aesthetic luminosity.[14]

Suleri stresses the performative entailments of the sublime, the implication
of any reading of the sublime in the yawning chasm between representation and event. The artifice of art calls attention to this gap; the power of
representation is a conceit, predicated on the ultimate powerlessness of all
representation. But the sublime is equally invested in the excess of all that
is signified, the horrible truth that both representation and affect fall so far
short of that which we seek to apprehend and understand. Culture in this
view is not simple sweetness and light; art does not necessarily contain
chaos.

Nevertheless, the sublime is hardly a revolutionary category; despite
Burke's strong, even obsessional, critique of England's colonial relationship
with India, his position on the French Revolution was entirely reactionary.
What is temporal disarray in Suleri's analysis is more generally, in Hayden
White's reading, the aestheticization of history.[15] As Thomas Weiskel has
suggested, "The dissociation or dualism at the core of the eighteenth-century
sublime had profoundly ideological implications, and the various forms of
alienation reinforced by the sublime ... could not be shaken until these ideological correlatives were questioned in the ferment of social revolution."[16]
The sublime was calculated to escape history, even if for a commentator such
as Burke the sublime could be produced by the extraordinary character of
history.[17] The enlightenment view of the sublime set the stage for the ideologies of Romanticism, in which the exquisite aesthetics of experience and the
quiet contemplation of beauty set art free from history at the same time that
history became not just ignored but suppressed by the rise of Romanticism
more generally.[18] And Kant's linkage of the sublime to the transcendental
properties of aesthetic judgement, in which the gap between signifier and
signified calls attention to the very limits of nature itself, provides the basis
for his understanding of the infinite: "The sublime is that, the mere capacity
of thinking which evidences a faculty of mind transcending every standard
of sense."[19] The sublime for Kant is "the disposition of soul evoked by a
particular representation engaging the attention of reflective judgement, and
not the Object."[20] In such a view, the sublime is about those glimpses, fragments, and perhaps even ruins that signify that which cannot be signified,
providing mere shadows for the quiet contemplation of aesthetic categories.
The sublime is thus about escape and transcendence, hardly the stuff either
of history or critique.

Kant's transcendental escape from history and materiality thus provided the philosophical basis for a romantic view of the world; Kant exempted all feelings of pleasure and displeasure from the realm of objective truth, consigning them instead to the autonomous domain of the aesthetic, "one whose determining ground cannot be other than subjective."[21] In addition to rejecting the didactic function of art, Kant delineated an aesthetic that was divorced completely from the social. Jerome McGann has written that "Kant's aesthetic has dominated western attitudes toward art and poetry for more than a hundred and fifty years,"[22] providing the justification for Coleridge's discussion of the harmonizing powers of Imagination, explaining the philosophical basis for poetry, such as Wordsworth's *Tintern Abbey,* that memorializes "certain private and intensely subjective moments of imaginative insight which he has known 'oft, in lonely rooms, and mid the din of towns and cities.' "[23] But if the romantic imagination took flight from the world not just of rational thought but also of materiality and history in poetry, it perhaps was lodged most extravagantly in the landscape where ruins, rather than lonely rooms, took pride of place; I refer here to the visual cartography of the picturesque.

By the last years of the eighteenth century, the cult of the picturesque had attained primacy in England as a general attitude to art and nature. Associated at first both with the classical landscapes of Claude Lorraine, Gaspar Poussin, and Salvator Rosa, and with the more naturalistic views of Ruysdael, Hobbema, Cuyp, and Van Goyen, the picturesque became the site for considerable argument about the character of the relationship between art and nature. The picturesque tradition frequently combined rigorous enlightenment attitudes about the need to depict the natural world scientifically and romantic convictions that art had to represent the experience of the beautiful and the sublime afforded by nature rather than nature itself. On the one hand, various proto-photographic techniques and devices sought to capture nature on paper, with the use of artist's viewers, the Claude glass, the camera obscura, and the camera lucida. On the other hand, while these processes were advocated because of the transparency they established between the real and representational, they were also thought to improve the picture, giving objects better perspective and more pleasing tinges and hues. Indeed, the mode of the picturesque increasingly sought to improve nature; the term itself could only be applied to certain kinds of natural settings, constituent features, and artistic compositions. Pictures often had to have mountains or hills as backdrops (even in lowland areas), lakes or rivers closer in, and gnarled trees, luxuriant vegetation, and ruined buildings closer still. Frequently, picturesque scenes seemed most readily obtainable in Hellenic or Oriental settings.

In England, the picturesque also became the site of a reaction to the transformations of history represented most dramatically by the French Revolution. The craze to redesign garden landscapes along classical lines in the middle decades of the eighteenth century was soon followed by serious rethinking. The magnificent prospects advocated by Addison and "Capability" Brown were attacked for their radical resort to reason rather than tradition and nature. The gothic imaginary of gentlemen gardeners such as Uvedale Price and Richard Payne Knight gave visible form to the critical concerns of Burke, who wrote that "the science of constructing a commonwealth is not to be taught a priori. . . . The nature of man is intricate; the objects of society are of the greatest possible complexity: and therefore no simple disposition or direction of power can be suitable either to man's nature, or to the quality of his affairs."[24] Ann Bermingham argues that Burke's conservatism and his concomitant commitment to complexity can be seen in the new picturesque aesthetic, where old gardens are preserved, and new gardens are wildly overgrown, even derelict. The new picturesque was steeped in nostalgia for the wildness of nature and the haunting call of grandeur, signified best by towering mountains and stupendous buildings. As for buildings, nostalgia was best conveyed through the image of ruins.[25]

The ruin was a sign of loss, of absence. Crumbling rock and fragments of shard stood for wholes that could never again be achieved, if even conceived. Ruins were approachable and representable, but only because they were but shadows of their former selves. Ruins made ancient truth both literal and literary. In ruins, the hollowed-out shells of ancient truth appeared majestic, approachable only through art—painting and poetry in particular. The science of archaeology was born in the attempt to recover the truth of the past concretely, but the allure of archaeology was always predicated on the impossibility of scientific fantasy (not to mention its inescapable relationship to plunder and the fantasy of instant wealth). Ruins also promised glory through recuperation rather than revolution, representing Burke's concern about the politics of the age, as well as about the relationship between history and the sublime. Perhaps more than anything, ruins made palpable the chasm between reality and representation, between desire and dejection, between now and then, lodging temporal alterity resolutely within the past rather than in some utopian future. The ruin not only housed culture, it stood for it: like culture itself, the ruin was at once material and ethereal, simultaneously about history and memory, a sign of achievement and a signal of failure, an inspiration for life as well as an intimation of death.

If culture's cavernous lack is the site of culture's power as well as the basis on which culture can be wielded as an instrument of power, the ruin helps us understand why culture must always be linked to the incommensurable. In Arnold, culture becomes both didactic and inspiring, containable but dangerous. For Burke, the danger is more palpable; the power of culture is in part its excess, the uncontainability of the sublime. And for the picturesque tradition, which sought to contain beauty by conventions of distantiation, the experience was always on the verge of leaking beyond the borders of carefully composed canvases and gardens. Representation turned out to be as uncontrollable as the referential affects of romantic aspiration. The modern career of culture has always had to negotiate these tensions, requiring the convictions and investments of class power to sustain any confidence in the controlled and controlling uses of culture. But it is precisely these tensions—the quarrels over the empty spaces between representation and reality—that produce the terrific for Kant, the terrible for Burke, and the horrible for Benjamin. No matter where we rest our critical position, we find that culture is not quite itself, not nearly as comfortable as Arnold would have us believe. For us all, culture is a site of extreme ambivalence, whether we refer to the ruin in the garden, the nude in the museum, or the harmony in a chorale. Now we attempt to clothe ambivalence in a different kind of distance, and we shift from the effort to describe and contain the sublime to a critical consideration of the political implications of the power of culture. But we are still drawn to culture as if to a spectre, the ghost of a past that still excites and the haunting possibility of a future we think we desire. Culture eclipses temporality itself even as we try to historicize it. Culture becomes a trace of its own representational artifacts that can be critiqued only when we are still compelled by the terrible pull of the sublime. As the impossible object of our critical conscience, culture either floats away into thin air as absence or takes the form and presence of the ruin.

In the Midrash story of the Tower of Babel, those who actually saw the ruins of the tower were doomed to forget the past, to lose sight of history altogether, to forfeit even their capacity to know themselves.[26] While ruins would seem to be about history, more often they are about the need to obliterate history, as well as signs of the death of history. Walter Benjamin distinguishes historical materialism from the history of Fustel de Coulanges, who "recommends...to historians who wish to relive an era...that they blot out everything they know about the later course of history."[27] Benjamin goes on to write, in his now famous passage, that "without exception the cultural treasures he [the historical materialist] surveys have an origin which he cannot contemplate without horror. They owe their existence not only to the efforts of the great minds and talents who have created them, but also to the anonymous toil of their contemporaries. There is no document of civilization which is not at the same time a document of barbarism."[28] The ruin is the document of civilization par excellence; it signifies the most onerous toil of the slaves and subalterns who executed the political and architectural ambitions of great civilizations, and the history of its contemplation generates nostalgia, which is the forgetting rather than the remembering of history, the forgetting of the conditions of possibility of history, not to mention its later course. But for those, unlike Benjamin, who have traditionally celebrated culture and civilization, the only horror attendant upon the contemplation of ruins is that of shock at the decline and fall of what once was great. The ruin is the only connection between the wonders of the past and the degradation of the present. The ruin puts us in awe of the mystifications that made civilization magnificent in the first place. The ruin is culture, both its reality and its representation.

If Benjamin teaches us more powerfully than perhaps any other modern critic that culture is a ruin, he betrays some measure of his own nostalgia when he defines the aura of traditional aesthetics. In Benjamin's early philosophy he had identified the aura, or uniqueness, or art as the source of its value; by the time he wrote his masterful essay, "Art in the Age of Mechanical Reproduction," he had reversed his view.[29] Whether it is produced by "cult value" (the ritual attribution of magical value) or by the logic of exhibition (the public presentation of works of art), Benjamin now views the aura of art, that quality of authenticity and presence that produces the sublime, as an endangered species. Art changes fundamentally once the technical means of reproduction enter the modern world with photography in the nineteenth century. In a flashback to his earlier position, the moment when the aura appears lost produces a "melancholy, incomparable beauty."[30] Nevertheless, Benjamin argues strongly that the loss of the aura opens up new possibilities for a revolutionary aesthetic, for the politicization and radicalization of art. Film is exemplary of the new aesthetic regime: according to Benjamin, film promotes a "revolutionary criticism of traditional concepts of art."[31] By its substitution of the camera for the public, film loses the aura of performance; by its reproducibility and accessibility, it makes every viewer an expert. Film embodies the principal of the mechanical reproduction of art, thus irrevocably changing "the reaction of the masses toward art." Benjamin had extraordinary confidence in the progressive implications of the new age of film.

But Benjamin's faith in the technologies of aesthetic reproduction and the critical capabilities of the masses (politically self-conscious if also absent-minded) was strenuously opposed by Adorno, who was far more distrustful of the "laughter of the proletariat in the movie house,"[32] and far more impressed by the capacities of the fascist state and the capitalist elite to appropriate the technologies of production. The argument between Benjamin and Adorno over popular and elite culture continues to haunt our understandings of culture in the final years of the twentieth century. Now the question is not whether culture, or the sublime, can be contained, so much as whether the modern technologies of the sublime will render containment that much more secure. Adorno's critique of the culture industry,[33] composed in its most complete and polemical form after his move to America, still provides the most eloquent critique of mass culture we have today. Adorno lamented that "real life is becoming indistinguishable from the movies."[34] He argued that "the stunting of the mass-media consumer's powers of imagination and spontaneity does not have to be traced back to any psychological mechanisms; he must ascribe the loss of those attributes to the objective nature of the products themselves, especially to the most characteristic of them, the sound film."[35] Adorno wrote more generally that "the culture industry as a whole has molded men as a type unfailingly reproduced in every product."[36] Anticipating current theoretical preoccupations with cultural hegemony and discursive domination, Adorno carefully dissected the ways in which the modern subject was converted into a consumer, a consumer whose needs, interests, and beliefs could be controlled and manipulated by the apparatuses of a mass media that produced pleasure (and incited further consumption) by stifling the possibility of critical reflection. With polemical rhetoric still unrivaled by other denunciations of the conceits of bourgeois liberalism, Adorno noted at the end of his essay that the methods of the fascists had reached their final apotheosis in modern America, where the "freedom to choose an ideology...everywhere proves to be freedom to choose what is always the same."[37]

Using Benjaminian language, if to rather different ends, Adorno wrote, "Today aesthetic barbarity completes what has threatened the creations of the spirit since they were gathered together as culture and neutralized."[38] The culture industry has rendered culture nothing but style, in which the commoditization of all aesthetic value reveals itself in the reduction of art to imitation. Adorno held up older and more classical forms of culture in contrast, noting that "the great artists were never those who embodied a wholly flawless and perfect style, but those who used style as a way of hardening themselves against the chaotic expression of suffering, as a negative truth."[39] While recognizing that art is always ideology, Adorno saw the confrontation with tradition in classical forms as the contradictory space for the expression of suffering, and for the necessary admission of failure through self-negation, the contradictions of any effort to transcend the particular limits of social existence. In this short aside, Adorno made reference to a lifetime of critical efforts to engage in ideology critique through great works of art, in particular the modernist musical experiments of composers such as Schoenberg.

Adorno's commitment to the critical potential of high modernist aesthetics and his despair about mass culture were functions of his experience of the normalization and appropriation of a classical tradition under the Nazi regime, as well as of the apparent utility of mass culture for totalitarian state systems and American capitalist market forces alike. Benjamin's belief in the potential of mass media was forged through his fascination with early film, as was his political and cultural affiliation with Brecht. Benjamin was convinced that the loss of aura represented by filmic media would render culture both more accessible and more political, but even if his commitment to Marxist doctrine and revolutionary praxis was far firmer than that of Adorno, it seems likely he would have worried along with Adorno about the production of new consumer subjectivities under the postwar American regime of capital, had he survived the war. The war itself, despite Adorno, left traditional European culture as a ruin, both architecturally—many of its most conspicuous symbols were literally ruined—and spiritually; it was clear to many that the heart of European culture had in some ways led to fascism and the holocaust. Ideology critique seemed woefully insufficient. At the same time, the ruins of Europe paved the way for the emergence of American hegemony over world culture, ruining cultural sensibility/possibility in precisely the terms laid out so eloquently by Adorno. Culture under the new regime became always already a ruin in the face of programmed obsolescence and the relentless advance of the new. After the war, culture was taken over by Eisenhower's military-industrial complex and Hollywood's fantasy factories. And the Cold War deployment of modernization, appropriating all the other uses of the modern to the world order of American power, affiliated the new with economic power, technological superiority, progress, and pleasure. The lure of the modern was more powerful than ever, and once again the modern came as a sign of Western power.

And so we return to the Villa San Girolamo. The Florentine shrine of culture was a ruin, its inhabitants shell-shocked. The image recapitulates the modernist critique of the sublime, forcefully set in motion by Nietzsche when, arguing that both the Apollonian and the Dionysian principles were conjoined in aesthetic production and experience, he took the Kantian tradition to task for failing to recognize that "the sublime is the artistic taming of the horrible."[40] Nietzsche's insistence on the Dionysian side of the sublime anticipated the later writings of Georges Bataille, who viewed cultural value and meaning as necessarily implicated in violence and excess. Focusing on rites of sacrifice and the close relations between ritual and war, Bataille interrogated the horror at the heart of culture, celebrating transgression as the fundamental modality of the sacred. For Bataille, as for Nietzsche, the moment of excess was both about sexuality and about death.[41] And even here, surveying the theoretical genealogies of our current condition, Ondaatje captures this sad sense of the sullied sublime. We see in his novel the necessary affiliation of love and violence; Almásy's love is obiterated by war, even as Hana and the Sikh sapper are torn apart by the nuclear explosion thousands of miles away.[42] Violence is what predicates love (in the colonial terrain of the desert or in the ruined villa), and violence is the force that ultimately disrupts it.

In the end, the English patient, the man who used Herodotus as his guide through the deserts of life, lay waiting for death, burned black beyond identity. He was a man who embodied the best of colonial knowledge and yet turned out to be not quite what he seemed; he belonged to all of Europe, erasing the distinctions between allies and axis by revealing the common heritage and fundamental flaws of both sides. The tragic elegy of his life provided the pretext for the ultimate intention of the novel, the devolution of cultural capital from Almásy and his Oxford education to the likes of Caravaggio and Hana, the one a streetwise though chastened thief, the other a young and beautiful woman who had already seen the empty deception of the domestic dream. And perhaps even more significantly, the position of critique is appropriated in the end by the silent sapper, the Sikh from India who recognizes the ultimate deception, the terrible tyranny of the West, the translation of European colonial power into American English. The ruin that haunts the final pages of the novel is that of Hiroshima and Nagasaki, cities instantaneously converted to rubble by the unprecedented power of nuclear explosion. When the sapper returns home, he does so to join in the final struggle of the nationalist movement, to attempt to free himself, for good, of the ruination of the West.

In this prelude, I have sought to capture, or at least evoke, the predicament of cultural theory today, fifty years after the end of the war; during these intervening years, American power has waxed and waned, popular culture has exploded across the globe, decolonization has transformed the cartography of colonial power, and the death of communism has led to the demise of the cold war and the epiphany of market capitalism. Ondaatje wrote his allegory from the perspective of these transformations; in an earlier novel set in Toronto he had written about the historical production of subjects such as Caravaggio and Hana (*In the Skin of a Lion*), and in a personal memoir, he had evoked the lush colonial past that had generated his own mediated relationship with his home, Sri Lanka (*Running in the Family*). In particular, Ondaatje tells his tale from the position of one who celebrates an escape from the West at the same time he is irrevocably trapped in its embrace. Decidedly not a postcolonial theorist, Ondaatje has reflected deeply on the entailments of the history and genealogy of the West for cultural migrants such as himself; he has immersed himself in the poetic possibilities of a colonial language at the same time he dreams of the authentic heat and passion of his youth; he has identified the hybrid formations that relentlessly enclose his own capacity for history and utopia. Without any explicit reference to Adorno, he exemplifies Adorno's own reflection about the dislocations of his life and times: "For a man who no longer has a homeland, writing becomes a place to live."[43]

Writing itself is not a neutral space. In the last fifty years we have learned how much it matters from where we write, to whom we write, and more generally how writing is positioned in geopolitical, sociohistorical, and institutional terms. If Ondaatje's *English Patient* can signify the monumental shifts in our cultural and intellectual landscape that have been brought about by decolonization and resurgent nationalism, it can also remind us that in cultural theory, postcolonial critiques are necessary features of all the new landscapes we inhabit or survey. Postcoloniality, in other words, is not just something out there; neither is it (nor should it be) simply a new name for a token inclusionism in our cultural business as usual. Rather, the postcolonial condition is the historical precipitate of centuries of Western political and economic domination, itself enabling, even as it was enabled by, centuries of cultural and intellectual colonization. Postcoloniality signifies those places and peoples that resist the universalization of positionality and perspective, even as it underscores the extraordinary power of the forces of universalization. Postcoloniality reminds us of the fact that culture and modernity were always flawed, always predicated on violence and domination even as they were the terms of seduction and conquest for colonization itself.[44] When the critique of the Enlightenment comes out of colonial history, we remember that Burke's eloquent defense of good government and disinterested despotism was in the service of massive force, monumental greed, unsupportable grandeur. We remember that culture has always been a spectre, haunting any attempt to reconstruct cultural authenticities untouched by colonial power even as it leaves a trace of violence in every moment of historical imagination and political utopia. The angel of history speaks with sadness not just about the atrocities of the past, but the atrocity of history itself, pro-pelled as he is into the future by the terrible storm called progress.[45] This is not a book about postcolonial cultural theory; but it is, necessarily, a book that begins with the critique and seeks to learn from some of the lessons of the postcolonial predicament.

If the postcolonial critique has subjected traditional notions of Western culture to serious scrutiny, it has also challenged the disciplinary integrity of another field heavily represented in the contributions to this volume: an-thropology. Should a field so tainted by its origins within the violence of colo-nialism continue as a privileged site of cultural critique in the postcolonial world? We are now well acquainted with reflexive positions within anthro-pology that adumbrate the horrors of the colonial past and the extent to which both the subjects and the imperatives of anthropological knowledge participate in those horrors. The nuclear calculus of Hiroshima was but a sign of the legacies of colonial history; the sapper's alienation from the nor-malizing technologies of Western warfare a token of nationalist resistance. But the anthropological concept of culture has survived both the implosion of the atom and the decolonization of empire; now the irony is that anthro-pological imaginaries are serving other purposes, sometimes justifying a wide variety of identity politics and national/subnational political claims, other times maintaining spaces for the delineation of difference within the normalizing and universalizing logics of continued forms of epistemological coloniza-tion. Here, we learn of new dangers even as we survey how the epistemo-logical battles we fight are not mere abstract debates but struggles that take on their particular meanings in discrete and different terrains. Culture can be used to critique the West at the same time that it can be deployed to de-flect any interrogation of local politics.

The essays in this book are fragments, the contingent residue of the in-stitutional history of a conference. But they are also fragments because the cultural field at the end of the twentieth century, from wherever we stand, is made of fragments. If traditional culture is still a (near) ruin, and much of popular culture still a (near) ruination, we have neither resolved the argu-ment between Benjamin and Adorno, nor fixed upon new ways to engage the field of culture that escape the problematic legacies of class hegemony, colonial domination, and capitalist exploitation. We are still uncertain about our place as intellectuals, and wherever we position ourselves, we are not completely sure what these places signify in relation to concerns of con-stituency and representation, let alone the politics of criticism. Each of the papers in this volume struggles with questions of critique and position; some focus on popular culture, others on high culture, still others on anthropological culture. None are content with the legacies of cultural theory; none are satisfied that general agreement about the need to politicize culture, on the one hand, or to provide spaces for multiple cultural representations, on the other, resolves the inherent contradiction between the two. The argument between Benjamin and Adorno continues to haunt us; we are not sure whether to find resistance in culture (whether "low" or "high"), to attempt to provoke subversion in culture through ideology critique, or to feel embarassment about the choice of culture as the field of criticism and interpretation in the first place.

But we keep coming back to the ruins of culture. We may feel horrified, but we also feel inspired; we may feel dispirited, as did Adorno, but we cannot escape the rhetorical echoes of Benjamin's utopian aspiration. When we confront the overdetermination of logics of cultural production and consumption, we may nowadays think more of Foucault than of Marx; when we experience the excess of cultural meaning and signification, we may refer more to Bataille than to Burke. But we keep coming back. We stroll across the dilapidated ramparts, we climb the devastated staircase, we sift through the sandy pieces of shard, we back up on a grassy knoll until we can see the grandeur and the beauty of the prospect. But there we are, and we cannot just stand back, despite the fact, perhaps because of the fact, that we now know the ruin is littered with unexploded mines. When we walk in the library, we know, as did Hana, that one wrong step may detonate the fuse of a deadly bomb. We pull books down from shelves knowing not what we may find, nor how old books might read again, now after the war. We plant flowers in the garden, never sure if the weeds we pull or the sharp blade of our trowel will trigger an explosion. We exist in a state of emergency; we live in near ruins.

Notes

I am grateful to Adela Pinch, Marilyn Ivy, Janaki Bakhle, Peter van der Veer, and Val Daniel for extensive conversations about an earlier draft of this essay.

1. Michael Ondaatje, *The English Patient* (New York: Vintage International Edition, 1993), 18–19.

2. Ibid., 143.

3. Ibid., 240–42.

4. Ibid., 234.

5. Ibid., 284–85.

6. Matthew Arnold, *Culture and Anarchy* (New York: Cambridge University Press, 1990), 68.

7. Ibid., 70.

8. Ibid.

9. Ibid., 204.

10. Ibid.

11. Ibid.

12. For a social history of the uses of culture in nineteenth-century Britain, see Tony Bennett, "The Exhibitionary Complex," in *Culture/Power/History: A Reader in Contemporary Social Theory,* ed. N. Dirks, G. Eley, and S. Ortner (Princeton, NJ: Princeton University Press, 1994), 123–54.

13. Edmund Burke, *A Philosophical Enquiry into the Origin of Our Ideas of the Sublime and Beautiful* (New York: Oxford University Press, 1990), 36.

14. Sara Suleri, *The Rhetoric of English India* (Chicago: University of Chicago Press, 1992), 39.

15. See Hayden White, *The Content of the Form: Narrative Discourse and Historical Representation* (Baltimore: Johns Hopkins University Press, 1987), 68.

16. Thomas Weiskel, *The Romantic Sublime: Studies in the Structure and Psychology of Transcendence* (Baltimore: Johns Hopkins University Press, 1976), 19.

17. This is Suleri's argument about Burke, that his notion of the sublime was in part a confrontation with the excessive recalcitrance and difference of Indian particularities; see Suleri, *Rhetoric of English India.*

18. See Jerome McGann, *The Romantic Ideology* (Chicago: University of Chicago Press, 1982).

19. Immanuel Kant, Critique of Aesthetic Judgement, cited in Ernst Cassirer, *Kant's Life and Thought* (New Haven: Yale University Press, 1981), 328.

20. Ibid., 328.

21. Jerome McGann, *Social Values and Poetic Acts* (Cambridge: Harvard University Press, 1988), 36.

22. Ibid., 39.

23. Ibid., 39–40.

24. Edmund Burke, *Reflections on the Revolution in France* (New York, 1973), 73–74.

25. Ann Bermingham, "System, Order, and Abstraction: The Politics of English Landscape Drawing around 1795," in *Landscape and Power,* ed. W. J. T. Mitchell (Chicago: University of Chicago Press, 1994), 78.

26. "The ruins of the Tower can be seen to this day. But he who sees them is cursed with the loss of memory. All the people on earth who go around saying, 'Who am I, Who am I,' are ones who have seen the ruins of the Tower of Babel." *Midrash Rabbah.* I am grateful to Anton Shammas for bringing this to my attention.

27. Walter Benjamin, *Illuminations* (London: Fontana Collins, 1982), 258.

28. Ibid., 258.

29. Susan Buck-Morss, *The Origin of Negative Dialectics: Theodor W. Adorno, Walter Benjamin, and the Frankfurt Institute* (New York: Free Press, 1977), 147.

30. Benjamin, *Illuminations,* 228.

31. Ibid., 233.

32. Buck-Morss, *Origin of Negative Dialectics,* 149.

33. See Max Horkheimer and Theodor Adorno, *Dialectic of Enlightenment* (New York: Herder and Herder, 1972), 120–67.

34. Ibid., 126.

35. Ibid.

36. Ibid., 127.

37. Ibid., 166–67.
38. Ibid., 131.
39. Ibid., 130.
40. Friedrich Nietzsche, *The Birth of Tragedy* (New York: Vintage Books, 1964), 60. I am grateful to Peter van der Veer for pointing this passage out to me.
41. See Georges Bataille, *The Accursed Share* (New York: Zone Books, 1991).
42. Again, I am grateful to Peter van der Veer for urging me to bring out this parallel more clearly.
43. Buck-Morss, *Origin of Negative Dialectics*, 190.
44. I refer here, of course, to the field that has been established in the wake of Edward Said's *Orientalism* (New York: Vintage Books, 1979); for Said's most recent treatment of the relation of imperialism to Western cultural legacies, see his *Culture and Imperialism* (New York: Knopf, 1993).
45. Benjamin writes, "The angel would like to stay, awaken the dead, and make whole what has been smashed. But a storm is blowing from paradise; it has got caught in his wings with such violence that the angel can no longer close them. This storm irresistably propels him into the future to which his back is turned, while the pile of debris before him grows skyward. This storm is what we call progress"; see *Illuminations*, 259–60.

2

The Culture of History

Gyanendra Pandey

The relationship between culture, nation, and history is closer than historians have generally been willing to acknowledge. At the end of the twentieth century, a curious twin movement has occurred in the matter of history writing. On the one hand, the "crisis" of nationalism—or at least the rethinking of the place of nationalisms and nation-states in the world—has been accompanied by a considerable debate on the privileged status of "history" as objective, scientific and "true." On the other hand, there has been a considerable renewal of extremist nationalism (perhaps because of this very crisis), and with it a renewal of some of the shallowest kinds of chauvinist, nationalist histories. I wish to examine one of these here in order to raise some questions about "the culture of history" as we know it.

Pronouncements of the death of history and of nationhood notwithstanding, the contest over history rages on everywhere. It is renewed time and again by a question that, far from going away, seems to be asked as insistently as ever by a growing body of right-wing opinion all over the world. The matter at issue is frequently articulated in the following terms: "What is the real culture of this nation?" which may also be translated as, "Whose country is this anyway?" In response to this question, new claims are made, or sometimes old claims are refurbished and put forward in an old style. It is this style, this mode of historical reconstruction, that I wish to reflect on in the following investigation of what I call the new Hindu history of India.

I

Over the past decade or so, a resurgent, right-wing Hindu movement has actively advanced what it sees as a new, alternative history of India, one that is said to be in tune with the unique character and traditions of its people. Peddled, promoted, and circulated in a number of recensions, this particular representation of the past has threatened to establish a new historical orthodoxy in that country, a new chronology of Hindu-Muslim military contests in the subcontinent, and, underlying this, a renewed belief in the inevitability of such contests, given the character of the people on the two sides.

The persuasiveness of this new Hindu history has been explained in various ways. That a powerful political movement, with massive financial and organizational resources, has been able successfully to disseminate its version of historical "truth" is hardly surprising, it is said. The argument is made too that economic misfortunes and the availability of a ready explanation (and scapegoat) for them have made for the widespread acceptance of this kind of history. While these suggestions are not irrelevant, they are plainly inadequate. They do not begin to tell us why other powerful political movements (e.g., of the left), and other available explanations have not had the same kind of impact. They seem not to recognize, either, that the widespread acceptance of the Hindu version of the history of the Muslims in India has contributed greatly to the rise of the new right-wing Hindu movement, not just the other way around.

To reopen the question of the appeal of Hindu history, let us first underline what seem to be its central claims to truth. Hindu history poses as a history of the local community, the society (*samaj* or, more accurately, Hindu *samaj*) as against the state: in other words, it claims to be a history that speaks in the language and voice of the people about their most deeply rooted beliefs and desires, which have (in this view) been too long suppressed. Further, and obviously in relation to the above claim, it asserts its position as an "authentic" Indian history, as distinct from the slavish imitation of Western histories produced by *deraciné* scholars ensconced in privileged positions in the universities and research institutions of the subcontinent.

A reexamination of the persuasiveness of different kinds of history may profitably begin with the question of language—in the sense both of the medium of speech and writing—and of the mode of constructing and framing historical, political, social-scientific arguments and statements. The critical importance of language in the production of knowledge, particular kinds of history, and particular kinds of politics is now widely recognized. Yet in India, perhaps in common with developments elsewhere, this recognition seems to have had little effect on practice. The notion of two Indias, India and Bharat, that populist politicians have promoted especially since the days of Rajiv Gandhi, retains considerable force in the country today. It is not that prominent secular historians never write in Hindi, Urdu, Bengali, Tamil, and so on; it is rather that they write predominantly in English and for a small, English-knowing, "modern," "secular," internationalist audience, whether living in India or abroad. Secular contributions to the debate in Hindi, Bengali, and Marathi, as it is conducted, say, in Delhi, Calcutta, and Bombay, are often translations. The regional-language press seems to have been handed over, as it were, to those who are not quite so "secular," "modern," or "cosmopolitan."

This "secular" inattention to language (and, therefore, to history, particularity, culture) is evident in other ways as well. The English-language press and social-scientific discourse in India have readily accepted the Hindu right-wing's chosen terms of self-description. For a long time now, we have spoken of Ram Janmabhumi, referring by that term to a precise spot once occupied by a small medieval monument, rather than to the general area of Ayodhya, which is, in Hindu belief, the *bhumi* (land, zone, region) of Ram's birth. We have taken to designating right-wing Hindu forces as the forces of Hindutva, thus conceding the entire heritage of "Hindu-ness" (or Hindu "tradition") to those who spuriously claim it, and surrendering the polemical charge of calling the right-wing's reactionary politics by its proper political name. Worse, we write of *sadhus* and *sants* (even translated as "saints" in the English press), of the *Sangh Parivar* (the "family" sprouted by the Rashtriya Swayamsevak Sangh), and the *Dharma Sansad* (religious parliament? parliament of religions? parliament of religious figures?).

Notice that there is not even a trace of irony in the secularists' use of these as descriptive terms. Consider, on the other hand, the terms used by journals like *Organizer* and *Paanchjanya* to describe the political opponents of the Hindu Right: "secular *giroh*" (gang of secularists), "pseudo-secularists" (and now the word *secularism,* having been associated so long with terms like *pseudo-* and *minorityism,* is often by itself enough of a condemnation), "slaves of the West," or "Westernism."

The Hindu Right's use of Hindi, Marathi, Malayalam, and so on for their political propaganda is of course important. But that use of local languages reflects, or perhaps produces, a sensitivity to language (and to linguistic/cultural sensibilities) that English-speaking secular academics and journalists in India could certainly learn from. Let me illustrate this by reference to the great importance attached by the so-called *Sangh Parivar* to the word used to describe the Babari Masjid, the disused sixteenth-century mosque in the small town of Ayodhya, in northern India, which became the focus of the Hindu Right's "Sri Ram Janmabhumi liberation movement" (or movement for the "liberation" of the birthplace of the God, Ram) between 1986 and 1992. In India today, it is a declaration of political position—or I suppose of position as a member of a "minority" Muslim community—to speak of the Babari Masjid. For the rest, for those who would reserve their political choices as well as for the Hindu Right, it is not, nor ever was, a *masjid* (mosque). It was the "so-called *masjid*." It was a *mandir* (Hindu temple) that had, nevertheless, to be destroyed. It was a "victory monument," "a sign of slavery" (*gulami ki nishani*), or of betrayal (*haram ki nishani*). It was, and astonishingly, given our ineptitude, may against all odds continue to be a "disputed structure." Certainly, the latter term has now passed into the vocabulary of elite political (and historical) discourse in India. Narasimha Rao, a prime minister hailed by the Hindu Right as the best in India since Lal Bahadur Shastri, is condemned forever from the moment he refers to the Babari Masjid as the Babari Masjid.

In the same way, the Hindu Right has played, and played to a large extent successfully, with notions of religion, culture, and politics. Hinduism is not a religion. It is the way of life, the manner of being, of people living in this part of the world. Everyone who lives in Hindustan is a Hindu; thus Bhai Parmanand could be asked in the United States whether every Hindu was a Muslim, and Imam Bukhari (the Shahi Imam of the Jama Masjid of Delhi), on a visit to Mecca, whether he was a Hindu. Ram is not a religious, but a national hero. The Ram Janmabhumi liberation movement is not a political but a religious movement—or the other way around.

Hindu history, like Hindu politics, has thrived on this play. It has moved unapologetically and unselfconsciously between the divine and the mundane. The opening paragraph of Ramgopal Pandey Sharad's *Shri Ram Janmabhumi ka Romanchkari Itihasa* (*The Thrilling History of Shri Ram Janmabhumi*) illustrates the point very well indeed:

> [Nine hundred thousand] years ago, the supreme ideal of manhood, Lord Shri Ramchandraji, took on his earthly incarnation in precisely this hallowed land/area. He rolled in the pure dust of this sacred spot... and, along with Bharat, Lakshman and Shatrughanji, thus enacted his rare and divine childhood. The Hindu rulers who graced the throne of India [Bharat] many centuries before Christ defended it all along. [Note this unheralded first reference to the site of Ram's birth, the Ram Janmabhumi, as a monument.] They repaired it from time to time, but at the time of the Kiratas and the Huna invasions, they turned their attention away from the site. As a result, the ancient temple [the first mention of this] was destroyed and no trace of it remained. In the end, a century or so before Christ, the shining light of the Hindu family, Em-

peror Vikramaditya, rediscovered the site after great effort and constructed a grand temple at the sacred spot.[1]

There is much to be said about the ease with which this paragraph moves from the alleged birth of Ram, nine hundred thousand years ago in the Treta Yuga, to the Hindu kings who graced "the throne of India" in the centuries (millennia?) before Christ, to the destruction of what could have been an "eternal," not just "ancient" temple (for its construction is nowhere mentioned), to the rediscovery of the site and the construction of another grand temple by Vikramaditya, a king who has still to be satisfactorily identified. But before entering into a more detailed discussion of these moves, it may be helpful to review some of the more obvious features of the new Hindu history.

II

The militant Hindu reconstruction of the Indian past is well illustrated in the Hindu Right's account of the history of Ayodhya, the claimed Ram Janmabhumi and site of the Babari Masjid. Perhaps the first thing that would strike the academic investigator about the histories of Ayodhya, produced in abundance in recent years by Hindu enthusiasts, is their pulp quality. Sold (or distributed) along with audiocassettes, badges, posters, images of gods and goddesses, other memorabilia, moral tales, and books of common prayer or devotional songs by Hindu right-wing sympathizers in Ayodhya and elsewhere, these pamphlets — produced in very cheap and short-lived editions, crudely written, and poorly printed on rough paper — seem scarcely worthy of our attention. Only the power of the political movement with which they are associated and which they reflect and reinforce has made us turn to them.

The next observation that one might make, if one bothers to collect and examine a number of these histories over the years, is that they are remarkably repetitive: so repetitive that they are hard to read with the best will in the world. Having looked at one or two, one is persuaded (perhaps rightly) that there is no need to look at any more. The repetitiveness is marked between publications, which often seem no more than quick copies of earlier productions with minor variations, as well as within individual histories. The uniformity and the repetitiveness start with the very titles of these productions. Here are five of them:

> *Shri Ram Janmabhumi: Sachitra, Pramanik Itihasa* (*An Illustrated and Authoritative History of Shri Ram Janmabhumi*; the booklet itself provides the translation as *An Illustrated and Authentic History,* and the

"authenticity" is underlined by the announcement that the author has an M.A. and Ph.D. in Archaeology and History), Ayodhya 1986.

Shri Ram Janmabhumi ka Pramanik Itihasa (*The Authoritative/Authentic History of Shri Ram Janmabhumi*), date and place of publication not given.

Shri Ram Janmabhumi ka tala kaise khula. Shri Ram Janmabhumi ka Romanchkari Itihasa (*How the Locks* [placed on the gates of the Babari Masjid/Ram Janmabhumi complex in 1949] *Were Opened. The Horripilating History of Shri Ram Janmabhumi*), Ayodhya, n.d.

Shri Ram Janmabhumi ka Rakt Ranjit Itihasa. Tala kaise khula? (*The Blood-Stained History of Shri Ram Janmabhumi. How the Gates Were Unlocked*), Ayodhya, n.d.

Mukti Yagya. Shri Ram Janmabhumi ka Sampurna Itihasa (*Sacrifice for Liberation. The Entire History of Shri Ram Janmabhumi*), Ayodhya, 1991.

The sequence of events (or chronology) that provides the core of these works is also noteworthy for its marked repetitiveness. This chronology appears as follows, with only slight variations of dates and numbers in different accounts:

1. 900,000 years ago—Birth of Ram and hence of Ram Janmabhumi (RJB)
2. 150 years B.C. (Greek and Kushana times)—Battle to liberate RJB
3. 100 years B.C.—Vikramaditya's rediscovery of RJB, and construction of grand RJB temple
4. Salar Mas'ud's time—two battles to liberate RJB
5. Babar's reign—Destruction of temple, construction of mosque; four battles to liberate RJB
6. Humayun's reign   ten battles to liberate RJB
7. Akbar's reign   twenty battles to liberate RJB
8. Aurangzeb's reign   thirty battles to liberate RJB
9. Sa'adat Ali of Avadh's reign   five battles to liberate RJB
10. Nasiruddin Haidar's reign   three battles to liberate RJB
11. Wajid Ali Shah's reign   two battles to liberate RJB
12. 1857: Attempted compromise between Hindus and Muslims over RJB (thwarted by British machinations)
13. British rule (1912 and 1934)   two battles to liberate RJB
14. December 1949: Appearance of Ram (in the form of the infant Ramlala), and installation of images of Ramlala inside the mosque. Building locked by administrative order to maintain the peace.
15. 1986: Opening of locks on Babari Masjid/RJB temple.[2]

Note that this chronology, based on one of the earliest in the new series of Hindu histories of Ayodhya, which is explicitly acknowledged as the source of some of the later accounts, gives a total of seventy-nine battles fought by the Hindus for the liberation of the Ram Janmabhumi. The magic number was, however, subsequently fixed at seventy-six, which is the number of battles supposedly fought since the time of the Mughals, with whom the history of Muslims in India is readily equated. The battle for the liberation of the RJB that was launched in the mid-1980s was, therefore, always referred to as the seventy-seventh, and I shall treat it here as that.

The point of this history is to enumerate the many occasions when the Hindus have risen in defense of the Janmabhumi and to catalog their enormous sacrifices. The opening pages of another early publication in this series, *Ham Mandir Vahin Banayenge*, illustrate the argument.[3] The first chapter begins with the title "Lakhon shish chadhe jis thaon. Shri Ram Janmabhumi ka itihasa — Amar balidangatha." ("Where *Lakhs* of Lives Were Offered Up. The History of Shri Ram Janmabhumi — A Saga of Eternal Sacrifice"). Above the title on the title page appears a note to say that seventy-seven battles have been waged and three hundred thousand lives sacrificed by the Hindus for the protection and liberation of the Ram Janmabhumi *mandir*.

The initial paragraphs of the history set the tone of the narrative that follows. After a statement on the antiquity of the town of Ayodhya, the text says,

> Foreign aggressions on Ayodhya also have a very ancient history. The first aggressor was the . . . notorious King of Lanka, Ravana, who destroyed Ayodhya during the time of the ancestors of Shri Ram Ravana's death, along with his entire family, at the hands of Shri Ram is a story known all over the world.
>
> In history, the second external attack upon Ayodhya was by the Greek king Milind or Mihirgupta (Menander), who was the first aggressor to have destroyed the Shri Ram Janmabhumi temple. But Indian pride arose to punish this irreligious foreigner for his evil deed [*dus-sahasa*; literally, "misguided (or foolish) bravery"], and within three months Raja Dyumatsena of the Sunga dynasty had killed Milind in a fierce war and again liberated Ayodhya. . . .
>
> The third aggressor to attack Ayodhya was Salar Masud, a nephew of the notorious Muslim plunderer, Mahmud Ghaznavi. Destroying temples as he went along, Masud reached [the environs of] Ayodhya and destroyed temples in the vicinity. But the united strength of the Rajas of Ayodhya and the surrounding areas and the attacks of the *sadhus* of the Digambari *akhada* prevented his conquering army from entering Ayodhya. He then moved to the north, but in 1033 A.D., 17 local Rajas led by Raja Suhail Dev surrounded that beastly irreligious tyrannical plunderer . . . in Bahraich, and sent the entire invading army to their graves. After this, all of Mahmud and Masud's successors were also beaten and driven from the country. . . .
>
> The next plunderer who attacked Ayodhya with the object of destroying the Shri Ram Janmabhumi temple was Babar. . . . This ungrate-

ful plunderer [who had been given refuge, food, and shelter by people in different parts of India] responded to India's native tolerance and hospitality by ordering his Commander-in-Chief, Mir Baqi, to destroy the huge, palatial Shri Ram Janmabhumi temple that had stood in Ayodhya since Vikramaditya's time, in order to simply please two evil Muslim *faqirs*. But . . . the people [the country] rose in fierce opposition to this vile attack on their national honor. The historian Cunningham writes [the reference is to *Lucknow Gazetteer*, pt. 26, p. 3], "At the time of the destruction of the Janmabhumi temple the Hindus sacrificed everything and it was only after 1 Lakh [= 100,000], 74 thousand Hindu lives had been lost that Mir Baqi succeeded in bringing down the temple with his cannons."[4]

Through the many recensions of the Hindu history of Ayodhya, it is this story of "foreign" aggression and native valor, of eternal Hindu activism and sacrifice, that is endlessly repeated. Context—the very heart of the historian's discipline, we might say—counts for nothing. I shall return to this point. For the moment, let me draw attention to two other fairly obvious features of Hindu history.

One is the importance of numbers. Numbers appear to be crucial here not only for their suggestion of statistical accuracy and historical precision: seventy-six (or seventy-seven, or seventy-nine as the case may be) battles fought for the "liberation" of the RJB; the seven hundred soldiers of Babar's army that Devi Din Pandey accounted for with his sword alone and in the face of a constant rain of bullets in just three hours (which, according to the Hindu account, Babar himself confirms); and, further, of Devi Din's inevitable offering of his own life in this process: "On 9 June 1528 A.D., at 2:00 P.M., Pandit Devi Din Pandey breathed his last." They represent the "excess" that characterizes all nationalist narratives. Hence we have Devi Din Pandey's seven hundred victims in a span of three hours; or the 174,000 Hindu lives sacrificed before Mir Baqi was able to bring down the temple; or the "hundreds" of monkeys who attacked the Mughal camp one day during the same period, engaged the soldiers in battle for several hours, and silenced their guns and cannons; or the ten thousand tong-wielding (*chimtadhar*) *sadhus*, who worsted Aurangzeb's army "with their tongs alone"; or, to take a non-numerical example, the "indescribably beautiful" Rani Jairaj Kumari, who formed a band of several hundred (or several thousand) female guerrillas to attack the Ram Janmabhumi on numerous occasions through the reigns of Babar, Humayan, and Akbar.

Numbers are important, too, in fixing the boundaries of the (unchanging) "community" (or "nation")—of "us" and "them." A pamphlet entitled *Angry Hindu? Yes, Why Not?* puts it as follows: "I (the "Hindus") form eighty-five per cent of this land: why should I be denied my rights?" The "Hindu" is these hundreds of millions of people — of one opinion and one vision. As *Ham Mandir Vahin Banayenge* has it, in a note that appears above the title on its title page, that title is the pledge, determination, and vision (*sankalp*) of "the 700 million Hindus of the entire world."

A final feature of these histories of Ayodhya that clearly deserves notice is their straddling of the worlds of religious and historical discourse. As I have mentioned, these histories are sold (or distributed) at pilgrim sites, along with images of deities, religious calendars, prayer books and the like, and bought perhaps as often for the decoration of a household shrine or prayer-room as for reading individually or in groups. They are prefaced or headed frequently by an "Om," a *mantra,* or a longer prayer to Shri Ram. They begin in the age of Ram, nine hundred thousand and more years ago, and they are marked by an easy (and, in a sense, unceasing) intervention of the divine or, to put it in other terms, a realization of the ineffable that lies behind the illusions of this fleeting world.

Thus, to take the most recent examples first, Hindu history tells us of the miraculous appearance of the infant Ramlala inside the Babari Masjid on a cold December night in 1949, attested to (in the Hindu account) by the Muslim policeman who was there on guard duty. We also have Ram, "unable to bear the suffering of his *bhaktas* (devotees) any longer," intervening through a local lawyer and a local magistrate in Faizabad to have the locks on the mosque/temple opened in 1986. There is evidence of divine intervention again in November 1990, when a number of *kar sevaks* "miraculously" scaled the Babari Masjid and attained the heights of the domes in a matter of moments (a feat, we are told, that took the trained commandos at the site, with all their equipment, over half an hour to accomplish). There is evidence also of the appearance of a large monkey which sat for a long time on top of the central dome, with the *bhagwa dhwaj* (saffron flag, emblem of the Hindu movement) in "his" hands: veritably, it is claimed, this was the monkey-god, the greatest Rambhakta of all, Hanuman himself.

The sequence of divine intervention began, of course, a long, long time ago. In historical times, its first startling manifestation occurs at the time of the Emperor Vikramaditya who "rediscovered" the Ram Janmabhumi. As the Hindu account has it, a tired Vikramaditya, accidentally separated from his companions, was resting by the river Saryu to regain his breath when he saw a handsome black prince, dressed from top to toe in black and mounted on a black horse, enter the river. When the horse and rider came out again a few moments later, an amazing transformation had taken place: the prince's mount, his clothes, his face, were all now shining white.

Overwhelmed, Vikramaditya went up to the strange prince and asked him to explain the meaning of this "vision." The prince explained: "I am Tirtharaj Prayag [the pilgrimage center, Prayag or Allahabad, personified]. Every year [at a certain time] I come with the countless sins I have taken onto myself from the millions of pilgrims who come to cleanse their sins at Prayag, and these are washed away by the Saryu" (which, therefore, becomes even more efficacious than Prayag as a site of pilgrimage and a step to salvation). Asked for further advice and guidance, Tirtharaj Prayag tells Vikramaditya to reestablish the Ram Janmabhumi. Aided by signs and measurements told to him by Tirtharaj, Vikramaditya rediscovers Ayodhya, establishes the exact site of the Janmabhumi by setting free a cow newly delivered of a calf (milk begins to flow automatically from her udders as soon as she reaches the sacred spot), and builds there a grand temple on the eighty-four pillars of black touchstone.

The subsequent history of the Ram Janmabhumi is in line with this half-human half-divine, "neither-this-nor-that" scenario—as indeed at "Ram Janmabhumi" it ought to be. The point is illustrated dramatically by the difficulties experienced by Babar in converting the temple into a mosque. After Babar had overcome "the Hindus" in a long and furious battle in which the Mughal forces were beaten back time and again, he left Ayodhya instructing his lieutenant, Mir Baqi Khan of Tashkent, to build a mosque on the site of the temple using the material of the temple. But this proved to be no easy task. "The walls that were built during the day came down [as if by miracle] at night," and this continued to happen day after day, until Mir Baqi in despair urged Babar to return and see things for himself.

Babar returned, and seeing that his people were completely frustrated, was forced to consult local *sadhus* (Hindu ascetics or holy men) and accept a compromise that gave him a way out. The *sadhus* said that Hanuman was against the construction of the mosque, and no building could occur until he was persuaded. In the end, as (according to our Hindu historians) Babar himself had written in his memoirs, the Hindus laid down five conditions: "The *masjid* was to be called 'Sita Pak' [Sita's *rasoi,* or kitchen]. The space for circumambulation around the central structure [*parikrama*] had to be preserved. A wooden door was to be erected at the main entrance. The turrets/spires were to be brought down. And Hindu *mahatmas* [religious leaders] were to be allowed to conduct prayers and recitations." Every one of these conditions negated the concept of a *masjid,* according to this Hindu account. Thus, it was not the Hindus but Babar who had ultimately to surrender. Even in the form of a mosque, the RJB remained a temple. Even in defeat the Hindus were (as, implicitly, they always will be) victorious.

III

I have suggested that a sense of eternal (and united) Hindu activism and sacrifice, of numbers (which testify again to Hindu strength), and of a divine "play" or "order" (once again revealing the power of "the Hindu"), actuates the Hindu history of Ayodhya. It is easy to mock this history for its obvious inconsistencies of time, place, and circumstance, its fallacious logic, its fraudulent use of sources, and its fabrication of many "historical" events.[5] It may be more interesting and effective however, to seek to unravel the organizing principles of such a history, its objects of analysis, the subject positions it affirms, and the notions of time that it works with. Through this exercise, it may be possible, too, to arrive at a somewhat better appreciation of the relation of this history to the modern, statist histories that it so vociferously condemns.

The Hindu history of Ayodhya, as found in all its recent versions, is not about the region, much less the people, of Ayodhya; it is not even about a spot now called the Ram Janmabhumi; it is about a building on that spot. This entire history is focused on a monument, which we can for the moment designate the "grand temple" built (and rebuilt) on the site of Shri Ram's "birth." Everything revolves around this monument. The narrative begins with the destruction of the monument, and returns to this point again and again. Two paragraphs that appear as a preface in one edition of *Shri Ram Janmabhumi ka Romanchkari Itihasa* and as postscript in another, illustrate this proposition.

I quote the opening line of the first paragraph, which is headed, "The Hindu Signs at the Janmabhumi": "Several Hindu features remained when the temple was demolished and given the form of a mosque: these are features that Babar was forced to retain because the walls [of the proposed mosque] kept falling down on their own." The second paragraph, headed "The Pillars of Black Touch-Stone," reads as follows:

> The ancient Shri Ram temple was built on 84 black touch-stone pillars. These had been constructed by King Aranya of the ... Surya dynasty. Ravana defeated Aranya in battle and carried the pillars away [to Lanka], from where they were brought back to Ayodhya by Shri Ram after his victory over Ravana ... The [Babari] *masjid* was built upon these very pillars, upon which the aforesaid images [of Hindu gods and goddesses] can still be seen, along with inscriptions of Maharaja Aranya, Ravana and Lord Shri Ram on some pillars. Of the 84 black touch-stone pillars, 11 are in the Babri Masjid, 2 at the entrance to the *mandir* [i.e., the same *masjid*] and [another 2?] at the [nearby] grave of Kajal Abbas [one of the Muslim *faqirs* said to have incited Babar to demolish the Ram Janmabhumi temple], and some are added to the glories of the museums in Lucknow, Faizabad and London.

What follows, in every account published in the last decade, is a longer or shorter description of battle after battle fought by the Hindus to liberate the site, remove the mosque, and rebuild the grand temple: seventy-six battles before the most recent one, which is the seventy-seventh. The monument, one could say, is the history.

This marks a significant change from earlier histories of the Ram Janmabhumi, the Krsna Janmabhumi, and so on, examples of which may still be found in Mathura. Here, at the site of the claimed Krsna Janmabhumi (or birthplace of the Lord Krishna), the pulp histories that are sold concentrate on the life of Sri Krsna, and stories of his exploits as a child and an adult are presented alongside a fairly bland account of the several temples built at various nearby sites, the destruction by Aurangzeb of the last "grand" temple, and the establishment of organizations to promote the worship of Krsna in Mathura and improve facilities for pilgrims, Indian and foreign.

Traces of a somewhat more open and tentative history of Ayodhya may also be found in some of the earlier publications associated with the latest round of Hindu agitation for the liberation of the Ram Janmabhumi from the mid-1980s. These begin with attempts to describe the grandeur of the "ancient city," as presented in the Valmiki *Ramayana,* for example, and acknowledge the gaps in our knowledge of this history: the difficulty of establishing who the "Vikramaditya" of tradition was and how he "rediscovered" Ayodhya; the fact that Ayodhya was built many times and many times fell into ruin; the long periods when the city had little habitation or activity (even down to the so-called Muslim period).

No such tentativeness or uncertainty is to be found in the "mature" Hindu history contained in works like *Romanchkari, Rakt-ranjit* or *Sampurna Itihasa.* The eighty-four black stone pillars, straddling the world from the age of Ram (and even earlier) to the age of colonial and postcolonial museums, capture the spirit of this history as it is evoked by the most recent Hindu historians of Ayodhya: its antiquity, its beauty and solidity, its destruction, and its continued existence.

It goes without saying that the eighty-four pillars stand for much more than a town called Ayodhya: they stand for the Ram Janmabhumi, for Hinduism, for the Hindu spirit and culture, the Hindu people, the nation. Ayodhya, or should we say the black stone pillars, are a symbol (*pratik*) of the "eternal," "undefeated" (Ayodhya means "that which cannot be defeated") Hindu nation. This is why this history refers constantly to the religious and national spirit of the native Hindu ever engaged in battle against the "irreligious, foreign invader"; the "Hindu kings who graced the throne of India [Bharat] in the centuries [even millennia] before Christ"; the united struggle of kings, *sadhus,* and the common people (Hindus) against any insult to the national honor—meaning almost always, to the Ram Janmabhumi.

Interestingly, however, the recent Hindu history of Ayodhya, which also stands for the Hindu history of India, is not about the *construction* of the Ram Janmabhumi temple. It is about its *destruction.* To that extent, it is a history, not of the temple but of the mosque built upon its ruins, not of the greatness of the "Hindu" but of the evilness of the "Muslim."

It is notable that the construction of the ancient temple is not mentioned, but simply assumed, and the construction of Vikramaditya's "grand" temple is never detailed (though his rediscovery of the site is). What is detailed is the destruction: how long it took, at whose hands it occurred, with what subterfuges and difficulties it was accomplished, and what features were left standing.

Even more significantly, the number of battles fought for the liberation of the Janmabhumi is fixed at seventy-six, which by the Hindu historians' own account is the number of battles fought for the liberation of the site since the time of Babar. The battles fought before Babar's time and listed by some early Hindu historians, including the two battles supposedly waged to fend off the invasion of Salar Mas'ud Ghazi, do not count in the end, for this is in fact a *history of the mosque* and attempts to obliterate it. It is no accident, then, that so many of these histories should begin their account of the history of Ayodhya with a statement of the "Hindu" signs still to be found in the mosque (until its destruction on 6 December 1992), or that the volume entitled *Shri Ram Janmabhumi ka Sampurna Itihasa (The Entire History of the Shri Ram Janmabhumi)* should add on its inside cover "from 1528 A.D. to today."

If the monument constitutes the history of Ayodhya/India, and the monument is in fact a mosque (by whatever name it may now be called), it follows that the Hindu account is very close indeed to the colonial account of the Indian past. As in the colonial account, "Hindu" and "Muslim" here are fully constituted from the start, and all of Indian history for centuries prior to the coming of the British becomes a history of perennial Hindu-Muslim conflict. The differences are minor, but noteworthy. What are "riots," "convulsions," or symptoms of a disease for colonialist writers are "wars" for the Hindu historian (though it must be noted that many colonialists were happy enough to describe Hindu-Muslim conflicts as "religious" or "national" wars). Wars have their heroes and villains, and Hindu history quickly runs up a long list of Hindu heroes and Muslim villains (joined just occasionally by Hindu villains), whereas for colonialist historiography Hindus and Muslims were uniformly villains (or at least beasts), with rare exceptions.

Another difference follows from the preconstituted character of the Muslims as congenitally evil, and the Hindus as tolerant, hospitable, liberal, and in an extension of colonial stereotypes that would surely have been unacceptable to the colonialist, part of the divine. Curiously, given the all-embracing character of Hindu philosophy, this modest status of being a small part of infinity is not accorded to the Muslim. Rather, the Muslim, "foreigner," "invader," and "irreligious being," who may be seen as scheming, greedy, lustful, and bigoted, is fully to be blamed for "his" actions (women figure, on both Hindu and Muslim sides, merely as property: extraordinary cases, like that of Rani Jairaj Kumari, are after all extraordinary). The Hindus, on the other hand—kings, landlords, *sadhus,* and even ordinary villagers—since they are all part of the divine, only serve a divine purpose and are, in that sense, not responsible for their actions. It is in that sense, too, I suggest, that they can never be defeated, according to the canons of Hindu history.

The remarkably different subject-positions occupied by Hindu and Muslim point to the vexatious interpenetration of different orders of time, indeed different domains of history, that take place in the Hindu account. The construction of the original Ram Janmabhumi temple, and its destruction, represent the quintessence of these different orders, different histories, the divine and the mundane.

From the time of Shri Ram (and even earlier), which can scarcely be described, which is beyond human time, to the ossified exhibits of colonial and postcolonial museums, divine time runs into historical (and archaeological) time. Hindu history is quite untroubled by this colossal chronological span, or by the huge gaps in it for example, between (1) and (2) in the chronological table given in section II above; or, on an altered, "modern" historical time-scale, between (3) and (4); or, in the greatly accelerated chronological arrangements of contemporary history, between (13) and (14).

There is a timeless, epic quality to this history in its proposition of beginnings that are not beginnings, destruction that is not destruction; in the circular character of the narrative, which returns to the same point again and again, and in which nothing changes; and in its suggestion that those participating in the "liberation" war against Babar (or against pseudosecularists today) are one with those who joined the war against Ravana. What the account does is to atemporalize events. Even the enumeration of battles fails to change this aspect of the narration. While enumeration usually implies linearity, the enumeration here has no such logic attached to it. It might be either random or entirely self-contained; and it does not necessarily grow. The seventy-six battles do not build up to different ends, not even somewhat different ends, but are in the end all the same.

The curious mixture of cyclical time and instrumentality found in these accounts has the structure of a rudimentary fable, where all events ultimately point one way. However, the collision of times is striking. Remote, golden, happy; overturned by a mythic cycle of bloodletting, savagery and valor; disrupted into linearity once again by the possibility of an "end" today. Mythic time schemes leak into positive, historical, realistic time. Marked by what Koseleck has called "the self-accelerating temporality of the 'modern,'"[6] epic time turns back upon itself in the demand for a final resolution now.

The "Muslim invasion" (equated frequently in both Hindu and colonialist historiography with the rule of the Great Mughals, dated to 1528, for Babar's attack on the RJB is the central motif) and "Indian independence" (the appearance of Ramlala in 1949 being a sign of this) are the two precisely dated historical events around which the discourse of Hindu history and politics turns. At one pole is Babar, the foreigner and invader, and with him all Indian Muslims, the progeny of that invader (*Babar ki aulad*) and a blot on India's history (not unlike the Babari Masjid). At the other end, this history is animated by the "continued slavery" of India (and especially of India's Westernized ruling class) even forty years after formal independence, which does not allow "us" (the Hindus: that is, the nation) to build a temple at this, "our" most sacred site, in "our" own country — the only Hindu country in the world (Nepal, of course, easily disappears). Eternal, epic conflict between the gods and the demons there was, at the Ram Janmabhumi, but final victory, it appears, is now at hand. Seven hundred million Hindus have awakened, and they will build the temple at precisely that spot, with their own hands, today.

In the end, then, this account belies its pretensions to epic status. If the epic tradition is distinguished by the absence of beginnings, middles, and ends, and of unidirectionality, by the refusal to privilege a single point of view, by the problematizing of the good and the bad, then Hindu history departs radically from it. In many senses, it is closer to the worst kind of realist melodrama, where Good is Good, and Evil is Evil, a thief is a thief, and that's all there is to that.

Hindu history seems to be a long way, too, from being the antistatist history that it claims to be, giving voice to society and "community." It is worlds apart, for instance, from the local nineteenth-century history of a weaver's *qasba* in northern India, in which the community is the subject of history and community honor the object of its analysis.[7] In the latter the idea of the community is valorized, but at the same time it has no fixed boundaries; it attaches itself to different collectivities and has multiple meanings, depending on context. In Hindu history, by contrast, the community ("Hindu" even more than the Muslim) is a clearly enumerated community, with boundaries that are fixed from the beginnings of time. In that sense, it has no history. What is more, this Hindu community can realize itself only through the capture of state power, which is, of course, the stuff of Hindu politics and Hindu history today.

IV

What does this Hindu history tell us about nationalist history, or even history in general? There are several themes here—the enumeration of forces and communities, the substantialization of cultures and national spirit in monuments, and so on—that are common to nationalist history. What is perhaps more notable is the demonizing of cultural modes and practices other than those of the groups in power, the putative "mainstream," in other words, of any mark of difference that, simply by being different, supposedly constitutes a threat to the nation and its culture.

This task of demonizing may be accomplished in numerous ways. One of the most powerful of these is to write histories of the obstinacy, the persistence, and the irreducibility of this difference, even in the face of mainstream accommodation and attempts at assimilation. Understandably, nationalist histories usually deny any evidence of change, or the possibility of change, among those whom they construct as different, even as they assert the changelessness of national culture.

However, history plays an even larger part in the construction of this argument about mainstream national cultures and the alien bodies (unfortunately welcomed or tolerated by a generous nation) that threaten it. It does so by positing a centralized, uniform, single history of each territory and people that has been constituted into a nation. One might argue in fact that this is the fundamental mode of history. History as we know it is framed from the start by the national project; and the nation must, by definition, have a uniform history. One consequence is that history cannot but demonize, or marginalize, certain aspects of the lives and conditions (past, present, and future) of particular populations, even as it celebrates those of others.

Secular, liberal, and left-wing historians in India—and I use the term broadly to include political figures, journalists, and others writing historical accounts—have worked consistently over the last hundred years and more to construct a unified, uniform, centralized, and (by extension) undifferentiated "Indian history." I think it can plausibly be argued that this is the very ground, the condition, of a unified, uniform, centralized, and undifferentiated "Hindu history." A second point, related to this, is that the secular historian, in common with all other "modern" social scientists in India, has insisted on a single language, a uniform vocabulary, a particular way of seeing, as the language, vocabulary, and approach of modern science and, therefore, of all scientific, historical, political, even philosophical, truth. One consequence has been a serious loss in the ability to acknowledge and manage difference.

There is little room in the formal intellectual life of social scientists for a recognition of contradictory strains and dissonant voices, whereas in their personal lives (in India, as elsewhere), difference, the diverse viewpoints of rationality and instinct, and the realm of the superstitious are easily (if often unconsciously) accommodated. There is little room in the approved academic history for an investigation of the historical content of different kinds of individualism, for questions about the direction of human progress, for self-doubt, or indeed for a sympathetic understanding of a religious sensibility.

I wish to suggest that this inflexible (and somewhat dated) scientism, based on an arrogant belief in the infinite power of nineteenth- and twentieth-century "man," has not only closed off many possibilities of reflection and debate, but also opened up the space for other arrogant believers to stake their claim to authenticity on the grounds of attention to particularity: a concern with indigenous (or, as it is quickly dubbed, "national") culture, religious sensibilities, and the rights of society as against the individual and the state.

Even after we have condemned Hindu history as myth or, more carefully, as a fraud that slides all too easily between myth and history; after we have pointed out its inconsistencies, ambiguity, duplicity, and refusal to account for so much of what it says, the question remains why this fraud persuades so many people of different classes, regions, and sexes, why such large numbers of our countrymen and women fail to notice what we see as its ambiguity and duplicity—or, at any rate, are untroubled by it.

The answers may lie not only in the kind of "authoritative" history of Muslim conquest and Hindu-Muslim strife that has been continuously and widely broadcast in India from early colonial times until today, or in the political manipulation and economic difficulties of recent decades. They may also lie in the persistence of world views that do not search for consistency in the way rationalist scientists do; that do not see the sharp distinctions that "modernists" make between religion and culture, or religion and politics (or, indeed, religion and history); that do not always expect human activity and history to be neatly compartmentalized, recognizing instead that ambiguity is central to the business of existence and survival, and working on the assumption that context determines meaning, so that the same things may have very different meanings in different contexts.

History and the search for persuasive, "scientific" histories are not going to disappear from our agendas. Yet "now after the war," to borrow a phrase from Nick Dirks's introduction to this volume, we may have to find new ways of "reading old books." It seems to me that we need to interrogate the philosophical assumptions that lie behind our own view of history and politics, even as we search for consistency, or inconsistency, in those of others. It is important that we ask unceasingly how particular unities— of nation, of culture, of history—came to be constructed as "mainstream" and even "natural," and how other mainstream unities, other histories, may still be constituted. That is surely a part of the intellectual, political agenda of our times.

Notes

Much of my investigation of the history and politics of Ayodhya took place in association with Professor Sudhir Chandra. I owe him thanks for many insights and suggestions. I am also grateful, for their comments, to participants in the CSST conference on culture and to participants in the "After Ayodhya" conference organized by the South Asia Research Unit, Curtin University of Technology, Perth, Western Australia, where earlier versions of this paper were presented.

1. Ramgopal Pandey Sharad, *Shri Ram Janmabhumi ka Romanchkari Itihasa* (Ayodhya: n.p., n.d.) 3–4.

2. Source: Pratap Narayan Mishra, *Kya Kahti Saryu Dhara? Shri Ram Janmabhumi ki Kahani* (1987; 2d ed., Lucknow: n.p., 1990), appendix, 144. To the battles listed in this appendix, I have added events 1 and 3, and numbers 13–15, which appear regularly in these histories of Ayodhya. The date of event number 3 varies, being given as late as the fifth century in Radhey Shyam Shukul's *Sachitra, Pramanik Itihasa*, which identifies Vikramaditya with the Gupta king, Skandagupta, who ruled at Pataliputra (modern Patna) from A.D. 455 to 467.

3. *Ham Mandir Vahin Banayenge* (New Delhi: Suruchi Prakashan, 1989).

4. *Ham Mandir Vahin Banayenge*, 10–11. It is noteworthy that while the attacks by Ravana and Milind (Menander) appear in these opening paragraphs, not even the latter forms part of the "77" battles listed by the author as having taken place for the protection/liberation of RJD. The reference to "the historian Cunningham" is to the civil servant who compiled the Lucknow *District Gazetteer* in the later nineteenth century. As with so many other references in these Hindu "histories," this is fraudulent in its failure to make an accurate identification, its modification of quotations, and its failure to acknowledge, in this instance, that unidentified, local oral sources were the authority for the author's statements and statistics.

5. To take only two relatively recent, and fairly well-documented instances, the 1912 and 1934 "riots," one *in* and the other *near* Ayodhya, automatically became "wars" over the Ram Janmabhumi in the Hindu account, even though neither was di-

rectly related to the question of the control of this site, but to other matters of property and local control.

6. R. Koselleck, *Futures Past: On the Semantics of Historical Time* (Cambridge: MIT Press, 1985), 18. The writing on this issue is now considerable: see, for example, Ashis Nandy, *The Intimate Enemy* (Delhi; New York: Oxford University Press, 1983); Ranajit Guha, *An Indian Historiography for India: A Nineteenth-Century Agenda and Its Implications* (Calcutta: Center for Studies in Social Sciences, K. P. Bagchi, 1988); Uma Chakravarti, "Whatever Happened to the Vedic Dasi?" in Kumkum Sangari and Sudesh Vaid, eds., *Recasting Women: Essays on Colonial India* (New Delhi: Kali for Women, 1989); Partha Chatterjee, *The Nation and Its Fragments* (Princeton: Princeton University Press, 1993); and Sudipta Kaviraj's analysis of Bankim's construction of the figure of Krishna in his forthcoming work on Bankimchandra Chattopadhya. See also the writings and speeches of Tilak and Syed Ahmad Khan; *Bal Gangadhar Tilak, His Writings and Speeches,* enlarged ed. (Madras: Ganesha, 1919), especially his comments on the *Gita,* 231 ff; and Christian W. Troll, *Sayyid Ahmad Khan: A Reinterpretation of Muslim Theology* (New Delhi: Vikas, 1978). For a fascinating comment on changing traditions in iconography, see Anuradha Kapur, "Deity to Crusader: The Changing Iconography of Ram," in G. Pandey, ed., *Hindus and Others: The Question of Identity in India Today.* (New Delhi; New York: Viking, 1993).

7. I have discussed this local history in my *Construction of Communalism in Colonial North India* (New Delhi; New York: Oxford University Press, 1990), chapter 4.

3

Check the Technique: Black Urban Culture and the Predicament of Social Science

Robin D. G. Kelley

Perhaps the supreme irony of black American existence is how broadly black people debate the question of cultural identity among themselves while getting branded as a cultural monolith by those who would deny us the complexity and complexion *of a community, let alone a nation. If Afro-Americans have never settled for the racist reductions imposed upon them—from chattel slaves to cinematic stereotype to sociological myth—it's because the black collective conscious not only knew better but also knew more than enough ethnic diversity to subsume these fictions.*

> — *Greg Tate,* Flyboy in
> the Buttermilk

The biggest difference between us and white folks is that we know *when we are playing.*

> — *Alberta Roberts, quoted
> in John Langston
> Gwaltney's* Drylongso

Once again, black urban culture—or what is believed to be black urban culture—has taken center stage. As in the late 1960s and early 1970s, publishers are offering huge advances for anything on the "real" situation in the ghettos. Filmmakers are searching out the crummiest locations so that they may better capture inner-city pathos. Black politicos and a rainbow of progressives debate whether contemporary black youth culture will prove to be the downfall of the community or the beginnings of a new revolution. Meanwhile, a growing number of young white kids are trying desperately to dress, speak, and walk like the ghetto youths who live in their TV sets or on the pages of *Vibe* or *Rolling Stone* magazines.

Keeping in the tradition beginning with Robert Park and his protégés to the War on Poverty–inspired ethnographers, academics have again stepped forward and significantly shaped, and in some cases defined, the current dialogue on black urban culture. In some respects, the central role that social science plays in shaping popular conceptions of "ghetto life" is also reminiscent of the research done in the late 1960s and early 1970s. Sociologists, anthropologists, political scientists, and economists compete for huge grants from Ford, Rockefeller, Sage, and other foundations to measure everything measurable in order to get a handle on the newest internal threat to civilization. With the discovery of the so-called underclass, terms like *nihilistic, dysfunctional,* and *pathological* have become the most common adjectives to describe contemporary black urban culture.

Unfortunately, too much of this rapidly expanding literature on the underclass provides less complexity about people's lives and cultures than a bad blaxploitation film or an Ernie Barnes painting. Many social scientists are not only quick to generalize about the black urban poor on the basis of a few "representative" examples, but more often than not, they don't let the natives speak. A major part of the problem is the way in which many mainstream social scientists studying the underclass define *culture*. Relying on a narrowly conceived definition of culture, most of the underclass literature use *behavior* and *culture* interchangeably.

My purpose, then, is to offer some reflections on how the culture concept employed by social scientists has severely impoverished contemporary debates over the plight of urban African-Americans. Much of this literature not only conflates behavior with culture, but when "expressive" cultural forms, or what has been called "popular culture," fall under the purview of social scientists (e.g., language, music, style, etc.), most reduce it either to expressions of pathology, compensatory behavior, or to creative "coping mechanisms" to deal with racism and poverty. While some aspects of black expressive cultures certainly help inner-city residents deal with and even resist ghetto conditions, most of the literature ignores what these cultural forms mean for the practitioners. Few scholars acknowledge that what might also be at stake here are aesthetics, style, and pleasure. Nor do they recognize black urban culture's hybridity and internal differences. Given the common belief that inner-city communities are more isolated than ever before and have completely alien values, the notion that there is one, discrete, identifiable, black urban culture carries a great deal of weight. By conceiving black urban culture in the singular, interpreters unwittingly reduce their subjects to cardboard typologies who fit neatly into their own definition of the underclass and render invisible a wide array of complex cultural forms and practices.

"It's Just a Ghetto Thang": The Problem of Authenticity and the Ethnographic Imagination

A few years ago Mercer Sullivan decried the disappearance of "culture" from the study of urban poverty, attributing its demise to the fact that "overly vague notions of the culture of poverty brought disrepute to the culture concept as a tool for understanding the effects of the concentration of poverty among cultural minorities."[1] In some respects, Sullivan is right: the conservatives who maintain that persistent poverty in the inner city is the result of the behavior of the poor, the product of some cultural deficiency, have garnered so much opposition from many liberals and radicals that few scholars are willing even to discuss culture. Instead, opponents of the "culture of poverty" idea tend to focus on structural transformations in the U.S. economy, labor force composition, and resultant changes in marriage patterns to explain the underclass.[2]

However, when looked at from another perspective, culture never really disappeared from the underclass debate.[3] On the contrary, it has been as central to the work of liberal structuralists and radical Marxists as it has been to the conservative culturalists. While culturalists insist that the behavior of the urban poor explains their poverty, the structuralists argue that the economy explains their behavior as well as their poverty.[4] For all their differences, there is general agreement that a common, debased culture is what defines the underclass, what makes it a threat to the future of America. Most interpreters of the underclass treat behavior not only as a synonym for culture but as the determinant for class. In simple terms, what makes the underclass a class is their common behavior, not their income, the poverty level, or the kind of work they do. It is a definition of class driven more by moral panic than systematic analysis. A cursory look at the literature reveals that there is no consensus as to precisely what behaviors define the underclass. Some scholars, like William Julius Wilson, have offered a more spatial definition of the underclass by focusing on areas of "concentrated poverty," but obvious problems result when observers discover the wide range of behavior and attitudes in, say, a single city block. What happens to the concept when we find people with jobs engaging in illicit activities and some jobless people depending on church charity? Or married, employed fathers who spend virtually no time with their kids, and jobless, unwed fathers who share in childcare responsibilities? How does the concept of underclass behavior hold up to Kathryn Edin's findings that many so-called welfare-dependent women must also work for wages in order to make ends meet?[5] More important, how do we fit criminals (many first-time offenders), welfare recipients, single mothers, absent fathers, alcohol and drug abusers, and gun-toting youth all into one "class"?

When we try to apply the same principles to people with higher incomes whom we presume to be "functional" and "normative," we ultimately expose the absurdity of it all. Political scientist Charles Henry offers the following description of pathological behavior for the very folks the underclass are supposed to emulate. This tangle of deviant behavior, which he calls the "culture of wealth," is characterized by a "rejection or denial of physical attributes" leading to "hazardous sessions in tanning parlors" and frequent trips to weight-loss salons; rootlessness, antisocial behavior, and "an inability to make practical decisions," evident in their tendency to own several homes, frequent private social and dining clubs, and in their vast amount of unneccessary and socially useless possessions. "Finally," Henry adds, "the culture of the rich is engulfed in a web of crime, sexism, and poor health. Drug use and white collar crime are rampant, according to every available index. . . . In sum, this group is engaged in a permanent cycle of divorce, forced child separations through boarding schools, and rampant materialism that leads to the dreaded Monte Carlo syndrome. Before they can be helped they must close tax loopholes, end subsidies, and stop buying influence."[6]

As absurd as Henry's satirical reformulation of the culture of poverty might appear, this very instrumentalist way of understanding culture is deeply rooted in even the more liberal social science approaches to urban poverty. In the mid-to-late 1960s, a group of progressive social scientists, mostly ethnographers, challenged the more conservative culture of poverty arguments and insisted that black culture was itself a necessary adaptation to racism and poverty, a set of coping mechanisms that grew out of the struggle for material and psychic survival.[7] Ironically, while this work consciously sought to recast ghetto dwellers as active agents rather than passive victims, it has nonetheless reinforced monolithic interpretations of black urban culture and significantly shaped current articulations of the culture concept in social science approaches to poverty.

With the zeal of colonial missionaries, these liberal and often radical ethnographers (mostly white men) set out to explore the newly discovered concrete jungles. Inspired by the politics of the 1960s and mandated by Lyndon Johnson's War on Poverty, a veritable army of anthropologists, sociologists, linguists, and social psychologists set up camp in America's ghettos. In the Harlem and Washington Heights communities where I grew up in the mid-to-late 1960s, even our liberal, white teachers, who were committed to turning us into functional members of society, turned out to be foot soldiers in the new ethnographic army. With the overnight success of published collections of inner-city children's writings like *The Me Nobody Knows* and Caroline Mirthes *Can't You Hear Me Talking to You?* writing about the intimate details of our home life seemed like our most important assignment.[8] (And we made the most of it by enriching our mundane narratives with stories from *Mod Squad, Hawaii Five-O,* and *Speed Racer.*)

Of course, I don't believe for a minute that most of our teachers gave us these kinds of exercises hoping to appear one day on the *Merv Griffin Show.* But, in retrospect at least, the explosion of interest in the inner city cannot be easily divorced from the marketplace. Although they came to mine what they believed was *the* "authentic Negro culture," there was real gold in them thar ghettos, since white America's fascination with the pathological urban poor translated into massive book sales.

Unfortunately, most social scientists believed they knew what "authentic Negro culture" was before they entered the field. The "real Negroes" were the young jobless men hanging out on the corner passing the bottle, the brothers with the nastiest verbal repertoire, the pimps and hustlers, and the single mothers who raised streetwise kids who began cursing before they could walk. Of course, there were other characters, like the men and women who went to work every day in foundries, hospitals, nursing homes, private homes, police stations, sanitation departments, banks, garment factories, assembly plants, pawn shops, construction sites, loading docks, storefront churches, telephone companies, grocery and department stores, public transit, restaurants, welfare offices, recreation centers; or the street vendors, the cab drivers, the bus drivers, the ice cream truck drivers, the seamstresses, the numerologists and fortune tellers, the folks who protected or cleaned downtown buildings all night long. These are the kinds of people who lived in my neighborhood in West Harlem during the early 1970s, but they rarely found their way into the ethnographic text. And when they did show up, social scientists tended to reduce them to typologies: "lames," "strivers," "mainstreamers," "achievers," "revolutionaries," and so on.[9]

Perhaps these urban dwellers were not as interesting, or more likely, they stood at the margins of a perceived or invented "authentic" Negro society. A noteworthy exception is John Langston Gwaltney's remarkable book, *Drylongso: A Self-Portrait of Black America* (1981). Based on interviews with black working-class residents in several Northeastern cities conducted during the 1970s, *Drylongso* is one of the few works on urban African-Americans by an African-American anthropologist to appear during the height of ghetto ethnography. Because Gwaltney is blind, he could not rely on the traditional methods of observation and interepretation. Instead—and this is the book's strength—he allowed his informants to speak for themselves about what *they* see and do. They interpret their own communities, African-American culture, white society, racism, politics and the state, and the very discipline in which Gwaltney was trained: anthropology. As one of his informants put it, "I think this anthropology is just another way to call me a nigger." What the book reveals is that the natives are aware that anthropologists are constructing them, and they saw in Gwaltney, who relied primarily on family and friends as informants, an opportunity to speak back. One, a woman he calls Elva Noble, said to him, "I'm not trying to tell you your job, but if you ever do write a book about us, then I hope you really do write about things the way they really are. I guess that depends on you to some extent but you know that there are more of us who are going to work every day than there are like the people who are git'n over."[10] While his definition of a "core black culture" may strike some as essentialist, it emphasizes diversity and tolerance for diversity. Granted the stylistic uniqueness of African-American culture, the central facet of this core culture is the deep-rooted sense of community, common history, and the collective recognition that there is indeed an African-American culture and a "black" way of doing things. Regardless of the origins of a particular recipe, or the roots of a particular religion or Christian denomination, the cook and the congregation have no problem identifying these distinct practices and institutions as "black."

Few ghetto ethnographers have understood or developed Gwaltney's insights into African-American urban culture. Whereas Gwaltney's notion of a core culture incorporates a diverse and contradictory range of practices, attitudes, and relationships that are dynamic, historically situated, and ethnically hybrid, social scientists of his generation and after, especially those at the forefront of poverty studies, treat culture as if it were a set of behaviors. They assume that there is one identifiable ghetto culture, and what they observed was *it*. These assumptions, which continue to shape much current social science and most mass media representations of the "inner city," can be partly attributed to the way ethnographers are trained in the West. As James Clifford observed, anthropologists studying non-Western societies are not only compelled to describe the communities under interrogation as completely foreign to their own society, but if these communities are to be worthy of study as a group they must be shown to possess an identifiable, homogenous culture. I think, in principal at least, the same holds true for interpretations of black urban America. Because it is conceived as a "foreign" culture, ethnographers can argue that inner-city residents do not share "mainstream" values. Behavior is not treated as situational, an individual response to a specific set of circumstances; rather, people are perceived to be acting according to their own unique cultural "norms."[11]

For many of these ethnographers, the defining characteristic of African-American urban culture was relations between men and women. Even Charles Keil, whose *Urban Blues* is one of the few ethnographic texts from that period that not only examines aesthetics and form in black culture but takes "strong exception to the view that lower-class Negro life style and its characteristic rituals and expresssive roles are the products of overcompensation for masculine self-doubt," nonetheless concludes that "the battle of the sexes" is precisely what characterizes African-American urban culture.[12] Expressive cultures, then, were not only constructed as adaptive, functioning primarily to cope with the horrible conditions of ghetto life, but they were conceived largely as expressions of masculinity. In fact, the linking of men with expressive cultures was so pervasive that the pioneering ethnographies focusing on African-American women and girls, notably the work of Joyce Ladner and Carol Stack, do not explore this realm, whether in mixed gender groupings or all-female groups. They concentrated more on sex roles, relationships, and family survival than on expressive cultures.[13]

Two illuminating examples are the debate over the concept of "soul" and the verbal art form known to most academics as "the dozens." In the ethnographic imagination, "soul" and, "the dozens" were both regarded as examples par excellence of authentic black urban culture as well as vehicles for expressing black masculinity. The bias toward expressive male culture must be understood within a particular historical and political context. In the midst of urban rebellions, the masculinist rhetoric of black nationalism, the controversy over the Moynihan report, and the uncritical linking of "agency" and resistance with men, black men took center stage in poverty research.[14]

"Soul" was so critical to the social science discourse on the adaptive culture of the black urban poor that Rainwater edited an entire book about it, and Ulf Hannerz structured his study of Washington, DC on it.[15] According to these authors, "soul" is the expressive lifestyle of black men adapting to economic and political marginality. This one word supposedly embraces the entire range of "Negro lower class culture"; it constitutes "essential Negroness." Only authentic Negroes had "soul." In defining soul, Hannerz reduces aesthetics, style, and the dynamic struggle over identity to a set of coping mechanisms. Among his many attempts to define soul, he insists that it is tied to the instability of black male-female relationships. Evidence for this is deduced from his findings that "success with the opposite sex is a focal concern in lower-class Negro life," and that a good deal of popular black music—soul music—was preoccupied with courting or losing a lover.[16]

Being "cool" is an indispensable component of soul; it is also regarded by these ethnographers as a peculiarly black expression of masculinity. Indeed, the entire discussion of "cool" centers entirely on black men. And cool as an aesthetic, as a style, as an art form expressed through langauge and the body, is simply not dealt with. Cool, not surprisingly, is merely another mechanism to cope with racism and poverty. According to Lee Rainwater and David Schulz, it is nothing more than a survival technique intended to "make yourself interesting and attractive to others so that you are better able to manipulate their behavior along lines that will provide some immediate gratification." To achieve cool simply entails learning to lie and putting up a front of competence and success. But like a lot of adaptive strategies, cool is self-limiting. While it helps young black males maintain an image of being "in control," according to David Schulz, it can also make "intimate relationships" more difficult to achieve.[17]

Hannerz reluctantly admits that no matter how hard he tried, none of the "authentic ghetto inhabitants" he had come across could define soul. He was certain soul was "essentially Negro" but concluded that it really could not be defined, for to do that would be to undermine its meaning: it is something one possesses, a ticket into the "in crowd." If you need a definition, you don't know what it means. It's a Black (Male) Thang; you'll never understand. But Hannerz obviously felt confident enough to venture his own definition of soul, based on his understanding of African-American culture, as little more than a survival strategy to cope with the harsh realities of the ghetto. Moreover, he felt empowered to determine which black people had the right to claim the mantle of authenticity: when LeRoi Jones and Lerone Bennett offered their interpretations of soul, Hannerz rejected their definitions, in part because they were not, in his words, "authentic Negroes."[18]

By constructing the black urban world as a single culture whose function is merely to survive the ghetto, Rainwater, Hannerz, and most of their colleagues at the time ultimately collapsed a wide range of historically specific cultural practices and forms and searched for a (the) concept that could bring them all together. Such an interpretation of culture makes it impossible for Hannerz and others to see soul not as a thing but as a discourse through which African-Americans, at a particular historical moment, claimed ownership of the symbols and practices of their own imagined community. This is why, even at the height of the Black Power movement, African-American urban culture could be so fluid, hybrid, and multinational. In Harlem in the

1970s, Nehru suits were as popular and as "black" as dashikis, and martial arts films placed Bruce Lee among a pantheon of black heroes that included Walt Frazier and John Shaft. As debates over the black aesthetic raged, the concept of soul was an assertion that there are "black ways" of doing things, even if those ways are contested and the boundaries around what is "black" are fluid. How it manifests itself and how it shifts is less important than the fact that the boundaries exist in the first place. At the very least, soul was a euphemism or a creative way of identifying what many believed was a black aesthetic or black style, and it was a synonym for black itself or a way to talk about being black without reference to color, which is why people of other ethnic groups could have soul.

Soul in the 1960s and early 1970s was also about transformation. It was almost never conceived by African-Americans as an innate, genetically derived feature of black life, for it represented a shedding of the old "Negro" ways and an embracing of "black" power and pride. The most visible signifier of soul was undoubtedly the Afro. More than any other element of style, the Afro put the issue of hair squarely on the black political agenda, where it has been ever since. The current debates over hair and its relationship to political consciousness really have their roots in the Afro. Not surprisingly, social scientists at the time viewed the Afro through the limited lense of Black Power politics, urban uprisings, and an overarching discourse of authenticity. And given their almost exclusive interest in young men, their perspective on the Afro was strongly influenced by the rhetoric and iconography of a movement that flouted black masculinity. Yet, once we look beyond the presumably male-occupied ghetto streets that dominated the ethnographic imagination at the time, the story of the Afro's origins and meaning complicates the link to soul culture.

First, the Afro powerfully demonstrates the degree to which soul was deeply implicated in the marketplace. What passed as authentic ghetto culture was as much a product of market forces and the commercial appropriation of urban styles as experience and individual creativity. And very few black, urban residents/consumers viewed their own participation in the marketplace as undermining their own authenticity as bearers of black culture. Even before the Afro reached the height of its popularity, the hair care industry stepped in and began producing a vast array of chemicals to make one's "natural" more natural. One could pick up Raveen Hair Sheen, Afro Sheen, Ultra Sheen, Head Start vitamin and mineral capsules, to name a few. The Clairol Corporation (whose CEO supported the Philadelphia Black Power Conference in 1967) did not hesitate to enter the "natural" business.[19] Look at this Clairol ad published in *Essence Magazine* (November 1970):

No matter what they say...Nature Can't Do It Alone!
Nothing pretties up a face like a beautiful head of hair, but even hair
that's born this beautiful needs a little help along the way...A little
brightening, a little heightening of color, a little extra sheen to liven up
the look. And because that wonderful natural look is still the most
wanted look...the most fashionable, the most satisfying look you can
have at any age...anything you do must look natural, natural, natural.
And this indeed is the art of Miss Clairol.

Depending on the particular style, the Afro could require almost as much
maintenance as the process. And for those women (and some men) whose
hair simply would not cooperate or who wanted the flexibility to shift from
straight to nappy, there was always the Afro wig. For nine or ten dollars,
one could purchase a variety of different wig styles, ranging from the "Soul-
Light Freedom" wigs to the "Honey Bee Afro Shag," made from cleverly la-
beled synthetic materials such as Afrylic or Afrilon.[20]

Secondly the Afro's roots really go back to the bourgeois high-fashion
circles in the late 1950s, when the Afro was seen by the black and white
elite as a kind of new female exotica. Even though the intention, among
some circles at least, was to achieve healthier hair and to express solidarity
with newly independent African nations, it entered public consciousness as
a mod fashion statement that was not only palatable to bourgeois whites
but, in some circles, celebrated. There were people like Lois Liberty Jones,
a consultant, beauty culturist, and lecturer, who claimed to have pioneered
the natural as early as 1952! She originated "Coiffures Aframericana" concepts of hair styling, which she practiced in Harlem for several years, beginning in the early 1960s.[21] More important, it was the early 1960s, not the late
1960s, when performers like Odetta, Miriam Makeba, Abby Lincoln, Nina
Simone, and the artist Margaret Burroughs began wearing the "au naturel"
style—medium-to-short Afros. Writer Andrea Benton Rushing has vivid memories seeing Odetta at the Village Gate long before Black Power entered the
national lexicon. "I was mesmerized by her stunning frame," she recalled,
"in its short kinky halo. She had a regal poise and power that I had never
seen in a 'Negro' (as we called ourselves back then) woman before—no
matter how naturally 'good' or diligently straightened her hair was." Many
other black women in New York, particularly those who ran in the interracial
world of Manhattan sophisticates, were first introduced to the natural through
high-fashion models in "au naturel" shows, which were the rage at the time.[22]

Helen Hayes King, associate editor of *Jet,* came in contact with the au
naturel style at an art show in New York, in the late 1950s. A couple of
years later, she heard Abby Lincoln speak about her own decision to go

natural at one of these shows, and with prompting from her husband, decided to go forth and adopt the 'fro. Ironically, one of the few salons in Chicago specializing in the au naturel look was run by a white male hairdresser in the exclusive North Side community. He actually lectured King on the virtues of natural hair: "I don't know why Negro women with delicate hair like yours burn and process all the life out of it. . . . If you'd just wash it, oil it and take care of it, it would be so much healthier. . . . I don't know how all this straightening foolishness started anyhow." When she returned home to the South Side, however, instead of compliments, she received strange looks from her neighbors. Despite criticism and ridicule by her coworkers and friends, she stuck with her Afro, but not because she was trying to make a political statement or demonstrate her solidarity with African independence movements. "I'm not so involved in the neo-African aspects of the 'au naturelle' look," she wrote, "nor in the get-back-to-your-heritage bit." Her explanation was simple: the style was chic and elegant, and in the end she was pleased with the feel of her hair. It is fitting to note that most of the compliments came from whites.[23]

What is also interesting about King's narrative is that it appeared in the context of a debate with Nigerian writer Theresa Ogunbiyi over whether black women should straighten their hair or not, which appeared in a 1963 issue of *Negro Digest*. In particular, Ogunbiyi defended the right of a Lagos firm to forbid employees to plait their hair; women were required to wear straight hair. She rejected the idea that straightening hair destroys national custom and heritage: "I think we carry this national pride a bit too far at times, even to the detriment of our country's progress." Her point was that breaking with tradition *is* progress, especially since Western dress and hairstyles are more comfortable and easier to work in: "When I wear the Yoruba costume, I find that I spend more time than I can afford, re-tying the headtie and the bulky wrapper round my waist. And have you tried typing in an 'Agbada'? I am all for nationalisation but give it to me with some comfort and improvement."[24]

Andrea Benton Rushing's story is a slight variation on King's experience. She, too, was a premature natural hair advocate. When she stepped out of the house sporting her first Afro, perhaps inspired by Odetta or prompted by plain curiosity, her "relatives thought I'd lost my mind and, of course, my teachers at Julliard stole sideways looks at me and talked about the importance of appearance in auditions and concerts." Yet, while the white Julliard faculty and her closest family members found the new style strange and inappropriate, brothers on the block in her New York City neighborhood greeted her with praise: " 'Looking good, sister,' 'Watch out, African queen!'" She, too, found it ironic that middle-class African woman on the continent chose to straighten their hair. During a trip to Ghana years later, she recalled the irony of having her Afro braided in an Accra beauty parlor while "three Ghanaians (two Akan-speaking government workers and one Ewe microbiologist)... were having their chemically straightened hair washed, set, combed out, and sprayed in place."[25]

No matter what spurred on the style or who adopted it, the political implications of the Afro could not be avoided. After all, the biggest early proponents of the style tended to be female artists whose work identified with the black freedom movement and African liberation. In some respects, women such as Abby Lincoln, Odetta, and Nina Simone were part of what might be called Black Bohemia. They participated in a larger community, based mostly in New York, of poets, writers, and musicians of the 1950s for whom the emancipation of their own artistic form coincided with the African freedom movement. *Ebony, Jet,* and *Sepia* magazines were covering Africa, and African publications such as *Drum* were being read by those ex-Negroes in the states who could get their hands on them. The Civil Rights movement, the struggle against apartheid in South Africa, the emergence of newly independent African nations, found a voice in recordings by various jazz artists, including Randy Weston's *Uhuru Afrika,* Max Roach's *We Insist: Freedom Now Suite* (featuring Abby Lincoln, Roach's wife); Art Blakey's *Message from Kenya* and *Ritual,* and John Coltrane's *Liberia, Dahomey Dance,* and *Africa.* Revolutionary political movements, combined with revolutionary experiments in artistic creation—the simultaneous embrace and rejection of tradition—forged the strongest physical and imaginary links between Africa and the Diaspora.[26] Thus it is not surprising that Harold Cruse, in one of his seminal essays on the coming of the new black nationalism, anticipated the importance of the style revolution and the place of the Afro in it. As early as 1962, Cruse predicted that in the coming years, "Afro-Americans... will undoubtedly make a lot of noise in militant demonstrations, cultivate beards and sport their hair in various degrees of la mode au naturel, and tend to be cultish with African- and Arab-style dress."[27]

Of course, he was right, but by the mid-1960s the Afro was no longer associated with downtown chic but with uptown rebellion. It was sported by rock-throwing black males and black-leathered militants armed to the teeth. Thus, once associated with feminine chic, the Afro suddenly became the symbol of black manhood, the death of the "Negro" and birth of the militant, virulent black man.[28] The new politics, combined with media representations of Afro-coifed black militants, profoundly shaped the ethnographic imagination. As new narratives were created to explain the symbolic significance of the natural style, women were rendered invisible. The erasure of women, I would argue, was not limited to histories of style politics but to ghetto ethnography in general.

The masculinism of soul in contemporary ghetto ethnography has survived to this day, despite the last quarter century of incisive black feminist scholarship. The ethnographic and sociological search for soul has made a comeback recently under a new name: the "cool pose." In a recent book, Richard Majors and Jane Mancini Bilson have recycled the arguments of Rainwater, Ulf Hannerz, Elliot Liebow, and David Schulz, and have suggested that the "cool pose" captures the essence of young, black, male expressive culture. Like earlier constructions of soul, they too believe that the cool pose is an adaptive strategy to cope with the particular forms of racism and oppression black males face in America: "Cool pose is a ritualized form of masculinity that entails behaviors, scripts, physical posturing, impression management, and carefully crafted performances that deliver a single, critical message: pride, strength, and control." Echoing earlier works, the "cool pose" is also a double-edged sword since it allegedly undermines potential intimacy with females.[29] By playing down the aesthetics of cool and reducing the cool pose to a response by heterosexual black males to racism, intraracial violence, and poverty, the authors not only reinforce the idea there is an essential black urban culture created by the oppressive conditions of the ghetto but ignore manifestations of the cool pose in the public "performances" of black women, gay black men, and the African-American middle class.

A more tangible example of black, urban expressive culture that seemed to captivate social scientists in the 1960s is "the dozens." Yet, in spite of the amount of ink devoted to the subject, it has been perhaps the most misinterpreted cultural form to come out of African-American communities. It has been called at various times in various places "capping," "sounding," "ranking," "bagging," "dissing," and so on, and virtually all leading anthropologists, sociologists, and linguists agree that it is a black male form of "ritual insult," a verbal contest involving any number of young black men who compete by talking about each other's mama. There is less agreement, however, about how to interpret the sociological and psychological significance of the dozens. In keeping with the dominant social science interpretations of the culture concept, so-called ritual insults among urban black youth were seen as either another adaptive strategy or an example of social pathology.[30]

The amazing thing about the sociological and ethnographic scholarship on the dozens, from John Dollard's ruminations in 1939 to the more recent misreadings by Roger Lane and Carl Nightingale, is the consistency with which scholars repeat the same errors. For one, the almost universal assertion that the dozens is a ritual empowers the ethnographer to select what appear to be more formalized verbal exchanges (e.g., rhyming couplets) and ascribe to them greater "authenticity" than other forms of playful conversation. In fact, by framing the dozens as ritual, most scholars have come to believe that it is first and foremost a "contest" with rules, players, and mental scorecards rather than the daily banter of many (not all) young African-Americans. Anyone who has lived and survived the dozens (or whatever name you want to call it) cannot imagine turning to one's friends and announcing, "Hey, let's go outside and play the dozens." Furthermore, the very use of the term *ritual* to describe everyday speech reinforces the exoticization of black urban populations, constructing them as Others whose investment in this cultural tradition is much deeper than trying to get a laugh.

These problems are tied to larger ones. For example, white ethnographers seemed oblivious to the fact that their very presence shaped what they observed. Asking their subjects to "play the dozens" while an interloper records the "session" with a tape recorder and notepad has the effect of creating a ritual performance for the sake of an audience, of turning spontaneous, improvised verbal exchanges into a formal practice. More significantly, ethnographers have tailor-made their own interpretation of the dozens by selecting what they believe were the most authentic sites for such verbal duels: streetcorners, pool halls, bars, and parks. In other words, they sought out male spaces rather than predominantly female and mix-gender spaces to record the dozens. It is no wonder that practically all commentators on the dozens have concluded that it is a boy thing. But evidence suggests that young women engaged in these kinds of verbal exchanges as much as their male counterparts, both with men and with other women. And they were no less profane. By not searching out other mixed-gender and female spaces such as school busses, cafeterias, kitchen tables, beauty salons, and house parties, ethnographers have overstated the extent to which the dozens were the sole property of men.[31]

Folklorist Roger Abrahams, who pioneered the study of the dozens in his book on black vernacular folklore "from the streets of Philadelphia," is one of the few scholars to appreciate the pleasure and aesthetics of such verbal play. Nevertheless, he argues that one of the primary functions of the dozens is to compensate for a lack of masculinity caused by too many absent fathers and domineering mothers, which is why the main target of insults is an "opponent's" mother. He writes, "By exhibiting his wit, by creating new and vital folkloric expression, [the dozens player] is able to effect a temporary release from anxiety for both himself and his audience. By creating playgrounds for playing out aggressions, he achieves a kind of masculine identity for himself and his group in a basically hostile environment."[32] David Schulz offers an even more specific interpretation of the dozens as a form of masculine expression in an environment dominated by dysfunctional families. He writes, "Playing the dozens occurs at the point when the boy is about to enter puberty and suffer his greatest rejection from his mother as a result of his becoming a man. The dozens enables him to develop a defense against this rejection and provides a vehicle for his transition into the manipulative world of the street dominated by masculine values expressed in gang life." It then serves as a "ritualized exorcism" that allows men to break from maternal dominance and "establish their own image of male superiority celebrated in street life."[33]

Allow me to propose an alternative "reading" of the dozens. The goal of the dozens and related verbal games is deceptively simple: to get a laugh. The pleasure of the dozens is not the viciousness of the insult but the humor, the creative pun, the outrageous metaphor. Contrary to popular belief, mothers are not the *sole* target; the subjects include fathers, grandparents, brothers, sisters, cousins, friends, food, skin color, smell, and hairstyles. I am not suggesting that "your mama" is unimportant in the whole structure of these verbal exchanges. Nor am I suggesting that the emphasis on "your mama" has absolutely nothing to do with the ways in which patriarchy is discursively reproduced. But we need to understand that "your mama" in this context is almost never living, literal, or even metaphoric. "Your mama" is a generic reference, a code signaling that the dozens have begun — it signifies a shift in speech. "Your mama" is also a mutable, nameless body of a shared imagination that can be constructed and reconstructed in a thousand different shapes, sizes, colors, and circumstances. The emphasis on "your mama" in most interpretations of the dozens has more to do with the peculiar preoccupation of social science with Negro family structure than anything else. Besides, in many cases the target is immaterial; your mama, your daddy, your greasy-headed granny are merely vehicles through which the speaker tries to elicit a laugh and display her skills. In retrospect, this seems obvious, but amid the complicated readings of masculine overcompensation and ritual performance, only a handful of writers of the period, most of whom were African-Americans with no affiliation to the academy, recognized the centrality of humor. One was Howard Seals, who self-published a pamphlet on the dozens in 1969 titled *You Ain't Thuh Man Yuh Mamma Wuz*. In an effort to put to rest all the sociological overinterpretation, Seals explains, "The emotional tone to be maintained is that of hilariously, outrageously funny bantering."[34] Compare Seals's comment with the words of linguist William Labov, who, while recognizing the humor, ultimately turns laughter into part of the ritual and thus reinforces the process of Othering:

> The primary mark of positive evaluation is laughter. We can rate the effectiveness of a sound in a group session by the number of members of the audience who laugh. . . . A really successful sound will be evaluated by overt comments . . . the most common forms are, "Oh!" "Oh shit!" "God damn!" or "Oh lord!" By far the most common is "Oh shit!" The intonation is important; when approval is to be signalled the vowel of each word is quite long, with a high sustained initial pitch, and a slow-fallng pitch contour.[35]

Without a concept of, or even an interest in, aesthetics, style, and the visceral pleasures of cultural forms, it should not be surprising that most social scientists explained black urban culture in terms of "coping mechanisms," "rituals," or oppositional responses to racism. And trapped by an essentialist interpretation of culture, they continue to look for that elusive, "authentic" ghetto sensibility, the true, honest, unbridled, pure cultural practices that capture the raw, roughneck "reality" of urban life. Today, that reality is rap. While studies of rap and Hip Hop culture have been useful in terms of nudging contemporary poverty studies to pay attention to expressive cultures, they have not done much to advance the culture concept in social science. Like its progenitor, the dozens, rap or Hip Hop has been subject to incredible misconception and overinterpretation. Despite the brilliant writing of cultural critics like Tricia Rose, Greg Tate, George Lipsitz, Brian Cross, James Spady, dream hampton, Seth Fernando, Jonathan Scott, Juan Flores, Toure, and others, a number of scholars have returned to or revised the interpretive frameworks developed by the previous generation of ethnographers.[36]

For example, in a recent book on poor, black youth in postwar Philadelphia, Carl Nightingale suggested that the presumed loss of oral traditions like toasting and the dozens and the rise of rap music and similar commercialized expressive cultures partly explain the increase in violence among young black males. The former, he argues, has played a positive role in curbing violence, while the latter is responsible for heightening aggression. He thus calls on young black men to return to these earlier, presumably precommercial cultural forms to vent emotions. Nightingale advocates resurrecting the ring shout, drumming, singing the blues, even toasting, to express black male pain and vulnerability.

The suggestion that rap music has undermined black cultural integrity is made even more forcefully in a recent article by Andre Craddock-Willis, who criticizes nearly all rap artists—especially hardcore gangsta rappers—for not knowing the "majesty" of the blues. The Left, he insists, "must work to gently push these artists to understand the tradition whose shoulders they stand on, and encourage them to comprehend struggle, sacrifice, vision, and dedication—the cornerstones for the Black musical tradition."[37] (A tradition, by the way, that includes the great Jelly Roll Morton, whose 1938 recording of "Make Me a Pallet on the Floor" included lines like, "Come here you sweet bitch, give me that pussy, let me get in your drawers / I'm gonna make you think you fuckin' with Santa Claus."[38])

The flip side are authors who insist that rap music is fundamentally the authentic, unmediated voice of ghetto youth. Tommy Lott's recent essay, "Marooned in America: Black Urban Youth Culture and Social Pathology," offers a powerful critique of neoconservative theories about the culture of poverty and challenges assumptions that the culture of the so-called underclass is pathological, but he nevertheless reduces expressive culture to a coping strategy to deal with the terror of street life. For Lott, the Hip Hop nation is the true voice of the black lumpenproletariat whose descriptions of "street life" are the real thing. "As inhabitants of extreme-poverty neighborhoods," he writes, "many rap artists and their audiences are entrenched in a street life filled with crime, drugs, and violence. Being criminal-minded and having street values are much more suitable for living in their environment." Of course, most rap music is not about a nihilistic street life but about rocking the mike, and the vast majority of rap artists (like most inner-city youth) are not entrenched in the tangled web of crime and violence. Yet Lott is convinced that Hip Hop narratives of ghetto life "can only come from one's experiences on the streets. Although, at its worst, this knowledge is manifested through egotistical sexual boasting, the core meaning of the rapper's use of the term 'knowledge' is to be *politically* astute, that is, to have a full understanding of the conditions under which black urban youth must survive."[39]

By not acknowledging the deep, visceral pleasures black youth derive from making and consuming culture, the stylistic and aesthetic conventions that render the form and performance more attractive than the message, these authors reduce expressive culture to a political text to be read like a less-sophisticated version of the *Nation* or *Radical America*. But what counts more than the story is the "storytelling," an MC's verbal facility on the mike, the creative and often hilarious use of puns, metaphors, and similes, not to mention the ability to kick some serious slang (or what we might call linguistic inventiveness). As microphone fiend Rakim might put it, the function of Hip Hop is to "move the crowd." For all the implicit and explicit politics of rap lyrics, Hip Hop must be understood as a sonic force more than anything else.

Despite their good intentions, ignoring aesthetics enables these authors not only to dismiss "egotistical sexual boasting" as simply a weakness in political ideology but to mistakenly interpret narratives of everyday life as descriptions of personal experience rather than a revision of older traditions of black vernacular poetry and/or appropriations from mainstream popular culture. To begin with rap music as a mirror image of daily life ignores the influences of urban toasts and published "pimp narratives," which became popular during the late 1960s and early 1970s. In many instances the characters are almost identical, and on occasion rap artists pay tribute to toasting by lyrically "sampling" these early pimp narratives.[40]

Moreover, the assumption that rappers are merely street journalists does not allow for the playfulness and storytelling that is so central to Hip Hop, specifically, and black vernacular culture, generally. For example, violent lyrics in rap music are rarely meant to be literal. Rather, they are more often than not metaphors to challenge competitors on the microphone. The mike becomes a Tech-9 or AK-47, imagined drive-bys occur from the stage, flowing lyrics become hollow-point shells. Classic examples are Ice Cube's "Jackin' for Beats," a humorous song that describes sampling other artists and producers as outright armed robbery, and Ice T's "Pulse of the Rhyme" or "Grand Larceny" (which brags about stealing a show).[41] Moreover, exaggerated and invented boasts of criminal acts should sometimes be regarded as part of a larger set of signifying practices. Growing out of a much older set of cultural practices, these masculinist narratives are essentially verbal duels over who is the "baddest." They are not meant as literal descriptions of violence and aggression, but connote the playful use of language itself.[42]

Of course, the line between rap music's gritty realism, storytelling, and straight-up signifyin(g) is not always clear to listeners, nor is it supposed to be. Hip Hop, particularly gangsta rap, also attracts listeners for whom the "ghetto" is a place of adventure, unbridled violence, erotic fantasy, and/or an imaginary alternative to suburban boredom. White music critic John Leland, who claimed that Ice Cube's political turn "killed rap music," praised NWA because they "dealt in evil as fantasy: killing cops, smoking hos, filling quiet nights with a flurry of senseless buckshot." This kind of voyeurism partly explains NWA's huge white following and why their album *Efil4zaggin* shot to the top of the charts as soon as it was released. As one critic put it, "In reality, NWA have more in common with a Charles Bronson movie than a PBS documentary on the plight of the inner cities." NWA members have even admitted that some of their recent songs were not representations of reality "in the hood" but inspired by popular films like *Innocent Man,* starring Tom Selleck, and *Tango and Cash.*[43]

Claims to have located the authentic voice of black ghetto youth are certainly not unique. Several scholars insist that Hip Hop is the pure, unadulterated voice of a ghetto that has grown increasingly isolated from "mainstream" society. Missing from this formulation is rap music's incredible hybridity. From the outset, rap music embraced a variety of styles and cultural forms, from reggae and salsa to heavy metal and jazz. Hip Hop's hybridity reflected, in part, the increasingly international character of America's inner cities resulting from immigration, demographic change, and new forms of information, as well as the inventive employment of technology in creating rap music. By using two turntables, and later digital samplers, DJs played different records, isolated the "break beats," or what they identified as the funkiest part of a song, and boldly mixed a wide range of different music and musical genres to create new music. And despite the fact that many of the pioneering DJs, rappers, and break dancers were African-American, West Indian, and Puerto Rican, and strongly identified with the African diaspora, rap artists wrecked all the boundaries between "black" and "white" music. DJ Afrika Islam remembers vividly the time when Hip Hop and punk united for a moment and got busy at the New Wave clubs in New York during the early 1980s. Even before the punk rockers sought a relationship with uptown Hip Hop DJs, Afrika Islam recalls, in the Bronx they were already playing "everything from Aerosmith's 'Walk This Way' to Dunk and the Blazers." Grand Master Caz, whose lyrics were stolen by the Sugarhill Gang and ended up in "Rapper's Delight" (the first successful rap record in history), grew up in the Bronx listening to a lot of soft rock and mainstream pop music. As he explained in an interview, "Yo, I'd bug you out if I told you who I used to listen to. I used to listen to Barry Manilow, Neil Diamond, and Simon and Garfunkel. I grew up listening to that. WABC. That's why a lot of the stuff that my group did, a lot of routines that we're famous for all come from all white boy songs."[44]

If you saw a picture of Caz, this statement would seem incongruous. He looks the part of an authentic black male, a real roughneck, hoodie, "G," nigga, criminal, menace. And yet he is a product of a hybrid existence, willing to talk openly about Simon and Garfunkel in a book that I could only purchase from a Nation of Islam booth on 125th Street in Harlem. He is also the first to call what he does "black music," structured noise for which the beat, no matter where it's taken from, is everything. Moreover, like the breakers who danced to his rhymes, the kids who built his speakers, the DJ who spun the records, Caz takes credit for his creativity, his artistry, his "work." This is the "black urban culture" that has remained so elusive to social science; it is the thing, or rather the process, that defies terms like *coping strategy, adaptive, authentic, nihilistic,* and *pathological.*

Revising the Culture Concept:
Hybridity, Style, and Aesthetics in Black Urban Culture

Aside from the tendency to ignore expressive/popular cultural forms and limit the category of culture to (so-called dysfunctional) behavior, the biggest problem with the way social scientists employ the culture concept in their studies of the black urban poor is their inability to see what it all means *to the participants and practitioners.* In other words, they don't consider what Clinton (George, that is) calls the "pleasure principle." If I may use a metaphor here, rather than hear the singer they analyze the lyrics; rather than hear the drum they study the song title. Black music, creativity and experimentation in language, that walk, that talk, that style, must be understood as sources of visceral and psychic pleasure. Though they may also reflect and speak to the political and social world of inner-city communities, expressive cultures are not simply mirrors of social life or expressions of conflicts, pathos, and anxieties.

Paul Willis's concept of "symbolic creativity" provides one way out of the impasse created by such a limited concept of culture. As Willis argues, constructing an identity, communicating with others, and achieving pleasure are all part of symbolic creativity—this is literally the labor of creating art in everyday life. Despite his distrust and vehement opposition to "aesthetics," he realizes that, in most cases, the explicit meaning or intention of a particular cultural form is not the thing that makes it attractive. The appeal of popular music, for example, is more than lyrical: "Songs bear meaning and allow symbolic work not just as speech acts, but also as structures of sound with unique rhythms, textures, and forms. Thus, it is not always what is sung, but the *way* it is sung, within particular conventions or musical genres which gives a piece of music its communicative power and meaning."[45] Indeed, words like *soul* and *funk* were efforts to come up with a language to talk about that visceral element in music, even if they did ultimately evolve into market categories. Over two decades ago, black novelist Cecil Brown brilliantly captured this "thing," this symbolic creativity, the pleasure principle, soul, or whatever you want to call it. Writing about the Godfather of Soul, James Brown, he argued that his lyrics are less important than how they are uttered, where they are placed rhythmically, and "how he makes it sound." He writes, "What, for instance, does 'Mother Popcorn' mean? But what difference does it make when you're dancing to it,

when you are feeling it, when you are it and it you (possession). It's nothing and everything at once; it is what black (hoodoo) people who never
studied art in school mean by art."[46]

Yet to say it's a "black" thing doesn't mean it is made up entirely of
black things. As Greg Tate makes clear in his recent collection of essays,
Flyboy in the Buttermilk, and in the opening epigraph, interpreters of the
African-American experience — in our case social scientists — must bear a
large share of the responsibility for turning ghetto residents into an undifferentiated mass. We can no longer ignore the fact that information technology, new forms of mass communication, and immigration have made the
rest of the world more accessible to inner-city residents than ever before.[47]
Contemporary black urban culture is a cultural hybrid that draws on Afro-
diasporic traditions, popular culture, the vernacular of previous generations of
Southern and Northern black folk, new and old technologies, and a whole lot
of imagination. Once again, James Clifford's ruminations on the "predicament of culture" are useful for exposing the predicament of social science.
He writes, "To tell . . . local histories of cultural survival and emergence, we
need to resist deep-seated habits of mind and systems of authenticity. We
need to be suspicious of an almost-automatic tendency to relegate non-
Western (read: black) peoples and objects to the pasts of an increasingly
homogenous humanity."[48]

Notes

The author is indebted to Diedra Harris-Kelley, Hazel Carby, Fernando Coronil,
Nick Dirks, Geoff Eley, David Freund, Kyra Gaunt, Guy Ramsey, Gerald Jaynes, David
Nasaw, Sherry B. Ortner, Tricia Rose, James Spady, Jeanne Theoharis, conference
participants at "Re-Configuring the Culture Concept" at the University of Michigan,
and the faculty fellows at the Robert Penn Warren Center for the Humanities (Vander-
bilt University) for their critical insights and suggestions. I would also like to thank the
faculty and students in the Graduate Program in History at CUNY, president Frances
Degen Horowitz, and Associate Provost Pamela T. Reid for inviting me to deliver this
essay as one of the four W. E. B. DuBois Distinguished Visiting Lectures.

1. Mercer L. Sullivan, "Absent Fathers in the Inner City," *The Annals* 501 (January 1989): 49–50.

2. Recent proponents of a new "culture of poverty" thesis include Ken Auletta,
The Underclass (New York: Random House, 1982); Nicholas Lemann, "The Origins of
the Underclass: Part I," *Atlantic Monthly* 257 (June 1986): 31–61, "The Origins of the
Underclass: Part II," *Atlantic Monthly* 257 (July 1986): 54–68, and *The Promised
Land: The Great Black Migration and How It Changed America* (New York: Knopf,
1991); Charles Murray, *Losing Ground: American Social Policy, 1950–1980* (New
York: Basic Books, 1984); Lawrence Mead, *The New Dependency Politics: Non-Work-
ing Poverty in the U.S.* (New York: Basic Books, 1992). This work is quite distinct in
scope, methods, and ideology from the pioneering studies by Oscar Lewis, who had

introduced the "culture of poverty" idea to American social science. Unlike the more recent work, he did not argue that poor people's behavior is the *cause* of their poverty. Rather, he insisted that capitalism impoverished segments of the working class who were denied access to mainstream institutions. The culture they created to cope with poverty and disfranchisement was passed down through generations and thus led to passivity and undermined social organization. Lewis had no intention of using the culture of poverty thesis to distinguish the "deserving" from the "undeserving" poor. See Oscar Lewis, *The Children of Sánchez* (New York: Random House, 1961) and *La Vida: A Puerto Rican Family in the Culture of Poverty, San Juan and New York* (New York: Random House, 1966).

Critics of the culture of poverty thesis are many, and they do not all agree with each other as to the relative importance of culture or the causes of poverty. See especially Charles Valentine, *Culture and Poverty: Critique and Counter-Proposals* (Chicago and London: University of Chicago Press, 1968); Herbert J. Gans, "Culture and Class in the Study of Poverty: An Approach to Antipoverty Research," in *On Understanding Poverty: Perspectives from the Social Sciences,* ed. Daniel Patrick Moynihan (New York: Basic Books, 1968); Sheldon Danzinger and Peter Gottschalk, "The Poverty of *Losing Ground,*" *Challenge* 28 (May–June 1985): 32–38; William Darity and Samuel L. Meyers, "Does Welfare Dependency Cause Female Headship? The Case of the Black Family," *Journal of Marriage and the Family* 46, no. 4 (1984): 765–79; Mary Corcoran, Greg J. Duncan, Gerald Gurin, and Patricia Gurin, "Myth and Reality: The Causes and Persistence of Poverty," *Journal of Policy Analysis and Management* 4, no. 4 (1985): 516–36.

3. Michael Katz, "The Urban 'Underclass' as a Metaphor of Social Transformation," in *The Underclass Debate: Views from History,* ed. Michael Katz (Princeton, NJ: Princeton University Press, 1993), 3–23.

4. The most prominent of the "structuralists" adopt some cultural explanation for urban poverty, suggesting that bad behavior is the outcome of a bad environment. William Julius Wilson's most recent work argues that the lack of employment has eroded the work ethic and discipline of the underclass, leading to behaviors that allow employers to justify not hiring them. See especially, William J. Wilson, *When Work Disappears: The World of the New Urban Poor* (New York: Knopf, 1996), and *The Truly Disadvantaged: The Inner City, the Underclass, and Public Policy* (Chicago: University of Chicago Press, 1987); David T. Ellwood, *Poor Support: Poverty in the American Family* (New York: Basic Books, 1988); Elijah Anderson, *Streetwise: Race, Class, and Change in an Urban Community* (Chicago: University of Chicago Press, 1990), and "Sex Codes and Family Life Among Poor Inner City Youth," *The Annals* 501 (January 1989): 59–78; Troy Duster, "Social Implications of the 'New' Black Underclass," *Black Scholar* 19 (May–June 1988): 2–9; Christopher Jencks, *Rethinking Social Policy: Race, Poverty, and the Underclass* (Cambridge: Harvard University Press, 1992); Mark S. Littman, "Poverty Areas and the Underclass: Untangling the Web," *Monthly Labor Review* 114 (March 1991): 19–32; Jacquelyn Jones, *The Dispossessed: America's Underclasses from the Civil War to the Present* (New York: Basic Books, 1992); Douglas G. Glasgow, *The Black Underclass: Unemployment and Entrapment of Ghetto Youth* (New York: Random House, 1981); William J. Wilson and Löic J. D. Wacquant, "The Cost of Racial and Class Exclusion in the Inner City," *The Annals* 501 (January 1989): 8–25; John D. Kasarda, "Caught in a Web of Change," *Society* 21 (November/Decem-

ber 1983): 41–47, and "Urban Industrial Transition and the Underclass," *The Annals* 501 (January 1989): 26–47; Maxine Baca Zinn, "Family, Race, and Poverty in the Eighties," *Signs* 14, no. 4 (1989): 856–74; Mary Corcoran, Greg J. Duncan, and Martha S. Hill, "The Economic Fortunes of Women and Children: Lessons from the Panel Study of Income Dynamics," *Signs* 10, no. 2 (1984): 232–48; Mary Jo Bane, "Household Composition and Poverty," in *Fighting Poverty: What Works and What Doesn't,* ed. Sheldon Danzinger and Daniel Weinberg (Cambridge: Harvard University Press, 1986); Ellwood, *Poor Support;* Barry Bluestone and Bennett Harrison, *The Deindustrialization of America* (New York: Basic Books, 1982); Richard Child Hill and Cynthia Negrey, "Deindustrialization and Racial Minorities in the Great Lakes Region, USA," in *The Reshaping of America: Social Consequences of the Changing Economy,* ed. D. Stanley Eitzen and Maxine Baca Zinn (Englewood Cliffs, NJ: Prentice-Hall, 1989); Elliot Currie and Jerome H. Skolnick, *America's Problems: Social Issues and Public Policy* (Boston: Little, Brown, 1984); Carl Nightingale, *On the Edge: A History of Poor Black Children and Their American Dreams* (New York: Basic Books, 1993); Staff of Chicago Tribune, *The American Millstone: An Examination of the Nation's Permanent Underclass* (Chicago: Contemporary Books, 1986). While most of these authors focus on deindustrialization and the effects of concentrated poverty, Douglas S. Massey and Nancy A. Denton have argued that racial segregation is the key to explaining the persistence of black urban poverty; see their *American Apartheid: Segregation and the Making of the Underclass* (Cambridge: Harvard University Press, 1993).

5. Kathryn Edin, "Surviving the Welfare System: How AFDC Recipients Make Ends Meet in Chicago," *Social Problems* 38 (November 1991): 462–74.

6. Charles P. Henry, *Culture and African-American Politics* (Bloomington, IN: Indiana University Press, 1990), 12–13. Likewise, social philosopher Leonard Harris asks us to imagine what would happen if we used the same indices to study the "urban rich": "Suppose that their behavior was unduly helpful to themselves; say they rarely married, had more one-child families, were more likely than previous rich to be sexual libertines practicing safe sex, were health conscious, and were shrewd investors in corporate and ghetto property without moral reflection." See Leonard Harris, "Agency and the Concept of the Underclass," in *The Underclass Question,* ed. Bill E. Lawson (Philadelphia: Temple University Press, 1992), 37.

7. Lee Rainwater, *Behind Ghetto Walls: Black Families in a Federal Slum* (Chicago: Aldine, 1970); Elliot Liebow, *Tally's Corner: A Study of Negro Streetcorner Men* (Boston: Little, Brown, 1967); Ulf Hannerz, *Soulside: Inquiries into Ghetto Culture and Community* (New York: Columbia University Press, 1969); Carol B. Stack, *All Our Kin: Strategies for Survival in a Black Community* (New York: Harper and Row, 1974); Betty Lou Valentine, *Hustling and Other Hard Work: Life Styles in the Ghetto* (New York: Free Press, 1978); Joyce Ladner, *Tommorrow's Tommorrow: The Black Woman* (Garden City, NY: Anchor, 1971); David Schulz, *Coming Up Black: Patterns of Ghetto Socialization* (Englewood Cliffs, NJ: Prentice-Hall, 1969).

8. Stephen M. Joseph, ed., *The Me Nobody Knows: Children's Voices from the Ghetto* (New York: Avon Books, 1969); Caroline Mirthes and the Children of P.S. 15, *Can't You Hear Me Talking to You?* (New York: Bantam Books, 1971).

9. These typologies are drawn from Hannerz, *Soulside;* William McCord, John Howard, Bernard Friedberg, and Edwin Harwood, *Life Styles in the Black Ghetto* (New York: W. W. Norton, 1969).

10. John Langston Gwaltney, *Drylongso: A Self-Portrait of Black America* (New York: Vintage Books, 1981), xxiv, xxxii.

11. James Clifford, "On Collecting Art and Culture," in *The Predicament of Culture: Twentieth-Century Ethnography, Literature, and Art* (Cambridge: Harvard University Press, 1988), 246. Don't get me wrong; the vast and rich ethnographic documentation collected by these scholars is extremely valuable because it captures the responses and survival strategies hidden from economic indices and illuminates the human aspects of poverty. Of course, these materials must be used with caution since most ethnographies do not pay much attention to historical and structural transformations. Instead, they describe and interpret a particular community during a brief moment in time. The practice of giving many of these communities fictitious names only compounds the problem and presumes that region, political economy, and history have no bearing on opportunity structures, oppositional strategies, or culture. For an extended critique, see Andrew H. Maxwell, "The Anthropology of Poverty in Black Communities: A Critique and Systems Alternative," *Urban Anthropology* 17, nos. 2 and 3 (1988): 171–92.

12. Charles Keil, *Urban Blues* (Chicago and London: University of Chicago Press, 1966), 1–12, 23.

13. Stack, *All Our Kin*; Ladner, *Tommorrow's Tommorrow*. This dichotomy also prevails in Elijah Anderson's more recent *Streetwise*.

14. Lee Rainwater, ed., *Soul* (New Brunswick, NJ: Transaction Books, 1970), 9.

15. Ibid. (especially essays by John Horton, Thomas Kochman, and David Wellman); Ulf Hannerz, "The Significance of Soul" in ibid., 15–30; Hannerz, *Soulside*, 144–58. For other interpretations of soul, see Keil, *Urban Blues*, 164–90; William L. Van Deburg, *New Day in Babylon: The Black Power Movement and American Culture, 1965–1975* (Chicago: University of Chicago Press, 1992), 194–97; Claude Brown, "The Language of Soul," in *Mother Wit from the Laughing Barrel: Readings in the Interpretation of Afro-American Folklore*, ed. Alan Dundes (New York: Garland, 1981), 232–43; and Roger D. Abrahams, *Positively Black* (Englewood Cliffs, NJ: Prentice-Hall 1970), 136–50.

16. Hannerz, "The Significance of Soul," in Rainwater, ed., *Soul*, 21.

17. Schulz, *Coming Up Black*, 78, 103; Rainwater, *Behind Ghetto Walls*, 372; see also John Horton, "Time and Cool People," in Rainwater, ed., *Soul*, 31–50.

18. Hannerz, "The Significance of Soul," in Rainwater, ed., *Soul* 22–23.

19. Robert L. Allen, *Black Awakening in Capitalist America: An Analytic History* (Garden City, NY: Doubleday, 1969), 163; Van Deburg, *New Day in Babylon*, 201–2.

20. Van Deburg, *New Day in Babylon*, 201–2.

21. Lois Liberty Jones and John Henry Jones, *All about the Natural* (New York: Clairol, 1971), n.p.

22. Andrea Benton Rushing, "Hair-Raising," *Feminist Studies* 14, no. 2 (1988): 334; Jones and Jones, *All about the Natural*; Helen Hayes King and Theresa Ogunbiyi, "Should Negro Women Straighten Their Hair?" *Negro Digest* (August 1963): 68.

23. King and Ogunbiyi, "Should Negro Women Straighten Their Hair?" 69–70, 71.

24. Ibid., 67–68.

25. Rushing, "Hair-Raising," 334, 326.

26. Harold Cruse, *Rebellion or Revolution?* (New York: Morrow, 1968); Norman C. Weinstein, *A Night in Tunisia: Imaginings of Africa in Jazz* (New York: Limelight

Editions, 1993); Penny von Eschen, *Democracy or Empire: African Americans, Anti-Colonialism, and the Cold War* (Ithaca, NY: Cornell University Press, 1997); Immanuel Geiss, *The Pan-African Movement* (London: Methuen, 1974); Robert Weisbord, *Ebony Kinship: Africa, Africans, and the Afro-American* (Westport, CT: Greenwood Press, 1973); P. Olisanwuch Esedebe, *Pan-Africanism: The Idea and Movement, 1776–1963* (Washington, DC: Howard University Press, 1982).

27. Cruse, *Rebellion or Revolution?* 73.

28. As Linda Roemere Wright's research reveals, ads and other images of Afrocoifed women in *Ebony* magazine declined around 1970, just as images of black men with Afros were steadily rising. See Linda Roemere Wright, "Changes in Black American Hairstyles from 1964 through 1977, as Related to Themes in Feature Articles and Advertisements" (M.A. thesis, Michigan State University, 1982), 24–25.

29. Richard Majors and Janet Mancini Billson, *Cool Pose: the Dilemmas of Manhood in America* (New York: Lexington Books, 1992), 4.

30. Historian Roger Lane treats the dozens as a manifestation of a larger pathological culture: "Afro-American culture was marked by an aggressively competitive strain compounded of bold display, semiritualistic insult, and an admiration of violence in verbal form at least. 'Playing the dozens,' a contest involving the exchange of often sexual insults directed not only at the participants but at their families, especially their mothers, was one example of this strain." See Roger Lane, *Roots of Violence in Black Philadelphia, 1860–1900* (Cambridge: Harvard University Press, 1986), 146–47. See also Roger D. Abrahams, *Deep Down in the Jungle: Negro Narrative Folklore from the Streets of Philadelphia* (Chicago: Aldine, 1970), 52–56; Herbert Foster, *Ribin', Jivin', and Playin' the Dozens* (Cambridge, MA: Ballinger, 1986); Thomas Kochman, *Black and White Styles in Conflict* (Chicago: University of Chicago Press, 1981), 51–58; Majors and Billson, *Cool Pose*, 91–101; Nightingale, *On the Edge*, 26–28. There are some remarkable exceptions, such as the work of linguists, historians, literary scholars, and first-person practitioners, who treat the dozens as a larger set of signifying practices found in black vernacular culture or focus on the art and pleasures of verbal play. For these authors, the dozens is not merely a mirror of social relations. See Claudia Mitchell-Kernan, "Signifying, Loud-Talking, and Marking," in *Rappin' and Stylin' Out: Communication in Urban Black America* (Urbana and Chicago: University of Illinois Press, 1972); H. Rap Brown, *Die, Nigger, Die* (New York: Dial, 1969); Geneva Smitherman, *Talkin' and Testifyin': The Language of Black America* (Boston: Houghton Mifflin, 1977), 128–33; Henry Louis Gates, Jr., *The Signifying Monkey: A Theory of African-American Literary Criticism* (New York: Oxford University Press, 1988), especially 64–88; Houston Baker, *Long Black Song: Essays in Black American Literature and Culture* (Charlottesville, VA: University Press of Virginia, 1972), 115. Despite disagreements between Baker and Gates, both try to make sense of black vernacular culture, including the dozens, as art rather than sociology. Although Lawrence Levine took issue with the functionalist approach to the dozens over fifteen years ago, he did not reject it altogether. He suggests that the dozens helped young black children develop verbal facility and learn self-discipline. See *Black Culture and Black Consciousness: Afro-American Folk Thought from Slavery to Freedom* (New York: Oxford University Press, 1977), 345–58.

31. Levine, *Black Culture and Black Consciousness*, 357. A beginning is Marjorie Harness Goodwin, *He-Said-She-Said: Talk as Social Organization among Black Children*

(Bloomington: Indiana University Press, 1990), especially 222–23. However, Goodwin emphasizes "ritual insult" as a means of dealing with disputes rather than an art form and thus is still squarely situated within the social scientific emphasis on function over style and pleasure.

32. Abrahams, *Deep Down in the Jungle*, 60, 88–96; see also Roger D. Abrahams, *Talking Black* (Rowley, MA: Newbury House, 1976).

33. Schulz, *Coming Up Black*, 68. In McCord, et al., *Lifestyles in the Black Ghetto*, Edwin Harwood argues further that the lack of a father leads to violent uprisings and low self-esteem among black male youth. "Negro males who are brought up primarily by mothers and other female relatives pick up from them their hostility toward the males who are not there, or if they are, are not doing worth-while work in society. In such an environment it must be difficult to develop a consructive masculine self-image, and the ambivalent self-image that does emerge can only be resolved in ways destructive both to the self and the society, through bold and violent activities that are only superficially masculine. If this analysis is correct, then the Negro youth who hurls a brick or an insult at the white cop is not just reacting in anger to white society, but on another level is discharging aggression toward the father who 'let him down' and females whose hostility toward inadequate men raised doubts about his own sense of masculinity" (32–33).

34. Eugene Perkins, *Home Is a Dirty Street: The Social Oppression of Black Children* (Chicago: Third World Press, 1975), 32.

35. William Labov, *Language in the Inner City: Studies in the Black English Vernacular* (Philadelphia: University of Pennsylvania Press, 1972), 325. David Schulz doesn't even trust the laughter of his subjects. He writes, "With careful listening one becomes suspicious of the laughter of the ghetto. So much apparent gaiety has a purpose all too often in the zero-sum contest system of interpersonal manipulation for personal satisfaction and gain." See Schulz, *Coming Up Black*, 5.

36. See, for example, Venise T. Berry, "Rap Music, Self Concept and Low-Income Black Adolescents," *Popular Music and Society* 14, no. 3, (fall 1990); Nightingale, *On the Edge*, 132–33, 162–63, 182–84; Wheeler Winston Dixon, "Urban Black American Music in the Late 1980s: The 'Word' as Cultural Signifier," *Midwest Quarterly* 30 (winter 1989): 229–41; Mark Costello and David Foster Wallace, *Signifying Rappers: Rap and Race in the Urban Present* (New York, 1990); Andre Craddock-Willis, "Rap Music and the Black Musical Tradition: A Critical Assessment," *Radical America* 23, no. 4 (June 1991): 29–38. The case of Hip Hop might be unusual since social scientists working on the black urban poor have been conspicuously silent, leaving most of the discussion to music critics and cultural studies scholars. The result has been a fairly sophisticated body of work that takes into account both aesthetics and social and political contexts. See, for example, Tricia Rose, *Black Noise: Rap Music and Black Culture in Contemporary America* (Hanover and London: Wesleyan University Press, 1994), and "Black Texts/Black Contexts," in *Black Popular Culture*, ed. Gina Dent (Seattle: Bay Press, 1992), 223–27; Greg Tate, *Flyboy in the Buttermilk* (New York: Simon and Schuster, 1992); Juan Flores, "'Puerto Rican and Proud, Boy-ee!': Rap, Roots, and Amnesia," in *Microphone Fiends: Youth Music and Youth Culture*, ed. Tricia Rose and Andrew Ross (New York: Routledge, 1994), 89–98; William Eric Perkins, *Droppin' Science: Critical Essays on Rap Music and Hip Hop Culture* (Philadelphia: Temple University Press, 1996); Joseph G. Eure and James G. Spady, eds., *Nation*

Conscious Rap (Brooklyn: P.C. International Press, 1991); James G. Spady, Stefan Dupree, and Charles G. Lee, *Twisted Tales in the Hip Hop Streets of Philadelphia* (Philadelphia: UMUM LOH Publishers, 1995); Brian Cross, *It's Not about a Salary . . . Rap, Race and Resistance in Los Angeles* (London: Verso, 1993); Michael Eric Dyson, *Reflecting Black: African-American Cultural Criticism* (Minneapolis: University of Minnesota Press, 1993); Jeffrey Louis Decker, "The State of Rap: Time and Place in Hip Hop Nationalism," *Social Text* 34 (1989): 53–84; Jonathan Scott, "'Act Like You Know': A Theory of Hip Hop Aesthetics" (unpublished paper in author's possession, 1994); S. E. Fernando, *The New Beats: Exploring the Music, Culture, and Attitudes of Hip Hop* (New York: Anchor/Doubleday, 1994); two good general histories are Steve Hager, *Hip Hop: The Illustrated History of Breakdancing, Rap Music, and Graffiti* (New York: St. Martin's Press, 1984); and David Toop, *Rap Attack 2* (London: Pluto Press, 1991).

37. Andre Craddock-Willis, "Rap Music and the Black Musical Tradition: A Critical Assessment," *Radical America* 23, no. 4 (June 1991): 37.

38. "Rockbeat," *Village Voice* 39, no. 4 (January 25, 1994): 76.

39. Tommy Lott, "Marooned in America: Black Urban Youth Culture and Social Pathology," in *The Underclass Question,* ed. Bill E. Lawson (Philadelphia: Temple University Press, 1992), 71, 72, 80–81.

40. Digital Underground's, "Good Thing We're Rappin'," *Sons of the P* (Tommy Boy, 1991) is nothing if not a tribute to the pimp narratives. One hears elements of classic toasts, including "The Pimp," "Dogass Pimp," "Pimping Sam," "Wicked Nell," "The Lame and the Whore," and perhaps others. Even the meter is very much in the toasting tradition. For transcriptions of these toasts, see Bruce Jackson, *"Get Your Ass in the Water and Swim Like Me": Narrative Poetry from Black Oral Tradition* (Cambridge: Harvard University Press, 1974), 106–30. Similar examples that resemble the more comical pimp narratives include Ice Cube, "I'm Only Out for One Thing," *AmeriKKKa's Most Wanted* (Priority, 1990) and Son of Bazerk, "Sex, Sex, and more Sex," *Son of Bazerk* (MCA, 1991).

41. Other examples include, Capital Punishment Organization's aptly titled warning to other perpetrating rappers, "Homicide," NWA's "Real Niggaz," Dr. Dre's "Lyrical Gangbang," Ice Cube's "Now I Gotta Wet'cha," Compton's Most Wanted, "Wanted," and "Straight Check N' Em," Ice T, *OG: Original Gangster* (Sire Records, 1991); Ice Cube, *Kill at Will* (Priority Records, 1992); Ice T, *Power* (Warner Bros., 1988); CPO, *To Hell and Black* (Capitol Records, 1990); NWA, *100 Miles and Runnin'* (Ruthless, 1990); CMW, *Straight Check N' Em* (Orpheus Records, 1991). See also chapter 8, "Kickin' Reality, Kickin' Ballistics: Gangsta Rap and Postindustrial Los Angeles," in Robin D. G. Kelley, *Race Rebels: Culture, Politics, and the Black Working Class* (New York: The Free Press, 1994), 183–227.

42. Ice T [and the Rhyme Syndicate], "My Word Is Bond," *The Iceberg/Freedom of Speech . . . Just Watch What You Say* (Sire Records, 1989); Ice Cube, "J.D.'s Gafflin'," *AmeriKKKa's Most Wanted* (Priority Records, 1990). West Coast rappers also create humorous countercritiques of gangsterism; the most penetrating is perhaps Del tha Funkee Homosapien's hilarious, "Hoodz Come in Dozens," *I Wish My Brother George Was Here* (Priority Records, 1991).

43. See John Leland, "Rap: Can It Survive Self-Importance?" *Details* (July 1991): 108; Frank Owen, "Hanging Tough," *Spin* 6, no. 1 (April 1990): 34; James Bernard, "NWA [Interview]," *The Source* (December 1990): 34.

66—Robin D. G. Kelley

44. Quoted in Spady and Eure, *Nation Conscious Rap*, xiii, xxviii. On the early history of Hip Hop in New York, see Rose, *Black Noise*; Hager, *Hip Hop*; and Toop, *Rap Attack 2*.

45. Paul Willis, *Common Culture: Symbolic Work at Play in the Everyday Cultures of the Young* (Boulder and San Francisco: Westview Press, 1990), 1–5, 65.

46. Cecil Brown, "James Brown, Hoodoo, and Black Culture," *Black Review* 1 (1971): 184.

47. For insightful discussions of the way information technology in the late twentieth century opened up new spaces for building cultural links between black urban America and the African diaspora, see George Lipsitz, *Dangerous Crossroads: Popular Music, Postmodernism, and the Poetics of Place* (London: Verso, 1994); Paul Gilroy, *The Black Atlantic: Modernity and Double-Consciousness* (Cambridge: Harvard University Press, 1993).

48. Clifford, "On Collecting Art and Culture," 246.

4

The Limits of Culture

E. Valentine Daniel

In my recent book *Charred Lullabies,* I attempted to confront the problem of representing violence ethnographically. This essay is an addendum as well as a postscript to the last chapter in that book, "Crushed Glass: A Counterpoint to Culture." I began that chapter by reviewing several dominant understandings of culture in anthropology and noted therein that despite their differences, all such understandings converged in taking culture to be a system (of thought or actions) of coherence. In recent years, it has become fashionable in anthropology and some of the other human sciences to invoke the word *contestation* in order to undermine a coherentist notion of culture. A little reflection, however, will show that most of these invocations submit as examples contestations that are only a subset within a larger domain of coherence. The threats of incoherence introduced by contestatory positions are merely of an agreeing-to-disagree kind of incoherence; they do not exceed the horizon of a universe in which you and I are parts or participants, a horizon illuminated by culture. Culture as a dense cluster of semeiosic habits has such recuperative and appeasing capabilities that it cannot be easily undermined or even challenged despite all the intellectual belligerence we may summon to mount such a challenge. Marx's celebrated "opiate" is only one—even if the most poignant—example where a major domain of culture, religion, offers persuasive ways of understanding aspects of the world that may otherwise remain incomprehensible. Marxism itself, like the Hegelianism it claims to have turned on its head, is another case in point. It is a cultural or cultured ideology. I believe that for those who bristle at the notion of culture and the sense of stasis it conveys, the problem is not with the word *culture* but with the idea of a system that accompanies it. The term *system* brings to mind something that is not merely coherent but closed rather than open, settled rather than dynamic, and if dynamic, then dynamic only within the bounds of cybernetic systematicity; above all, it is something that is governed by clearly articulatable rules rather than improvisational forays and strategies into the radically unknown. In the view of one of the more sophisticated theorists such as Clifford Geertz, I argued, the work of culture is seen as given to making sense, also beauty, and sometimes even truth. An absolutely fugitive idea, action, or thing, fugitive from the sense-making power of culture, is almost impossible *to seek and find*. This is not because of culture's stability, but because of its protean nature, its absolute dynamism. The act of *seeking and finding* in this context is akin to Descartes's mental or meditative exercise in doubting that led him to the *eureka* of the *cogito ergo sum,* an act which Peirce, in one of the most brilliant anti-Cartesian essays ever written, belittled as mere "paper doubt," which he contrasted with real doubt. Real doubt has a brute quality to it, it cannot be easily willed in nor wished out. And yet I want to argue that in life, one does encounter moments that make it possible, even necessary, to interrogate the limits of culture's totalizing mission and capacities. Such moments are encountered, mind you, not willed. But to question such capacities is not to appeal to culture's contraries, such as Kant's *ding an sich* or the concept of the individual agent, as the solution, as the way out of the confines of culture. The limits of a culture's recuperative powers or its meaning-making capacities are to be found elsewhere; they are to be found at the threshold of a relatively dense cluster of semeiosic habits.[1] Such a cluster might constitute anything from a discourse (in the Foucauldian sense), or an intensely commensurate dialogue between two or more persons, to an individual's sensory limits. Even though hazards lurk at all such thresholds, the work of culture literally *comprehends* such hazards either by the bounding of such thresholds by routine, redundancy, and regularization or by providing such thresholds with the power to colonize, to convert, or to conquer fugitive elements that may drift within their expanding semeiosic field. But it is also at these very thresholds that semeiosis runs the risk of failing to tame, its expansion being abruptly obstructed and the action of semeiosis held at bay by the reaction of something that we can only call an object(ion). This is the point at which there is an encounter between an inner world with an outer existent, an encounter that can be best characterized as a clash without resolution, a precipitation of a counterpoint against a point, an encounter with an Other whose face, voice, and look pierce my world and shatter my monistic ontology that has hitherto been made possible by my cultured being.[2]

There are times in the life of a person or the history of a people when a counterpoint to culture appears that cannot be easily subsumed and tamed by the powers of culture. The counterpoint to culture I have in mind is not the analogue of the counterpoint in music rendered with such brilliance and beauty by Johann Sebastian Bach, that contrapuntal genius whom the Dutch sociologist, Wim Wertheim (1974) extolled as providing a metaphor to enable us to better understand violent revolutions and rebellions required for social change. The counterpoint I speak of is something that resists incorporation into the harmony of a still higher order of sound, sense, or society. It resists the recuperative powers of culture; it runs parallel to without ever crossing the dialectic. It resists normalization; it is a shock that impairs *habitus,* it is a point of irresolution in a semeiosically realized inner world and a semeiosically unrealizable (at least for a time being) but all too real (or even surreal) existent.

I divide this chapter into two parts. Part I incorporates material from my chapter, "Crushed Glass," that describes an incident and a moment in the ongoing ethnic conflict in Sri Lanka where the taming capacities of culture fail. In Part II, I turn to a more general and theoretical examination of recalcitrant realities, or what I call with greater exactitude existents, that resist their realization by culture to one degree or another, but I first show when and how such a realization takes place when it works, when the taming by and into semeiosis is successful, a success so commonplace as to go unremarked upon. Next, by "indicating" (pointing to) the unrealizability of certain entities and experiences by semeiosis, I attempt to enable the appreciation of the recalcitrance of the counterpoint to culture. What follows as part I appeared in almost the same form in *Charred Lullabies* (Daniel 1996, 202–10).

Part I

Allow me to indicate more clearly what I have called the counterpoint of culture by the only way I know how: by intimation, by example. The example is violence, though violence is not the only event that is constituted of the culturally unrecoverable surplus I speak of. Let me plunge into ethnography and tell you of an event that was described to me by two brothers. It concerns the senseless deaths of two men and the suffering of two survivors. These two brothers narrowly escaped being killed by a gang of Sinhala youth during the 1983 anti-Tamil riots in a northeastern village in Sri Lanka. They witnessed the murders of their elder brother and father.[3]

Selvakumar is twenty-two years old and works as a teller in one of the local banks. When arrangements were made for me to interview him about the events that led to his father's and brother's deaths, I was not warned that

whenever he recalled these events, he suffered episodes of loss of consciousness. The day of my interview with him was no exception. During our interview, which lasted for over four hours, Selvakumar lost consciousness
thrice. The first time was after the first half-hour of the interview, and it took
twenty-five minutes for him to recover. On the second and third occasions,
he remained unconscious for about ten minutes each time. During these
episodes his pulse and temperature fell sharply, his color drained to an
ashen gray, he responded neither to pin pricks nor to smelling salts, and he
lost control of his bladder. By the physician's orders, a warm poultice of
medicinal herbs was applied to his temples and forehead, and his lips were
moistened with *tippili* tea. When Selvakumar regained consciousness he did
not remember having lost it. What follows is a partial description of what
happened on "that day," as he calls it.

> That day my father and the Chairman [of the Urban Council] went to
> the police and told them that we had heard with our own ears that this
> Gunasene had collected the other boys in the soccer team and had ob-
> tained long knives and sticks and that they were planning to come and
> beat up all the Tamils in this housing settlement. This Gunasene had
> already served some time in jail. He is not from this area. He is from
> Nawalapitiya, from where you come. He has been here for many years,
> though. This place, this housing colony, was in really bad shape when
> my father moved in. But he organized the place. He cleaned up the
> well, cleared the jungle, and cut drains for the rain water to flow. My
> brother. Oh, my brother they killed him. They killed him and I couldn't
> even help. I was afraid. They beat him to death: "thuk," "thuk." [He
> passes out].
>
> [Later:] The police inspector told the Chairman that if we had a
> complaint, we should take it to the navy post. So my father and the
> Chairman went to the navy post. The sentry did not let them through
> at first. They waited there all morning. Then the commander's car came.
> He must have been going into town. The Chairman waved him to a
> stop. They asked him if they could talk to him for a moment. The Chair-
> man had known him personally. "Say what you have to say. I have a
> lot of work." "Can we go into your office?" the Chairman wanted to
> know. "There is no time for that," replied the commander. So my father
> and the Chairman told him what they had heard. The commander told
> them that they did not have any right to approach him on such matters
> and that he should have taken his complaint to the police station. They
> told him that they had already been there and the police inspector had
> told them to come to him [the commander]. "If you are so smart, why
> don't you control your own people," said the commander to the Chair-
> man. My father and the Chairman walked back to the police station.
> On the way, another friend, a Tamil, told us that some Sinhalas from
> Vavuniya had also joined Gunasene's gang and that he had heard

Gunasene say to the boys not to worry, that he had taken care of the police. My father and the Chairman walked back to the police station.

We were met there by Nitthi [Selvakumar's younger brother], who came to tell us that all the Sinhala taxi-drivers were telling the Tamil taxi-drivers that they were going to be killed today. There were no taxis in the Tamil taxi-stand. They [the Sinhala taxi-drivers] had told my younger brother that the rain had delayed things a little, but when it ceases, to be prepared for "Eelam."[4] It was raining heavily. The inspector finally came out and said, "So what, the commander did not want to see the tigers?" The Chairman said, "Look, you know all these boys. You know this man. They are good people. They have lived with the Sinhalas in peace. They are neither tigers nor bears. There are rowdies who are threatening to kill them." He said things like that. The inspector laughed and said, "Looks like the tigers are afraid. They have become pussy cats." The other constables joined in and laughed. "Why don't you go to Appapillai Amirthalingam.[5] He will take care of you. What do you say?" (He was talking to my brother). "They tell me that you are the big man in the area. What, are you afraid too?" My brother did not say a word. He just clenched his teeth and looked down and walked away. All the constables were laughing. [Then he said] "Now go home and take care of your women and children. And beware! If any of you dare call a Sinhala a rowdy. I am warning you. That is how you start trouble." Then what was there to do? The Chairman went to his home; my father and I came home and shut the doors and put bars against them. Then the rains stopped.

Then they came. About half an hour later. My father was old and not as strong as he used to be. He was not feeling well in his body. But my brother was very strong. He was a big man. He was a good soccer player. That was something else this Gunasene had against him. He used to play soccer with us. We heard this loud noise at a distance. It sounded like one hundred saws were sawing trees at the same time. They were shouting something in Sinhala. Nitthi looked out through the crack in the front door and told us that there were two navy personnel standing on the side of the road. We felt relieved. Our neighbor, she is a Sinhala woman who is married to a Tamil. Her husband works in Anuradhapura. He is a government servant. He used to come once in two weeks. So this little girl, about three years old, used to spend most of her time in our place. This woman treated my mother like her own mother, and she used to leave this child with us. That day this child was with us. And the gang started coming closer and closer. My sister and my mother were hiding. Where can they hide? The house has only three rooms. They were in the kitchen behind the firewood. Then suddenly there was silence. All the shouting stopped. Nitthi looked through the crack in the door and the two navy personnel were talking to Gunasene. Then we saw the navy personnel leave. My father told my younger brother to bar the two windows. But then we heard footsteps in the mud outside. Then they started pushing down the door. My father had fallen to the ground. My brother was still holding the door. But they used crowbars to break it. I ran into the kitchen out of fear. Another gang broke through the kitchen door. They surrounded the house. But the men who entered through the kitchen door didn't look for us in the kitchen; they walked on into the front room. Then I heard the beating. My mother and sister took the child and ran out of the back door into the fields. Then I heard the beating again. I slowly stood up and looked through the kitchen door into the front room. Nobody saw me. They were looking at the ground. I knew it was my brother on the ground. I wanted to help him. There was a knife in the kitchen. I wanted to take it and run and cut them all up. But I was a coward. I was afraid. My brother would have certainly done that for me. [He becomes unconscious. He is laid flat on the floor on a mat. A single tear trickles down his cheek. The man who had arranged this interview tells me, "The boy can't cry. That is the trouble."]

[Later:] Then someone said, "The old man is out there near the well." They looked out and laughed. "He is trying to draw water." They said things like that and were making fun of him. Some of them moved out, and now I could see my brother. They had cut him up. My younger brother had fainted behind the stack of firewood. I left him and ran into the field. Someone shouted, "There, over there, someone is running." I sat down behind some old tires. I must have fainted. When I woke up it was dark. There was smoke coming from where the house was. They had set their torches to it. I went looking for my mother and sister in the dark.

Nitthi is sixteen. He believes that he was in school, waiting for the rains to stop, when his father and brother were killed and his house was set on fire. Most of the time he has total amnesia about the events of that day. There are two exceptions. The first is when he wakes up with a start from a nightmare. From the time he wakes up, he begins to describe certain events of that awful day in great and minute detail. And then, as suddenly as he awakened, he falls back onto his mat and falls asleep. In the second typical occasion, he loses consciousness during the day as his brother does, but he then wakes up, not into his wakeful amnesia but into detailed recall. The recalling and retelling lasts for about five minutes, and then he falls asleep. He may sleep for several hours before waking up again. What follows are several of Nitthi's accounts taped by his brother for me during several episodes. The statements are all Nitthi's, but are drawn from four different "dream episodes" and two separate "post-unconsciousness" episodes. I was asked by the family not to play back the tapes to Nitthi. I have, with Selvakumar's help, edited the tapes so as to arrive at a narrative that makes reasonable chronological sense. Apart from rearranging the utterances for such a purpose, I have edited only to omit the highly repetitive utterances (ranging from exclamations such as "*Aiyo*" to phrases and full sentences) and those sounds that made no sense to either Selvakumar or me. In this edited version, I mark shifts from utterances drawn from one episode to those drawn from another by rendering the first word of the "new" utterance in boldface type.

The middle hinge is coming loose. They are pushing the door. Someone is kicking the door. Listen. **He** has put his foot down now. Now he is lifting it out of the mud. Now he is kicking the door. **Kick,** Kick, Kick. Now he is resting his foot again in the mud. It is like a paddy field outside. For all the kicking the door is not loosening. . . . **The** bottom hinge is still holding. The screws in the top hinge have fallen. The wood is splitting. A crowbar is coming through. **It** appears that father has been poked in the back. He can't breathe. He has fallen down. **My** elder brother has turned around and is trying to hold the door back with his hands. **I** see his (Gunasene's) toes from under the door. I know them from seeing him play soccer. He has ugly toes. Mud is being squeezed from in between his toes. **Knives** are cutting through the wood of the window. There is smoke coming through the window. **Gunasene** is shouting, "Not yet, not yet" (*dämma epa, dämma epa*). **My** brother's leg is moving. It is moving like the goat's leg. (He is supposed to have witnessed the slaughtering of a goat when he was younger.) **The** front door is open and they are going around to the back. They are going to the back to kill my father. Look through the door. The two navy men are near the *dhobi*'s house (a house at some distance across the main road). My eyes are filling with tears. The navy men look like they are very close. I squeeze my eyes. The navy men are far away again, near the dhobi's house. **Father** is crying. "Give me some water for my son, *Sami*. (god or Lord) Kill me but give my son some water. Let me give my son some water. The son I bore, the son I bore, the son I bore . . ." **Piyadasa** is asking, "How are you going to draw water like this, lying in the mud. Stand up to draw water from the well, like a man." They are all laughing. **Karunawathi** has come. The tailor boy has come. [The tailor boy is telling her,] "They ran to the field with your child. They are all right. Don't go. They might follow you." **They** are kicking my father. Karunawathi is shouting, "Leave that old man alone. Leave him alone. He is almost dead." "We know your man is a Tamil too. And we'll do the same thing to him if we find him." Karunawathi is crying: "What a shameful tragedy this is" ("*mona aparadede meke*"). **Someone** is calling the men to the front. They want someone to drag my big brother to the road and leave him there. Listen! Karunawathi drawing water from the well. She tells the tailor boy, "He is dead."

I was not able to meet Gunasene. He was in police custody. However, I was able to find out two things about him. First, he was not from Nawalapitiya, where I had spent part of my childhood, but from a neighboring town called Kotmale. Second, using a police constable as a messenger, he had sent Selvakumar Rs.500 and a message, the gist of which (according to Selvakumar) was, "What has happened has happened. Let us forget what has happened. This money is for you to rebuild your house. You can stay in our house if you want until you finish building your house."

Social scientists have tried to understand or even to explain communal violence in Sri Lanka. The grandest, and in many ways the most admirable, attempt so far in this regard is the one put forth by Bruce Kapferer (1988), who sought to understand Sinhala against Tamil violence in terms of Sinhala cultural ontology. He argued that Sinhala-Buddhist ontology required that it hierarchically encompass and dominate a subdued antithesis, in this case the Tamils. Insofar as such a contained antithesis might rebel from within, it was seen as demonic, and Sinhala Buddhism was called upon to exorcise this demon by ritual. The available ritual in the context of ethnic rebellion was violence. Such is a rough summary of *Legends of People, Myths of State*. The thesis is perfectly Hegelian, except of course for its terminus not at a summum bonum in equipoise but in an ontology condemned to violence. The only problem was that no sooner had this and similar theses been put forth than Tamil violence rose to match Sinhala violence. Furthermore, violence was no longer interethnic but intraethnic, with more Tamils killing Tamils and Sinhalas killing Sinhalas than Sinhalas killing Tamils or Tamils killing Sinhalas, and with the Sri Lankan state killing the most, both Tamils and Sinhalas.

I must pause to emphasize here that my description of a violent event in which Tamils were the victims and Sinhalas the aggressors is fortuitous. Conditions in 1983 and 1984 when I did fieldwork on this topic yielded more tales of violence by Sinhalas against Tamils. Rest assured that there are plenty of equally gory examples of violence in which the Sinhalas were the victims. An altogether separate book needs to be written on behalf of the thousands of Tamils and Sinhalas who watch from afar and from within the violence their own people are capable of and who abhor what they hear and see. Here are two symmetrical statements, one from a Sinhala and one from a Tamil. The first statement was made to me by the nephew of the Minister of State at that time, Dr. Anandatissa de Alwis. At a party in Colombo in December 1983, he had this to say: "After I saw what happened that day (July 23, 1983), I am embarrassed to say I am a Sinhalese. I hate the Sinhalese. They are shameless. Cowards. I have never seen so much hate in my life and hope I never will." In 1993, a Tamil gentleman, a retired civil servant and now a refugee in Tamil Nadu, had this to say following the assassination of Rajiv Gandhi: "The Tamils are a cursed race. A low race. Those Tamils there (meaning Sri Lanka) and these Tamils here (meaning South India), are both a cursed race. Barely human. Woe unto me who was born a Tamil!"

These are strong expressions of self-loathing and frustration, expressions of disbelief that make the core of their very beings revolt and tremble.

The point is this: Violence is an event in which there is an excess of passion, an excess of evil. The very attempt to label this excess (as I have done) is condemned to fail; it employs what Georges Bataille (1988) called *mots glissants* (slippery words). Even had I rendered faithfully, without any editing, the words, both coherent and incoherent, of Nitthi, I would not have seized the event. Everything can be narrated, but what is narrated is no longer what happened.

I have also interviewed young men who were members of various militant movements and had killed fellow human beings with rope, knife, pistol, automatic fire, or grenade. "You can tell a new recruit from his eyes. Once he kills, his eyes change. There is an innocence that is gone. They become focused, intense, like in a trance." Such was the account of a veteran militant, who has since left the movement in which he fought. Violence, like ecstasy (and the two at times become one) is an event that is traumatic, and interpretation is an attempt at mastering that trauma. Such an attempt may be made by victim (if she is lucky enough to survive), villain, or witness. Those of us who are forced or called upon to witness the event's excess either flee in terror or are appeased into believing that this excess can be assimilated into culture, made, in a sense, our own. Regardless of who the witness is—the villain, the surviving victim, or you and I—the violent event persists like crushed glass in one's eyes. The light it generates, rather than helping us to see, is blinding. Maurice Blanchot, in *Madness of the Day,* writes thus:

> I nearly lost my sight, because someone crushed glass in my eyes. . . . I had the feeling I was going back into the wall, or straying into a thicket of flint. The worst thing was the sudden, shocking cruelty of the day; I could not look, but I could not help looking. To see was terrifying, and to stop seeing tore me apart from my head to throat. . . . The light was going mad, the brightness had lost all reason; it assailed me irrationally, without control, without purpose. (Quoted in Shaviro 1990, 3)

More ethnography: Piyadasa (a pseudonym) is a Sinhala in his late twenties. I knew him as a young boy who played soccer in the town of Nawalapitiya, where I grew up. He lived in a village near Kotmale and used to ride the bus back and forth to his school with Tamil school children who came to Nawalapitiya from the tea estates. At times, after a game of soccer, he and his bus-mates would feel so famished that they would pool all their small change, including their bus fares, to buy and eat buns and plantains from the local tea shop. Having eaten, they would start walking up the hill to Kotmale, all of six miles. His village now lies buried under the still waters of a reservoir built by the Swedes as part of the Mahaväli river-damming project.

In 1983, the *pantaram* (the boy who makes garlands) of the local Hindu temple was killed. I was informed by another Sinhala man, a close friend of one of my brothers, that Piyadasa was among those who had killed the *pantaram* and that he too had wielded a knife. I visited Piyadasa, who has been resettled in the North-Central province, and asked him to describe to me what had happened. He denied that he had directly participated in the violence but was able to give me a detailed account of the event. The following are a few excerpts:

> He was hiding in the temple when we got there. The priest, he had run away. So they started breaking the gods. This boy, he was hiding behind some god. We caught him. Pulled him out. So he started begging, "*Sami,* don't hit. *Sami,* don't hit." He had urinated. He pleaded, "O gods that you are, why are you breaking the *samis?*" They pulled him out to the street. The nurses and orderlies were shouting from the hospital balcony. "Kill the Tamils! Kill the Tamils!" No one did anything. They all had these long knives and sticks. This boy was in the middle of the road. We were all going round and round him. For a long time. No one said anything. Then someone flung at him with a sword. Blood started gushing (*O gala lee ava*). Then everyone started to cut him with their knives and beat him with their sticks. Someone brought a tire from the Brown and Company garage. There was petrol. We thought he was finished. So they piled him on the tire and set it aflame. And can you imagine, this fellow stood up with cut up arms and all and stood like that, for a little while, then fell back into the fire.

The constant shifting from the including *we* to the excluding *they* is noteworthy. This was in the early days of my horror-story collecting, and I did not know what to say. So I asked him a question of absolute irrelevance to the issue at hand. Heaven knows why I asked it; I must have desperately wanted to change the subject or pretend that we had been talking about something else all along. "What is your goal in life?" I asked. The reply shot right back: "I want a VCR."

I have struggled to understand this event in which reality overtakes the surreal, to speak *about* it, and thereby to master it, but I have literally been struck "speechless." I am not alone, quite clearly. During my work in 1983–84 and since, in Sri Lanka, India, Europe, and North America, I have met many witnesses of the excess of violence who have been stricken likewise by abominations that stagger belief. Shaviro puts it eloquently when he describes such a silence as "not a purity before or beyond speech. It does not indicate calm or appeasement. It is rather a violent convulsion, a catastrophe that overwhelms all sound and all speaking" (1990, 84).

There are, to be sure, interpretations of such events that friends and "friendly texts" offer me, but no sooner do I seize them than they escape the grasp of my understanding, although sometimes I think that I do understand. But, to return in closing to the optic metaphor, there remains a blind spot in all such understandings. Georges Bataille considers this blind spot to be

> reminiscent of the structure of the eye. In understanding, as in the eye, one can only reveal it with difficulty. But whereas the blind spot of the eye is inconsequential, the nature of understanding demands that the blind spot within it be more meaningful than understanding itself. To the extent that understanding is auxiliary to action, the spot within it is as negligible as it is within the eye. But to the extent that one views in understanding man himself, by that I mean the exploration of the possibilities of being, the spot absorbs one's attention: it is no longer the spot that loses itself in knowledge, but knowledge which loses itself in it. In this way existence closes the circle, but it couldn't do this without including the night from which it proceeds only in order to enter it again. Since it moved from the unknown to the known, it is necessary that it inverse itself at the summit and go back to the unknown (Bataille 1988 [1954], 110–11).

Part II

Based upon the manner in which I have ended part I, several conclusions are possible.

> **1.** Violence (especially in such extreme forms as discussed above) is something ineffable; it is something about which we cannot speak because we can neither come to know it nor understand it. Since language, knowledge, understanding, and the regularization of behavior in *significant* practices are the ultimate manifestations of culture, the ineffable quality of violence places it outside of culture. Such a position would concur with the Kantian notion of the *ding an sich*. It also provides a justification for the semeiological (in contradistinction to the semeiotic) method to account for the workings of all manner of signs and signification, not only linguistic ones, as if they functioned inside a hermetically sealed discourse, unaffected by the extra-semeiological context. This is a method that has been most blatantly and unapologetically employed by structuralists. But it is also one adhered to, in the final analysis, by most poststructuralists and postmodernists who are not only like their structuralist counterparts but paradoxically also like the positivists they shun: they are nominalists in the extreme. The explication of such a sweeping charge must await another day and time. To think of positivists as realists is to partake of a widespread misunderstanding.

2. Another response would be to say that it is contradictory to hold that something (violence, in this instance) is unknowable, for to say that it is unknowable is itself to know it in some manner or the other. This would be the position held by Peirce at one time or another in his critique of Kant's ultimate concession to nominalism. Or as Hegel put it somewhere, Kant's *ding an sich* is, after all, some thing "in-itself *for us.*" Peirce's point, exactly.

3. A third response would be to say that to hold something such as a particular act of violence to be a thing in itself, unknowable and ineffable, is nothing more than errant and sentimental hyperbole.

I shall not discuss the third response at any length except to say that anyone who holds such an opinion is unlikely to have encountered unspeakable violence or to have met victims of violence who are unable to speak of their experience, for anyone who has experienced acts of violence will at first sympathize at least with a quasi-Kantian stance of the existence of things-in-themselves. My own characterization of the relationship of particular acts of violence to culture will settle upon a modification of the first two of the above positions, a modification that will ironically lead to a conclusion somewhat like the third, but without the irresponsible charges of hyperbole and errant nonsense. In the process of explicating my position, the justification for the manner of my treatment of the event that ends with "I want a VCR" will also become clearer; this is my purpose.

My own understanding of why a particular existent is or is not taken up by culture derives from Peirce's account of the representation of an external reality in the cognizing mind through the dynamics involved in the transformation of a percept into a concept. Alternatively stated, the transformation of the first sensory impression, the percept, to the status of a concept serves as a paradigmatic instance for what is true more generally when the external and the internal are bridged, or a dividing threshold is crossed. In the paradigmatic case of the sentient human person, who is commonly called "the individual" in the West, the senses, or more characteristically, the skin, serve as the breach across which the external object of experience is taken into the internal world of cognition, but to state it so is to get ahead of our story. Let us develop the argument systematically, even if painstakingly.

C. S. Peirce claimed that this universe is perfused with signs, but this is not to say that all there is in the universe are signs. What is a sign? It is many things, among which, "A [SIGN] is a subject of a triadic relation TO a second, called its OBJECT, FOR a third, called its INTERPRETANT, this triadic relation being such that the [SIGN] determines its interpretant to stand in the same triadic relation to the same object for some interpretant" (Peirce 1931–35, 1.541).[6] The triadic relation may be represented as follows:

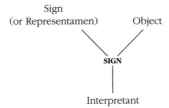

Sign
(or Representamen)   Object

SIGN

Interpretant

And at the end of yet another definition Peirce amplifies on the nature of the third correlate, the interpretant, so as to provide us with a greater understanding of the semeiotic process. "The Third... must have a second triadic relation in which the Representamen, or rather *the relation thereof to its Object,* shall be its own (the Third's) Object, and must be capable of determining a Third to this relation. All this must equally be true of the Third's Third, and so on endlessly" (Peirce 1931–35, 2.274).

Note, then, that the interpretant-sign serves as a further sign to the same object as represented by the first sign for another interpretant, and this process, theoretically, continues ad infinitum. This may be diagrammed as follows (adapted from Sheriff 1989):

S   O
(Sign)   (Object)

I (Interpretant)

I   S-O
(Sign)   (Object)

I (Interpretant)

I   I-(S-O)
(Sign)   (Object)

I (Interpretant)

And so on endlessly

To render this in quasi-anthropomorphic terms, it is as if the "First" sign[7] represents an object—which Peirce calls a "Second"—that then comes alive, turns around, as it were, and does two things. It "determines," or rather, constrains, the sign's representational freedom on the one hand,[8] but on the other, incites it to invite ("determine" or constrain in its turn) another sign, the interpretant (which Peirce calls a "Third"), to represent the same object in an even more developed if not identical fashion to yet another sign. The latter continues the same process of representation and determination in the same manner that the first interpretant (now, a "second sign" in this string) represented and determined, by inviting another interpretant-sign to participate in the ongoing process of semeiosis, a process that is, for all practical purposes, open and indefinite. In the human world, which is dominated by symbolic signs (i.e., signs of convention), the representations are rarely identical, and the determinations are never absolute. This slippage in representation and determination provides room not only for growth and transformation of signification and meaning but also for error as well as for the recognition of error, and possibly change. In what we have come to separate out as nature, the processes of semeiosic growth, error, and change are much less dynamic; for nature is largely constituted of petrified habits.[9] It is out of this, the quick (as opposed to the dead) and predominantly symbolic world of indeterminacy, that we carve out a vague domain that we then call culture,[10] a domain of *relative* permanence and persistence where the capricious dynamism of symbolic growth and change is constrained by an environment of coexisting and codetermining symbolic signs, with some help from nonsymbolic signs as well.

Whatever we know, we know through representations or signs. Knowledge by definition is mediated; it is an inferential process. Any notion of unmediated knowledge, whatever else that may be, is not knowledge. *Intuition* is often proffered as a term that describes what is claimed to be direct knowledge when it is only the operation of tacit inference. However, in Peircean semeiotics (unlike many other approaches to the study of signs and sign activities that go under the name of semeiology and semeiotics) knowing is not only about representations but is also about determination and effects. In fact, the interpretant, or the third correlate within the triadic sign, is defined as "the significate *effect*" of the sign.[11] But Peirce complicates the picture further by claiming that a human being is himself/herself a sign, and in so doing not only brings back the question of ontology so radically alienated by modern philosophy since Descartes, but creates a nondualistic relationship between knowing and being. (Deely 1994) One may restate this claim more precisely by saying that a human being is a dense cluster of a multitude of signs that forms the basis for the phenomenon of individuation. Once we admit that a human being is a sign, we do not have merely a semeiosic epistemology but a semeiosic ontology: to be is to be significantly. Human beings are perfused with culture and are themselves tokens of culture. If individuation is brought about by the dense clustering of signs, so is culture, which is what gives it the appearance of an essence. Or we may say that human life is shot through with that relatively dense cluster of signs called culture, whose density constitutes and contributes to a very great part of human being in the world.

The greater preponderance of signs that densely cluster are signs of habit, that is, signs that through their activity (sign activity = semeiosis) tend to reproduce themselves by bringing the signs in their immediate environment into concordance with themselves. But most important, one of the habits that humans have by virtue of their human being is that of changing habits. This is the source of human agency. There are clustered densities of signs that are not coterminous with what we in the West have come to name the individual, to whom we attribute agency. Both supra- and infra-individual clustered densities of signs may be said to have the capacity for agency. Examples of the former would be the collective transformative force of a group or a movement, a sorority or a society, a culture or a nation; an example of the latter would be the force of an internal dialogue that gradually builds momentum and results in habit change.[12] Therefore, any clustered density of signs that contains within it the habit for habit change may be deemed to have agency.[13] This would therefore include not only human beings but also the products of human labor, corporal or imaginative. For example, the American Constitution has agency in this sense because the habit for habit change is part of its impress, part of its constitution, although its operation is determined only by historical circumstances and contexts.

The semeiosic concordance brought about by habit is one of the qualities that gives a human being his or her sense of coherence and integrity of being and ability to act. (This would, by extension, hold for the aforementioned infra- and supra-individual agents as well.) Such a semeiosic concordance is what makes the greater part of the consequences of one's actions predictable.

How does all this contribute to our understanding and answering the question that led Descartes to invoke God and Kant to invoke the theory of an unknowable *ding an sich*? How do elements of the "external world" cross over into the cognizing mind or, more generally, into the inner world? Or as Dan Nesher poses the problem in three unfolding questions, "How can we know that our cognitions are signs representing external reality? How can we be justified in defining a sign as a cognitive representation of external reality? How can we cognize the real objects beyond our cognitions themselves?" (1997, 212). The answers to these questions contribute to our understanding of why and how certain entities of the "external world"—certain violent acts, for instance—are barred at the threshold or confined to the periphery of the internal world, forbidden, as it were, from engaging with the sign activity of an inner world, be it that of a person or a culture, made familiar by habit.

If we are to take the semeiosic reality of our being seriously, then we need to replace the image of the cognizing mind as either a mirror that reflects external reality or a container in which external reality is or is not faithfully represented with an image of thresholds. These would be thresholds that bound or rather demarcate a domain of densely clustered semeiosic activity sustained by a high degree of habit from semeiosic activities with different epicenters or from sign movements that are far less dense and far more free-floating, even fugitive. Such a threshold then does demarcate, more or less tightly, an inner from an outer world. As I indicated earlier, the paradigmatic threshold is the one that divides human cognition from sensory input that comes from beyond that threshold. This threshold is not to be understood as necessarily (though it may be) coterminous with our skin, but as coincidental with the limits of our semeiosic capacity to engage with objects that are presented to us by virtue of the limitations of and the reach of our habits. Furthermore, the customary notion of the mind, typically confined to the brain, needs to be expanded to include a mindful body as well, where percepts and perceptual judgments may or may not mature into the generality and the generalizability of the cognitive order of concepts that are amenable to reflection and available to consciousness. To anticipate, our semeiosic capacities may be incapable of accommodating a certain act of violence that exerts its brute force upon our habit-constituted world, our inner world of a semeiosically ordered meaningfulness. Such was the case when I, as a human constituted of a certain cultural and personal history, encountered the brute Otherness (or Secondness) of the violent incident I described and its summation in the statement, "I want a VCR." It was, in the strictest sense, incomprehensible. This brute Second is the unassimilated or unsignified presemeiosic object; it is the objection to the conceit of semeiosic expansion, serious or playful.

What does it take for an external (presemeiosic) object to traverse the threshold (sensory or otherwise) and become part of the flow of signs within a quasi-bounded semeiosic domain? One may begin to understand this more general traversing of and transformation across a threshold through a better understanding of the manner in which a percept is transformed into a concept, which in turn will require a closer scrutiny of the sign structure, sign types, and their dynamic interplay. What follows will be a highly abbreviated sketch of a more detailed argument that may be found in a recent essay by Dan Nesher (1997) with the caveat that his essay is tethered to the questions of analytic philosophy and the individual body, whereas mine is intended to engage questions of ontology and culture in which the body serves only as a metaphor.

According to the above definition of the sign, the sign is a First, its object a Second, and their interpretant a Third. These three correlates of the sign are but species of three modes of being: the being of positive qualitative possibility, the being of actual fact, and the being of law that will govern facts in the future (these correspond to Peirce's triune categories, which he called, Firstness, Secondness, and Thirdness; see Peirce 1931–35, 1.300–1.353).

The type of relationship that holds between a sign and its object is called the "ground" of their signification. And the possible grounds of/for signification may be seen as broadly falling under one of Peirce's three categories. In the most commonly known types of ground, iconicity (signification by virtue of the sign's similarity to, including identity with, the object) is a relative First; indexicality (signification by virtue of the contiguity between sign and object, often a causal relationship) is a relative Second; and symbolization (signification by virtue of the bringing together of object and sign by convention) is a relative Third. In this chapter what concerns me most are Thirds and Seconds, especially Seconds.

In the idea of reality, Secondness is predominant; for the real is that which insists upon forcing its way to recognition as something other than the mind's creation. (Remember that before the French word, *second,* was adopted into our language, *other* was merely the ordinal numeral corresponding to two; see Peirce 1931–35, 1.325.)

In the cognitive dimension of cultural life, Thirdness predominates over Secondness: process over haecceity, suasive power over brute force, knowing over willing, conceiving over sensing, symbol over index, the general over the actual and particular. Thus, for the most part, every Second becomes both logically and ontologically overcome or assimilated by a Third. Conversely, by the rule of hierarchic inclusion, every Third contains a Second, and every Second contains a First, but not the other way around. Therefore, in every element of cognition there is an element of duality, of struggle, of interaction with some other forcing itself on our cognition, and it is this (force) that we call actuality or external reality. In the experience of reaction, effort, and resistance, we cannot avoid the actuality of independent objects.

Peirce distinguishes between the immediate and the dynamic object, a distinction that is crucial to our analysis. The immediate object is the object internal to the sign. Or as Nesher phrases it, the immediate object (he also calls it the "internal object") "*stands in*" a triadic relation to its representamen and its interpretant. The dynamic object is the object that the representamen *"stands for."* The immediate object that is cognized in the sign is an idea (what we also commonly call the meaning of the sign). The dynamic object, by contrast, is what offers resistance and exerts a constraint on free-floating semeiosis or semeiosic drift. The dynamic object is not necessarily an individual thing exerting physical force. It is not the same as a "real object," or an existent, or an actual, though it could be that too. The dynamic object could also be a possible (a goal for instance) or even an instance of a general law (Liszka 1996, 215). As we have already noted, in the semeiotic sign's most elementary structure, the object is the second correlate of the sign. Its secondness is compounded, as it were, when this object is a dynamic (rather than an immediate) object; and it is compounded further when this dynamic object's manifest form is an existent/actual. Thus, we could say that when the semeiotic object happens to be an existent in its dynamic mode, the Cartesian, Kantian, and Humean question gets posed in its starkest form. The question is, How does the representing sign in the "mind" come in contact with this independent real object, this object that so insistently asserts its otherness? (Nesher 1997, 215).

The link between the immediate and the dynamic object is human experience. Nevertheless, Peirce did not assume that we can separate experience from our background knowledge, our cultural heritage, or from our semeiosic capacities, capabilities, and endowments. Since all its elements are signs, even experience, then, is a cognitive process that falls under the Peircean category of Thirdness. "However, the most prominent [or even dominant] elements of experience belong to the sub-category of Secondness" (Nesher 1997, 225). Experience is a cognitive process, albeit a cognitive process in which external reality asserts itself as a duality recognizable in the Secondness of Thirdness that occupies a dominant position in the cognitive process in question. For those who are more familiar with Kant than with Peirce, it may be helpful to think of Peirce's immediate object and his dynamic object as approximately corresponding to Kant's objects of appearance (phenomenal object) and his transcendental object (the object as it is in itself) respectively. But for Kant, the transcendentalist, the reality of the outer sense in which we perceive objects in space is no more than "the reality of some sort of representation inside our minds" (Nesher 1997, 225). For Peirce, however, "the two kinds of sign representations are two aspects of our knowledge of external (independent) reality" (Nesher 1997, 213).

In the clash between ego and non-ego, a dynamic double consciousness, of an inner and an outer world, is precipitated into perception. Even though this dynamic duality, in becoming part of a percept, becomes a component of a triadic process, "It appears forcefully and beyond our control and criticism, and therefore as duality between our cognitive mind and external reality" (Nesher 1997, 223). Our inner world is a world we know *habitualiter*. We consider the semeiosic workings, the dispositions, and the expectations of this inner world to be natural. In our everyday commerce with the world, our inner world is ready and able to accommodate elements of the outer word without any threat to its habit, more often as enforcers and enhancers of the reproduction of habit. The encounter with an element of the outer world with which the inner world is unfamiliar is an encounter with a "stranger," who shoves aside all "expectation into the background and occupies that place"(Peirce 1931–35, 5.57). It is an encounter that reveals the clash between the inertia of expectation and its failure to maintain that inertia in the face of the unfamiliar. Unfamiliarity is, of course, a matter of degree, and so are surprises and the failures of expectation. This degree is determined by the semeiosic capacities, capabilities, and predispositions the inner world has for accommodating itself to the stranger's entry. Such an accommodation entails a semeiosic appropriation of the stranger, a comprehension of the Other, by the prevailing habits of the inner world. Such an appropriation or comprehension happens, if at all, in stages. The argument in the following three paragraphs, represented in the accompanying diagram, is intended to convey the evolving, many-dimensional process of semeiosis in its movement from percept to habit.

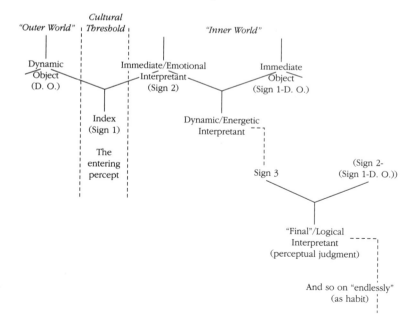

Every new perception is a surprise to one degree or another. At the very first level, this perception is translated into a feeling-sign: a feeling of surprise, a feeling for the strange, an uncanny feeling, or a feeling of shock even, sometimes a feeling of absolute awe. This first interpretation of perception is effected in an "emotional interpretant." An emotional interpretant is a relative First among significant effects pertaining to human and humanized agencies. The emotional interpretant may be considered a specific manifestation of the more inclusive, paradigmatic category called the "immediate interpretant." The second stage of interpretation involves the sense of duality brought about by the exertion of the "outer world" and the resistance to it by the counterexertion of the "inner world." In this dyadic sense of exertion and resistance, "we are internally compelled to react differently to two different feelings: one is of the past, the feeling of the expected percept, the second is of the present, the feeling of the actual percept frustrating our expectation" (Nesher 1997, 236). At this stage, the percept is interpreted in an "energetic interpretant." The energetic interpretant, relative to the emotional interpretant, is a Second in the triad of interpretants pertaining to human agents. "The energetic interpretant . . . is the effect of exertion any sign has on an interpreting agent" (Liska 1996, 26). It captures the moment of action and reaction. The paradigmatic, more inclusive counterpart of the energetic interpretant is the "dynamic interpretant." That is, the dynamic interpretant is a Second, relative to the immediate interpretant. The dynamic interpretant cannot harbor the meaning of the sign, but only its *singular effects*. The same is true of its analogue, the energetic interpretant. The effect of the violent incident that was condensed in the "I want a VCR" statement was, for me at least, a "singular effect" without meaning, incomprehensible.

In the third stage, the percept is interpreted through the "logical interpretant" (a Third, relative to the emotional and the energetic), which is the "conceptual import, the meaning of the sign" (Peirce 1931–35, 5.475). The logical interpretant is understood as the "would-be" of the sign, as Peirce suggests (5.482), that is, the *expression* (5.491) of the generalizable outcome of the sign (see Peirce 1931–35, 5.483, and Liszka 1996, 27). It is at this point that we may say that the percept has been translated into a perceptual judgment.

Following our parallel tracing of the category of interpretants pertaining to human agencies to the more purely formal and paradigmatic categories of interpretants, we shall find that the logical intepretant is the analogue or counterpart of what Peirce called the "final interpretant." Thus even as the logical interpretant is a relative Third to the emotional (First) and energetic (Second) interpretants, the final interpretant is a Third relative to the immediate (First) and the dynamic (Second) interpretants. The nomenclature, "final" may be misleading, giving the impression that it indicates an absolute termination of further semeiosic interpretation. This need not be the case. All that is meant by "final" is that it introduces a provisional state of rest or settlement of doubt or irritation that was triggered by the initiating percept, or that the interpretation arrived at has settled into habit. What is most important to note is that in Peirce's hierarchic scheme the logical (or final) interpretant contains (in both senses of "contain," to possess and to restrain) its genealogical predecessors, the emotional and the energetic interpretants. Whether and to what extent the disturbing potential of these two are appeased remains an open and empirical question.

The cognitive process that we have followed so far is the development of a percept from being an immediate/emotional/feeling interpretant to a dynamic/energetic/reactive interpretant to a final/logical/assimilating interpretant. The movement is from apparent immediacy to directness to familiarity. All these are still only relations among stages of cognition, and cognition is a semeiosic process, a process carried forth in and through signs. In other words, we are still talking of triadic processes that include the immediate objects in their progression from feeling to familiarity. With all its surprises and shocks to and intrusions into and disturbances of an order of habits, this is a diagnosis of a process that is still confined to the inner world of signs and their movement through mediations. What is special about percepts, however, is that they carry with them undeniable and forceful traces or aspects of the outer world of dynamic objects. Where and how does the dynamic object enter this inner world?

How can we speak of "that knowledge that is directly forced upon" us or support the claim that we do "have *direct experience of things in themselves?*" (Peirce 1931–35, 6.95). Nesher rightly suggests that this can be resolved by a Spinozistic theory of the mind/body connection as the union of two aspects in the same person. This view of the mutual immanence of body and mind tallies with Peirce's own view that matter is but effete mind (Peirce 1931–35, 6.25). "Peirce sometimes echoes Spinoza's idea, in so far as the cognitive sign and the effect of the represented object in the perceiver's body are [seen as] two aspects of the same whole (Nesher 1997, 238). Note the following quasi-figurative statement of Peirce concerning the nature of an indexical sign (which is, in the icon-index-symbol triad, a Second): "If the Sign be an Index, we may think of it as a fragment torn away from the [dynamic] Object, the two in their existence being one whole or a part of such a whole" (Peirce 1931–35, 2.230).

The combination of some aspect of the "stranger" from the outside world with a component of an inner world (or an aspect of the "real object" with the human body, as Nesher prefers to formulate it in his attempt to understand the formation of the percept) results in a hybrid that Nesher calls a "physical operation." The relationship is not a causal one but an ontological unity, an indexical First. The indexical sign is a constrained sign, constrained by the dynamic object, which it "attempts" to draw into the semeiosis of the inner world. This is done by its translation, stage by stage, into an emotional interpretant, an energetic interpretant, and a logical interpretant. With the very first translation of the object into/by the immediate/ emotional interpretant, an immediate object—that is, an object internal to the sign—is created, and the resulting triadic sign relationship becomes the elementary percept-sign. With each subsequent translation by/into subsequent interpretants, this immediate object undergoes further modification, and so does the percept-sign. In the energetic/dynamic interpretant, the immediate object gains specificity. In the logical interpretant, the immediate object gains generality. Once the immediate object and therefore the entire percept-sign within which it is lodged attains generality of the most primitive kind, the percept-sign is transformed into a perceptual judgment, and as such is prepared to enter the conceptual order, available for reflection as well as for habit making and habit taking.[14] The percept is the first impression of sense of the inner world. It is the immediate object that will be invoked by signs of the inner world in memory, when the dynamic object as such no longer exists.

The above explicates the relatively "successful" appropriation of elements or aspects of the "outer world" into an "inner world." But such appropriations are not always successful. The semeiosic process of incorporation can be stopped in its tracks so to speak, at the very gate of the inner world. It could be arrested in its initial hybridity; it could progress into its translation by an immediate/emotional interpretant and not move beyond it. Or it may go as far as being translated into an energetic/dynamic interpretant, arrested in its specificity, and be stuck there as nothing more than a trace of action and reaction, a reminder of the Secondness, the uniqueness, the incomparability, and the ungeneralizability of the event of the "stranger's" entry into the inner world, who was then condemned to remain there as a stranger. Does this make the "stranger" a Kantian unknowable? No. In principle, if not in practice, the inner world in question is a world in movement and evolution, transition and translation, a world that acquires other, more accommodatable and translatable aspects of the outer world even as it sheds some furnishings of the inner world. With time, such subsequent acquisitions, enrichments, and even impoverishments, may enable the world in question to construct an adequate interpretant, which in its turn, facing the prevailing signs in the inner world, will summon an immediate object such that it could be iconic to the Other and thereby successfully absorb the "stranger" in question into the semeiosis of the inner world. But at the same time, this is not to deny that for however long it takes, the "stranger" in question—that uninterpretable event, that unspeakable act—may be held up in progress at one stage or another.

To return now to the event of the "I want a VCR," for me and for many of my friends who were "cultured" like me, the significant effect of this event remains restless and unsettled in a state of hybridity, pulsating now as an immediate/emotional interpretant and then as a dynamic/energetic interpretant, without quite becoming transformed into a final/logical interpretant. One hopes that time, further readings, and further experiences will enable me and others to nudge at least some aspect of the event forward into the translation by logical interpretants and into the conceptual domain of theory, reflection, and culture: in a word, into history. And there are signs that such a process has begun. For this reason, I have provided in my book an alternate closing to the chapter in question. But even so, whenever I return to the tape recording of that interview or to the notes taken that day, the immediate object seems to carry with it a trace, no, an excess, of the dynamic event that has been only very partially translated at best, only partially assimilated into history. Yes, the event may never have been *a ding an sich* in principle, but neither has it arrived at a perceptual judgment of any certainty. And even when and to the extent that a translation into a fuller, final/logical interpretant is effected, the intensity of the encounter between the dynamic object and the semeiosic inadequacies of the inner world and the subsequent birth-trauma of an immediate object itself will persist in the semeiosis of the inner world in one form or another. In the case of the "I want a VCR" statement, it persists as an acute pain that lingers at the limits of culture without having acquired for itself its own pulse in the flow of cultural comprehension, its own angle of repose in the convolutions of history.

One final and important dimension of what I have been calling "the event" must be faced. What happened was not a mere event, a thing, or an object. In fact, the semeiosic language that speaks of the second, the Other, as an object is somewhat infelicitous for the purpose at hand. The mode in which the problem has been posed involved the comprehension of an object by and into that supreme semeiosic process we call thought. But the event in question was a person, the object was a human being, the Other was evil. The French philosopher, Emmanuel Lévinas, writes, "What distinguishes thought which aims at an object from the ties with a person is that the latter is articulated in the vocative; what is named is at the same time that which is called. The essence of discourse is prayer" (Lévinas 1996, 7–8). Such should be our predisposition toward the radical Other, he argues, and this is the only ethical stance one can and should take. Regardless of whether one does, like Lévinas, deny that ontology is fundamental, or whether one is a Peircean such as myself who believes that a semeiosic ontology is fundamental for human being in the world, the question remains: What stance does one take toward the Other when the Other is evil? The question is held at bay at the limits of culture.

Notes

My special thanks to Kristin Ruppel, who helped me with the diagrams and some of the more difficult passages in the text of this chapter.

1. Adjective form of "semeiotic," the general theory of signs. I adhere to this spelling in order to remain faithful to C. S. Peirce's own spelling and differentiate my own (broadly Peircean) approach to the study of signs from other (predominantly Saussurean) approaches. For further justification and elaboration, see Daniel 1996, 213.

2. For a discussion of the Other and "face," see Lévinas 1996, 8–12 and 68–70.

3. The killings took place in April 1983. My interview with Selvakumar was in December of the same year.

4. This is a sarcastic reference to the name that Tamil separatists have given to their hoped-for, separate nation-state.

5. Mr. Amirthalingam was the head of the Tamil United Liberation Front, which had constituted in 1975 of the former (major Tamil) Federal Party and several smaller parties and groups. In its 1976 platform the TULF proclaimed the right of self-determination for the Tamils, even if that were to entail the formation of a separate state. In August 1983, the constitution was amended so as to outlaw parties advocating secession. Members of parliament were required to take an oath of allegiance to the new constitution. The elected members of the TULF refused. Consequently the party was outlawed, the members lost their seats in the legislature, and the Tamils largely unrepresented.

6. In keeping with the convention of citing from Peirce (1931–35), the number to the left of the decimal point indicates the volume, and that to the right indicates the paragraph.

7. It is the "first" only in the sense and to the extent that it has been chosen as an arbitrary starting point and not because it is the absolute first in any sense. This "first" sign, it must be noted, has its own genealogy and history, which for the purposes of explication have bree bracketed out.

8. In other words, a sign does not have the infinite freedom assumed by some semeiological traditions to represent the object in any way whatsoever without constraints.

9. See Peirce 1931–35, 6.25 (hereafter cited without the date).

10. See Peirce, 5.447 and 5.505, for further discussion of the notion of the "vague."

11. See Peirce, 5.475.

12. Peirce considered thought to be a form of a dialogue. Thus, we could say that a stream of thought that flows uninterrupted is essentially dialogic.

13. My treatment of "agency" is in broad agreement with that of Webb Keane (1997).

14. To be sure, habits are not limited to the conceptual order of symbolic operations but are dispersed into other less "mindful" Second- and First-order habits.

Works Cited

Bataille, Georges. 1988 [1954]. *Inner Experience.* Albany: State University of New York Press.

Daniel, E. Valentine. 1996. *Charred Lullabies.* Princeton, NJ: Princeton University Press.

Deely, John. 1994. *New Beginnings: Early Modern Philosophy and Postmodern Thought.* Toronto: University of Toronto Press.

Kapferer, Bruce. 1988. *Legends of People, Myths of State.* Washington, DC: Smithsonian Institution Press.

Keane, Webb. 1997. *Signs of Recognition.* Berkeley: University of California Press.

Lévinas, Emmanuel. 1996. *Basic Philosophical Writings.* Edited by A. D. Peperzak, S. Critchley and R. Bernasconi. Bloomington: Indiana University Press.

Liszka, James Jakób. 1996. *A General Introduction to the Semeiotic of Charles Sanders Peirce.* Bloomington: Indiana University Press.

Nesher, Dan. 1997. "Peircean Realism: Truth as Meaning of Cognitive Signs Representing External Reality." *Transactions of the Charles S. Peirce Society* 23 (winter): 201–57.

Peirce, Charles S. 1931–35. *Collected Papers.* Vols. 1–6. Edited by C. Hartshorne and P. Weiss. Cambridge: Harvard University Press.

———. 1958. *Collected Papers.* Vols. 7–8. Edited by A. Burks. Cambridge: Harvard University Press.

Shaviro, Steven. 1990. *Passion and Excess.* Gainesville: University of Florida Press.

Sheriff, John K. 1989. *The Fate of Meaning: Charles S. Peirce, Structuralism, and Literature.* Princeton, NJ: Princeton University Press.

Wertheim, W.F. 1974. *Evolution and Revolution.* Baltimore: Penguin.

5

Mourning the Japanese Thing

Marilyn Ivy

It has become a truism to say that national culturalism is a powerful force
in Japan. A range of insistences on Japanese uniqueness is pervasive in public discourse, yet what those insistences mark out is precisely the fear of somehow *not* being unique. They designate moments of cultural anxiety and category trouble, which then obscure the dialectically entwined status of both
the United States (as the paradigmatic "west") and Japan as national-cultural
imaginaries. And therein lies the historical rub: Japan is literally unimaginable
outside its discursive positioning vis-à-vis the "west." Like other colonized
or near-colonized polities, Japan as a *nation-state* was instaurated in response
to the threat of domination by the Euroamerican powers in the mid-nineteenth century. It is arguable that there was no discursively unified notion
of the "Japanese" before the eighteenth century, and the particular articula-
tion of a unified Japanese ethnos with the "nation" to produce "Japanese
culture" is entirely a *modern* configuration.[1] What I mean by modern—as
if one could simply define it—indicates not only the urban energies, capitalist structures, and mechanico-electrical forms of reproduction that came
into sharpest relief in the Japan of the 1920s but had matured through the
nineteenth century in Europe and elsewhere.[2] It indicates the very problem
of the nation-state and its correlation with a capitalist colonialism that ensured that Japan (for example) would be pulled into a global geopolitical
matrix.

In the process of warding off the intrusions of the west after Perry's
1853 arrival in Japan, the newly instituted Japanese state bent all efforts toward rapid industrialization and the formation of a unitary Japanese polity,

often with brutal force and violent exclusions. The formation of a modern nation-state that could enter into the geohistorical nexus of western world history demanded the repression of internal differences in the service of what Slavoj Žižek has called the "national thing," one that could stand apart from and up to the powers of the west (*seiyō*).[3] By the national thing, or the "nation thing," Žižek means the particular nexus of national identification that is organized around what he calls "enjoyment" (*jouissance*) and that bears a particular relationship to the problem of national others. Žižek leans on Lacan and his notion of the "Thing," which derives from his anatomy of demand and desire and their emergence from an irrevocable lack within human subjects, such that the object of desire is always the desire of the Other: within the realm of human signification, desire is always directed toward another. But that desire is a "non-object"; it can never be specified as such but is always displaced: "The object signified in the demand becomes the signifier of something else (of that impenetrable 'Thing,' *das Ding*, that Freud locates in the *Nebenmensch* [another human].)"[4] The "Thing" is precisely not a thing—an object of knowledge—and in the psychoanalytic scenarios that Lacan drew upon, one word for the "Thing" would be "love," the love that no amount of proof can ever demonstrate. In the demands that I make upon another, the "satisfaction of the demand always leaves something to be desired—something that is nothing but is nevertheless always carried beyond the object of demand, as what this object is not: the paradoxical 'object' of desire."[5] Another name for this mysterious "Thing" is Žižek's "enjoyment" when he turns to the register of the national:

> What holds together a given community can never be reduced simply to the point of symbolic national identification: A shared relationship toward *the other's* enjoyment is always implied. Structured by means of fantasies, this thing—enjoyment—is what is at stake when we speak of the menace to our "way of life" presented by the other. . . . National and racial identities are determined by a series of contradictory properties. They appear to us as "our thing" (perhaps we could say *cosa nostra*), as something accessible only to us, as something "they," the others, cannot grasp; nonetheless, "our thing" is something constantly menaced by "them."[6]

The "nation qua Thing" thus subsumes contradictory imperatives: it is both something that is by definition *not* appropriable by another national community, because it is "our" thing, yet it is constantly menaced. If we try to specify what this national "Thing" is, according to Žižek, we are left with a series of tautologies: we can only specify it by reciting disconnected fragments of "our way of life," the "way we are," the details of the "American way of life," or "Japanese culture": "It's a national thing, you wouldn't understand." (Or, as I prefer, "It's a national-cultural thing, you wouldn't understand.") Yet the "Thing" can't be reduced to those details themselves; there is something more that causes them to cohere into a nexus of identification and belief, into "our" national thing as a fantasy of shared enjoyment (with the specific resonances that the idea of "enjoyment" generates).[7]

It's not entirely coincidental that Žižek turns to Japan as an example of American paranoia about national "theft of enjoyment," the way that national groups resent the excessive forms of others' structures of enjoyment. This projection onto others mirrors an interior, intimate alienation at the core of national identifications. So, for example, he lingers on

> the obsession of the American media with the idea that the Japanese don't know how to enjoy themselves. The reason for Japan's increasing economic superiority over the USA is located in the somewhat mysterious fact that the Japanese don't consume enough.... What American "spontaneous" ideology really reproaches the Japanese for is not simply their inability to take pleasure, but the fact that their very relationship between work and enjoyment is strangely distorted.[8]

This relationship is perceived as a threat to American superiority, one that inevitably reflects American desires: we find enjoyment in fantasizing about the Other's excessive relationship to enjoyment.

But what is left unstated in this proposition is the way that the desire of the Other is retranslated in Japan, and the forms of mirroring that determine the difficult contours of that retranslation. The internal antagonisms of capitalism produce an excess that can then be transmuted into the hatred of others who seem themselves the excessive producers of that excess (too many Japanese products; too much work). Yet a common Japanese view echoes this spontaneous ideology: "We Japanese work really hard; Americans are lazy." The American perception of Japanese excess is ambivalently echoed in Japan as well, along with the uneasy recognition that the specific structure of Japanese enjoyment might be at stake as well within the relentless requirements of advanced capitalism. That is to say, because of the specific history of Japan and the United States (as the exemplar of the western "Thing"), the Japanese organization of its national particularity bears a phantasmatic relationship to the American (western) fantasy of the Japanese thing (which itself is a refraction of an internal alienation): the Japanese national-cultural thing became recognizable as *Japanese* because of its imbrication with the west.[9]

Recent works on colonialism and nationalism have tried to account for the working of mimetic desire in colonial discourses; in Homi Bhabha's terms, the colonized responds to colonial domination via a complex "mimicry," a mimicry that can never succeed in effacing the difference between the (western) original and the colonized copy. Colonized "mimics" remain as "not white/not quite" in Bhabha's formulation.[10] Is it any wonder that Japanese have been extolled (and denigrated) as adept "mimics," good at copying but lacking "originality"? Or that the South African government had, at one time, given the Japanese an official racial designation as "honorary whites" (in deference to Japan's status as South Africa's primary trading partner)? Yet the mimetic attempts of the colonized also contain an element of menace (in Bhabha's formulation) because of their dangerous doubling and uneasy proximity to the colonizer's position: there is always an excess, a slippage that reveals mimicry as something more (and less) than the object of mimesis. It is no doubt Japan's presumption to have entered geopolitics as an entirely exotic and late modernizing nation-state instead of as an outright colony that has made *its* "mimicry" all the more threatening. As the one predominantly nonwhite nation that challenged the dominance of western colonizers on a global scale during the Second World War—and did so by becoming colonialist, imperialist, and fascist—Japan's role as quasi-colonized "mimic" has finally exceeded itself: now it is American companies, educators, and social scientists who speak of the necessity of "learning from Japan" in the hopes of copying its economic miracles, its pedagogical successes, its societal orderliness. If modernity and its apparatuses, particularly the American versions, are installed in the interior of the Japanese national imaginary, "Japan" conversely indicates a loss at the heart of American self-perceptions: "The Cold War is over, and Japan won." Japan's very devastation in World War II has allowed it to emerge belatedly victorious in the current wars of trade. Japan's martial loss thus prefigured a victory, a deferred victory that now marks the defeat of the United States. In the American national rhetoric of deficit, Japan marks out a nation-space of excess operating as the nameable supplement of the United States, the defeated term that comes both to add to and invasively supplant the victorious one (even American cars are made with Japanese parts).

The excesses of mimicry remarked both by westerners and Japanese indicate the instabilities that founded the difference between quasi-colonial original and quasi-colonized copy in the first instance. And they point as well to the impossibility, in a radical sense, of instituting a sheer difference between Japan and the west, although the attempts to do so are far from abating. Euroamerican attempts to place Japan as unassimilably alter and Japanese attempts to live up to, to assert, that difference cannot be easily dissociated, despite the numerous efforts to maintain the distinction between the

two unities. The efforts to sustain difference have never been without re-
mainders, losses, violences not only within the "island nation" but outside;
violences enacted not only against Japanese but by them. But those remain-
ders have tended to be recuperated within the unitary national-cultural totality of Japan.

That supplemental relationship and the phantasms of history — the temporal deferral that retrospectively inscribes Japan as the winner in the global
market wars, for example — point to a way to begin to loosen the entangle-
ments of Japanese modernity. Japan's national successes have produced,
along with Corollas and Walkmans, a certain crucial nexus of unease about
cultural transmission and stability. This anxiety indicates the lack of "success" at the very interior of national self-fashioning. And the thematic of loss
at the interior of this cultural anxiety, and questions of its representation,
forms a recurring motif of critical import in thinking about the instabilities
of what is often depicted as uncannily stable. That is, there is widespread
recognition in Japan today that the destabilizations of capitalist modernity
have decreed the loss of much of the past, a past that is sometimes troped
as "traditional." At the same time, there is a disavowal of this recognition
through the massive investment in representative survivals refigured as elegiac resources. Through tourism, folklore studies, education, and mass media, and through everyday moments of national-cultural interpellation and
identification, Japanese of all generations seek a recognition of continuity
that is coterminous with its negation. As culture industries seek to reassure
Japanese that everything is in place and that all is not lost, the concomitant
understanding arises (sometimes obscurely) that such reassurance would
not be necessary if loss, indeed, were not at stake.

The linkage of recognition and disavowal describes what in psychoanalytic criticism is known as the logic of the fetish, indicating the denial of a
feared absence that is then replaced with a substitute presence.[11] But this
very replacement inevitably announces the absence it means to cover up,
thus provoking anxiety. This concurrent recognition and disavowal can only
be sustained by a certain splitting of the subject, a certain topological segregation of the subject who knows (something is missing) and the subject
who, fixed on the replacement of absence, doesn't. Anxiety appears as the
symptomatic effect of a self-sameness that can only be different from itself.[12]

The movements of national-cultural self-fashioning often retrace the lines
of fetishistic investment in the most general sense (we are reminded again
of Bhabha's ambivalence). In Japan, refined high culture is one such site
where, for example, Noh theater, tea ceremony, and Kyoto politesse attain
the realm of desirable banality for the domestic bourgeoisie and approved

export status as icons of Japaneseness. Another locus we might call the generalized, customary everyday, where chopsticks, kimono, and sushi materially demarcate the Japanese thing (without, of course, subsuming it). Yet another asserts the sublimity of the Japanese language and the inscrutabilities of Japanese selves diametrically opposed to western logocentric individuals.[13] Allied with this are the varieties of state-approved anthropological arguments for Japan as a "household" (ie) society.[14] Arguably the most charged topos of all is the position of the emperor, who by the postwar denial of divine status and his placement as a powerless, "symbolic" monarch who nevertheless still remains in place as a deified icon for nationalists, literally embodies the logic of fetishistic denial, with all its troubling political effects.[15] These registers of investment are of course not mutually exclusive; rather, they are interimplicated in the formation of a national-cultural imaginary and the contours of enjoyment specific to the Japanese thing.[16]

Yet the simultaneously realized and denied loss of the Japanese thing is delineated perhaps most sharply where ethnos, voice, and nation-culture problematically coincide: the register of what is sometimes called the folkloric, sometimes temporalized as the essentially "traditional," concurrently located as the "marginal."[17] Located in the ever-receding "countryside" (inaka) or on the edges of advanced capitalist prosperity, that is, distanced in some fashion from metropolitan sites of representation, these practices compel as recalcitrant spectacles of the elegiac, as allegories of cultural loss that Japanese often link, viscerally, with personal loss.

Not strictly confined to the enclosure of the pastoral (although located most paradigmatically there), they index the investment in the survival of a continuous communality, guaranteed by the thought of tradition (dentō) as unbroken transmission. This transmission is often assured by the redemptive mode of the dialogic presumed in its most unmediated form. "All returns to the past are a return to the voice": Michel de Certeau's assertion points to the intimate linkages of voiced speech and nostos, or the desire for origins.

I want to look at one site in contemporary Japan that allegorizes, in strange ways, the complexities of recouping the Japanese thing and the possibilities of mourning its dispersal. It is a site that is explicitly devoted to the work of memorializing the dead; it is also formed by illicit practices of mourning that then trouble the dominant discourses of memorialization there. Memorialization and mourning operate as a crossed pair of tropes for coming to terms with the anxieties at the foundation of the modern Japanese thing.

The place is called Osorezan (its Japanese name could be translated as Mt. Dread or Mt. Terror), a mountain dominating the northernmost peninsular tip of Honshu, Japan's main island. Mt. Osore, as a singular, foreboding presence in what is sometimes romantically described as an "unexplored region" (*hikyō*), rises out of the center of the peninsula; covered with thick cypress forests, it precipitously reverses its slope at the summit. Almost coincident with this downslope comes something equally surprising: the unmistakable, overpowering odor of sulfur. The incongruous smell of sulfur announces what lies ahead, at the bottom of the downslope. For the summit of Mt. Osore is a crater, and the mountain itself is a dormant volcano.

The crater is an expanse of volcanic rocks, steam vents, bubbling sulfuric pools, and hot springs extending to the shoreline of a deep blue, deadly still lake (the sulfur kills fish). Deployed on this landscape, which resembles the aftermath of an atomic explosion whose residual radioactivity precludes the reemergence of life, is a Buddhist temple complex; some of its buildings have stainless-steel roofs to stave off the corrosive effects of sulfur. The complex resembles a frontier outpost, guarding what is said to be one of the last remaining approaches to the other world in Japan, as the buildings make no particular attempt to master or surpass their surroundings. The other "three great holy places" (*sandai reijō*) in Japan with which Mt. Osore is ranked (Mt. Kōya and Mt. Hiei) are topped with monumental, ancient, and enormous complexes: gates, pagodas, subtemples, massive statuary, graveyards. Mt. Osore's bleakness undercuts the basis for a focus on architectural grandeur. More than most such famous sites managed by Buddhist institutions, the terrain itself overshadows its managing institution. In northeastern Japan, Mt. Osore has long been the final destination of spirits of the dead, the ultimate home where the dead continue to live a shadowy, parallel "life." More than just the home of the dead, Mt. Osore is a place of practices for consoling, pacifying, memorializing, and communicating with the dead.

Historically, Mt. Osore was a specific, local topos of death. To many folklorists of Japan, this specific locating of death in nearby mountains forms an original stratum of Japanese folk beliefs. Mountains were often actual burial sites, abodes of dead spirits and of gods at one and the same time. The projection of death and its aftermath onto mountains, called *sanchūta-kaikan* (the "belief in the 'other world' in the mountains"), fused with post-medieval Buddhist conceptions that projected symbolic itineraries of pure lands (*jōdo*) and polluted hells (*jigoku*) onto mountains to create a doubled structure of mountains as both literal and allegorical domains of death. Mt. Osore's strange topology and its remoteness augmented its image as an uncanny "other world" (*takai*) where the dead and the living exist simultaneously.[18]

The feast day of the deity Jizō (a deity who rescues the dead and is the special protector of children, especially dead children) falls on the twenty-fourth of each month and is the occasion for a gathering of a wide range of religious associations, many of them devoted to the figure of Jizō. The biggest of these feast days falls on the twenty-fourth of the sixth month of the old calendrical system, the so-called Jizō-bon. All of Jizō's feast days are connected with death, but Jizō-bon is the one most explicitly regarded as a day of return for the dead.[19]

Jizō-bon awakens the temple, which is usually as fitfully dormant as the steaming crater on which it is built, into preparations for the biggest event of the year on the mountain, the Osorezan *taisai* (big festival). Hundreds of Buddhist priests, workers, local faithful, curious tourists, and hopeful bereaved from throughout Japan ascend the mountain during the five-day festival (now fixed at July 20–24). This "festival" is the greatest attraction of Mt. Osore, its main source of fame. The temple on the mountain (Entsūji) then holds an official range of rites and rituals aimed at memorializing the dead (*kuyō*). These memorial rites have as their aim the pacification of the dead by remembering them with rites and offerings.[20] By correctly remembering the dead through these practices, the living hope to pacify and console them as well as keep them from troubling this world. At the same time, practices and beliefs that are not subsumed by official Buddhist methods for controlling the dead appear. What is unusual, however, at Mt. Osore is the simultaneous occurrence of mourning. Even though Buddhist temples form themselves around the managing of death, and temple fairs can also be occasions for memorializing the dead, it is not usual for people actively and openly to mourn the dead in close, confused juxtaposition to the space of festivity. Mt. Osore was and is a divided territory where this juxtaposition could occur. In addition to official memorialization and its various practices—practices that aim to settle the dead person and to distance, in effect, the living from a too-close association with the dead—other practices supplement or even overturn, with a profusion of voices and ghostly epiphanies, official memorialization.

In conventional Buddhist memorialization in Japan, a distinction is made between the "newly" dead and the "settled" dead. The newly dead are those that have died, usually, within the last forty-nine days and thus are not yet settled. There are many other kinds of unsettled dead, but in all cases, memorial services are performed to settle them. That is the primary goal of many Buddhist rites (*segakie*, for example) and the domestic household rites connected with so-called "ancestor worship."[21]

Memorialization is really the remembering of the dead in order to settle them. When correct remembrance (i.e., memorialization) has occurred, the dead can become settled "ancestors" (*senzo*) who will benefit and protect the living. The opposition between *shirei* (newly dead) and *sorei* (ancestral dead) reveals the clarity of the distinction between the two. By definition, the settled dead are those who are memorialized and remembered; in most cases they are the ancestors. The unsettled are those that are not remembered, or who have not been remembered adequately, and are thus on the loose, dangerous. If the living do not correctly remember the dead, if they forget or neglect to remember the dead, then the dead can become dangerous: they can "haunt" the living as ghosts. Ghosts indicate that the structure of remembering through memorialization is not completely efficacious, that the line between life and death that remembering the dead institutes is not secure.

Memorial practices allow the living to work through grief, to idealize the dead, and to substitute images of the person as really "dead" for the memory of the person as he or she was in life. Through memorialization, memory becomes once-removed from all the images that surround the thought of the person and evoke grief.[22] By "remembering" the dead, by carrying out practices that ensure that they will settle into Buddhahood and become beneficial ancestors, the living are able to relinquish grief. Memorializing the dead is intimately connected with the fear of misfortune (provoked by the unsettled dead) and the hope for blessings (afforded by the settled dead). Both depend on the failure or efficacy of the living's remembrance of the dead.

Mt. Osore is constructed as one vast memorialization apparatus, through which the dead are properly remembered. Buying stupas, giving offerings, performing rituals to console *muenbotoke,* the "unconnected dead"—all these fall within an official round of memorial practices. They are practices that fall within the purview of the temple's ritual specialists, or that culminate in marked, designated, allegorical inscriptions of space through which worshippers walk and follow along performing acts of *kuyō* (Buddhist memorialization).

Access to *mourning,* however—to a bodily recalling of the dead instead of a bracketed "remembering"—is set aside, left for the intercessions of blind female spirit mediums called *itako.* Encounters with the mediums, attempts to speak with the dead, to hear their voices, become the real occasions for mourning at Mt. Osore. But within this doubled structure of reassuring memorialization on the one hand, and the cathartic recalling of the dead on the other, a third term intervenes: that of fear of the dead, specifically the fear of meeting with the unsettled dead. The circulation of ghost stories and tales of uncanny occurrences at the mountain attest to the prevalence of this fear.

The mention of Osorezan to contemporary Japanese elicits predictable adjectives: *bukimi* (weird), *fushigi* (mysterious), *kimochiwarui* (creepy or disgusting). Something that is weird often inspires a sharing of stories, of rumors. Stories told about Mt. Osore are correspondingly unearthly, as befits a place which links conceptions of otherworldliness with fear (again, *osore*). When Japanese refer to Mt. Osore as *bukimi,* they are referring to the general of aura of death there, but they are often specifically thinking of an untoward meeting with the dead. There are both desirable and undesirable meetings with the dead; an undesirable encounter is always with a ghost, someone who should be absent but is uncannily present.

Although all memorial practices at Mt. Osore are aimed at ensuring the passage from unsettled, dangerous, new death to settled, stable, and beneficial old death, the stories of ghosts (*yūrei*) at the mountain indicate that these practices are not always effective. There are gaps in the edifice of memorialization, and through these gaps the dangerous, unsettled dead appear. A ghost is a sign that memorialization is not fully adequate. Ghosts appear where they should not, at places where no one should be, at times when no one is expected to be present: a transgression of expectation. This undercutting of expectation about reality shows itself as a split between a phenomenon and its origin. In the descriptions of ghostly apparitions and auditions at Mt. Osore, and of tales told about ghosts, there is a often a gap, a discrepancy, between the aural and the visual. One hears a sound, looks to see, and no one is there. It is not just that one "hears voices," but that one hears voices emanating from places where no one is supposed to be, and where on inspection no one is: voices without a visual source. If an apparation appears, it is wordless, only peripherally apprehended. The voices of ghosts displace the visual origins of sound. This rift between an auditory phenomenon and its visual source appears as well in the spirit recallings of the blind mediums.

Buddhist narratives of redemption and the procedures and rationales for rites for the dead lie in the public domain. Enscripted and formalized, they set the outer limits of Osorezan's Buddhist control of the dead. The repeated telling, the enunciation, of reports of ghosts forms a circulating reserve of private, minute experiences not subject to formal verification. Ghost stories circulate, rarely promising or describing an actual communication with a specific dead one. Hearing a sound without a source or seeing a specter (again, rarely are the two conjoined) is an unsettling reminder of a failure in memorialization. Encounters with the dead are limited to those few who claim them, yet narratives of these encounters vicariously extend the possibility.

If ghost stories augment Mt. Osore's national image as a site of lingering mysteries by telling of the properly absent (the dead) becoming problematically present, then the blind mediums go a step further with their promise of an actual communication with the dead. *Kuchiyose* (the calling down of spirits by mediums) not only promises a dialogue with the specific dead, it also becomes a source of knowledge about the future. Encounters with *itako* are both occasions for hearing and talking to the dead (which also involves mourning the dead) and for receiving predictions and recommendations from them. There is a double trajectory of wishfulness: toward the past, when the dead one was alive, and toward the future, which the dead have the power to foresee and to "protect" (*mamoru*).

A notice at the entrance to the temple proclaimed, "Osorezan is not the itako mountain and this is not an itako festival. We only lend the itako space at the time of the festival." The temple disclaims any official sponsorship of the itako and has asserted various controls over the gathering. The itako formerly set up their places throughout the temple grounds; through negotiations with representatives of the itako, the temple has, since the early 1960s, confined them to the area directly around the main Jizō hall.[23] There were about fifteen itako in 1984. Unlike the arrangement shown in photographs of earlier festivals, in which the itako had spread mats on the ground and were conducting their callings of the dead in the open air (surrounded by crowds and sometimes protected from the sun by assistants holding parasols), the itako now individually occupied identical, army-fatigue-green, nylon tents arrayed in two facing rows. The itako (and the others) worked continuously throughout the five days of the festival, late into the night. At one end of the tents was an herbalist, keeping up the nonstop persuasive patter for which peddlers and salesmen in Japan are noted. At the other end was an equally garrulous young man dressed in Buddhist black, imitating the demeanor of a priest and selling magical rings. Both were reminiscent of carnival barkers with the insistence of their voices and the extravagance of their claims. The rows of identical tents, with lines of people waiting to have an audience with the blind mediums hidden inside, indeed resembled a carnival sideshow (known to Japanese as *misemono goya*, "spectacle tents"). By linking the mediums in their tents with the "quacks and peddlers" outside, the organizers were stating that they belonged in the same place: that the medium's disclosures of the dead and predictions of the future were of the same order as the amulet seller's or herbalist's assurances and vice versa. A conjoining of voice and commerce was kept out of the precincts of "proper" death and its inscribed places and prescribed routings of piety.[24]

The customers take their turns one by one in the tents. Many bring offerings to the itako, such as fresh fruit, candy, packaged crackers; they put them down in front of the itako as they kneel, facing her. There is a prescribed set of questions that the itako asks the customer. Without fail, the itako must know the day of death (the *meinichi*), the sex, and the age of the person to be contacted. She also often asks the relationship of the dead to the living questioner and how the person died; she does not ask the name of the dead person. This knowledge allows her to search for and locate the dead, and it also allows her to describe the present condition of the dead one accordingly. She then begins an incantation in which she calls up the dead person from the other world.

At the beginning of the incantation, the itako states that she is calling a *hotoke* who died on such and such a date and invokes myriads of *kami* to descend and watch over the kuchiyose. At an unspecified point in the incantation, the person of the speaker shifts to the hotoke, who then addresses the patron directly. This moment also marks a shift from an almost incomprehensible incantatory style to one that is more conversational.

The dead often start by thanking their living interlocuters for calling them back to this world. They sometimes say that they "never dreamed" they would be able to meet the living again. They state that they are now satisfied (*manzoku*) and can now hold their heads up and face the other dead ones. The hotoke then recount the conditions of the after-death state. The portrayal and revelation of the dead's experiences are consistent with their status and age at death. Although itako conventionally make a number of distinctions between new and old spirits, at Osorezan the purity of the distinctions is not always maintained.[25] The overriding tonality of this recounting of the after-death state is one of sorrow and regret, of unsatisfied desire.

There is then a shift toward recollections of life. These recollections focus on the experiences the dead person shared with the living interlocutor. After recollections of life comes a recital of wishes and unfulfilled desires, and ways to fulfill them. The customer can interrupt to ask questions: "Is there anything you want?" "Do you ever get to see Papa?" "Is your cancer completely cured?" Sometimes the dead answer directly; sometimes the itako comes in to answer or to clarify the question.

The dead one then gives a few general cautions and admonitions for the future (some of them on the order of "Be careful not to catch cold" or "Work hard"), as well as specific predictions: Don't go out of the house on

August 25; watch out for fires on December 11. They say farewell, and then there is a return to the voice of the itako speaking in her own persona as she chants the *hotokeokuri,* the ritual send-off of the dead back to the other world. At Osorezan this whole process may take only five minutes, ten or fifteen at most. The fee for one kuchiyose, for each "mouth" (*kuchi*) opened, was ¥1500 in 1984, which the customer gives the itako at the end.[26]

The kuchiyose, then, follows an order, and this order is repeated at each calling. Unlike sightings of ghosts, there is no suprise here. It is a repeatable, conventionalized, predictable, yet *specific* encounter with the dead. The itako's voice does not change; there is no perceptible shift in her voice when the dead speak through her. For example, if she is calling down a man, there is no change in the pitch of her voice, although the use of status language changes accordingly. There is no explicit attempt to "sound" like the dead person. Why is it then that so many of the questioners, both those from the area and those from far away, are overwhelmed with grief?

To folklorists and anthropologists of Japanese religion, kuchiyose at Osorezan calls into question the authenticity of trance. Most agree that itako exhibit no trace of "real" trance: they are merely performing a series of patterned roles for their customers:

> Clearly the itako were simply reciting the most suitable among a repertory of fixed chants learnt by heart in the course of their training as purporting to come from the dead. Their performance belonged to the category of *geinō* or folk drama, and at the same time functioned as a kuyō or requiem comfort for the dead.
>
> On their audiences, however, the effect of these hackneyed effusions was pathetically touching. Round each itako was to be seen a little group of sobbing women, old and young, their faces screwed up with emotion. . . . Here and there I noticed women sitting in rapt attention, as though at the theatre, and eagerly begging with proffered coins for "One more!" as soon as the itako's chanting stopped.[27]

Carmen Blacker, the author of this description, puts these "hackneyed effusions" within a framework of theatrical or performative conventions: "That such utterances should still strike the sobbing audiences as convincing communications from the dead argues a suspension of disbelief of the same order as that which sees the invisible world behind the sacred drama, the ritual mask, or the recital of a myth."[28] What Blacker is questioning here is how the stereotypical could be believable, and therefore moving. In her analysis, only if one really believes that he or she is hearing the voice of the dead could one legitimately cry; otherwise, tears could only be the result of theatrical illusion. Because the itako's words are repetitive, they cannot be believable; that is, they cannot be mistaken for authentic, spontaneous communications from the dead obtained in trance.

Blacker argues that "what passes for a trance among them is seen on shrewd inspection to be mere imitation."[29] She contrasts the authenticity of trance with the imitative (i.e., false) performance of trance that is kuchiyose. Thus Blacker supports the description of Japanese folklorists that the itako are *gisei shaman* (fake shamans). Later she implies that the itako do not even imitate trance: "They exhibited none of the usual symptoms of stertorous breathing and convulsively shaking hands."[30] Hori Ichirō adduces evidence why the itako are not shamans: they do not go into trance or "ecstasy" (*eku-sutashī*) and their kuchiyose is monotonous, songlike, performatized.[31] Blacker also states that kuchiyose is only a dilapidated trace of what used to be an authentically transgressive rupture. Kuchiyose claims to be transgressive, to broach a rupture between life and death, but it is not even that: it is a spurious transgressive.

The convulsive hands and gasps of the shaman indicate "trance," which further indicates an authentic contact with the dead. Descriptions of trance in Japanese anthropology are not only concerned to maintain the integrity and authenticity of something called "shamanic trance"; they are also concerned to say that this trance state has something to do with authentic communications from the dead. It is as if these descriptions postulate a real sphere of extraordinary knowledge that is signaled by the convulsed body. They imply that the message emanating from a gasping mouth has more truth value than the itako's performatized recitation. The convulsed hands of the shaman become the last guarantee of authenticity, a guarantee that the itako do not give.[32]

The convulsive sobbing of the listeners, however, remains as the anomalous guarantee of kuchiyose's effects. Despite its depictions as merely a spurious reenactment of genuine trance, kuchiyose produces effects (for example, sobbing) that only a real communication with the dead should produce. It produces effects it has no right to produce, but we must start with those effects (specifically, expressions of grief) as indications beyond any suspension of belief: the genuine effects of a spurious spectacle.

Much of kuchiyose consists of what might be called ritual language: formalized, archaic, formulaic. These utterances are repeated at each kuchiyose. They set up the encounter with the dead; they predict it. The patterns (*kata*) of the performance are prescribed, yet this prescriptive patterning does not indicate that the itako is therefore unbelievable. On the contrary, it indicates the itako's words as magical. In such language, the conventionality of language comes to the fore; the words are meaningless; they refer not in the least to the desired effect of the ritual or performance. Their unintelligibility and formalization mark them as exotic, as coming from without, and thus as socially determined. Only the force of society can ensure that the conventional is believable, and signs of trance are evidently not necessary to induce authentic effects: sobs, protestations of belief, action based on the dead's predictions.

In its overall movement, the repeated, formalized unintelligibility of the itako's chants thus effects a disassociation between signifier and signified: language is unbound as the chanting foregrounds itself as pure utterance, divorced from meaning. The form itself is emphasized; content is marginalized. Any signifier can refer to innumerable signifieds, and since there is no intrinsic connection between them, the force of language makes itself felt compellingly.[33] It is in this milieu of indeterminate utterance that itako compels the dead to descend. The function of this moment of kuchiyose is not to present the dead as "alive" again. On the contrary, its purpose is to establish the dead as "dead": as somewhere else, as inhabiting another scene. It thus establishes the dead person as recallable, retrievable.

The kuchiyose is not entirely unintelligible, however. There is instead a shift between incomprehensible, formulaic moments and understandable ones; between monologic chanting and dialogic exchange; between the medium as speaker and the dead as the ostensible communicator. This shifting between levels divides the authority of the speaker; there is no one source of speech, yet through this shifting, the itako's voice qua voice does not change. The voice comes from the medium's body, but the words come from somewhere else outside the body, from the dead. The unity of the voice and the presence of the person behind it are thrown into question, as the speaking subject and the subject of speech move away from one another.

In the chanted moments, the unity of signification is rent; the signifiers acquire an authority of their own. In the moments of dialogue, this rent is re-stitched—there is a message here—but the source of the message is claimed to be elsewhere: a second rift, one between the medium and the message opens up. It is in this part of the kuchiyose that patterns of speech appear that correspond to different kinds of spirits: grandparents, children, fathers, wives. In both moments something outside the medium compels her speech: in the first case, language itself seems autonomously authoritative; in the second, the dead person, not the medium, becomes the source of speech.

There is thus a dual function in kuchiyose. One is to establish the dead as dead, as "not here"; they are somewhere else, and thus can be recalled. An ensemble of repetitions, patterns, and unintelligibilities embodying the force of language thus sets up the dead as, indeed, dead. Yet the other function of kuchiyose is to recall, literally, the dead and through the voice to embody them, to establish them as "here." This moment occurs when the itako starts speaking in the first person of the dead, describing the after death state and its insufficiencies.

What was striking to me in listening with the crowds to the kuchiyose (which, I should say, is clearly accepted; crowds of listeners indicate an effective itako), was the realization that the point of transference of voices, when the dead speak through the voice of the itako, is also the point when most of the questioners started crying, when mourning in the sense of the expression of grief began in cathartic earnest. To wonder why this particular moment empowers grief is to wonder further about the fraught relationships between memory and language energized at Osorezan.

The dead person is still idealized—thus the role of the kata—and the dead speak as they should speak, according to their statuses.[34] Through this patterned description, they retain their place as authoritatively dead, yet they speak directly to the questioner in the medium's voice: the subject of speech is different from the speaking subject. The idea is sometimes expressed that the silent dead borrow (*kariru*) the medium's voice, her body. But there is an immediate and stunning difference between the dead one's remembered voice and the voice of the medium, unlike other forms of possession where the strangely altered voice of the medium mimetically doubles the spirit's voice. The itako at Mt. Osore do not attempt to imitate the timbre or pitch of the spirit's voice; there is no confusion between her voice and the remembered voice of the dead one. This would seem to be a moment of disillusionment, as it were, with the patent realization that the medium's words are *not* those of the beloved dead.

Yet this is the moment of grief, and I believe it is provoked not so much by a belief that the dead one is speaking, but precisely because of the difference that is instituted through the itako's voice. Here is the moment of realizing the irretrievability of what is lost, signaled by the irresolvable gap between the voice of the medium and the dead person's remembered voice. Expressions of grief occur as much from the realization of this gap, of the impossibility of a communication, as from any easy insistence that the dead have actually spoken. If mourning, as Freud said, has to do with the realization of loss, a process that must occur (at least, it seems, for many people in Euroamerica and Japan) before the comforts of memorialization, then kuchiyose is a scene for encountering this bodily loss, this "hole in the real" that death institutes. A split between the body and voice of the medium, and that which is disembodied and voiceless, thus effects a bodily recalling that exceeds the idealized status of the dead enframed by official memorialization.

Am I thus saying that the auditors don't believe that the dead are really speaking, and that this realization of impossibility inspires their grief? Not simply so. What occurs constitutes a phenomenon that cannot become an object of positive knowledge, as in the case of the "uncanny." The medium's voice emerges as a "thing," a sublime (non)-object of desire. The contours of fetishistic remembrance come into view here through Octave Mannoni's understanding: "I know but nevertheless..."[35] "I know that the dead do not speak, but nevertheless [I believe that they do]": a split between knowledge and belief that is sutured by the embodiments of the itako. And the resolutions are correspondingly precarious, suspended. Many of the people I spoke to at the site and elsewhere did not express a strong belief that they had spoken to the dead. They instead talked about the comfort they had received through the attempt at communication, of which I shall say more later.

The movements between registers of language and the senses redouble those at other sites on the mountain. Like a ghost story, kuchiyose uncovers a difference between seeing and hearing. One does not see the dead in kuchiyose, however; one only hears them. Hearing itself is already divided by the difference between the medium's voice and the remembered voice of the dead person. Yet the itako provides a visible source for the language of the dead, a source that is missing in reports of ghosts at Osorezan. The itako embodies the split that ghosts imply: she provides the visible source of ghostly discourse. She embodies that difference between the dead and the living, the invisible and the visible. Her blind body becomes the sign of difference, of loss itself.

All the mediums at the mountain claimed to be blind or partially blind. Those who were fully blind had more customers at Osorezan than those who were not, suggesting that blindness was perceived as somehow allowing a more compelling access to the dead. In encounters with ghosts, the visual and the aural do not coincide. Yet with the itako, this discrepancy is not a problem because they cannot see. For them, voices never have a visual origin; voices always emanate from an invisibility. It is not simply that the itako "are blind and therefore they can see the invisible world," a logic of reversal that links blindness and insight. It is precisely because they are blind and they *cannot* see the invisible world that they can hear the voices of the dead and become the visible form of the properly invisible.

Blindness is an image of primal loss, a bodily mark of something lacking. There is something missing in the itako, and what is missing is the imperative of sight to demand a visual origin for sound. This lack is supplemented by the itako's place as the visual and vocal point of origin for the speech of the dead; their gendered status as women undoubtedly augments these images of privation and loss.[36]

The elderly women from the area see kuchiyose as kuyō, as an occasion for grief, and as a source of knowledge about the future. It is repeatable, scheduled. Kuchiyose ends by redrawing the border between death and life that it worked to erase by recalling the dead; as a result it operates as a kuyō, the "best kuyō," as the devotees from Shimokita would say. The desperate metropolitan visitors who come to Osorezan expressly to contact the dead regard kuchiyose as an extreme measure, as a means to work through grief. In the first instance, the kuchiyose does contain the force of social convention, as kuchiyose has been a scheduled, almost necessary part of the household's relationship to the ancestors: the ancestors must be called at regular intervals, and these callings often require interhousehold cooperation. In the second, the urban visitors have no particular relationship to the itako and no long-standing group investment in kuchiyose.

Many people who have traveled long distances to Mt. Osore to have an audience with an itako have come there out of a sense of desperation; they approach the itako as a last resort. They cannot forget the dead person and are still driven by thoughts of the dead person as "alive." They are still in a state of incomplete mourning, and presumably all the various resources of kuyō have not allowed them to relinquish their grief. They come to remember (in the sense of memorialization: to remind oneself that the dead person is "dead") the dead so that they can then forget the memories that haunt them.

I met two sisters, one from Tokyo, the other from northeastern Japan. The older one from northeastern Japan told me this:

> My husband died last year. I wanted to come to Osorezan but I didn't want to come alone—that's why my sister came. My husband got sick two years ago. He was really sick for one and one-half years. Then he died. It's still so new, it's like he's still alive. [Her younger sister later said that he was *yōki* (spirited), that he liked to drink and sing *enka* (Japanese popular songs)]. Somehow or other I understood some of what the itako was saying. He said he had been "returned" [*modosareta*] to some place, but when I asked where he was, he said he didn't know. He said he was thirsty—for three months before he died he was always hungry and thirsty, but he could hardly drink anything. So it was strange that he said he was thirsty. The itako didn't have any particular recommendations . . . [but later her younger sister said that she was supposed to give him water every day].

I asked if the purpose of having kuchiyose done was to console the dead spirit. She said, more than that, it was to be able to hear the person once again. She said she did not know if she believed, but somehow or other *she* was consoled. She felt she had to try to talk to him again; there was much left unsaid, and that is why she wanted to go and try to talk to him.

This woman's recounting of her reasons for coming to Osorezan and of her experience with kuchiyose were similar to others I heard. The weight of words "left unsaid" compelled her to try to complete a communication that was incomplete. She tried to fill this lack by calling the absent other into presence again. To try to "hear the voice of the dead" just once more overrides the motive of consolation and propitiation through remembrance (kuyō) that is also said to be a result of kuchiyose. And it is the effort of communication that seems to offer self-consolation, even though she is not sure whether the dead one has spoken or not: "I know but nevertheless . . ."

The woman from Tokyo stated that "somehow or other" (*nantonaku*) she understood much of what the itako said. Yet on the important matter of suggestions from the itako on how ritually to take care of the dead, she and her sister had reached different understandings. This question of intelligibility is central to unraveling the efficacy of kuchiyose, because the itako speak in a dialect barely, if at all, understandable to the vast majority of Japanese who retain their services at the festival. The itako use, as well, a lexicon of "taboo words" (*imikotoba*) whose origins the itako themselves do not comprehend.[37] Only the most experienced people from the locale can understand the itako, and even they run up against a modicum of unintelligibility; even they, as well, sometimes misunderstand the itako from other parts of northeastern Japan attending the festival.

People standing around the tents, spectators from Tokyo, remarked that they could not understand a word. Others asked me how I could possibly understand anything, when "even we Japanese can't understand."[38] Some people carried tape recorders into the tents so that they could play back the itako's words later; sometimes the itako's attendants or one of the elderly local women who stayed in the tents through hours of others' kuchiyose would translate into standard Japanese. The unintelligibility of the dialect (usually Tsugaru, not Shimokita dialect) and the taboo words was further heightened by the style of the recitation, sometimes whispered, often almost inaudible. The persistent calls of the sellers and the subdued talk of the crowds huddled outside augmented the difficulty of understanding for the customers in the tents. Often they would have to get as close to the mediums as possible in order to hear, and would ask the itako to repeat what she had said any number of times. There was a straining to hear, to understand what was often unintelligible.

For speakers of standard Japanese, then, kuchiyose is twice unintelligible. Not only is its "ritual" language incomprehensible, but the messages from the dead are as well. This incomprehensibility then requires a translator, a local person who will put the medium's words into standard Japanese. This person is a "secondary medium," yet another voice in a transmission conveying the words of the dead.

The kuchiyose and the words of the dead are exotic, outside the body of standard Japanese and standard understandings. Because of that they convey an even greater force to those who do not understand them: they relay the interior difference at the core of the national thing at the same time that they speak of an intimate loss. Mediums and their callings of dead spirits are supposed to incorporate what is most authentic about Mt. Osore. Yet even as these voiced recollections of loss are grasped as quintessentially Japanese, they appear, as they must, in the guise of something ineluctably Other.

In its common Japanese translation, "tradition" (*dentō*) implies an authoritative, conventional, oral transmission. In the Japanese case, this transmission has a history of being legitimated ultimately by the ancestral dead. It is striking that this definition of "tradition," then, could describe kuchiyose itself: an authoritative oral transmission from the dead. But as we have seen, kuchiyose is also a figure for falsity, for theatricality, for obscurity, for unreliability, for what is scandalous and marginal from a certain contemporary perspective of national-cultural order. It becomes "traditional" *because* of these negativities. And thence the duplicity of "tradition" itself: a transmission that always contains the possibility of betrayal, of an arbitrary selection from the past.[39] Kuchiyose becomes a figure for the essence of Japanese national-cultural identity at the moment it is farthest removed from understanding; as such, it reveals the estranged familiarity of the nation thing itself.

What makes kuchiyose a particularly sharp reminder of an entire spectrum of modern losses are the modalities of voicings and the registers of desire it embodies. The expansion of those possibilities of desire, such that kuchiyose appears to become the site for a doubled form of mourning work, is located within current Japanese encounters with loss. If all returns to the past, personal or national-cultural, are linked to returns to the voice, then the seduction of kuchiyose at Mt. Osore might mean this: the voices of the dead disclose both the promise and the betrayal of mourning the Japanese thing as the disappearing (non)-object of desire.

Notes

1. Naoki Sakai claims that Japanese language and "culture" were born in the eighteenth century, but he recognizes the difference between this eighteenth-century unification and the post-Meiji modern configuration. This difference is intimately en-

twined with the rise of the nation-state, in which "the unity of the Japanese and the 'interior' were equated to the existing language and community without mediation. . . . The Japanese language and its ethnos were brought into being and made to exist in the present and were thereby transformed into unobjectionable certainties as if they were entities observable in experience. Thus the Japanese were resurrected from the dormant past and, as a nation, began to play the role of the subject to and for the modern state. . . . Needless to say, this was the process in which the modern nation-state of Japan was appropriated into the nineteenth-century discourse of global colonialism, cultural essentialism, and racism." See *Voices of the Past: The Status of Language in Eighteenth-Century Japanese Discourse* (Ithaca, NY: Cornell University Press, 1991), 336.

2. The historian Miriam Silverberg has written with great insight about Japanese modernity, modernism, and mass culture, particularly during the interwar years. See her *Changing Song: The Marxist Manifestos of Nakano Shigeharu* (Princeton: Princeton University Press, 1990); "Constructing the Japanese Ethnography of Modernity," *Journal of Asian Studies* 51, no. 1 (February 1992): 30–54; and "Remembering Pearl Harbor, Forgetting Charlie Chaplin, and the Case of the Disappearing Western Woman: A Picture Story," *Positions* 1, no. 1 (spring 1993): 24–76, for a range of arguments about the distinctiveness of Japanese modernity (as opposed to conflations of the "modern" with the "western," say). Late twentieth-century Japan poses other problems for a rethinking of the modern.

3. Slavoj Žižek, "Eastern Europe's Republics of Gilead," *New Left Review* 128 (September/October 1990).

4. See Mikkel Borch-Jacobsen's discussion of the relationship among need, demand, and desire—and the status of the "Thing"—in Lacan's thinking in his *Lacan: The Absolute Master,* trans. Douglas Brick (Stanford: Stanford University Press, 1991), 207.

5. Ibid., 209.

6. Slavoj Žižek, "The 'Theft of Enjoyment,'" *Village Voice,* May 1993.

7. As Žižek argues, it is important not to conflate his notion of "enjoyment" with what we think of as "pleasure." In the Lacanian economy to which he is complexly faithful, enjoyment is, "precisely 'pleasure in unpleasure'; it designates the paradoxical satisfaction procured by a painful encounter with a Thing that perturbs the equilibrium of the 'pleasure principle.' In other words, enjoyment is located 'beyond the pleasure principle.'" See Žižek, "Eastern Europe's Republics of Gilead."

8. Ibid., 56.

9. Having established the special valences of Žižek's "Thing," I will use the lowercase.

10. Homi Bhabha, "Of Mimicry and Man: The Ambivalence of Colonial Discourse," *October* 28 (spring 1984): 125–133.

11. Freud's classic essay on fetishism—although he repeatedly addressed the issue throughout his career—is (not surprisingly) his "Fetishism" (1927), in *The Standard Edition of the Complete Psychological Works of Sigmund Freud,* trans. James Strachey, in collaboration with Anna Freud, assisted by Alix Strachey and Alan Tyson (London: Hogarth Press, 1955). The peculiar workings of the notion of "fetishism"—the correlate display and disavowal of absence through a substitute—is of course put into the register of the economic in Marx's "commodity fetishism." Recent work has pushed

the fetishistic dynamic into new realms of analysis. See, for example, the recent volume *Fetishism as Cultural Discourse*, ed. Emily Apter and William Pietz (Ithaca, NY, and London: Cornell University Press, 1993). See also the *Princeton Architectural Journal* 4, which is devoted to the fetish.

12. As Žižek, following Octave Mannoni states, "We could thus say that the formula of fetishism is 'I know but nevertheless...' ('I know that Mother doesn't have a penis, but nevertheless...[I believe that she has]')." There is thus a movement of identification that exists only in difference, described as a split between knowledge and belief. See Slavoj Žižek, *For They Know Not What They Do: Enjoyment as a Political Factor* (London: Verso, 1991), 245.

13. Those works included within the *Nihonjinron* genre usually assert such diametrical opposition to western individualistic selves. The genre finds its provenance in many of the prewar texts of Japanese philosophy, which probed the distinctiveness of a Japanese national subjectivity in the face of western domination. The difficulties of asserting difference from the west lay, of course, in the dialectical terms predicating those assertions. That is, in a necessity well-known to critics of orientalism and colonialism, the colonized must always assert its difference *in relation to* the west, and as such even its difference is dependent on the other term. This dilemma has often led to an ever-greater hypervaluation of difference.

14. See Murakami Yasusuke, Kumon Shunpei, and Sato Seizaburō, *Bunmei to shite no ie shakai* ["Household Society" as Civilization] (Tokyo: Chūō Kōronsha, 1981).

15. Norma Field uncompromisingly reveals the dangers of the "harmless" symbolic emperor through the stories of contemporary Japanese who have relinquished the comforts of the imperial fetish in her powerful *In The Realm of a Dying Emperor: A Portrait of Japan at Century's End* (New York: Pantheon, 1991).

16. H. D. Harootunian spoke of the "Japanese thing" in analyzing late-twentieth-century ideologies of the "holonic" society and state-sponsored theories of Japanese "culture." The "Japanese thing" operated as a literal translation of the ideologically charged phrase *Nihontekina mono*, which was used repeatedly in the texts that he examined. See his "Visible Discourse/Invisible Ideologies," in *Postmodernism and Japan*, ed. Masao Miyoshi and H. D. Harootunian (Durham, NC: Duke University Press, 1989), 63–92.

17. I use the notion of discourse in ways inspired by Foucault: discourse as a mode of language use that is articulated with forms of power, institutional and otherwise. But I am also indebted to Michel de Certeau's somewhat more open-ended perspective on discourse, in which he is acutely attuned not only to discourses as orders of representation, but also to the problem of alterity: that which is not representable. Discourses are constituted as much by their relationship to the nonrepresentable as by their status as representations. That is why the question of the irrational and the logics of psychoanalysis particularly engage de Certeau as a theorist of the "heterological" dimensions of modern discourses. See in particular his collection of essays *Heterologies: Discourse on the Other*, trans. Brian Massumi (Minneapolis: University of Minnesota Press, 1986).

18. An enormous amount of research in Japanese folklore studies is centered on the significance of mountains. For a brief description of *sanchūtakaikan*, see Sakurai Tokutarō, "Minkan shinkō to sangaku shūkyō," in *Sangaku shūkyō to minkan shinkō no kenkyū*, ed. Sakurai Tokutarō (Tokyo: Meichō shuppan, 1976), 27–32. Sakurai ini-

tially makes a distinction between the other world as a strange or foreign land (*ikyō*) and the other world as the after-death state (*shigo takai*), but then says the two distinctions have much in common, particularly when mountains become the loci of conceptions of the other world. See also Hori Ichirō, *Folk Religion in Japan: Continuity and Change,* ed. Joseph M. Kitagawa and Allan L. Miller (Chicago: University of Chicago Press, 1968), especially chapter 4, "Mountains and Their Importance for the Idea of the Other World," 141–79; and Komatsu Kazuhiko, "Yosute to sanchūtakai," in *Kamigami no seishinshi* (Tokyo: Dentō to Gendaisha, 1978), 177–98. Komatsu's essay was an early (first published in 1972) structuralist analysis of mountains as liminal "other worlds." Historically, mountains have been powerful locations of alterity in Japanese culture. They have represented the unknown, the unconceivable: sites of "terrible multiplicities" (Nakazawa Shin'ichi, personal communication). In both what is "terrible" (terror-inducing or awe-inspiring) and what is "multiple" (excessive, beyond language), mountains function as representations of what might be called a Japanese sublime. There is a whole discourse built up around mountains in Japan which fuses "death" and "mountains" as sublime unknowns, with attendant practices of framing, bounding, limiting, and troping this sublimity.

19. Hori, *Folk Religion,* 207–10.

20. Kuyō is defined by *Kenkyūsha's New Japanese-English Dictionary* as a "memorial service." Kuyō is a complex concept that refers to any Buddhist-influenced ritual performed in remembrance of living beings who have died or of objects that are broken or have outlived their usefulness. Thus there are *senzo kuyō* for the ancestral dead; *segaki kuyō,* for *muenbotoke,* the dead who are "unconnected," who have no known living kin to memorialize them; and *hari kuyō,* performed for old or broken needles. In Japan, kuyō also refers generally to any Buddhist *matsuri,* or festival. Kuyō is used almost interchangeably with another key term in Japanese Buddhism, *ekō,* translated by Buddhologists as "merit transference": the idea that the living can store up merit and transfer it to others, in particular the dead, but defined popularly (and in the same Kenkyūsha dictionary as above) as a "memorial service" for the dead. For a discussion of all aspects of memorialization and veneration of the dead, see Robert J. Smith, *Ancestor Worship in Contemporary Japan* (Stanford: Stanford University Press, 1974).

21. The most comprehensive English-language work on Japanese ancestor worship, memorial practices, and spirit beliefs is Smith, *Ancestor Worship in Contemporary Japan.*

22. Freud explores this process of working through memories in his 1917 essay, "Mourning and Melancholia"; see Sigmund Freud, *General Psychological Theory,* ed. Philip Rieff (New York: Macmillan, 1963), 164–80. Freud states in this essay that the survivor must recall and work through all the memories of the loved person, confirming the reality of loss and withdrawing all attachments to those memories. Only after this lengthy and painful process is completed can the dead person be "remembered" without grief; only then can the dead's memory be set aside. In Japan this process is helped along by the idealization of the dead that occurs through memorialization and accession to ancestral status. In another context, Java, there seems to be an almost complete lack of mourning as Freud describes it: the dead person is almost instantly idealized. James T. Siegel describes the interworkings of language, memory, and sensory experience in interpreting this Javanese absence of mourning

in his "Images and Odors in Javanese Practices Surrounding Death," *Indonesia* 36 (October 1983): 1–14. A strongly contrasting essay that describes the interweaving of grief, memory, and rage in Ilongot culture is Renato Rosaldo's "Grief and a Head-hunter's Rage: On the Cultural Force of Emotions," in *Text, Play, and Story: The Construction and Reconstruction of Self and Society,* ed. Edward M. Bruner (Washington, DC: The American Ethnological Society, 1984), 178–95.

23. Sakurai, Tokutarō *Nihon no shamanizumu,* 2 vols. (Tokyo: Yoshikawa Kōbunkan, 1974), 1:151.

24. This marginalization reflects the itako's historical position as well. Plural etymologies of the word *itako* (a word disliked by Shimokita mediums for its subsidiary connotations of "beggar" or "vagabond") lead not to any certain historical origin, but to a series of possibilities. One etymology derives itako from *eta no ko* (a "child of the *eta*"), one name for the so-called outcast groups in Japan. The word *eta* itself is replete with different readings, but most of them point to an association with death and defilement. Another origin of the word *itako* is traced to the writing of the dead person's posthumous Buddhist name (*kaimyō*) on a slat (*ita*), which the itako would use for Buddhist memorial services (*ekō* or *kuyō*). Thus the origin of the medium's local name is traced to a writing of the dead person's name, a function that we have seen is a priestly one in Buddhist institutional contexts. That this etymology would point to a replacement by the itako (who are blind) of the properly priestly function of inscribing the wooden stupa is all the more striking when we consider that the itako function as mouthpieces of the dead, that their powers are based on an oral recalling of the departed. This orality in itself and its tendency to get out of control is what is untrustworthy about the mediums from the standpoint of authority: the impossible promise of a communication with the dead, enacted indiscriminately for money from hordes of bereaved visitors to the mountain.

25. Sakurai states that at the newly formed itako machi, kuchiyose of *shinbotoke* (the "newly dead," also called *niibotoke* in some regions) cannot be performed. The itako say that the dead person will not speak until one hundred days after death. Even if the dead person appears, he or she will not say anything. Thus, only kuchiyose for the settled dead (*furubotoke*) will work. His partial explanation for this is as follows. In *shinkuchi* (the kuchiyose of the newly dead), the person who has recently died is called and speaks in turn to each of his survivors. It is thus a group calling, and the dead person speaks to the survivors following the status order of the people who offered incense at the funeral. But in calling people who have been dead more than one hundred days (the length of time varies according to region), *one* supplicant requests the calling of one or more dead people and asks questions in relation to only him or herself. There is usually an order to the dead called in this pattern also (although sometimes it is random): sometimes it parallels the nearness of kinship to the supplicant; sometimes the calling starts from the oldest (measured by date of death) spirit. Only individuals request kuchiyose at Mt. Osore; therefore, the itako can legitimately perform furukuchi in the absence of a larger legitimating kinship group. Sakurai, *Nihon no shamanizumu,* 1:132–33.

26. In 1973, the fee was ¥200; in 1974, ¥700; and in 1975, ¥1000. There is an agreed-upon price that all the itako charge at Osorezan during the festival and that also holds in the hotoke kuchiyose in the villages of Shimokita. The old women of the region used kuchiyose primarily for memorializing the dead, and they could

afford to call many dead relatives any number of times at one sitting. Now this function of repeated memorialization is unthinkable because of the expense. Takamatsu Keikichi, *Shimokita hantō nominkan shinkō* (Tokyo: Dentō to Gendaisha, 1983), 85.

27. Carmen Blacker, *The Catalpa Bow* (London: George Allen & Unwin, 1975), 160–61.

28. Ibid., 163.

29. Ibid., 140.

30. Ibid., 160.

31. Hori Ichirō, *Nihon no shamanizumu,* Kōdansha gendai shinsho, vol. 256 (Tokyo: Kodansha, 1971), 185–86. Hori also gives other characteristics of the itako that disqualify them as bona fide shamans.

32. I do not question a typology of outward symptoms that would indicate or contraindicate a particular state as "trance." Clearly by the typologies that Eliade and others have constructed, the itako are not in trance. They cannot even be said to pretend to be. What I am questioning is an analysis that regards symptoms of trance as somehow naturally expressing a communication with the dead, that believes that trance is any less "performative" than any other mode of approaching the dead. What seems to be at stake in these discussions of trance, genuine and spurious, is false belief: if a shamanic trance is extreme, if it exhibits those convulsive or extraordinary characteristics that go beyond everyday experience, then trickery should not, could not, be involved. There is a notion of purity here, of authenticity that disregards Mauss's discoveries concerning the conventional power of magic and belief. Lévi-Strauss retells the remarkable story of a Kwakiutl Indian, a native skeptic, who stumbled into the shamanic profession by an urge to learn the tricks of the trade. And so he did, as his "narrative recounts the details of his first lessons, a curious mixture of pantomime, prestidigitation, and empirical knowledge, including the art of simulating fainting and nervous fits, the learning of sacred songs." Yet this fake shaman had great success as a healer, and what Lévi-Strauss elicits from the facts of this narrative is the power of a socially based complex of beliefs in determining "reality," even a reality as impervious to manipulation as illness. What Lévi-Strauss has uncovered is the role of trickery, of duping, in any system of conventions that calls for belief; he thus discounts the possibility of any "pre-performative" trance. Lévi-Strauss strangely denies the power of this insight later on in the same essay, however, by reverting to an explanation that now sees shamanic trance as reproducing an initial series of revelations "in all their vividness, originality, and violence." To this representation he assigns the psychoanalytic term *abreaction,* and calls the shaman a "professional abreactor." He thus both asserts and denies the constitutive possibility of trickery in producing effects like "healing." See Claude Lévi-Strauss, "The Sorcerer and His Magic," in *Structural Anthropology,* trans. C. Jacobson and B. Grundfest Schoepf (New York: Doubleday, 1963), 161–80.

33. This is close to Lévi-Strauss's concept of zero symbolic value, which he uses in elucidating the concept of *mana,* the central organizing indeterminable of *A General Theory of Magic.* Mana is the concept that designates the compelling force of language as social convention. As Lévi-Strauss states, "Always and everywhere notions of this (*mana*) type intervene . . . to represent a value of indeterminate meaning (*signification*), which being itself empty of meaning (*sens*) is therefore susceptible to the reception of any meaning . . . whatsoever. Its unique function is to make good a

discrepancy between signifier and signified, or, more exactly, to draw attention to the fact that in certain circumstances...a relation of inadequacy exists between signified and signifier to the detriment of the anterior relation of complementarity." See Lévi-Strauss, "Introduction a l'oeuvre de Marcel Mauss," in Marcel Mauss, *Sociologie et anthropologie* (Paris: Presses Universitaires de France, 1950), xliv; translated in David Pocock, "Foreword" to *A General Theory of Magic,* 4.

34. In Japan the notion of conforming to a status pattern is widespread and accepted. The notion of *rashisa,* of "likeness" and of performing according to an ideal typical model also occurs in Japanese theater as well; thus, a female impersonator or a woman is *onnarashii,* "ladylike," "like a woman," in accordance with Japanese conventions of ladylikeness. Kata are the performance conventions that produce conventional likenesses. That dead spirits should speak just as dead spirits should speak, repeatedly, is perhaps less of a cause for disbelief or skepticism than it might seem.

35. In the idiom of psychoanalytic notions of fetishism, the formula would be rendered as follows: "I know but nevertheless..." ("I know that Mother doesn't have a penis, but nevertheless...[I believe that she has]").

36. If one were to take a certain psychoanalytic logic further, blindness becomes the bodily mark of "castration" as the name for a primal loss. Women's bodies become the site for Oedipal fantasies around the loss of the phallus: women as "castrated" men. A blind woman, then, becomes a doubly invested embodiment (and reminder) of loss.

37. Sakurai gives examples of these words, also called *idako kotoba* (itako words). A man is called *yumitori,* a woman *kagami* (mirror), a husband and wife, *ai no makura* (pillow of love), and a child, *takara* (treasure). The dead spirits descend through the use of these terms of address. In calling the dead person, then, the itako use formulaic substitutes that have no particular relationship to the person called (*ai no makura* might be an exception) and are used at the point where one would use the normal term of address for a living person. He states that these words are almost all understood by the local clientele, but they are not generally understood by the one-time visitor to Osorezan. Sakurai, *Nihon no shamanizumu,* 1:59.

38. For an increasingly standardized Japanese cultural landscape, a perceived "internal exotic" becomes problematic. Remaining dialects, of which there are many in Japan, become held up, valorized as languages of difference within a much-valued culture of consistency. What is only marginally understood, from the standard perspective, becomes an exemplar of what is most traditional: the exotic and the traditional coincide at the farthest reaches of the Japanese national-cultural imaginary.

39. See Raymond Williams's discussion in *Keywords: A Vocabulary of Culture and Society* (New York: Oxford University Press, 1976), 268–69.

6

Disorienting Culturalist Assumptions: A View from "Java"

John Pemberton

This unique balance— between mechanical, inert matter which passively resists pressure, and informing spirituality which pushes upward— breaks, however, the instant a building crumbles. For this means nothing else than that merely natural forces begin to become master over the work of man: the balance between nature and spirit, which the building manifested, shifts in favor of nature. This shift becomes a cosmic tragedy which, so we feel, makes every ruin an object infused with our nostalgia; for now the decay appears as nature's revenge for the spirit's having violated it by making a form in its own image. . . . For this reason, the ruin strikes us so often as tragic— but not as sad— because destruction here is not something senselessly coming from the outside but rather the realization of a tendency inherent in the deepest layer of existence of the destroyed.

— *Georg Simmel,*
"The Ruin"

By a logic of historical convergence that some might call coincidence, in 1911, precisely the same year that "The Ruin" was restored in print within Simmel's *Philosophische Kultur: Gesammelte Essays,*[1] the restoration of the massive Central Javanese Buddhist monument Barabudur was at last, under the supervision of the Dutch scholar Dr. Th. van Erp, complete. Some two million cubic feet of stone, containing, as the art historian Claire Holt has put it, "1,460 pictorial and 1,212 decorative panels, adding up to 27,000 square feet of stone surface carved in high relief," had been reassembled, rescuing the Barabudur, once more, from ruins.[2] I say "once more" because not quite a century earlier this Buddhist structure had experienced a similar rebirth of form during the brief British interregnum in the Indies under the rule of Sir Thomas Stamford Raffles. By the turn of the twentieth century, however, the ineluctable forces of nature's revenge had taken root, the grounds for Simmel's cosmic tragedy had slid into place, and van Erp would enter, center stage.

Van Erp, of course, would not be the last actor to occupy this central role of guardian of the Javanese cultural spirit manifested so majestically, it would seem, in the image of the Barabudur. Enter Indonesia's President Soeharto in the early 1970s, with a 25-million-dollar project and UNESCO support, to reclaim the monument from potential ruin yet again.[3] By 1983, the Barabudur was at last once more ready for dedication: "As a modern nation we are, indeed, classified as young," observed the president, "but we are an old people, possessing a history, traditions, and a culture that is old."[4] As chief cultural guardian, he dwelled at length in his dedication address on a special concern, warning the people not to "spoil this precious cultural inheritance of ours with writing, scratched scribbling, or doodling on the monument proper or any of its parts. What is important and necessary is not writing or scribbling as a sign that we visited this monument but attendance that is whole and does not deface the Barabudur, which stands in the very middle of our society as a unique cultural inheritance of mankind."[5] Having apparently thwarted nature's revenge (Indonesian government officials now reckoned that the Barabudur would be able to "withstand a thousand years"), Soeharto thus moved to thwart the signed revenge—graffiti traces, teenage tags, miscellaneous "doodlings"—of the people.

Yet what if already etched within the monument's ancient reliefs were scenes that appeared to threaten its modern status as a grandiose icon of spiritual heritage, the sublime essence of Javanese culture? Just months before the dedication, it was made public that archeologists had unearthed scenes of classic lust—"Karma Gangga" exhibitions of carnal desires so compelling that they could only be transcended, of course, by one's steady path upward, away from lowly distractions—scenes said to have been covered up, thanks to nature, for centuries. "After Restoration," Indonesian news headlines announced, " 'Porno' [porno] Relief Exposed on Barabudur's Foundation." Such momentary setbacks have not in the least diminished obsessions with spiritual heritage and cultural origins on the part of Soeharto's self-proclaimed New Order regime. Indeed, in light of occasional untoward exposures, the drive to locate truly authentic (asli) origins becomes all the more intense.

The political implications of these sorts of obsession with the location of an authentic Javanese culture (kebudayaan Jawa), with traditions (tradisi-tradisi) that must be preserved at all costs, and so on, are obvious: effaced, in the name of cultural continuity and stability, is a history of political activism opened by the Indonesian revolution in the late 1940s and closed with Soe-harto's seizure of control in the mid-1960s when highly politicized massacres left one-half to one million Indonesians dead and hundreds of thousands imprisoned. Genealogically founded on issues of origins and continuity, cul-turalist discourse facilitates conditions under which a history of New Order terror is not spoken about, as political activism is routinely disappeared. I am not referring to some Machiavellian ruse that simply legitimizes power by reference to constructs like "traditional culture" as a means of social control. Instead, the issue of origins goes well beyond such a ruse as it re-doubles the attention focused precisely on those cultural sources that New Order authorities assume they themselves are serving. For the New Order regime is utterly devoted to the idea of an authentic Javanese culture just as surely as it is dedicated to the preservation of the Barabudur, undisturbed by modern Indonesian graffiti.

So one might ask how it is that this peculiar obsession, this intense fo-cus on culture as an object of desire that would recall origins, reclaim ruins, and institute a siting of the past in place, could come to hold such sway. Of course, one thinks, this *is* Javanese culture, this is culture. And yet, if one looks to Javanese (or Malay) writings inscribed before the late nineteenth century, the terms that would inform culturalist discourse, precisely the terms used in Soeharto's 1983 address, "culture" (*kebudayaan*), "tradition" (*tradisi*), "ritual" (*upacara*), and so on, are conspicuously absent. From the turn of the twentieth century on, however, Javanese (and nationalist Malay, soon to become Indonesian) writings exhibited, with increasing refinement and in terms most recognizable now in retrospect, the sense of a vast cultural discourse. General encyclopedias, ethnographic compendia, journals, maga-zines, newspapers, schools textbooks, radio programs, and so on — some in Dutch, others in Javanese, still others in Malay — all recorded and displayed, through various effects, evidence on or for "culture," particularly "Javanese culture" in light of Java's crowning position as the centerpiece of the East Indies empire. Of course, one thinks again; for such discursive frames are precisely those drawn under colonial conditions, which in the "East," at least, facilitated properly Orientalist pursuits and institutes like Central Java's own Javanologie Instituut, formally established in 1919, whose proceedings were published in Dutch, yet whose personnel were drawn in many cases from the ranks of Javanese literati, crossing languages with increasing ease, as if the translation of essential cultural terms appeared almost transparent.

While such historical insistences have their place, especially, for our purposes here, in countering culturalist assumptions (that is, the assumption of culture), they all too often simply reinstate a classic analytic dichotomy when it comes to colonial encounters, typically expressed in terms of within versus without, of interior versus exterior. For if patently culturalist interpretation would attempt to transcend historical insistences (even while taking historical forces into consideration) by essentially arguing from within, as it were, then historicist explanation tends, in the case of colonial encounter, to amass evidence for the effects of modern technologies and epistemologies conveyed by the colonizers and imposed on colonized subjects who gradually imitate, adopt, appropriate, and incorporate these essentially foreign logics. Through a series of reflections on Javanese manuscripts composed between 1745 and the late 1930s (that is, from the years of Dutch East India Company intervention and the subsequent establishment of a formal colonial government in the Indies in 1800, across the British interregnum of 1811–16, until the eve of the collapse of the Dutch East Indies empire in 1942), I want to trouble the stabilizing effects conveyed by such dichotomies, effects that in their most reduced form might institute a distinction between, say, culture and history.

In the Central Javanese city of Surakarta are royal archives belonging to the palaces whose mid-eighteenth-century emergence first put this city on the map. Although these archives are rarely visited by contemporary Indonesians (who would find in their volumes many surprises more stunning, even, than Barabudur "porno"), they are imagined to contain the textual traces of all that might represent Java's glorious past. Housed in these scriptoria are almost three-quarters of a million pages comprising some five thousand texts composed by Javanese and penned in Javanese script: manuscripts whose subject matter ranges from historical chronicles in verse or prose to Sufi speculative lyrics, illuminated catalogues of magical talismans, and much more.[6] Alongside these Javanese texts stand other texts, printed in Dutch, which once variously organized the colonial state of affairs into well-ruled compendia of financial records, programs for social reform, reports from incumbent East Indies officials, and much more. But these Dutch materials are not the only texts inscribing the contours of a colonial presence and an eventually abandoned civilizing mission, for this presence is everywhere to be found, in fact, within the Javanese manuscripts. In many manuscripts the contours of that presence loom large as, for example, a Javanese king salutes the Governor-General of the Netherlands Indies with a glass of Madeira. In other texts that focus on what would seem more typically indigenous concerns (divinational calculations, for instance), that presence assumes the quasi-invisible form of a Dutch watermark fatefully recalling the origins of the very paper against whose grain Javanese scribes were writing: a watermark like GOD ZY MET ONS, that is, GOD BE WITH US.

Such a watermark poses a question of alternatives that reiterates questions concerning colonial encounter I alluded to a moment ago. How might one write an account of Central Java's colonial past that fully acknowledges the force of Dutch rule without reducing the native subjects of that past to the status of mere (cultural?) victims increasingly overpowered by the technologies of a modern knowledge imposed from without, a knowledge that effectively invested theological certainty into the secular cause of a civilizing mission? And how might one do so without simply resorting to a certain sense of cultural priority? In turning primarily to Javanese manuscripts, as I am about to do, I do not mean to present these indigenous sources simply as evidence for the "other" point of view that, when combined with the one framing the colonizer's vision, might eventually provide a completed portrait of colonial encounter. I do not intend, that is, to treat the manuscripts simply as representative traces of another culture increasingly overtaken by a colonizing power coming from without, for locating these sources within a fundamentally cultural framework would mean overlooking the very modernity of constructs like "culture," "tradition," and so on. It would mean missing, as well, a significant ambivalence sustained within many Javanese manuscripts concerning the origins of what would appear to lie always just beyond the limits of colonial conquest, a figuration of difference that moves discursively, anticipating its future recollection as a sign of culture: that is, the figure of "Java." That this figuration occured in contradistinction to the invasively constant yet only partially incorporated presence of the Dutch goes without saying. Yet just as the figure of "Java" was not a legacy of precolonial times, neither was it simply an issue of imitating foreign orientalist epistemologies; rather, it was a prefiguration, even anticipation, of what would become a properly cultural subject, orientalist or otherwise. Given a certain ambivalence of origins, this figure eventually would also prove immensely capable of anticipating its own demise, thus prophetically signaling the limits, if not the end, of Javanological and, by extension, other more contemporary cultural certainties. In anticipation of such an ending, I turn now to the first of five extended discursive moments. I do so by way of a 1939 celebration recalling cultural origins along somewhat elliptical temporal contours similar to those informing the dedication of Barabudur in 1983, or in 1911, or even, perhaps, under the rule of Raffles almost a century earlier.

Seminal Contradictions

In April 1939, the Central Javanese palace ruled by a dynasty of kings reigning under no less a title than "Axis of the Cosmos" (*Pakubuwana*), celebrated its bicentennial by holding a grand nightfair. A two-hundred-year reign was a first in Javanese history; never before had such a dynasty managed to live in one palace for so long. The rationale behind the celebration was also a first. It had not occurred to the occupants of this palace to observe, say, a one-hundred-year commemoration in the mid-nineteenth century. In the past, royal commemorations were tied directly to the body of the king himself and acknowledged the cosmological import of a monarch's age or the length of His Majesty's reign. Now, however, near the unexpected end of Dutch East Indies colonial rule, they celebrated the age not of a king but a kingdom and an abstracted image of kingliness soliciting, in turn, devotion to a far more generalized sense of royalty, empire, and particularly high culture. The site of this abstraction was the Kraton Surakarta Hadiningrat, the "Palace of Surakarta, Finest in the World."

For the two-hundred-year celebration in 1939, the Surakarta Palace published a commemorative volume of precisely two hundred pages: "Royal Deeds" (*Sri Radya Laksana*), the official story of Surakarta kings and their state. Drawing on passages from eighteenth-century Javanese chronicles, the volume opens with a description of the king's move to the village of Solo in 1745, the move by which the Palace of Surakarta was founded. This highly celebrated move from the palace's former site just seven miles west of Solo is in fact the only story found in the commemorative book. The events surrounding the old palace's abandonment, a complex mix of rebellions and political maneuverings that left the old palace in shambles, are not cited; nor are later events of the high colonial era recorded in nineteenth- and early-twentieth-century chronicles. It is as if the formal ceremonial procession created by the move were all that one really needed to know about Javanese history.

Now the eighteenth-century manuscripts cited in "Royal Deeds" do indeed describe in detail a royal progress of unparalleled completeness. The king rode in his carriage, "Sir Venerable Eagle," a gift from the Dutch East India Company. Accompanying him were the golden icons of kingship, a sea of ceremonial parasols, and palace troops numbering fifty thousand. Like Javanese royal progresses of the past when kings toured the realm, the 1745 procession was meant to display a kingdom in well-ordered glory. This formal move in which the remnants of a sacked palace were simply picked up and ceremonially deposited a few miles away was, however, without precedent in Javanese history. In the past, displaced monarchs had scattered to the periphery of political power, where they secluded themselves in ascetic retreat. It was thus the novel fate of an eighteenth-century, retreating "Axis of the Cosmos" not to be transformed into a legendary ascetic, but to be transferred to a new political position by means of a procession headed by a Dutch company commander and graced by royal banyan trees uprooted from their old turf and carted off like potted plants, as well as by the old palace's gilded throne-room transported in one piece like a mobile home.

All of this had a marvelous effect. A new order of things suddenly appeared at the procession's destination, as an eighteenth-century palace scribe records:

> Upon the arrival of
> His Highness at Solo,
> the Gilded Throne-room was set up
> . . . .
> the troops sat in order, attending.
> The King sat in the Throne-room
> with the officers and the Dutch Commandant
> standing on the right side
> of the Royal Sitting-hall;
> the soldiers were in long rows,
> Dutch and Javanese.
> . . . .
> The religious officials
> then prayed for the well-being of the kingdom;
> His Highness ordered
> the planting of the fenced banyan.
> . . . .
> Now His Highness the King indeed
> took up residence in the city of Surakarta;
> there was no misfortune,
> everything was now in good order.[7]

Forming a procession of state at the very moment in a kingdom's demise when convention demanded ascetic retreat, the displaced court performed a most original act. In the customary guise of a royal progress, and with Dutch East India Company escort, it ceremoniously founded a new kingdom. One of the many unintended consequences of this act through which Surakarta was created was the eventual transfer to the Dutch of most powers of state, save the significant symbolic shell of what later would come to be thought of as "traditional" Javanese authority. A second, related consequence was the appearance of ritual as a supplementary sign of displacement. For the procession to Solo represented both a displaced kingdom *and* a denial or deferral of that displacement, that is, an epistemological displacement in which the classic difference between a royal progress (when a king is displayed as the reigning icon of kingship in a flourishing kingdom) and a royal retreat (when a defeated king abandons kingship for the peripheral powers of refuge) was bypassed. The 1745 progress was performed as a sign of what the move to Surakarta was *not:* namely, the manifest image of a flourishing, already well-ordered kingdom. Ritual thus emerged as a new form of power, a particularly privileged process for transforming the contradiction between what was and what was not into a novel royal state.

The suspension of the contradiction contained in the origins of Surakarta initiated what would become a vast discourse on things "Javanese." From the late eighteenth century on, palace scribes and courtiers articulated, in Javanese, an other "Java," an exemplary realm ideally removed from the encroachment of Dutch colonial rule, a realm whose perpetual displacement guaranteed that the contradictions of its own creation would be constantly recovered. As this discursive figure of "Java" was repeatedly reinvested with all that might *not* represent Dutch colonial presence, the contours of what much later would be readily identified as "Javanese culture" began to emerge. The emergence of these contours was, of course, most gradual. For this figuration of difference called "Java" was motivated not so much by a grand logic of representation that assumed from the outset an abstracted structure to be filled in with so many identifiable types—the grammar of orientalism, perhaps—but instead by a particular logic of the concrete.

Fashioning "Java"

Soon after the founding of Surakarta, two other Central Javanese courts were similarly founded, again through Dutch intervention. The first was located only forty miles away in nearby Yogyakarta under Sultan Hamengkubuwana ("Lap of the Cosmos"), and the second just across town under a semi-independent Surakarta prince with the title Mangkunagara ("Lap of the Realm"). By the 1760s, with military confrontation past, the rulers of these three rival courts now devoted themselves to a domesticated politics of marriage diplomacy. Underlying much of the conjugal knotting detailed in these chronicles was the late-eighteenth-century hope of tying together the loose ends of Javanese royalty that had separated since 1745. Court chronicles thus turned their attentions from war to in-house affairs of state.

Of particular interest in these chronicles is the image of the Dutch company representative assigned to the palaces, an image that shifts dramatically between the 1760s and 1780s. Consider, for example, the behavior of the Dutch *Opperhoofd* (Commander), or "Huprup," as this title sounded in Javanese, in the following 1760s manuscript tracking a Yogyakarta prince who sought the hand of a Surakarta princess. Invited to demonstrate his skill as a dancer, the bashful prince declines and at once the Dutch Huprup, thoroughly drunk, turns on him:

"Your father the Sultan of Yogyakarta
is wise and of religion devout,
not stubborn like you.
He'd go along for a drink or two,
because he knew what's correct,
the Company set him up as Sultan."[8]

The Huprup then aims his words at the prince's Javanese escort:

" . . . you animal,
did you train this Crown Prince?
Your prince is a little shit,
. . . .
and [you, sir,] are a dog!"[9]

Unnerved by the Huprup's behavior, the Surakarta king (Pakubuwana III)
seeks consolation from his chief counsel. The response?

"It is nothing to worry about if you consider,
[the Huprup is] just a little different,
a crazy Dutchman to be sure."[10]

It is precisely in light of such apparent craziness—that little difference—
that "Javanese custom" then emerges as a powerful tutor. Although this power
is still uncertain in the 1760s, its effects are beginning to be felt, as the following passage from the manuscript quoted above indicates. The scene here
focuses on a royal wedding procession in the streets of Surakarta. The Huprup
is the same fellow.

Now then, the head of the procession
having reached the Company fortress
. . . the [Javanese] Commander
Jayanagara,
. . . .
shouted out while still on horseback.
'Twas the Huprup who was ordered out,
the startled Huprup
came out in a rush.
Jayanagara straightway said,
"Huprup, fast,
fire the cannons at once!"

The Huprup replied, "Hey, Jayanagara,
the groom is still far off,
are you drunk?"
Said Jayangara,

"To the west of the outermost palace gate
    has come the groom,
so go ahead and fire at once."

Thus compelled by Commander Jayanagara,
the Huprup quickly obeyed,
signaling his gunners,
thunderously the cannons sounded forth.
Jayanagara spoke calmly,
"Now follow this,
let me tell you,

by Javanese rules [*adat Jawa*] a groom is
    the same as a general [*jéndral*]
so sound cannons galore!"
And so Huprup Béman
just obeyed,
the cannons shot over and over again.
From his great pleasure,
Jayanagara danced,
jumping up and down twirling his moustache.
The Huprup enjoyed the show
and invited Jayanagara to have a seat
before the groom arrived.[11]

    When Jayanagara appeals to "Javanese rules" and thereby elevates the status of a Javanese groom to that of a general, the military official in question is not a Javanese general but, in fact, a Dutch general, for the term Jayanagara employs is *jéndral*. It is as if "Javanese rules" somehow not only transcended the rules of respect demanded by Javanese royalty but exceeded even the restrictions on Javanese behavior imposed by Dutch intervention into Surakarta political affairs, for such a sounding of cannons was normally reserved for a king or jéndral. All of this was to Jayanagara's great pleasure; it was left to the Dutch Huprup to "enjoy the show." In a series of substitutions articulated from the late eighteenth century on, the customary figure of a Javanese groom would gradually overlap with figures of higher authority. Everyday grooms would become replica "kings-for-a-day," as Javanese idiom would have it, and the king himself would be tranformed into the reigning icon of Javanese custom: a model "king-for-a-day."

    The contemporaneous account of a 1780s wedding discloses a sense of the new interior space of customary orderliness surrounding this royal model. After making a brief appearance at the wedding of his crown prince son, who is being ceremoniously "treated *like* a king [*rinatu-ratu*]," Surakarta's monarch returns to the inner palace where he too will sit in state, "treated like a king":

> Then exiting west the King
> returned within the palace
> where places were arranged all in order.
> Sitting on chairs [*kursi*] alongside the Dutch,
> were the princes,
> lined up in a row before the King.[12]

The construction of interior scenes of palace order was organized around the *kursi:* a European-style, straightback chair, the central prop in Javanese court life. Royalty and privileged guests were seated and then dutifully observed as they themselves observed the ceremonial events unfolding around them.

Sitting in state was, of course, nothing new for Javanese kings, but the rows of chairs were, and so too were the Dutch guests that now routinely filled the chairs. The Dutch intruders thus became irreversibly involved in court etiquette and systems of seating that supported a Javanese sense of order. The extent of this involvement is immediately apparent in the stanza that follows the passage just quoted. In an almost instantaneous switch,

> without delay, entering the inner palace
> and changing his clothes, the King
> dressed in the Dutch fashion [*cara Walandi*].
> All the royal family dressed Dutch;
> only Prince Mangkunagara
> remained in ceremonial batik.[13]

The chronicle later notes that by wearing this batik, only the rival Javanese prince, Mangkunagara, "remained firm." The obvious implication—that by dressing "Dutch," the Surakarta king exhibited his submission to Dutch influence—is complicated by the fact that there was no apparent need for the king, along with his entire family, to adopt this fashion for such an event. This was not a Dutch protocol affair, but a patently Javanese wedding.

"Dressing Dutch" no doubt held a certain novelty value for Javanese royalty, whose ceremonial appearance in cultural drag displayed a special familiarity with Dutch ways. To dress Dutch was to share, somehow, in the strange power that the persistent presence of the Dutch must have represented to Javanese rulers by the late eighteenth century. The king's cross-dressing exhibited a privilege that even the Dutch did not enjoy: it was unthinkable for a Huprup to make a formal appearance in Javanese royal attire.

"Dutch fashion" was appropriated and entered into the Javanese court catalog of ceremonial costume, a catalog now able to place the foreigners in an
identifiable style: these folks also "dressed Dutch." The Huprup and his Dutch
cohorts thus were drawn into a ceremonial scene which was, at bottom,
thoroughly Javanese. That such an attempt at ritually bracketing the presence of the Company should occur in the context of a wedding simply un-
derscored the process of domestication implicitly at work.

One need only recall the 1760s disorderly Huprup, that rude reminder
of a Dutch presence still precariously primitive and unpredictable, not yet
cultured in the Javanese terms that would develop to place the intruder in
context, to get a sense of just how far the 1780s Huprup had been pulled
into ceremonial line. Sitting in state alongside his Javanese royal companion had become completely routine. This incorporation into Javanese affairs
of state was due, in part, to the king's appropriation of "Dutch fashion," an
act of cultural transvestitism that gave the Dutch an identifiable and implicitly
subordinate place in Javanese court ceremony. Although such an act may
have achieved the partial domestication of Dutch foreignness, it nevertheless raised questions regarding the status of Javanese kings. Was His Majesty
not "firm" enough? Was he somehow turning "Dutch"?

Just five years after the 1783 wedding and at the impressionable age of
twenty, the crown prince groom acceded to the throne as Surakarta's new
king (Pakubuwana IV). Provoked by his father's actions, as well as the
palace's failure at preventing Dutch intrusion into state affairs, this king
banned the use of Dutch dress by Javanese. A singular optional style of attire became identifiable. No longer was the conceptual alternative to Dutch
dress expressed in the limited terms of batik specifics. Emerging in opposition to "Dutch fashion" (*cara Walandi*) came the immensely significant, generalizable cultural figure *cara Jawi:* "Javanese fashion," or better yet, "Javanese
style." The "Javanese"/"Dutch" distinction highlighted by the king's wardrobe
options, pivoted on *cara,* a rather generic term that in everyday usage (both
past and present, by most accounts) referred simply to a "manner" of behavior, a certain sense of style. In the context of nineteenth-century Surakarta
chronicles, however, the term *cara* conventionally designated, in combination with "Dutch" or "Javanese," *attire.* It is as if, for ceremonial purposes,
an entire world of differences between Dutch and Javanese ways were reducible to choice of dress, as if what really stood behind world views were
wardrobes. Through a logic of the concrete, the root of Javanese custom,
or so it would appear, was costume.[14]

Once cara Jawi became fixed as a logical alternative to cara Walandi, it
facilitated the creation of a substitute world, an imagined option to the state

of affairs brought to Java by the Dutch: a self-contained, ideally invulnerable, thoroughly "Javanese" world. During the nineteenth century, the self-contained world implicit in the cara Jawi figure would expand to identify "Javanese" language, cuisine, literature, customs, and so on down the line demarcating, eventually, classic cultural difference. The "Javanese" figure, thus, would emerge in contradistinction to what *already* had been discursively construed and inscribed in Surakarta texts as its "Dutch" counterpart. The supplementary "Javanese" figure then would appear to counter the force of the other fashioned as "Dutch" by fashioning itself in a certain priority, as if "Javanese culture" had always been self-evident. In short, the supplement would come first.

The lines drawn by this form of Javanism ran deep. By the turn of the nineteenth century, the ban on Dutch dress was lifted. The king might dress "Dutch" one day and "Javanese" the next, for both of these clearly belonged to a palace catalog of fashion. Built into the "Javanese"/"Dutch" distinction was a peculiar remove that treated each style as if equally weighted. Rather than express the Javanese stance toward outsiders — that potentially looming Other — in explicitly (and classically anthropological) we/they terms, Javanism subsumed, as it appropriated, both "Jawi" and "Walandi." The long-term effect of this appropriation was a sense of self-assurance strong enough to seal foreignness out while bracketing "Dutch" (and others) in and, at the same time, refined enough to attract and draw the foreigner into a "Javanese" world that was, by definition, impenetrable. Regardless of how many Spanish figurines, French chandeliers, Italian sculptures, or Dutch portraits might be crammed into the Palace of Surakarta, it would all, eventually, be viewed as "authentically [*asli*] Javanese."[15]

"Java" Doubles

In the years following the formal establishment of the Dutch East Indies colonial state in 1800, the alternative, substitute world implicit in the figure "Javanese style," that is, cara Jawi, assumed a certain reality, an everyday realness, and the quotation marks framing "Javanese" slowly began to fade into a kind of invisible permanence. This is not to say that future Javanese would not cite "Java," quite frequently in fact, as a privileged site of cultural authenticity. On the contrary, they could do so with increasing self-assurance that such a citation had a well-founded referent. And with this permanence came a newfound confidence, regardless of extraordinary changes brought by colonial rule. In 1812 the British took control of the colonies; in 1816 they left, and the Dutch reclaimed control. No great matter it seems, for when the British flag in front of Surakarta's colonial headquarters was replaced by its returning Dutch counterpart, a palace chronicler recorded the event thus:

> The English flag upon being lowered
> received a twenty-one cannon salute,
> and when Holland had raised its colors,
> the salute was just (more of) the same.[16]

An increasing sense of routine would inform the ceremonial presentation of "Java" from the early nineteenth century on. An 1847 manuscript detailing the events of the palace's annual grand assembly of the realm (Garebeg Mulud) thus becomes ordered diachronically, synchronizing movement precisely with colonial clock time. Under the heading "Ten-thirty," for example, we read,

> As His Highness Mister Resident [the Dutch colonial official overseeing Surakarta] reaches the edge of the Central Pavilion, His Majesty His Highness the King of Surakarta stands in respect and then shakes hands with His Highness Mister Resident...Mister Resident then takes his seat on His Majesty's left.[17]

The two sit briefly in state. At no point is there recorded a ceremonial mishap that might historically situate the document. The 1847 account remains temporally suspended in a prescriptive present and may be read either as a report modeled on the 1847 ceremony or a model for ceremonies sometime in the future. Almost a century later, at the conclusion of Dutch rule in the Indies, the very same scene was still reenacted annually. A 1940 account makes this eerily perceptive comment:

> His Majesty...takes his place on the throne positioned just to the east of the seat prepared for the Mister Governor. An *invisible line* divides the pavilion into two parts, forming a boundary between His Majesty and the Mister Governor.[18]

Once the Dutch official is seated next to the king, these immobile authorities exhibit a remarkable detachment, as if even the invisible line itself did not exist. The overall effect is that of a pair of "kings" set up side by side, both staring dead ahead in nearly parallel vision, permanently suspended in ritual stalemate.

The maintenance of such an invisible line of course depended on a mutual recognition of the central figure to which both authorities were, somehow, devoted. Even the commanding Dutch official would invariably make a final grand toast: "To the land of Java!" No doubt the single most elaborated scene of this devotion in the nineteenth century was the royal wedding. Before the 1830s, it apparently was unimaginable that a Javanese manuscript should devote itself entirely to such an affair, for older chronicles characteristically allotted weddings only a few stanzas within a broader narrative structure concerned more with the historical intrigue of alliance and rivalry than with ceremony per se. From the 1830s on, however, the royal wedding developed into a topic demanding an entire volume, a respectable subject warranting a place all its own on the shelves of palace archives. As this subject attracted the imaginations of palace scribes, the royal wedding began to write itself onto the figure of "Java"; this figure, in turn, discovered new discursive space in which to move.

And the Dutch were not to be left out in demonstrating their devotion to this figure of emerging cultural desire. An 1850s manuscript finds both the Dutch Resident and his wife obsessed with the finest of details in preparing for the wedding of Surakarta's junior palace (noted earlier) of Prince Mangkunagara. The Resident informs the prince,

> "and if there's anything lacking, I'll take care of it." ... Her Lady the Mistress added: "Again, Prince, whatever you'd like in terms of decorations and costumes, only the finest, with jewels. So that you have them soon, I myself'll go to Semarang. Or bought goods, fine things, if there's something you still don't have, I'll go myself. Whatever you want, just jot it down, how many and what kinds."[19]

"Java" emerges as a world equipped with its own undeniable attractions and obligations through which Dutch colonial authority is circumscribed. Throughout this mid-nineteenth-century chronicle, the Resident performs as if he has become thoroughly acculturated or, better yet, as if upon reflection he turns out to be really a good "Javanese" after all.

In light of an underlying sense of insecurity vis-à-vis the formal Palace of Surakarta regarding its status as a truly royal house, this junior palace of Prince Mangkunagara proved particularly energetic in its efforts to articulate the contours of "Java." By the 1870s, the Mangkunagara's palace was producing a world of treatises on ceremony, literature, ethics, and so on that today are recalled as the hallmarks of an exquisitely refined, lavishishly inscribed, cultural past. An 1870s exemplary wedding text from this palace reflects at length on a nuptial scene enveloped, alliteratively, by a "mood most deeply moving" and arrives at this fantasy:

> The competing rays and radiances within the hall,
> truly fitting when viewed,

added to the noble ladies' pleasure;
it was as if Sedana and Sri
had descended into
the great wedding hall.[20]

The benevolent appearance of Sedana and Sri, the Javanese god and goddess of prosperity and fertility, finds its companion fantasy just a few stanzas later when the bride and groom are formally introduced to the Resident and his wife,

who with handshakes bestowed their blessings.
Following behind
the Dutch ladies crowded around

and with the Dutch gentlemen gave their blessings
coming forward one after another.
Upon reflection, one had the impression that
gods [jawata] and goddesses [apsari]
had descended bringing good fortune
to the newlyweds.[21]

Now this last lucky bestowal of blessings, ostensibly from Dutch dignitaries and guests, "upon reflection" turns out to come from "Javanese" gods and goddesses: these jawata and apsari are *indigenous* spiritual benefactors, not some sort of foreign *goden*. With this, coverage of the wedding celebration proper is complete as the Dutch are made respectable, yet again, precisely with respect to the authority of "Java."

Meanwhile, however, just across town in the Palace of Surakarta, the routine nineteenth-century spectacle of customary order had become *so* routine that a marked desire for the eccentric began to motivate this long-term bastion of "Javanese" centrism, a desire represented in court events as well as the texts inscribing them. An 1865 wedding of His Highness, "Axis of the Cosmos," experienced, for example, the following astonishing interruption as magically charged court servants (dwarves, the so-called *édanan,* or "crazies") burst onto the scene:

The crazies loved a good laugh,
free was the mood as they entered
from the cookery into the courtyard
prancing to and fro like horses,
some shouldering a penis [dakar]
the size of a man's calf, painted

black, the head reddened,
outrageously beating about.
Delighted were those who looked on,

the court women
scattering, not wishing to be dizzied
by a form so great.[22]

The crazies had long been essential figures in entourages of Javanese rulers, but their antics were never really spotlighted in early chronicles, at least not with the flare produced in this 1865 manuscript. A ceremonial scene like the royal wedding first had to be conceived as a self-contained event, a discrete textual subject demanding a manuscript all its own, for such familiar follies to find space for, and deserve, inscription. Moreover, the routine sense of "Javanese" order now ran deep enough not only safely to allow the crazies' intrusion but to *need* it. As monstrous wooden phalluses flailed about the courtyard on the king's wedding day, "delighted were those who looked on."

While the junior palace of Mangkunagara cultivated a "Javanese" world of refinement, a world immensely recognizable to European visions of what the Orient should be, the senior Palace of Surakarta, under its ninth "Axis of the Cosmos" king, Pakubuwana IX (r. 1862–93), appeared increasingly unrecognizable as it attempted to reclaim a world of "Java" beyond the reach of colonial rule, a reiteration of Surakarta's origins as a (displaced) "Javanese" kingdom. On the outskirts of the city this king thus built an extensive pleasure/meditation retreat to explore what were, by late-nineteenth-century standards, strange pleasures and to renew cosmological contacts with this other "Java." That is, while one "Java" was busy presenting itself front and center for cultural recognition, the other, reiterating a logic of self-displacement, was headed for cultural eccentricity.

The difference between these two "Javas" was all too apparent to European visitors. Consider, for example, the 1889 response of a British merchant, one Arthur Earle, touring what he took to be the "East." Reflecting upon his visit to Pakubuwana IX's pleasure retreat, Earle entered the following in his journal:

> In the afternoon we drove to see the Emperor's summer house at Langenardjo. It is some six miles distant, on the banks of the river. His Dutch guard follows him here. A more grotesque looking place I never saw. It contains a large collection of European rubbish, and the gardens are full of fountains, ornamented by numberless China dolls and animals.[23]

This king had "the character of being the most impudent barbarian ruler in existence," Earle added.[24] Then, that evening, at the junior palace of Mangkunagara:

Here we were courteously received by "His Highness," who was the very opposite of the Magnate who had given us the opportunity of seeing his truly Native Court in the morning. . . .

We mounted the audience chamber, and after tea had been served, went to a large gilded open platform with a white marble floor, used for ceremonies. On the magnificent gamelang [sic] (of some hundred performers) striking up, two men (professional dancers) at once emerged from the back, dressed in the most magnificent costumes I ever beheld. The value of these dresses is very great, and no one possesses such a fine collection as the Prince. He has sent several splendid costume specimens to the Java Court at the Paris Exhibition, and has arranged after that is closed, to present them to one of the museums in the French capital. . . . The scene was, as one of the gentlemen who accompanied us said, more akin to those depicted in the "Arabian Nights," than anything one could well imagine.[25]

In contrast to the truly disorienting otherness of Pakubuwana IX's world ("a more grotesque looking place I never saw") Prince Mangkunagara's palace graciously provided Earle with the "very opposite," an "Arabian Nights" evening, a representation of Other so classic for those late-nineteenth-century travelers who believed that they were touring the Orient, that it had been admitted to the Java Court of the Paris Exhibition.

From the late eighteenth century on, the figure of "Java" had expanded discursively as if in anticipation of precisely this sort of international recognition. While the 1870s Palace of Surakarta partially distanced itself (quite literally, in the case of its pleasure retreat) from such a figure, Prince Mangkunagara's exhibitionism would, in contrast, present "Java" up front for full cultural approval. In this junior palace, even the prince's gamelan orchestra sounded "magnificent" to Earle. Only hours earlier in the older palace, essentially the same sounds had confronted him with a "monotonous wail." There was thus a pronounced mutual exaggeration between the two "Javas." The more eccentric and inaccessible the senior palace's "Java" became, the more strangely powerful it appeared to Prince Mangkunagara and hence the more devoted the junior palace became to recovering the cultural secrets of a displaced realm.

Figures for Replication

By the turn of the twentieth century, "Java" was, of course, already the focus of considerable European orientalist attention. As I noted earlier, the field of this inquiry was called "Javanologie," and the formal organization, established in 1919 and dedicated to "advancing" such inquiry, was the Java Institute, whose proceedings were attended by Dutch and Javanese scholars and conducted in Dutch. A Mangkunagara prince, Mangkunagara VII, became the first honorary chairman of this institute. No one was better suited. Mangkunagara VII soon became known for his eloquent testimonial lectures on the "very high civilization" (*zeer booge beschaving*) of "Java" and particularly on the essence of the "Javanese spiritual self." In a (now) classic 1932 lecture to the Institute's Cultural-Philosophical Study Circle (Cultuur-Wijsgeerigen Studiekring) concerning the mystical elements of Javanese shadow-puppet theater (*wayang kulit*), the prince began,

> In the address to follow... I have dared to lift a small tip of the veil to show how in the wayang lies hidden the secret Javanese knowledge [*de geheime Javaansche wetenschap*] concerning the deepest significance of life.[26]

He concluded,

> It is all reflected in the rhythms of [the puppeteer's] beats against the wayang-chest [the *kothak*, the wooden chest containing puppets for performance and used for sound effects], which is supposed to represent the accelerated heart-beats of the meditation-practitioner and the noises heard by him in the phase when the "spiritual self" [*"geestelijk ik"*] is being crystallized.[27]

It was precisely this culturalized figure of a spiritual self, this crystallized "I," that the prince hoped to reveal, as if it were his own, to the Javanological audience, a figure that could be promoted and disseminated, in the spirit of Javanology, through acts of repeated recognition. In a very real sense, this figure depended on and was constituted by just such moments of revelation, moments that could *only* be achieved through dissemination. That is, knowledge of such an "I" required an audience to whom it could be revealed and through whom it might be recognized. For at stake was a secret: the "secret Javanese knowledge." Thus, the prince had to speak as if exposing, momentarily, an essentially esoteric knowledge—as if lifting, in true orientalist fashion, a small tip of the veil. With Mangkunagara VII, the "Java" that had long anticipated translation found its ideal translator and patron. In the modern age of reproduction, the subject of that knowledge *crystallized* (as the prince put it, just as certainly as Mangkunagara sugar was now scientifically produced) within the newly charted census space of "Javanese" identity in the form of an identifiably indigenous "self," a Javanized *geestelijk ik*, in short, a refined, personalized figuration of "Java" perfectly suitable for replication.

Mangkunagara VII's philosophical commentary on the "Javanese" spirit was part of a much broader discourse on identity developing in the Indies in the early twentieth century, a discourse increasingly mediated by newspapers, magazines, catalogs of advertisements, and books devoted to customs, manners, beliefs, and much else that might inform the subject of "Java." It is tempting, in retrospect, to assume a certain universalist priority of the notion of self in Mangkunagara VII's lecture, as if its "I" must always stand behind particular articulations of identity. This is especially so when rereading nationalist thought of the period, characteristically cast in the form of a natural awakening of spirit or identity in the Indies as elsewhere. But the crystallizing subject of "Java" in the early twentieth century discloses not so much a figure of identity as a figure *for* identification. For just as the Javanized *ik* emerged to spiritually inhabit the modern, replicable space created for "Java," the very figure of "Java" that made such an identification possible emerged much earlier, as we have seen, not out of expressions explicitly pertaining to self or person but, most fundamentally, to costume: cara Jawi. Wrapping itself within precisely the terms by which the deepest significance of life might appear to exist, the "Javanese spirit" thus represented, in effect, the final layering of signification onto the subject of "Java" by refashioning it as subjectivity.

Nowhere was the sociocultural space that this spiritual figuration was fashioned to fill better illustrated than in the mail-order catalogs produced for Javanese colonial civil servants, catalogs distributed by Surakarta's clothing stores. Appealing to a sense of "Javanese" genuineness virtually identical to that informing Mangkunagara VII's reflections but expressed in commercial-media Malay rather than Javanological Dutch, a 1928 catalog introductory page opens as follows:

THE KNOWLEDGE OF THE BATIK DYEING OPERATION

> *This* is a knowledge of dyeing that exists as an heirloom from the land of Java, which for such a long time the Europeans—despite their many noble knowledgeable skills—to this day still haven't been able to achieve like the genuine product from Java.[28]

Batik-dyeing is presented here as yet another form of a "Javanese secret knowledge" unequaled in the West, a means of production whose products are as identifiably genuine as the numerous "Javanese" souls who would identify themselves through them. Although "genuine Javanese" batik from Surakarta formed the core of this clothier's business, the store supplied its customers with much more than batik. The catalog was a means of outfitting countless native colonial administrators from top to bureaucratic bottom, from Buitenzorg to Borneo. Every form of official character was provided for, from full-dress uniform costumes for top-ranking regional regents ("A Regent suit [*costuum Boepati*] with yellow ceremonial parasol, No.1 quality: 250 guilders, No.2: 175") to a village headman's hat with a Queen Wilhelmina *W* sewn on the front ("6 guilders"). Moreover, the store was famed for its *blancon,* or "ready-to-wear," breakthrough in design. Turbans no longer needed to be wrapped repeatedly by their wearers but instead were already sewn into form. Borrowed from the Dutch *blanco,* a term used in the Indies for bureaucratic and commercial blank forms designed to be filled in for completion or endorsement, blancon fashion fitted its subjects into a prefabricated interval that was at once patently modern and thoroughly "Javanese."

The subjective effect of such replicable expressions of "Javanese" identity was readily apparent in the dozens of satisfied-customer testimonials that filled the back pages of the catalog. For example,

> Although I did not come in person for a fitting, it didn't need even the slightest alteration. The formal jacket you made for me was finely tailored both in cut—*snit*—and detail, and is a pleasure to its wearer. In light of such diligence, I will not hesitate to recommend this to all my friends.[29]

Like most outfitted customers who mailed in their measurements, this "Javanese" official was amazed at the uncanny fit of his Regent Suit. Now he could just snap on his costume and in an instant, as so many others testified for the catalog, look grand. Finely tailored, both in cut and detail, the figure of "Java" could, at last, express the gratitude of the person it contained in the form of an endorsement from a figure who never came for a fitting in person.

While Mangkunagara VII's Javanologically rendered self provided the newly individualized figure of "Java" with a reflection on inner character, Surakarta clothiers provided that figure a blancon format with which, once filled in, the "Javanese" character might emerge as immediately recognizable. There was thus a certain creative tension between these two takes on identification. The more persuasive the effects of the clothiers' "Javanese" voguing ("I will not hesitate to recommend this to all my friends"), the more effective the prince's appeal ("I have dared to lift a small tip of the veil") to a genuine "Javanese" spirit. It was as if behind the veil of a Regent Suit with yellow ceremonial parasol such a character *had* to exist. And yet, given the specific genealogy of the "Javanese" figure, born as it was from a wardrobe distinction with cara Jawi fashioned in contradistinction to cara Walandi, its newfound subject appeared cloaked in a style that might not fully translate the ontological weight of an *ik,* and thus remain partially unsuitable to a modern rhetoric of individuality. It was in light of this shadowy logic of veils, this unusual fit between subject and style, that yet another, related, early-twentieth-century discourse on the subject of "Java" would prove so compelling.

In 1893, a Surakarta author and "native informant" for Dutch linguists began work on a book in Javanese entitled *Customs and Manners: The Customary Practices and Behavior of Javanese People Who Still Adhere to Superstitions.*[30] In his introduction, the author, Ki Padmasusastra, noted that he felt "crowded out" by all the formal Javanological knowledge produced by Dutch scholars, "as if no place had been allotted him." In response he decided to write the "life of a Javanese person," *any* Javanese. This was quite novel, for never before had there been a book in Javanese on this form of generalized character. His approach was also novel: the story of the "customary practices of a Javanese person, beginning as a baby... until a person's death."[31] The colonized subject thus would be rescued from global anonymity and given a "place," a frame for individuality, and a character whose life as a "Javanese" was endowed with individual ritual meaning.

While Arnold van Gennep was still busy, back in Europe, theorizing the ritual framework that would make his *The Rites of Passage* a foundational classic in anthropological discourse for generations to come, Padmasusastra had already arrived at essentially the same, albeit less grandiose, conclusion. Van Gennep wrote, "[A] man's life comes to be made up of a succession of stages with similar ends and beginnings: birth, social puberty, marriage, fatherhood, advancement to a higher class, occupational specialization, and death."[32] Both writers were responding to the demands on or, more precisely, for identity posed by the advent of modernity. If van Gennep's approach was theoretically universalist, Padmasusastra's was typically generalist.

Composed in dialogical style (resembling that of language primers he had produced for Dutch linguists), the story of a "Javanese life" unfolds serially as a domestic minidrama. Consider the following excerpt from the massive *Customs and Manners* as "Mr. and Mrs. T" prepare for their daughter's wedding:

MR. T: "Have you taken care of all the necessary requirements and preparations for someone about to marry off a daughter?"

MRS. T: "Yes I have, if I haven't missed anything."

MR. T: "What for example?"

MRS. T: "Offerings buried: clay pots filled with dried fish, mung beans, soybeans, macadamia nuts (long ones and flat ones), a wad of betel leaves, chicken eggs, buried in front of the

inner room, near the front door, near the kitchen, and at the
crossroads — with half a bottle oil, and half a bottle water,
mixed together, to be impervious to black magic and other
evil intents... [and on Mrs. T goes, through several pages of
prepared offerings, finishing up with] that's all."

MR. T: "Good, seems as if nothing's been overlooked."[33]

"Javanese" identity emerges here in the form of a trajected composite:
the end product of a prolonged series of customary rites dutifully completed.
Padmasusastra's story is written as if it could be taking place at any time and
anywhere there is a good "Javanese" home. Depicting ritual practices neither rural nor royal, *Customs and Manners* invests its identity with a kind of
eternal transience, a generically "Javanese" state of being compelled to recover its own uncertain origins, always haunted by the sense that something crucial may have been forgotten.

This fear of the forgotten inspires much of the book's dialogue. No
sooner does Mr. T declare, "Good, seems as if nothing's been overlooked,"
than Mrs. T is off again, running down lists of details to reassure him once
more that she has not missed a thing. Such scenes of potential forgetting
underscore Padmasusastra's own fears concerning a "place" in a world now
overtaken by knowledge that is crowding him out. For what the author
seems to have feared most was the possibility that no space would be left,
that the past might no longer be recoverable except through the hands of
European scholars, which is to say that his "Java" might be lost forever. It
was in anticipation of such a loss that Padmasusastra devoted himself to the
character conveyed by *Customs and Manners*. By persistently reminding
his readers of what they may have forgotten, of what might, one day, even
be lost, the author would give that character a place: busy at work as a ritual
subject, repeatedly redeeming its customary identity by self-consciously *not*
forgetting what might have been forgotten.

Future foreign ethnographers searching out instances of rites of passage would find here a perfectly recognizable type referenced within an indigenous rhetoric in much the same manner that nineteenth-century Dutch
scholars had discovered an object of orientalist desire already prefigured as
"Java" in the palace archives and through royal ceremony. Anticipating van
Gennep's formulations of rites of passage by a decade, the Javanese author
effectively reconfirmed the modernist certainty of the reality of tradition,
just the sort of certainty from whose imperial, epistemological framework he
was, as a colonial subject, trying to escape. Later generations of ethnographers
tracking down instances of van Gennep's formulations in Java could now

cite an indigenous account to reaffirm their certainty that such a tradition did exist. Conversely, through such international recognition, "Java" itself became all the more certain of its own being.

From the early 1920s on, and with the founding of the Java Institute, there was such a densely articulated coalescence of formal Javanological interests expressed in Dutch, and similar discursive interests in "traditional Java" expressed in Javanese or Malay, that the underlying subjects of these interests appeared virtually identical. Mangkunagara VII's 1932 appeal to a native *geestelijk ik* would be particularly persuasive because the subject of his lecture, although delivered in Dutch, previously had been introduced by a discourse on the "Javanese person" in Javanese. An initial translation had *already* begun. It remained for the prince to expand the interior space of that subject by lifting a tip of the veil as if to reveal, for a moment, a re-covered spirit. In a similar fashion, Surakarta clothiers' cultural customers could not only easily slip into a "genuinely Javanese" suit, but feel fully comfortable within that blancon form, with its uncanny fit, and say so by expressing themselves in the form of a testimonial letter. The "Java" that seems to have long anticipated cultural recognition could now present itself as a wholly identifiable, individualized subject, front and center. But what of the other "Java" of the displaced realm, the "Java" headed increasingly toward eccentricity and inaccessibility?

Prophetic Conclusions

With this question, we return to our point of departure and the 1939 bicentennial. Just two months before the event, the Palace of Surakarta's tenth "Axis of the Cosmos," Pakubuwana X, a king best known for his power of prophecy, died. The king's prophecies—often numerologically concealed in the exact numbers of trees, pillars, and ornaments built into the design of timely palace additions—pointed to the end of an era, indeed, the end of an entire world that once appeared to revolve around His Majesty's axial being. With his death, the power of "Java" would, in essence, evaporate. Of the king's dozens of offspring by palace concubines, none would be endowed with the special talents associated with kingship. Pakubuwana X thus dubbed his youngest son Prince Barja, a name that in the 1980s the elderly prince still took great pleasure in deciphering: "Prince Barja, that's me, 'the end of prosperity' [bu*bar* ing rahar*ja*]!"

When Pakubuwana X died on February 20, 1939, he did so, amazingly, on the highly charged first day of the Javanese new year, the most powerfully endowed moment cosmologically conceivable. Even the palace's largest and notoriously potent gong, Sir Surak (*surak*: "the noise of spectators cheering"), ceased to sound and would, in fact, remain silent ever after. It was as if the prophecies had been realized, the royal progress of 1745 had arrived at its logical destination, and the contradiction of "Java's" creation had reached a terminal perfection and come to a close entirely of its own accord. Thus, just as the force of "tradition" emerged in works like *Customs and Manners* and signaled the recovery of a world on its way to being past, that past knew that its days were numbered.

Faced with the prophetic conclusions the king's portentous death ushered in, as well as the emergence of the idea of "tradition" as that which would counter such conclusions, the 1939 bicentennial thus recalled the palace as a sign of origins celebrated, rather than rule perpetuated. It was in this spirit that the commemorative volume *Royal Deeds* selected the passages it did from eighteenth-century manuscripts detailing the progress of 1745. Focusing on a scene of origins in which an eighteenth-century Javanese ruler was rescued from retreat within the rhetoric of a royal progress, a "progress" that, quoted out of context, recovered the contradiction of Surakarta's creation, the 1939 volume and event ceremoniously *reiterated* the conditions of that creative contradiction; it did so in the form of a novel bicentennial celebration held at the very moment when the palace was being drained of all dynastic power. The celebration recognized in Surakarta a particularly well-endowed site for recovering the past of "Java": a place immensely capable of discovering its own origins by repeating them.

This repetition prefigured, in turn, future efforts at recovery. On the night of January 31, 1985, the core buildings of the Palace of Surakarta burned to the ground. While official government reports cited electrical short-circuiting as the cause of the fire, members of the royal family and many older Surakartans thought otherwise: "It was already predetermined," noted one palace-affiliated mystic.[34] Long before the fire, prophecies had, in fact, already revealed that the palace itself would not survive two hundred and fifty years. The year 1985 marked two hundred and forty Western years, or two hundred and forty-seven Javanese years, depending upon one's calendrical preference. The contradiction of the creation of "Java" had yet again retraced its origins to a prophetic conclusion, only this time *nothing* would remain save, perhaps, memories of what should now have disappeared.

Enter President Soeharto with a 3.73 billion rupiah "Committee for the Reconstruction of the Surakarta Palace" and this decree: "Traditional rituals *must* be continued!"[35] In 1987, a newly recuperated Surakarta Palace of cultural origins was dedicated, a palace, as newspapers put it, of "even greater elegance and greater authority."[36] But the customary comment from long-term court servants faced with their reconstructed palace was far from enthusiastic:

"Quite handsome, but..." Within the space of this ellipsis remained a difference that reiterated, through absence, the gap across which the authority of "Java" is instituted. For while those with powers of prophecy are particularly gifted at foreseeing an end—in the case of "Java," *the* end—the modern power of cultural discourse, leaning as it does on a sense of essential continuity, appears as that which is perfectly incapable, like the Soeharto regime itself, of really believing that its own days may be numbered.

In near ruins, the charred palace exposed, for a moment, the predetermined logic informing the contradictions of its own construction and, hence, the certainty of its eventual destruction. Exposed, if only for a moment, was "the realization," as Simmel noted at the outset, "of a tendency inherent in the deepest layer of existence of the destroyed." Yet it is precisely the specter of this prophetically endowed moment foreshadowing total disappearance, signaling a point beyond even the strange comfort of ruins, that makes the peculiar power of culture, it would seem, so compelling.

Notes

1. For a translation, see Georg Simmel, "The Ruin," in *Georg Simmel, 1859–1918: A Collection of Essays with Translations and a Bibliography,* ed. Kurt H. Wolff (Columbus: Ohio State University Press, 1959), 259, 263.

2. Claire Holt, *Art in Indonesia: Continuities and Change* (Ithaca, NY: Cornell University Press, 1967), 42.

3. For numerous insights into the status of the Barabudur during Soeharto's New Order times, see Shelly Errington, "Making Progress on Borobudur: An Old Monument in New Order," *Visual Anthropology Review* 9, no. 2 (1993): 32–59.

4. *Suara Merdeka,* February 24, 1983.

5. Ibid., June 6, 1982.

6. For a wonderful introduction to these archives and a brilliant translation and analysis of one particularly provocative text, see Nancy K. Florida's *Writing the Past, Inscribing the Future: History as Prophecy in Colonial Java* (Durham, NC: Duke University Press, 1995).

7. Soepomo Poedjosoedarmo and M. C. Ricklefs, "The Establishment of Surakarta: A Translation from the *Babad Gianti,"* *Indonesia* 4 (1967): 105–108. I have altered the translation here somewhat; all other translations in this essay are my own.

8. R. Ng. Yasadipura, *Babad Prayut* (composed in Surakarta, late eighteenth century; inscribed Surakarta, 1854). Ms. RP B32b; SMP MN 212,161 recto.

9. Yasadipura, *Babad Prayut,* 161 recto–161 verso.

10. Ibid., 163 recto.

11. Ibid., 125 recto–125 verso.

12. *Babad Nitik Mangkunagaran wiwit taun Alip 1707 ngantos dumugi Jé 1718* (composed in Surakarta, 1791; inscribed Surakarta, 1930). RP B29 (typed transliteration of Koninklijk Instituut Ms. KITLV Or. 231), 42 (Ms. 22a).

13. *Babad Nitik,* 42 (Ms. KITLV, 22a).

14. An occasional exception finds *cara Walandi* indicating the Dutch language and *cara Jawi* Javanese language (particularly High Javanese). This is increasingly true of *cara Jawi* from the late nineteenth century on. Refined language, like costume, was displayed with style.

15. An English visitor to the Palace of Surakarta recorded the following in his account of an 1828 royal wedding: "The Pendopos were well lighted with chandeliers, lamps and candles, and a large company was assembled, Europeans and half-caste as well as natives. All the military and Civil Officers, all the Christian population of Solo had been invited. The Susunan [Pakubuwana VI] was also present in an European dress, the coat being an imitation of the full uniform of a general of the Netherlands army, with epaulettes of real gold, very well made and a brilliant star on each breast; he wore a dress sword and military hat with feathers corresponding with the coat, the rest of his dress was plain except the diamond knee and shoe buckles, with white silk stockings, and large clumsy shoes.... He opened the ball with the Resident's lady in an English country dance, in which he performed with more activity than grace, one or two nobles followed his example, the bride's father led out the wife of the commandant, and Lieutenant-Colonel Prince Poroboyo [the future Pakubuwana VII] another European lady, these two princes danced with more ease and grace than the Emperor. After some time, waltzing succeeded, in which also the Emperor performed, first with a very tall gentleman and afterwards with a very little lady, this was a failure. His Highness had sent his billiard table to the party, and during the evening played frequently with some of the Europeans, in pools, as did many of the native nobles. Many of these wore the Dutch military uniform, with Major's or Colonel's epaulettes, some of them were mere boys, the relatives of the Susunan, and it was curious to see them squatting around his chair or running messages for him, reflecting as I thought no distinction on the dress they wore." "Journal of an Excursion to the Native Provinces on Java in the Year 1828, During the War with Dipo Negoro," *Journal of the Indian Archipelago and Eastern Asia* 7 (1853): 17. The author is identified as "J. D. P."

16. *Babad Sangkala* (composed in Surakarta, circa 1831) in [*Klempakan Warniwarni*] (inscribed Surakarta, circa 1831). Ms. SP 6 Ta; SMP KS 1C, pt. 2, 111.

17. Reksadipura, *Pratélan Miyos Dalem Ingkang Sinuhun Kangjeng Susuhunan Pakubuwana VII Kaprabon Garebeg Mulud ing Taun Dal 1775* (composed in and inscribed Surakarta, 1847/8). Ms. RP H42; SMP MN 271C, 6.

18. *Soeloeh Sekatèn* [compiled by "Chronos, Free-lance journalist Indonesier"] (Solo: B. T. Tjioe, 1940), 15 (emphasis added).

19. *Sajarah kanthi Babad Lalampahanipun Kangjeng Gusti Pangéran Adipati Arya Mangkunagara ingkang kaping IV ing Surakarta* (composed in and inscribed Surakarta, 1853–1863). Ms. RP B66; SMP MN 224, 81.

20. K. G. P. A. A. Mangkunagara IV, *Wiwahan Dalem Kangjeng Pangéran Adipati Ariya Prabu Prangwadana*, in *Serat Serat Anggitan Dalem K. G. P. A. A. Mangkunagara IV*, vol. 1, ed. Th. Pigeaud (Soerakarta: Java-Instituut [de Bliksem], 1927), 204.

21. Mangkunagara IV, *Wiwahan Dalem*, 205.

22. R. Atmadikara, *Babad Krama-dalem Ingkang Sinuhun Kangjeng Susuhunan Pakubuwana kaping sanga ing Nagari Surakarta-Adiningrat* (composed in Surakarta, 1865–1866; inscribed Surakarta, mid–late nineteenth century). Ms. Rp 310; SMP RP 59, 52 verso.

23. Arthur Earle, "A Month in Java in 1889" (unpublished manuscript), 36. I am grateful to Nancy Florida for bringing her photocopy of this diary to my attention.

24. Ibid., 32.

25. Ibid., 37–38.

26. K. G. P. A. A. Mangkunagara [Mangkunagoro] VII, *On the Wayang Kulit (Purwa) and Its Symbolic and Mystical Elements,* trans. Claire Holt, Southeast Asia Program Data Paper, no. 27 (Ithaca, NY: Cornell University Press, 1957), 1 (brackets added).

27. Mangkunagara VII, *On the Wayang Kulit,* 19 (brackets added).

28. Sidho-Madjoe, *Geillustreerde Prijscourant* (Surakarta: Tjan Tjoe Twan, 1928), 1.

29. Ibid., 34.

30. Ki Padmasusastra, *Tatacara: Adat sarta Kalakuwanipun Titiyang Jawi ingkang Taksih Lumengket dhateng Gugon Tuhon* (Batavia: Kangjeng Gupremèn, 1907).

31. Padmasusastra, *Tatacara,* iv–v.

32. Arnold van Gennep, *The Rites of Passage* (Chicago: University of Chicago Press, 1966), 3; first published in 1908.

33. Padmasusastra, *Tatacara,* 327–30 (brackets added).

34. K. P. H. Mloyomiluhur, *Kedaulatan Rakyat,* February 4, 1985.

35. *Kedaulatan Rakyat,* February 7, 1985.

36. *Suara Merdeka,* December 10, 1987.

7

Rubber Bands and Old Ladies

Adela Pinch

I

The spectre of a Victorian old lady can be seen haunting contemporary think-ing about culture and gender. I'd like to begin exploring this admittedly ex-travagant hypothesis by introducing a Victorian old lady who emerges in a debate between two of British cultural studies' ancestor figures, Raymond Williams and E. P.Thompson, over what culture and cultural criticism should be. In his 1961 *New Left Review* essays on *The Long Revolution* and *Culture and Society,* Thompson raises some crucial questions about the notions of culture that emerge in those books. He wonders whether Williams's "culture" places too much stress on a shared, coherent community of ideas and feel-ings, and argues for a concept of culture that could instead embrace con-flict and difference. Williams's culture is in Thompson's view simultaneously too broad and too genteel: he points out the costs of Williams's engagement with a single "Tradition" of cultural thought. For Thompson, the figure who characterizes Williams's vision of culture is an old lady:

> At times, in *Culture and Society,* I felt that I was being offered a pro-
> cession of disembodied voices — Burke, Carlyle, Mill, Arnold — . . . the
> whole transmitted through a disinterested spiritual medium. I sometimes
> imagine this medium . . . as an elderly gentlewoman and near relative of
> Mr. Eliot, so distinguished as to have become an institution: The Tradi-
> tion. There she sits, with that white starched affair on her head, knitting
> definitions without thought of recognition or reward (some of them
> will be parcelled up and sent to the Victims of Industry) — and in her
> presence *how one must watch one's* LANGUAGE! The first brash word,
> the least suspicion of laughter or polemic in her presence, and The Tra-

dition might drop a stitch and have to start knitting all those definitions over again.[1]

Thompson is trying to portray the tradition Williams describes as disembodied, detached from the social, and incapable of accommodating conflict. He casts the "disembodied" quality of this view of culture by, conveniently, embodying it in a woman. Vaguely spiritual, mildly neurasthenic, and certainly archaic, this figure is both hypersensitive and maddeningly complacent. She bespeaks the elitism of a culture that gets parceled out to the uncultured masses, and she represents both the intractable, persistent quality of this view of culture (she is like a "near relative" you can't shake) and its fundamental fragility. In an essay that brought this passage to my attention, Laurie Langbauer comments, "A polemic so brash that she would drop her yarn completely, Thompson implies, is the very antidote to the outdated and elitist malaise of history this figure represents." He uses the figure of the old woman, she points out, to "conjure and dispel Williams's Leavisite reliance on the great tradition and to assert instead a culture that really is ordinary."[2] Appearing at the opening of his long essay on Williams, the old lady allows Thompson to begin to replace the vestiges of a reverential, high Arnoldian culture he detects in Williams's work with a culture that might include the "Victims of Industry" as well as its captains.

Why should this debate take place through the figure of a Victorian old lady? Where does this old lady come from, and who exactly does the old lady in Thompson's conceit actually represent? On the one hand she is "The Tradition," high culture's quite masculine parade of Carlyle, Arnold, Eliot, and company, strangely cross-dressed. But on the other hand she represents Raymond Williams himself. Williams is the one who is, famously, "knitting definitions" in *Culture and Society,* tracing out the histories of *culture, class, industry,* and other key words. Thompson's criticism of Williams's concept of culture is inseparable from his objections to Williams's tone and method—including, pointedly, his predilection for *definitions:* "He must be aware that definitions alone are sterile ... to adumbrate a theory of culture it is necessary to proceed from definitions to evidence and back from the evidence to definitions once again."[3] For Thompson, however, the fundamental methodological and conceptual weakness of Williams's excavation of the history of culture is his strategic refusal to engage explicitly with a socialist tradition of cultural thought. Later he casts the battle between Williams's "Tradition" and the social theorists he neglects as a match between a team of sissies and a team of real men: "If Williams had allowed himself to look beyond this island, he might have found a very different eleven of Players fielding against him, from Vico through Marx to Weber and Mannheim, besides whom his own team might look, on occasion, like gentlemen amateurs."[4] The subtext of the old lady passage is quite similar: there Thompson challenges Williams's inattention to class and class struggle by casting it as feminine. The gendered language forms part of the debate over Williams's and Thompson's relationships to Marxism.[5]

It is worth dwelling a little longer on the question of who exactly this old lady is: Where did Thompson get her? She is indeed a relative of Mr. Eliot; Thompson is probably remembering Eliot's early poem "Aunt Helen":

> Miss Helen Slingsby was my maiden aunt,
> And lived in a small house near a fashionable square
> Cared for by servants to the number of four.
> Now when she died there was silence in heaven
> And silence at her end of the street.
> The shutters were drawn and the undertaker wiped his feet—
> He was aware this sort of thing had occurred before.
> The dogs were handsomely provided for,
> But shortly afterwards the parrot died too.
> The Dresden clock continued ticking on the mantlepiece,
> And the footman sat upon the dining-table
> Holding the second housemaid on his knees—
> Who had always been so careful while her mistress lived.[6]

The interest of this poem lies in the way its lines keep making deliberate, small readjustments in what it is saying about the marginality or centrality of this figure in her world; and the story of the poem is the story of the passage from Thompson: the replacement of an old high culture, embodied in the Victorian old lady, with something at once more banal and more vital. It ends with the footman sitting on the dining room table, the housemaid on his knees. In addition to being T. S. Eliot's aunt, Thompson's old lady is also the sister, if she is not positively the same dame, of another endlessly knitting old lady, the "uncanny and fateful" figure who sits outside the company office in *Heart of Darkness*. The "white starched affair" that Thompson's lady wears is, on Conrad's lady's head, a "starched white affair." ("She wore a starched white affair on her head, had a wart on one cheek, and silver-rimmed spectacles hung on the tip of her nose.") In the midst of his mission in Africa, Marlow recalls, "the knitting old woman with the cat obtruded herself upon my memory as a most improper person to be sitting at the other end of such an affair."[7] Like Thompson's gentlewoman, the Fate-like figure in Conrad's book is a ludicrously genteel, feminine figure for an institution she would seem to be antithetical to.

My point in noting these echoes in Thompson's transformation of Williams's "culture" into an old lady is not simply to argue that Thompson's imagination is shaped precisely by the high culture he wishes to displace, or even to tar him with the brush of modernism, though the early modernist resonances of Eliot and Conrad give Thompson's ambivalence further historical substance.[8] For Thompson's purposes (as for Eliot's and Conrad's), this figure's femininity is inseparable from her obsolescence. The phrase "Victorian old lady" always threatens to become triply redundant.[9] Rather my point is to suggest the availability of this figure for such discussions, her ubiquity. What these old ladies share is a logic through which they come to centrally embody institutions—high culture, imperialism—to which they seem to be, *from that very perspective,* marginal.

The second section of this paper is devoted to a Victorian book populated entirely by knitting old ladies who wear starched white caps on their heads and who are likely to drop a stitch when provoked or disturbed. Originally published serially between 1851 and 1853 in Dickens's periodical *Household Words,* Elizabeth Gaskell's novel *Cranford* is about life in a town of genteel spinsters. Like Thompson's gentlewoman, the ladies of Cranford often parcel up the products of their knitting for the "Victims of Industry"; or they may be victims of industry themselves. Like Thompson's old lady, they must be seen as icons in a larger discussion, embodiments of conflicts over conceptions of British culture. Gaskell's old ladies, I will argue, are especially positioned to articulate the nature of a historical moment that is central to both E. P. Thompson's and Raymond Williams's influential visions of "tradition," of culture, of British class-consciousness, the 1840s; and they do so by articulating their relationship to that era's own icons: the new manufactured goods of the industrialized city. In order to determine the place of old ladies in British society, I will argue, Gaskell had to write a book about things. This argument will require an excursus into the meanings of *fetishism,* a term that does not appear in *Cranford,* but to which Dickens's *Household Words* devoted its attention.[10]

But I'd like first to suggest briefly that contemporary feminism, like cultural studies, may have its own Victorian old lady problem. The old Victorian lady seems to appear in popular accounts of the kinds of feminist thinking that are derived from cultural feminism. Cultural feminism, as is well known, is generally taken to be a product of the 1970s, evolving out of a political crisis in the women's movement: it was originally a feminism that conceived of culture as the realm of women's oppression and held that women could be liberated through an alternative "women's culture," a postrevolutionary, authentically female way of life that could itself bring about social transformation.[11] Over the years, the term *cultural feminism* has come to be applied not only to lifestyle feminisms but also to any number of feminisms that believe in and seek to preserve fundamental differences — cultural, moral, psychological, even biological — between men and women. Thus, for example, the widespread dissemination of Carol Gilligan's notion of a feminine "ethics of care" is seen to be an instance of the dominance of cultural feminist ideas. The political costs of this kind of feminism are well known: it seems to renounce political struggle, as well as the principle of equality, and by imagining "woman" as a culturally unified group, minimizes differences of race, ethnicity, class, and sexuality.

Recently, popular media critics of cultural feminism have attacked it by drawing an analogy between its valorization of women's difference and ideas that are believed to be Victorian: the idea that women and men inhabit "separate spheres," and that women's fundamental differences are to be cherished and preserved for the sake of society. Discussing Gilligan's work and Sara Ruddick's *Maternal Thinking* in *The Nation,* Katha Pollitt locates this kind of thinking by arguing that

> the peaceful mother and the "relational" women [put forth by Ruddick and Gilligan] are a kinder, gentler, leftish version of "family values," and both are modern versions of the separate-spheres ideology of the Victorians. In the nineteenth century, too, some women tried to turn the ideology of sexual difference on its head and expand the moral claims of motherhood to include the public realm.

In *Backlash,* Susan Faludi makes very much the same argument, warning that feminists who celebrate women's special characteristics "risked clothing old Victorian conceits in modern academic dress." And in a *New York Times* op-ed piece that served as a warm-up for her controversial book, *The Morning After,* about how we are all too worried about rape, Katie Roiphe suggested that the date-rape manuals penned by "feminists" sounded "like Victorian guides to conduct."[12]

The old Victorian lady, it seems, can represent either a bad version of culture or a bad version of feminism. Such accounts of cultural feminism are certainly right to see a long and problematic history behind current appeals to women's moral superiority, separate-sphere thinking, and sexual vulnerability; nothing is easier to criticize than cultural feminism. In both the discourses of popular feminism and the debates of cultural theory, moreover, the Victorian old lady is likely to evoke and problematize a feminism, or a "culture," that is very white. I'd like simply to raise the following questions: Why does the spectre of Victorianism seem so compelling as an argument against cultural feminism? Is it easier and more convenient to cast the enormous sway of cultural feminism as a version of a past we think we understand than to articulate exactly what role cultural feminism plays in our own political, cultural moment? Does it have to do with feminism's struggle to find a usable past?

II

The prestige of the cultural feminism of the 1970s was crucially extended by the pioneering work in feminist literary criticism of that decade, much of which looked to nineteenth-century literature, and identified there a woman's tradition. Feminist criticism in the 1970s transformed Gaskell's *Cranford* from quaint satire to a novel about women's community. The book is devoted to an almost entirely female village ("Cranford is in the possession of the Amazons," the first sentence tells us) in the 1830s and 1840s and its relation to "the great neighboring commercial town of Drumble" [Manchester] located a distance of "twenty miles on a railroad."[13] To the women who run Cranford—hardly Amazons, but rather proud, impoverished, shabby-genteel spinsters—that relation is one of difference: they pride themselves on their independence, their cultural superiority to the world of Drumble and the world of men. The few masculine figures who do appear pop briefly in and out of the novel in alarming ways. One unfortunate man who moves to Cranford gets run over by the train; another dies promptly after a trip to Paris, only pages after he appears. "A Man," observes one of the Cranford old ladies, "is *so* in the way in the house."[14] While E. P. Thompson casts his Victorian old lady as a reverent guardian of a high literary culture, Gaskell's old ladies's relation to the masculine world of letters combines strong opinion and utter indifference. One of them, Miss Deborah Jenkyns, affiliates herself with Samuel Johnson; but the book's narrator points out repeatedly that Cranford society as a whole simply does not read. They are disdainful of Victorian high culture, falling asleep over Tennyson,[15] hostile to Dickens.[16] Their lives are an endless round of charitable acts and formal social occasions at which they all deludedly conceal their poverty from each other.

Not surprisingly, *Cranford* appears as a crucial text in Nina Auerbach's *Communities of Women: An Idea in Fiction*. For Auerbach, *Cranford* adjudicates between the powers of a "separatist" female community and those of the masculine world.[17] The novel represents a world in which a "cooperative female community defeats the warrior world that proclaims itself the real one."[18] Speaking of the end of the novel, in which Gaskell might seem to establish an alternative economy by setting up the town's main old lady, Matty Jenkyns, with a tea shop (as rumours filter in of businesses collapsing in Drumble), Auerbach sees the town "'triumphing' over the failure of economic and masculine reality": "The atomized city of Drumble lacks the power that makes Matty's tea shop thrive on love and incompetence and the silent cooperative gifts of 'our society.' "[19] While Auerbach carefully balances such moments of her analysis with a sense of the fragility and complexities of this "power," her discussion of *Cranford* and her book as a whole is quite explicitly situated within cultural feminist goals: establishing the legitimacy and the distinctiveness of feminine community. For Auerbach, as for other critics and historians writing in the 1970s, the study of nineteenth-century culture could serve to prove "that female self-sufficiency is not a postulate of this or that generation of feminists, but an inherent and powerful component of our shared cultural vision."[20] Describing women's writings can help create and fill in an adequate picture of the specificity of a woman's culture: "We lack," she laments, "an agreed-upon common denominator of womanhood."[21] Critical activity is designed to create a consensus. From such a perspective *Cranford*'s old ladies, with their knitting needles, starched caps, strange rituals, and genteel sociability, do indeed come to stand for a feminist's vision of a separate culture.

A shift in historical perspective, however, can yield a rather different view of the relationship between Cranford and Drumble. If we see the twenty miles of railroad between them not as the distance between a fading, feminine way of life and the new masculine world of industry, but rather as the distance between the new manufacturing city and the railway suburbs they spawned, this relationship changes. While Cranford is often said to be based on the small town of Gaskell's youth, it clearly also represents the new railway suburbs that by 1850 had become home to a significant portion of the urban-based middle class. The novel's narrator, a shadowy young woman named Mary Smith, describes herself as having "vibrated all my life between Drumble [where her father is a man of business] and [the woman's world of] Cranford."[22] In their massive study, *Family Fortunes: Men and Women of the English Middle Class, 1780–1850,* Leonore Davidoff and Catherine Hall document the ways in which provincial middle-class cultural identity in the first half of the nineteenth century was consolidated precisely through the "vibrations" between the commercial and manufacturing center and the "separate sphere" of the home increasingly located at a distance in the suburb and organized around elaborate concepts of gentility, femininity, and domesticity.[23] From this perspective, Cranford's "women's culture" — its quaintness, its domestic concerns, its obsession with creating gentility in the absence or defiance of the "cash nexus," its disdain for the ways of men — is significant not for the promises it holds of a separatist culture, but as an instance of the gendered nature of mid-Victorian, middle-class identity-formation.

When pushed, moreover, the Cranford women will identify with Drumble rather than against it, as for example when Miss Matty assumes personal responsibility for a Drumble bank in which she holds shares. In a study of transgression in Gaskell's fiction, John Kucich has stressed the aggressive, competitive, and mendacious aspect of the old ladies's world: "Female Cranford society is a world that aggressively pretends to be better than it is, or ever was. Its fundamental lie is that it is different from the commerical world of men in its freedom from competition, in its solidarity and compassion."[24] "It's coming very near!" exclaims Miss Matty on hearing, in another scene, that the prospect of marriage is closer to the spinster world of Cranford than she imagines.[25] Perhaps, we could say, it is the world of Drumble, with its banks, its men, and its "horrid cotton trade"[26] that comes much nearer to Cranford than the Cranford ladies like to think.

Drumble may come closest to Cranford, however, in the form of the manufactured goods—the cotton umbrellas, dresses, and starched white caps, and as we shall see, the rubber bands—it provides; and it is to these goods that I would like to turn our attention. *Cranford* seems at times to be about the petty tyranny of the material world over the human. Goods frequently displace and overwhelm people. On the second page of the book, for example, we learn the history of an umbrella:

> I can testify to a magnificent family red silk umbrella, under which a gentle little spinster, left alone of many brothers and sisters, used to patter to church on rainy days. Have you any red silk umbrellas in London? We had a tradition of the first that had ever been seen in Cranford; and the little boys mobbed it, and called it a 'stick in petticoats.' It might have been the very red silk one I have described, held by a strong father over a troop of little ones; the poor little lady—the survivor of all—could scarcely carry it.[27]

The language of testimony here reflects the narrator's role as reporter to the civilized world about the quaint ways of Cranford. Her question, "Have you any silk umbrellas in London?" signifies how utterly outmoded this umbrella is: by the mid–nineteenth century, silk umbrellas had largely been replaced by cotton umbrellas in drab shades.[28] Vigilant about the social semiotics of objects, the Cranford women are militantly, rather than indifferently, unfashionable: "Their dress is very independent of fashion; as they observe, 'What does it signify how we dress here at Cranford, where everybody knows us?' And if they go from home, their reason is equally cogent: 'What does it signify how we dress here, where nobody knows us?' "[29] Their unfashionableness, I will suggest later, is itself testimony to how seriously the women take material things, their recognition of their uncanny life. Antiquated as it might be, the red silk umbrella is more socialized than the old spinster, the only member of her family left. Decked out and personified, a "stick in petticoats," it takes center stage in this family history, dominating and replacing the woman who totters under it as the subject of narrative.

Gaskell persistently subordinates persons. *Cranford* is a book about the transformations and histories of things rather than people: there is very little human event in Cranford. Men appear and disappear precipitously; the women, with the exception of one discreet death and one notable marriage, persist. (It has been argued that the book's narrator, Mary Smith, develops into a substantial character over the course of the novel, but she remains very much a Mary Smith, a faceless voice.) Things, however, like the red silk umbrella, have life histories. There is the history of the "decline and fall" of a certain muslin gown, now recycled into a window-shade;[30] the history of a twenty-five-year-old pair of boots;[31] the narrative of a lace collar that gets cycled through the digestive system of a cat.[32] We could call the narrator's tendency to put things before people a species of fetishistic digression. After two paragraphs describing the caps and brooches of the ladies at a particular party, the narrator checks herself: "But I am getting on too fast, in describing the dresses of the company. I should first relate the gathering."[33] But Mary Smith is more interested in the hallucinogenic lifelikeness of the brooches, which seem to contain the whole world and to travel around the wearer's body (they are worn "up and down and everywhere"), while the ladies are strangely nonpresent, described as ostriches with their heads buried in their caps, unconscious of the rest of themselves.[34]

Gaskell's experiment in narrating the histories of things takes place amidst a general perception that England was witnessing an unprecedented flow of material goods. During the years *Cranford* was appearing serially in its pages, *Household Words* was full of articles about things, particularly about things as they cycle about in often unpredictable and errant ways. Dickens's essay "Railway Waifs and Strays" evokes a country being crisscrossed, via train, not so much by people but by objects, as lost or forgotten items pursue their own sad journeys. The bundles in the terminal "depositories," or lost-and-founds, "tie up unwritten histories, and journals of travel." "Valentine's Day at the Post-Office" itemizes the many things (toothpicks, fishing flies, samples of hops and corn, a Greek manuscript, pawn tickets, etc.) to be found at the Dead Letter Office, sent unsuccessfully through the mail.[35] 1851, the year *Cranford* began its serialization, was of course a crucial year in the history of things. It was the year of the Great Exhibition of the Works of Industry of All Nations, held in the Crystal Palace in London's Hyde Park. In six months, it was estimated, one-fifth of England's population came to the Crystal Palace to witness its vast display of goods. The Exhibition, organized under the auspices of Prince Albert, was designed to exemplify a new spirit of international peace and diplomacy, a world in which science, entrepreneurship, and industry had replaced war. Though the exhibits of things themselves were organized according to an elaborate taxonomy that grouped things according to both origin and kind (so that, for example, all rubber products appeared together), the Exhibition effectively divided the world up through the world of things.[36]

The power of material goods to redescribe and reorder the globe is in evidence in *Cranford*. For example, one of the advantages of seeing the novel as a book about things is that its things can reveal how the distance between Cranford and Drumble is mediated by a third place: India. The fortunes of the Lancashire cotton trade were completely intertwined with overseas markets, and increasingly with Indian markets. And goods from India crucially cycle into Cranford. When she is ruined by a bank failure, Miss Matty Jenkyns sets up to support herself as an agent of the East India company: the selling of tea from her parlour-turned-shop is deemed to be dramatically less damaging to her gentility than any other business. At the end of the book, Cranford is visited by the Jenkynses' brother Peter, who has been living mysteriously as the "Aga Jenkyns" in India; he returns to rescue Matty and to restore the town to tranquillity and harmony. Cranford thrives not only on infusions of cash and goods from the empire, but on a cultural logic that makes the production and accumulation of such goods appear untainted by the masculine, ungenteel world of Drumble trade. It thus recalls a long history in mercantilist thought that associates women with imported luxury goods. The story things tell, then, is that the Victorian old lady's ability to stand for a female culture may be connected to her ability to represent an imperial economy: Nina Auerbach's Victorian old lady and Joseph Conrad's may be closely related.[37]

But if exotic, foreign commodities afford Cranford a fantasy of its difference from the economy of Drumble, they also speak forcefully of the alien, uncanny ability of things in a commodity system to be transformed, to circulate illicitly, and live endlessly. A mysteriously foreign, turbaned magician comes to Cranford to perform; his visit is closely followed by a panic about a roving band of household thieves, and the old ladies go to strange measures to prevent their household goods from doing disappearing acts like the magician's props. Dangerous, magical powers also attend the white shawl that the Jenkynses' mother is buried with. When Peter Jenkyns runs away to India, his mother dies of grief. The day after she dies, a shawl arrives: "a large, soft, white India shawl, with just a little narrow border all round; just what my mother would have liked...just such a shawl as she wished for when she was married, and her mother did not give it her."[38] The shawl is not simply just what she would have liked; the white shawl that Peter sends also appears as the repetition and transformation of other objects of desire associated with the mother. This sad piece of family history emerges, for example, when Miss Matty Jenkyns and Mary Smith set themselves to sorting through the preceding generation of Jenkyns's letters. The future Mrs. Jenkyns always ends the letters of her courtship by reminding her suitor of a "white 'Paduasoy' ":

> His letters were a curious contrast to those of his girl-bride. She was evidently rather annoyed at his demands upon her for expressions of love, and could not quite understand what he meant by repeating the same thing over in so many different ways; but what she was quite clear about was her longing for a white 'Paduasoy'—whatever that might be; and six or seven letters were principally occupied in asking her lover to use his influence with her parents....to obtain this or that article of dress, more especially the white 'Paduasoy.'[39]

In typical Cranfordian fashion, the white Paduasoy, which the bride succeeds in getting, has its own life history: it turns up in a later letter, recycled into a christening gown.[40] The white India shawl that arrives too late, moreover, documents a historical transformation of the earlier object of desire, the passage of the typically eighteenth-century luxury good—a white Padua silk—of Mrs. Jenkyns's youth, to the archetypical nineteenth-century luxury good: as all readers of Victorian novels know, the India shawl is a recurrent object of desire.[41] But the white shawl turned shroud is also like another pale, fluttering thing, the ancient letters themselves, which Miss Matty decides to burn, watching each one as it rises up the chimney, "in faint white, ghostly semblance."[42] Buried with the dead mother, the shawl is an anomaly. This commodity finds the terminus to its life history in a dead woman's coffin; it is not handed down, passed on, recycled further, like most of the things in Cranford. The white shawl is an angel of death, a ghost, and we can't help sensing that it itself has killed Mrs. Jenkyns, or that at least the decision to bury it with her stems from a recognition of the paradox of material things. The more things are perceived to have a kind of life, the more deathly they become. I am reminded of something Norman Bryson says about the enduring, everyday objects in still-life paintings: "They have the look of dead man's clothes."[43]

In Gaskell's novel, the power of things to explain a social world is inseparable from their frequent appearance as alien intrusions. We may further specify the status of the thing in the text—Gaskell's particular economies of representing them—by focusing our attention on the passage where she most explicitly explores what people actually do with small things. In this passage, an object is withdrawn from circulation and buried, not in a woman's coffin, but in a woman's pocket. I focus on the "India rubber ring," or rubber band, in this passage because unlike the feminine shawls, umbrellas, brooches, and bonnets that make up much of the catalog of Cranford's fetishized objects, the rubber band seems so indifferent to gender, and thus poses a particular problem in a study of women's relation to the material object. I quote this digression into rhopography (the depiction of the small or trivial) in full because it suggests the interplay between the literary paradoxes of representing things and the politics of such an enterprise.[44] The passage begins by defining what the narrator calls the "private economies" that people practice in their everyday lives, putting forth the example of a man who hates the waste of paper:

> I have often noticed that almost every one has his own individual small economies—careful habits of saving fractions of pennies in some one peculiar direction—any disturbance of which annoys him more than spending shillings or pounds on some real extravagance. An old gentleman of my acquaintance, who took the intelligence of the failure of a Joint-Stock Bank, in which some of his money was invested, with stoical mildness, worried his family all through a long summer's day, because one of them had torn (instead of cutting) out the written leaves of his now useless bank-book; of course, the corresponding pages at the other end came out as well; and this little unnecessary waste of paper (his private economy) chafed him more than all the loss of his money. Envelopes fretted his soul terribly when they first came in; the only way in which he could reconcile himself to such waste of his cherished article, was by patiently turning inside out all that were sent to him, and so making them serve again.[45]

(The discussion of envelopes refers to the fact that until the early nineteenth century, letters were folded up, sealed, and mailed without envelopes.) This brings the narrator to a confession of her own in this regard:

> I am not above owning that I have this human weakness myself. String is my foible. My pockets get full of little hanks of it, picked up and twisted together, ready for uses that never come. I am seriously annoyed if any one cuts the string of a parcel, instead of patiently and faithfully undoing it fold by fold. How people can bring themselves to use India-rubber rings, which are a sort of deification of string, as lightly as they do, I cannot imagine. To me an India-rubber ring is a precious treasure. I have one which is not new; one that I picked up off the floor, nearly six years ago. I have really tried to use it; but my heart failed me, and I could not commit the extravagance.

The next paragraph begins,

> Small bits of butter grieve others. They cannot attend to a conversation, because of the annoyance occasioned by the habit which some people have of invariably taking more butter than they want. Have you not seen the anxious look (almost mesmeric) which such persons fix on the article? They would feel it a relief if they might bury it out of their sight by popping it into their own mouths, and swallowing it down.[46]

The digression ends by describing Miss Matty Jenkyns's own particular fixation, the proclivity of candles to melt away.

This passage begins a chapter of *Cranford*; its strings, rubber-bands, and small bits of butter have no relation to the narrative at hand. It raises some questions about what is at stake when one represents the trivial by quite noticeably drawing attention to its status as a digression. The narrator's practice bears a strange relation to the practices she muses on, insofar as she is getting stuck on small things herself, fixing on them an "almost mesmeric" look. That this digression begins with a man who dreads the wasting of paper (and I have left out one sentence in which this man frets whenever he sees his daughters wasting a whole sheet with a letter of a few lines) suggests that we reflect on the narrator's own writerly economy, or extravagance. From this perspective, the passage begins to look like a ludicrous digression on digression. My point is that Gaskell's representation of the small material world is quite different from, say, Dickens's catalog-like evocations of a personified world of objects giddily circulating through the country. It is not, moreover, akin to the *effet de reel* that Barthes famously described in the work of other nineteenth-century realists, in which insignificant material details stand out to signify precisely that they *are* insignificant and empty, and hence signify "the real" that realist narrative aspires to. In this passage from *Cranford,* insignificant things interrupt narrative, foster digression; they get caught up in the nonfigural aspects of the text. From Gaskell's perspective, nineteenth-century material culture — the bank-book, the newly invented envelope, the rubber band — demands a mode of attention that disrupts the formal, representational mode that is thought to be nineteenth-century capitalism's literary mode: the realist novel.[47] This suggests that the real workings of nineteenth-century industrial capitalism, particularly as they affect the sphere of Victorian old ladies, may require an alternative to realist narrative, something more like narrative fetishism.

In its discussion of "small economies," this passage actually describes several different kinds of objects, and different investments in objects. Most notably, while the paper envelopes at the beginning of the passage, and the small bits of butter at the end, are to be *used up,* the narrator's own instances of a "private economy," the string and the rubber band, consist of taking things out of use. In this respect the narrator's insignificant-things-of-choice stand out; and the rubber band, treasured and deified, particularly attracts our mesmeric attention. What is this woman doing with the rubber band?

For this we ourselves must go into a digression on the history of rubber and rubber bands. India-rubber, or *caoutchouc* (which came not from India but largely from Brazil, as rubber plantations in the East Indies were not a significant source of European rubber until after 1870), was one of the miracle products of the nineteenth century. Though samples of "Indian" rubber were brought back as curiosities from South America by early explorers, its use as a manufactured good began in the late eighteenth century. But it was the efforts of Thomas Hancock (inventor of "vulcanized" rubber) and Charles MacIntosh (of rubber raincoat fame) in England in the 1820s (and of Charles Goodyear, of blimp fame, simultaneously in the United States) that transformed rubber into hundreds of everyday uses. Hancock and MacIntosh went into partnership in 1825 and established the largest rubber factory in the country, located as it happens in Manchester (i.e., Drumble). Rubber goods earned their own display at the Great Exhibition in 1851, and contemporary accounts of rubber are full of excitement.[48] An article on "India-rubber" appeared in *Household Words* during the period of *Cranford*'s serialization there; it is full of rubber's ubiquitous bouncings and stretchings:

> Who is not familiar with the coats and capes, the wrappers and over-alls, the sou'westers and leggings, the gloves and gaiters, the air-beds and air-cushions, the neat little India-rubber bands or rings, the maps and prints, the bags and balloons? What with our elasticity and our impermeability, we are certainly becoming a redoubtable race in this nineteenth-century.[49]

Both the writer's identification with rubber goods ("our elasticity and our impermeability") and his sense that all of this rubber qualifies his contemporaries as a specially modern race, comes out elsewhere as well:

> To be elastic, to bend rather than break, is a good old Anglo-Saxon quality for India-rubber, and India-rubber users, to possess. We certainly live in an elastic age. If we cannot break that which opposes us, we bounce away from it with great agility and feel not much the worse for the encounter. There is a fair amount of caoutchouc in the human mind—a useful quality; else we should never bear the knockings and thumpings which the struggle through life brings to us.[50]

I hardly need to comment on the wonderful logic here, whereby the natural properties of the Indian material pass to the Anglo-Saxon manufacturer, becoming perfectly expressive of an imperial, philosophical attitude, an English *sang-froid*. Rubber, with its flexibility, adaptability, and resilience, has an easily personified "character," and that character is an English one.[51] The passage culminates in a description of a Victorian Gumby:

> Look at this little India-rubber gentleman, just purchased brand-new from a toy-shop: you may open his jaws to any extent you please; you can make him laugh, cry, yawn, grin, frown, simper, stare, doze — it is all one to him: he returns into himself again and to the original expression of his countenance, when the pressure from without is removed. He is a self-contained man; a man sufficient unto himself.[52]

The true essence of rubber for the Victorians lies in its flexibility, both its literal flexibility and a metaphorical flexiblity that allowed it to accommodate a wide range of references. But in the description of the Gumby, this supremely anthropomorphic flexibility is combined with an inhuman self-sufficiency. One last quotation from Victorian rubber-mania will further suggest something of rubber's place as a wonder commodity, its relation to the human and the superhuman. In his *Personal Narrative* of his adventures with rubber, inventor Thomas Hancock recounts an old man's reaction to a slab of the stuff in the 1820s: "I remember at that time, when exhibiting a piece of my solid rubber to an old gentleman, he examined it, and on returning it made this remark (which bids fair to be realized): '*The child is yet unborn who will see the end of that.*' "[53] Finally, we should note that "elasticity" — the quality of rubber that for the *Household Words* writer typified the age — is exactly the term introduced by nineteenth-century economic theorists (and particularly the "Manchester School" of economics) to describe the market itself.[54] Rubber was the apotheosis of the commodity, living endlessly, stretching to accommodate the entire commodity system in its image.

 The centrality of rubber to the commodity imagination of mid-Victorian England could be confirmed by looking at the rubber band's place in Gaskell's "private economy" passage. What kind of logic is it that moves the narrator from paper to string, to rubber bands, to butter, to candles? The sequence of the passage charts out very different kinds of material objects with different relations to the material world. Butter and candles are certainly unfortunate choices for the object fetishist: it is part of their essence that their sojourn in the material world is a brief one, as all that is solid melts into grease. Their malleability, their consistency, their relatively unprocessed nature, however, make them more familiar to the human; they are like bodily substances.[55] In the context of this passage, paper and string occupy the other end of the spectrum: relatively durable, less anthropomorphic. In between paper and string on one end and butter and candles on the other, the rubber band combines the fleshliness and flexibility of the latter, with a permanence that transcends that of the former: this rubber band is, we are told, nearly six years old. In this passage the India-rubber ring declares itself the overlooked, the idiosyncratic obsession, but it is also a historically resonant, handily capacious, ur-thing.

Let me dwell on the fleshliness of this particular rubber band: *Cranford,* as I've argued, concerns itself with the often magical processes through which things get recycled and transformed into other things. The rubbber band itself appears to the narrator as a magical transformation, a "deification" of string. I must confess that as I thought about it, this used rubber ring picked off the floor and treasured by a woman began to transform itself, in my mind, into the latex ring of a condom. Have I stretched this rubber band too far? Certainly: there is a critic's as well as a narrator's fetishism. However, it is true that one of the uses to which the exciting new rubber of the nineteenth century was eventually put, though it does not appear in any of Thomas Hancock's exhaustive lists of rubber products, "domestic," "medical," or "nautical," was contraception. Rubber was used for condoms and, later in the century, for the *capote anglais,* or female condom, and "womb veils" and pessaries inserted into the vagina.[56] Rubber's association with fleshliness was close indeed. I point this out as a way of helping us hear the transgressive tinge of the fetish language in this passage. Where has the narrator kept this rubber ring for almost six years: in her pocket, along with the pieces of string? A "precious treasure," a guilty fetish ("my heart failed me"), a "human weakness" she must own to, the rubber ring carries some of the vaguely sexual energy that, as William Pietz has argued, always surrounds discourses of the fetish.[57]

The overdetermined energies—imperceptibly sexual, vaguely transgressive—with which Gaskell invests this encounter between woman and rubber band must now be set back into the context of this digression as a whole. The digression on "private economies" in which the rubber band appears pretends that the practices it describes are, precisely, private and that they run completely counter to real economic rationality. But the passage itself is framed by a reminder of the volatility of the "real" economy: the first example of a "private economy" is a man's careful preservation of a bank book rendered useless by the failure of a joint-stock company. In other words, Gaskell composes this discussion of private economies in the margins of the larger economy, just as the man writes in the blank pages of the bank book.[58] The passage is particularly troubled by women's relationship to the economy represented by the bank book: it is the man's daughters who tear out its leaves. This passage reminds us that *Cranford,* which takes as its subject a community of "poor" spinsters, looks at the mid-Victorian economy from the perspective of a peculiar kind of poverty. The "poverty" that prompts people to practice private economies, irrational scrimpings and savings of the trivial, is obviously not to be measured in financial terms; it speaks of other needs. It redefines poverty in ways particularly appropriate to the paradoxes of the Cranford ladies' poverty. The Cranford ladies are "poor": they are spinsters with no incomes, redundant women who must recycle old dresses into curtains and hide tea-trays under the sofa. But they are solidly members of a middle class; their gentility is unassailable. And as the history of this novel and the history of the figure of the Victorian old lady suggest, their very poverty — the extent to which they appear to be operating on the margins of the "real" economy — has conspired to make them and the gender-based gentility they represent, culturally central.[59]

"What is the proper labor of the consumer?" asks Susan Stewart: "It is a labor of total magic."[60] That the Cranford woman should find a rubber band a treasure, a deification of string, is surely a sign of her alienation from the world in which labor is exploited and rubber bands made, an impoverished or limited perspective on the world. For Marx, writing about capitalism from the point of view of the factory, the labor of the consumer necessarily appeared as a mystification of production that caused things themselves to appear through a superstitious "mist." It may seem strange to invoke Marx on the fetishism of the commodity, a characterization of a systematic misrecognition of the relations between persons and things, in connection with the woman pocketing the rubber band. Surely this is something more rudimentary than what Marx means. Marx's chapter on the fetishism of the commodity and its secrets, however, is as much a Victorian exercise in rhopography ("the commodity appears, at first sight, a very trivial thing...") as is Gaskell's novel. But what Gaskell can suggest to us is the extent to which Marx is descriptively right. That is, Marx may be right in pointing out that people are mistaken in trying to locate the source of value *in* the mysterious properties of things themselves (rather than in relations between persons); but he may also be right that this is what people *do*. To deify, to treasure, to give the ordinary object a history, to overinvest in it, to misread it, is to illuminate the ways in which things in capitalist culture *are* overinvested; from some perspectives, the thing may be the most visible — the only visible — form that such social relations take. *Cranford* can suggest ways of seeing commodity fetishism itself, even as it is described by Marx, not simply as a delusion of capitalism, but as a viable strategy for coping with its effects.[61]

To be a single Victorian old lady, for example, is precisely to have such social relations mediated by and embodied in things.[62] We might specify the "magic," that is, both the politics and the ontological status of the thing, in a commodity fetishism practiced by old ladies by drawing an analogy to the female fetishism theorized by psychoanalytic feminist critics; for, as many theorists have pointed out, Freudian fetishism and Marx's fetishism of the commodity share structural similarities as well as common debts to Victorian thinking. Naomi Schor and Emily Apter have found the possibilities of a fetishism that could be wrested from Freud's emphasis on the masculine fetishist lurking in the very structure of Freudian fetishism itself. Freud's fetishism depends upon a logic of *denegation:* the fetishist attempts to disavow woman's castration by substituting an object for the "missing" phallus, an object that he *knows* is a mere substitute but that he believes in anyway. Schor proposes a female fetishism that appropriates the fundamental oscillations of the fetishist's *denegation,* turning his either/or predicament ("either I recognize the truth of women's castration, or I have the fetish") into an undecidable both/and: the female fetishist embraces wholeheartedly the substitute object in the knowledge that what it substitutes for (the phallus) is itself a substitute.[63]

Like the female fetishist, the Cranford women simultaneously denaturalize the commodity and refuse to dematerialize its fetish nature. They denaturalize things by focusing on their histories, their transformations, and their substitutions rather than on their essences. And we can see their insistence on the *materiality of things* in the women's rigorous unfashionability, their outmoded accessories. The Cranford ladies love to go shopping, but they always desire the *wrong things:* their sense of the magic of things exceeds the participation of those things in a fashion system. Appropriately, one of the central episodes of *Cranford* involves (as I noted earlier) a conjuror coming to town to perform magic tricks with things. The old ladies of Cranford respond to the magician in their usually contradictory ways: "Conjuration, sleight of hand, magic, witchcraft were the subjects of the evening."[64] They are alternately credulous, mystified and sceptical. One, Miss Pole, takes out the encyclopedia to read up on conjuring and declares, wonderfully, that "conjuring and witchcraft is a mere affair of the alphabet."[65] But conjuring is not something the Cranford ladies need to study up on; they are performing a labor of magic on things all the time.

Gaskell is pointing to some of this labor in her digression on private economies, and in particular by narrating the woman's pocketing of the flexible and overdetermined commodity, the rubber band. As we have noted, both the metaphorical concentration of rubber in Victorian culture, and the place of this rubber band along the syntagmatic chain of objects in this passage, point to its centrality, its status as an embodiment of the commodity market itself, and its ability to mediate between the fleshly, the industrial, and the global. A stretching thing, the rubber band is an exemplary embodiment of the way things get stretched. The woman who deifies and treasures the rubber band may be profoundly alienated, but in pocketing it she is also articulating a relationship to an entire commodity system and a particular historical moment.

Can we stretch this rubber band even further and suggest that this highly elastic object of fascination itself images women's flexible conceptual place in the novel? We should not forget that the woman in this passage is the book's narrator, Mary Smith, a not-yet-old Victorian lady, who spends her life "vibrating" between Drumble and Cranford. But more generally, is it not the flexibility of these seemingly unflexible Cranford ladies, the betweenness that makes them both marginal and culturally central, that allows them, moreover, to keep snapping back, like rubber bands as modernism's, or cultural criticism's, or feminism's image of culture?

III

This paper ends with Victorian old ladies as fetishists; it began with the Victorian old lady as a kind of fetish in cultural criticism. Fetishism, as both Apter and Schor point out, engenders fetishism (and the critic who finds that she has written ten pages about a rubber band in a book begins to wonder what is the thing she is writing about).[66] It could be said that in this paper I have replaced a Victorian old lady I don't like—one representing a moribund, coherent, highbrow view of culture or a bad and regressive feminism—with one that I do. The relationship, or the difference, between these old ladies could be further situated within the ambivalent oscillations of fetishism described above. On the one hand, *Cranford* suggests that overvaluing the Victorian old lady is a useful way of understanding capitalism, that the old lady provides a crucial vector or perspective from which to view its effects (and in a society in which currently the average income for women over sixty-five and living alone is currently well below the poverty level, I would suggest that old women are still a useful vector for talking about capitalism's effects).[67] On the other hand, the Victorian old gentlewoman who turns up in the discourses of cultural criticism and popular feminism returns as a fetish when these discourses repress certain things that they know: that "culture" is gendered in its very definitions, for example. Feminism, for one, may not be able to get rid of the Victorian old lady until it comes to terms with the way in which much of its terms are intertwined with nineteenth-century ways of thinking.[68]

I would like to end this discussion by mentioning briefly one final Victorian old lady. Or is she a sheep? Or a shawl? I am referring to the lady shopkeeper in the form of a sheep that Lewis Carroll's Alice encounters in *Through the Looking Glass*. Sitting behind her counter, wearing a "white starched affair" on her head, spectacles at the end of her nose (see Tenniel's illustration) and knitting, this sheep, I would contend, is a demonic version of *Cranford*'s Matty Jenkyns, who also knits behind the counter of her tea shop. Carroll's sheep knits furiously with fourteen knitting needles (she is a veritable multiplying porcupine of knitting needles), as if she were doing the knitting of all the knitting Victorian old ladies rolled into one. This sheep, moreover, owes her appearance in the narrative itself to a process of transformation and condensation: she is a product of the previous scene in the story, in which the hapless White Queen becomes completely muffled up in her wayward white wool shawl, which seems to have a life of its own and travels around her body: "The Queen . . . seemed to have suddenly wrapped herself up in wool."[69] This sheep is thus the natural *source* of the commodity, the commodity itself, the producer (she knits), the female consumer, the shopkeeper, all bundled together, an embodiment of the whole cycle of the object. It makes sense that the circulation of commodities in her shop is giddily accelerated: the objects for sale will not rest, but maddeningly travel around the room "Things flow about so here!" complains Alice; and indeed they do.[70] In this speeded-up tiny shop, the only thing one can possibly grasp is the figure of the Victorian old lady.

Notes

My thanks to Julie Burch for her assistance with the research for this paper, and to Austin Booth, Ann Cvetkovich, Anne Herrmann, Stacy Carson Hubbard, John Kucich, Erin O'Connor, Sherry Ortner, Roger Rouse, Athena Vrettos, and John Whittier-Ferguson for their suggestions.

1. E. P. Thompson, "The Long Revolution," *New Left Review* 9 (1961): 24–25.

2. Laurie Langbauer, "Cultural Studies and the Politics of the Everyday," *diacritics* 22 (spring 1992): 54.

3. Thompson, "Long Revolution," 30.

4. Ibid., 30.

5. See Joan W. Scott's discussion of the gendering of class consciousness in Thompson's work, "Women in *The Making of the English Working Class*," in *Gender and the Politics of History* (New York: Columbia University Press, 1988), 68–90.

6. T. S. Eliot, "Aunt Helen," from *Prufrock and Other Observations* (1917), in *Collected Poems, 1909–1962* (London: Faber and Faber, 1935).

7. Joseph Conrad, *Heart of Darkness* (New York: St. Martin's Press, 1989), 25, 80.

8. Stacy Carson Hubbard has suggested to me that for the modernist writers themselves, this archaic lady might have had a local name and habitation: Virginia Woolf. Wyndham Lewis, for example, conflated Woolf herself with her own icons of "Victorian" old ladyhood—the knitting Mrs. Ramsay, the aging Mrs. Dalloway, the little old lady on the train in her essay "Mr. Bennett and Mrs. Brown"—in order to

scapegoat her as the antithesis of truly modern. Lewis's vision of Woolf is remarkably like E. P. Thompson's old lady: "Mrs. Woolf...apeeping in the half-light...those... half-lighted places of the mind — in which, quivering with a timid excitement, this sort of intelligence shrinks, thrilled to the marrow, at all the wild goings-on! A little old-maidish...I think. And when two old maids...shrink and cluster together, they titter in each other's ears...pointing out to each other the red-blood antics of this or that upstanding figure, treading the perilous Without." See Wyndham Lewis, "Virginia Woolf: 'Mind' and 'Matter' on the Plane of a Literary Controversy," in *Men without Art* (1934; Santa Rosa: Black Sparrow Press, 1987), 139.

9. I would speculate, however, that Thompson's Victorian association of femininity with a culture that seems "disembodied," in some way autonomous from economics and politics, can be heard echoing faintly through more recent and more positive assessments of the relationships between gender and culture. Both commentators who speak from within feminist studies and those who don't tend to affirm the importance of connecting feminist studies with cultural studies on the grounds that women's lives have had a special connection with the realm of culture, that feminism can truly keep the "culture" in cultural studies. This assumption is articulated, for example, in Richard Johnson's account of the relationship between feminism and cultural studies in his essay "What Is Cultural Studies Anyway?" *Social Text* 6 (1987): "[feminism and antiracism] have kept the left new," rescuing it from focusing too exclusively on economics and politics; feminism has contributed by bringing " 'aesthetic' concerns to bear on social issues" (40). Feminist accounts of cultural studies often yield similar positions. See for example Sarah Franklin, Celia Lurie, and Jackie Stacy, "Feminism and Cultural Studies: Pasts, Presents, Futures," *Media, Culture and Society* 13 (1991): 171–92; Cora Kaplan, "Introduction," in *Sea Changes: Culture and Feminism* (London: Verso 1986), 1–12.

10. See John Hollingshead, "Fetishes at Home," *Household Words* 17 (April 24, 1858): 445–47. On Thompson's and Williams's conflicting visions of the 1840s, see Thompson, "The Long Revolution," where Thompson says of William's vision, "I have spent a good deal of time in the 1840s, and his 1840s are not mine" (28).

11. For an interesting account of the emergence of cultural feminism, see Alice Echols, *Daring to Be Bad: Radical Feminism in America, 1967–1975* (Minneapolis: University of Minnesota Press, 1989). Proponents of a women's culture in the 1970s truly focused on culture: in an interview published in 1975, Robin Morgan spoke of ·vomen's culture, their women's poetry and art, as an "absolute necessity....It is not cultural nationalism, it is not self-indulgence....Culture is breath, it is oxygen to us as an oppressed people who have never spoken in our own voice." See "Adrienne Rich and Robin Morgan Talk about Poetry and Women's Culture," *The New Woman's Survival Sourcebook* (New York: Knopf, 1975), 106. See also Barbara Burris et al., "The Fourth World Manifesto," *New Woman's Survival Sourcebook*, 341: "A FEMALE CULTURE EXISTS. IT IS A CULTURE THAT IS SUBORDINATED AND UNDER MALE CULTURE'S COLONIAL, IMPERIALIST RULE ALL OVER THE WORLD. UNDERNEATH THE SURFACE OF EVERY NATIONAL, ETHNIC, OR RACIAL CULTURE IS THE SPLIT BETWEEN THE TWO PRIMARY CULTURES OF THE WORLD — THE FEMALE AND THE MALE CULTURE." For a discussion of how the principles of cultural feminism became enshrined in feminist theory, see Linda Alcoff, "Cultural Feminism versus Poststructuralism: The Identity Crisis in Feminist Theory," *Signs* 13 (1988): 405–36.

12. Katha Pollitt, "Are Women Morally Superior to Men?" *The Nation,* December 28, 1992, 804; Susan Faludi, *Backlash: The Undeclared War on American Women* (New York: Crown, 1991), 327; Katie Roiphe, "Date Rape Hysteria," *New York Times,* November 20, 1991. Roiphe repeats this charge in her book, where contemporary feminists' responses to sexual harrassment are also likened to the views expressed in one particular Victorian lady's text, Charlotte Perkins Gilman's *Herland, The Morning After: Sex, Feminism, and Fear on Campus* (Boston: Little, Brown, 1993), 60, 87.

13. Elizabeth Gaskell, *Cranford* (Harmondsworth: Penguin, 1976), 39. Two excellent recent essays have focused on the material object in *Cranford* from perspectives different from my own. Andrew H. Miller's "The Fragments and Small Opportunities of *Cranford,*" *Genre* 25 (spring 1992): 91–111, discusses the writing of detail and of every life from the perspectives of Michel de Certeau and Henri Lefebvre; in *"Cranford* and the Victorian Collection," *Victorian Studies* 36 (winter 1993): 176–206, Tim Dolin places the novel's mode of organizing things in the context of Victorian women's household collections.

14. Gaskell, *Cranford,* 39.

15. Ibid., 76–77.

16. Ibid., 47–48.

17. Nina Auerbach, *Communities of Women: An Idea in Fiction* (Cambridge: Harvard University Press, 1978), 98.

18. Ibid., 87.

19. Ibid., 86.

20. Ibid., 6.

21. Ibid., 31.

22. Gaskell, *Cranford,* 211.

23. Leonore Davidoff and Catherine Hall, *Family Fortunes: Men and Women of the English Middle Class, 1780–1850* (Chicago: University of Chicago Press, 1987).

24. John Kucich, "Transgression and Sexual Difference in Elizabeth Gaskell's Novels," *Texas Studies in Language and Literature* 32 (1990): 204.

25. Gaskell, *Cranford,* 166.

26. Ibid., 106.

27. Ibid., 40.

28. For fashions in umbrellas, see Alison Adburgham, *Shops and Shopping: 1800–1914* (London: Allen and Unwin, 1964).

29. Gaskell, *Cranford,* 40.

30. Ibid., 164.

31. Ibid., 169.

32. Ibid., 125–26.

33. Ibid., 120.

34. Ibid.

35. Charles Dickens,"Railway Waifs and Strays," *Household Words,* December 20, 1850; Charles Dickens and W. H. Wills,"Valentine's Day at the Post Office," *Household Words,* March 30, 1850, 6–12; see also George Sala,"Old Clothes!" *Household Words,* April 17, 1852, 93–98; W. H. Wills and Charles Dickens, "My Uncle," *Household Words,* December 6, 1851, 241–46.

36. On the Great Exhibition, see Christopher Hobhouse, *1851 and the Crystal Palace* (London: John Murray, 1951); C. H. Gibbs Smith, *The Great Exhibition of*

1851 (London: Victoria and Albert, 1964). For an account of the effects of the Exhibition on Victorian anthropological thinking about culture, see George Stocking, *Victorian Anthropology* (New York: The Free Press, 1987). Thomas Richards's *The Commodity Culture of Victorian England: Advertising and Spectacle, 1851–1914* (Stanford: Stanford University Press, 1990) sees as the fundamental problem of Victorian culture the question of how to go about representing the commodity. For Richards, the dominant mode of the commodity from the mid–nineteenth century on was the semiotics of spectacle. See especially his interesting discussion of the cultural effects of the Great Exhibition of 1851, "The Great Exhibition of Things," 17–72.

37. This line of reasoning has become a familiar old Victorian story: see Gayatri Spivak, "Three Women's Texts and a Critique of Imperialism," *Critical Inquiry* 12, no. 1 (1985): 243–61.

38. Gaskell, *Cranford,* 102.

39. Ibid., 86.

40. Ibid., 87.

41. In the first chapter of Gaskell's *North and South* (1855), for example, the heroine stands as a mannequin so that the India shawls of her wealthy cousin's trousseau may be displayed before envious eyes. See Adburgham, *Shops and Shopping,* 98–100.

42. Gaskell, *Cranford,* 86.

43. Norman Bryson, *Looking at the Overlooked: Four Essays on Still Life Paintings* (Cambridge: Harvard University Press, 1990), 144.

44. I follow Norman Bryson's use of the term *rhopography;* see *Looking at the Overlooked,* 60–95, especially chapter 2, n. 2, 182–183.

45. Gaskell, *Cranford,* 83.

46. Ibid., 83–84.

47. This is not the only place in *Cranford* where material objects are paired with a consciousness of unseemly narrative excursion. It happens as well in the passage where Mary Smith tells of the ladies' brooches before she tells of the ladies (120). There is also Mrs. Forrester's epic history of the lace collar that gets eaten and regurgitated by a cat (125–26), recounted by the narrator as an instance of socially inappropriate narrative.

48. For the history of rubber, see Thomas Hancock, *A Personal Narrative of the Origin and Progress of the Caoutchouc or India Rubber Manufacture in England* (London, 1857); Charles Goodyear, *Gum-Elastic* (1853); William Woodruff, *The Rise of the British Rubber Industry in the Nineteenth Century* (Liverpool: Liverpool University Press, 1958). The rubber band of the kind found in *Cranford* was patented in the 1840s. On rubber in the Great Exhibition of 1851, see Asa Briggs, *Victorian Things* (London: Batsford, 1988).

49. George Dodd, "India-Rubber," *Household Words,* March 12, 1853, 32.

50. Ibid., 29.

51. The possibilities of rubber for matters of character were fully exploited by Dickens. *Pickwick Papers* is apparently full of instances of the elasticity of mind and body: a Mr. Dowler, for example, "bounced off the bed as abruptly as an india-rubber ball." Mr. Carker in *Dombey and Son* has a smile like india-rubbber. Thanks to Erin O'Connor for bringing these passages to my attention.

52. Dodd, "India-Rubber," 29.

53. Thomas Hancock, *Personal Narrative,* 14; italics in the original.

54. For the use of the notion of the elasticity of supplies and demands in the work of David Ricardo and others, see William Grampp, *The Manchester School of Economics* (Stanford: Stanford University Press, 1960), 20–21.

55. On the fleshliness of butter, see Harriet Martineau, "Butter," *Household Words,* December 25, 1852, which proposes that all peoples of the world, especially those in dry climates, need to eat butter to keep their flesh from drying out: "An effusion of oil into the human frame is necessary to life" (344). Thanks to Erin O'Connor for this reference.

56. See Angus McLaren, *A History of Contraception* (Oxford: Basil Blackwell, 1990); Marie Carmichael Stopes, *Contraception: Its Theory, History, and Practice* (London: J. Bale, Sons, and Danielsson, 1929).

57. William Pietz, "The Problem of the Fetish," pt. 1, *Res* 9 (1985). On the fetish as something that is pocketed, Pietz notes in his complex genealogy of the concept, that a common thread of fetish discourse is the material fetish's relationship to the embodied individual. Medieval Portuguese, for example distinguished the *feitico,* a fabricated object worn about the body, from the *idolo* (10).

58. The failure of a joint-stock company is later central to the events of *Cranford;* the failure of such a bank "ruins" Miss Matty Jenkyns, causing her to go into the tea business. Rumours of the failure of Matty's bank are accompanied by general rumblings about bad business in Drumble, effecting even the narrator's father. *Cranford* is as concerned with the economic volatility of industrial England as are Gaskell's "Condition of England" novels. See Andrew H. Miller, "Subjectivity, Ltd: The Discourse of Liability in the Joint Stock Companies Act of 1856 and Gaskell's *Cranford,*" *ELH* 61 (1994): 139–57.

59. For a discussion of the way the power of one extremely dominant Victorian old lady, Queen Victoria herself, was linked to the image of the queen as the archetypal female consumer (and to the use of her image in advertising), see Thomas Richards, "The Image of Victoria in the Year of the Jubilee," in *Commodity Culture of Victorian England,* 73–118. Regarding the history of the novel, *Cranford* gained its enormous popularly only after Gaskell herself had become a dead Victorian old lady in 1865, and it reached the height of its popularity in the period between 1899 and 1910, during which time it was reprinted *seventy-five times.* In other words, *Cranford* was most popular around the time of Conrad and Eliot: its gender has always been central to its obsolescence.

60. Susan Stewart, *On Longing: Narratives of the Miniature, the Gigantic, the Souvenir, the Collection* (1984; Durham: Duke University Press, 1993), 164.

61. For a reading of Marx to which I am much indebted here, see Ann Cvetkovich, "Marx's *Capital* and the Mystery of the Commodity," in *Mixed Feelings: Feminism, Mass Culture, and Sensationalism* (New Brunswick: Rutgers University Press, 1992), especially 191–97.

62. For a glimpse of a "real life" Cranford lady, with Cranford-like attachment to material goods, see Davidoff and Hall's account of the will of Maria Cadbury (1800–87), unmarried daughter of a Birmingham draper: "Her will provides a testimony of the social and emotional world of a single woman of modest independent means. . . . Her favorite family memorabilia were left to her beloved sister Emma . . . and precious teaspoons, sauce ladles, and sugar tongs were left to her many neices and nephews," in *Family Fortunes,* 58–59.

63. See Naomi Schor, "Female Fetishism: The Case of George Sand," in *The Female Body in Western Culture*, ed. Susan Rubin Suleiman (Cambridge: Harvard University Press, 1986), 363–72, and *Reading in Detail: Aesthetics and the Feminine* (New York: Methuen, 1987); Emily Apter, *Feminizing the Fetish: Psychoanalysis and Narrative Obsession in Turn-of-the-Century France* (Ithaca, NY: Cornell University Press, 1991). Schor is particularly indebted to Sarah Kofman's valorization of fetishism in "Ca Cloche," in *Les fins de l'homme: A partir du travail de Jacques Derrida*, ed. Philippe Lacoue-Labarthe and Jean-Luc Nancy (Paris: Galilee, 1981), 89–132. Kofman asks, "Pourquoi c'est si mal d'etre fetichiste?" (99). Fetish discourses of various kinds have been revalorized from a number of different perspectives recently: these discussions seem to address historical conjunctions between heterogenous social systems (Western and non-Western for example); they seem to embrace practices of signification that subvert enlightenment thinking. See, for example, in addition to the works by Apter, Schor, and Pietz cited above, *Fetishism as Cultural Discourse*, ed. Emily Apter and William Pietz (Ithaca, NY: Cornell University Press, 1993); Arjun Appadurai, "Introduction" to *The Social Life of Things: Commodities in Cultural Perspective* (Cambridge: Cambridge University Press, 1986). On the significance of the outmoded, I am indebted to Michael Taussig's discussion of Benjamin's essay on surrealism,"Surrealism: The Last Snapshot of the European Intelligentsia," in *Mimesis and Alterity* (New York: Routledge, 1993), 212–35.

64. Gaskell, *Cranford,* 131.

65. Ibid., 132.

66. Apter, *Feminizing the Fetish,* 2; Schor, "Female Fetishism," 363.

67. Statistic reported on National Public Radio, August 11, 1993.

68. On how feminism's terms have been shaped and limited by their persistent debts to nineteenth-century social theory, see Rosalind Coward's *Patriarchal Precedents: Sexuality and Social Relations* (London: Routledge and Kegan Paul, 1983); and Michelle Z. Rosaldo, "The Use and Abuse of Anthropology in Feminist Theory," *Signs* 5 (1980): 389–417.

69. Lewis Carroll, *Alice in Wonderland and Through the Looking-Glass* (1871; reprint, New York: W. W. Norton, 1971), 153.

70. Ibid., 154.

8

Live Sex Acts
[Parental Advisory:
Explicit Material]

Lauren Berlant

I am a citizen of the United States, and in this country where I live,
every year millions of pictures are being made of women with our legs
spread. We are called beaver, we are called pussy, our genitals are tied
up, they are pasted, makeup is put on them to make them pop out of a
page at a male viewer. . . . I live in a country where if you film any act
of humiliation or torture, and if the victim is a woman, the film is both
entertainment and it is protected speech. Now that tells me something
about being a woman in this country.[1]

I open with the preceding passage not simply to produce in advance the
resistances, ambivalences, and concords that inevitably arise when someone
speaks with passion and authority about sex and identity, but also to foreground here the centrality, to any public politics of sexuality, of coming to
terms with the conjunction of making love and making law, of fucking and
talking, of acts and identities, of cameras and police, and of pleasure in the
text and patriarchal privilege, insofar as in these couplings can be found
fantasies of citizenship and longings for freedom made in the name of national culture.

I'm going to tell you a story about this, a story about citizenship in the
United States. It is about live sex acts, and a book called *Live Sex Acts,* and
a thing called national culture that, in reference to the United States, I mean
to bring into representation here—which is hard, because the modality of
national culture in the United States that I will describe exists mainly as a
negative projection, an endangered species, the shadow of a fetish called
normalcy, which is currently under a perceived attack by sex radicals, queers,

173

pornographers, and pop music culture. This perceived attack on national morals raises a number of questions. What kinds of forces in national life are being both marked and veiled by the culturally defensive demonization of atypical sexualities? And if sex and sensuality radicals were really circulating a kind of pleasure acid that could corrode the American Way of Life, what about it exactly would they be attacking?

Three vulnerable spots on the national terrain should be flagged from the very outset: the first is the national future. Because the only thing the nation form is able to assure for itself is its past, its archive of official memory, it must develop in the present ways of establishing its dominion over the future. This is one reason reproductive heterosexuality and the family always present such sensitive political issues. Reproduction and generationality are the main vehicles by which the national future can be figured, made visible, and made personal to citizens otherwise oblivious to the claims of a history that does not seem to be about them individually. The anxieties surrounding the process of making people into national subjects confirm that the hegemonic form of national culture is fragile and always in the process of being defined, even when it appears as a thing with an essential character that can be taken prisoner, like the soul in fierce battles between rival gangs of angels and devils.

Once it is established that national culture demands a continuous pedagogical project for making people into "private citizens" who understand their privacy to be a mirror and a source for nationality itself, it becomes equally important that the national culture industry generate a mode of political discourse in which the nation form trumps all other images of collective sociality and power. However, the content of the nation's utopian project has been complicated during the rise of the Reaganite right. One axiom of this ideology has been to destroy an image of the federal state that places its practice at the center of nation formation. The right's attempt to shrink domestic government and thereby to hack away at the hyphen between the nation and the state has required the development of new technologies of patriotism that keep the nation at the center of the public's identification while shrinking the field of what can be expected from the state.[2]

During the last twenty years as well, the sexual minorities of the United States—heterosexual women, gays, and lesbians—have developed sexual publics that not only demand expanded protections from the state and the law but also challenge the practices, procedures, and contents of what counts as politics, including questioning whether the nation form as such should continue to organize utopian drives for collective social life. Additionally, using the forms of publicity that capitalist culture makes available for collective identifications, some of these sex publics have exposed contradictions in the free market economics of the Right, which names nonmarital sex relations as immoral, while relations of economic inequality, dangerous workplaces, and disloyalty to employees amount to business as usual, not provoking any ethical questions about the privileges some citizens enjoy. These complex challenges, posed by a diverse set of sex and sensual publics, are therefore both central to how citizenship must be thought of as a question of sexuality, and convenient distractions from the conservative project of installing a sanitized image of normal culture as the nation's utopian aspiration.

One result is that the national culture industry is also in the business of generating paramnesias, images that organize consciousness not by way of explicit propaganda, but by replacing and simplifying memories people actually have with images—traces of political experience about which people can have political feelings that link them to other citizens and to patriotism. This process veils, without simply suppressing knowledge of, the means by which the nation's hegemonic contradictions and contingencies are constructed, consented to, displaced, and replaced by images of normal culture that "the people" are said already to accept. In this chapter the space of crisis is held by the image of extremist and hypersexualized citizens that has been recently generated in the struggle over what will count as the core national culture. Most of the time political discourse about sex in this modality is a way of creating instant panic about the fragility of people's intimate lives; most of the time, extravagant sex is a figure for general social disorder, and not a site for serious thinking and criticism about sexuality, morality, or anything. But the relation between national knowledge and amnesia is not one of mutual negation. Instead, we never really know whether the forms of intelligibility that give citizens access to political culture are monuments to false consciousness or are the inevitable partial truths of publicly held information. Michael Taussig argues that state knowledge is a site of the full "coming together of reason and violence" that generates paradoxes of knowing and unknowing, such that ordinary pragmatic detail, good-enough comprehensions of national activity, and traumatized pseudoknowledges together can be said to constitute the ongoing lived relations among states, national ideology, and citizens.[3] Along with drawing attention to sexuality and its place in the contemporary construction of U.S. citizenship, the sex culture wars I investigate here provide a way of exploring what different kinds of national worlds are brought into being by different conceptions of sex.

This chapter began as a review of some recent feminist work on pornography.[4] In it I take no position on "pornography," as such, but discuss it in terms of how, more broadly, the U.S. citizen's vulnerability and aspiration to a nationally protected identity has been orchestrated by a national culture industry that emphasizes sexuality as the fundamental index of a person's political legitimacy. In this regard the chapter refocuses the discussion of sex and representation away from the domain of the politics of sexual difference and toward the conjunction of sexuality, mass culture, and mass nationality.

In particular, I am interested in tracing some meanings of privacy, a category of law and a condition of property that constitutes a boundary between proper and improper bodies, and a horizon of aspiration vital to the imagination of what counts as legitimate U.S. citizenship. Privacy here describes, simultaneously, a theoretical space imagined by U.S. constitutional and statutory law; a scene of taxonomic violence that devolves privilege on certain actual spaces of practical life; a juridical substance that comes to be synonymous with secure domestic interiority; and a structure of protection and identity that sanctions, by analogy, other spaces that surround, secure, and frame the bodies whose acts, identities, identifications, and social value are the booty over which national culture wages its struggle to exist as a struggle to dominate sex.

Thus, this story will indeed contain graphic images, parental advisories, and magical thinking, that is to say, the usual dialectic between crassness and sublimity that has long dressed the ghosts of national culture in monumental forms, and made it available for anxious citizens who need to invoke it on behalf of stabilizing one or another perceived social norm. This story has real and fictive characters, too: John Frohnmayer, Andrea Dworkin, Tipper Gore, and some fat, queer Nazis who try to join the military; but its main players are a little girl and an adult, both Americans. The little girl stands in this chapter as a condensation of many (infantile) citizenship fantasies. It is in her name as future citizen that state and federal governments have long policed morality around sex and other transgressive representation; the psychological and political vulnerability she represents has provided a model for other struggles to transform minority experience in the United States. And it is in her name that something other to her, called, let's say, "adult culture," has been defined and privileged in many national domains, although not without its contradictions: we have the "adult" by whose name pornography is marked, as in "adult books," and the one who can, on the other hand, join with other adults to protect the still unhistorical little girl whose citizenship, if the adults act as good parents, might pass boringly from its minority to what has been called the "zone of privacy" or national heterosexuality that "adult" Americans generally seek to inhabit.

"Zone of privacy" is a technical phrase, invented in a Supreme Court opinion of 1965. It was Justice William O. Douglass's opinion in *Griswold v. Connecticut* that designated for the first time the heterosexual act of intercourse in marital bedrooms as protected by a zone of privacy into which courts must not peer and with which they must not interfere. Justice Douglass's rezoning of the bedroom into a nationally protected space of privacy allowed married citizens of Connecticut for the first time to purchase birth control. It sought to make national a relation that it says precedes the Bill of Rights. It consolidated the kind of thinking that happened when the Justices recently, in *Bowers v. Hardwick,* confirmed the irreducible heterosexuality of the national bedroom, as it established once again that homosexuality has no constitutionally supported privacy protections in the United States. It could have been otherwise. Writing a memo to be circulated among Supreme Court Justices, Daniel Richman, a clerk for Thurgood Marshall, sought to instruct the Court about oral and anal sex. He wrote to the Justices, in capital letters, "THIS IS NOT A CASE ABOUT ONLY HOMOSEXUALS. ALL SORTS OF PEOPLE DO THIS KIND OF THING."[5] He does not name the "sorts" of people. But in almost referring to heterosexuality, that sacred national identity that happens in the neutral territory of national culture, Richman almost made the "sex" of heterosexuality imaginable, corporeal, visible, public.

Thus, I mean to oppose a story about live sex acts to a story about "dead citizenship." Dead citizenship, which haunts the shadowland of national culture, takes place in a privacy zone, and epitomizes an almost Edenic conjunction of act and identity, sacred and secular history. It involves a theory of national identity that equates identity with iconicity. It requires that I tell you a secret history of acts that are not experienced as acts, because they take place in the abstract idealized time and space of citizenship. I use the word *dead,* then, in the rhetorical sense designated by the phrase "dead metaphor." A metaphor is dead when, by repetition, the unlikeness risked in the analogy the metaphor makes becomes so conventionalized as to no longer seem figural, no longer open to history: the leg of a table is the most famous dead metaphor. In the fantasy lifeworld of national culture, citizens aspire to dead identities: constitutional personhood in its public abstraction and suprahistoricity; reproductive heterosexuality in the zone of privacy. Identities not live, or in play, but dead, frozen, fixed, or at rest.

The fear of ripping away the privacy protections of heteronational culture has led to a national crisis over the political meanings of imaginable, live, and therefore transgressive sex acts, acts that take place in public either by virtue of a state optic or a subcultural style. By bringing more fully into relief the politics of securing the right to privacy in the construction of a sexuality that bears the definitional burden of national culture, I am in part telling a story about preserving a boundary between what can be done and said in public, what can be done in private but not spoken of in public, and what can, patriotically speaking, neither be done nor legitimately spoken of at all in the United States. Thus there is nothing new about the new national anthem, "Don't Ask, Don't Tell, Don't Pursue." I am also telling a story about transformations of the body in mass national society, and thinking about a structure of political feeling that characterizes the history of national sentimentality, in which, at moments of crisis, persons violate the zones of privacy that give them privilege and protection in order to fix something social that feels threatening: they practice politics, they generate publicity, they act in public, but in the name of privacy. I mean to bring into representation these forms of citizenship structured in dominance, in scenes where adults act on behalf of the little girl form that represents totemically and fetishistically the unhumiliated citizen.[6] She is the custodian of the promise of zones of privacy that national culture relies on for its magic and its reproduction.

Looking for Love in All the Wrong Places: Live Sex Acts in America

When John Frohnmayer made his pilgrimage to serve the National Endowment for the Arts (NEA) in Washington, he was a "babe in the woods" of politics who hoped to "rekindl[e]" the "free spirit" of the nation, a spirit now endangered by television and other mass-mediated forms of alienation in the United States.[7] He initially imagined using the NEA to reproduce the nation through its localities, emphasizing not cities (which are, apparently, not localities), but the rural and provincial cultures whose neglected "vitality" might help return the mass nation to a non-mass-mediated sense of tribal intimacy. Frohnmayer's autobiography, *Leaving Town Alive: Confessions of an Arts Warrior,* describes in great detail the deep roots of the nation in aesthetic genealogies of an organic citizenry: for example, he tells of the gospel roots of rap, the spirit of fiddling in an age of "overamplified electronic music," native American weaving, ballet, and other arts that make "no mention of homosexuality, foul words, or nudity,"[8] which, according to this logic, become phenomena of cities and of mass culture.

Yet his ambitions for cultural reformation did not protect Frohnmayer's tenure at the NEA, which was so riddled by the competition between a certain metropolitan and an uncertain national culture that he was driven out of office. The cases of the X, Y, and Z portfolios of Robert Mapplethorpe, of the NEA Four, and of *Tongues Untied* are famous examples of how sex-radical performance aesthetics were inassimilable by the homophobic and mock-populist official national culture-making machine that currently dominates Washington. But what got Frohnmayer actually fired was the NEA's support of a *literary* publication project in New York City that dragged the nation into the dirt, the waste, and the muck of sex and other gross particularities. This project, managed by a press called "the portable lower east side," produced two texts in 1991: *Live Sex Acts* and *Queer City*. The Reverend Donald Wildmon made these texts available to every member of Congress, President George Bush, and Vice President Dan Quayle. He also wrote a letter to them citing an excerpt from a poem as evidence for the virtually treasonous use of taxpayer money to support art that besmirched national culture.

My first exhibit, or should I say, my first "inhibit," is the poem "Wild Thing," written by the poet "Sapphire" (Ramona Lofton), and published in *Queer City*. "Wild Thing" is written in the fictive voice of one of the boys whose wilding expedition in 1989 resulted in the rape and beating of the woman called "the Central Park jogger." Here is the excerpt from the poem that Wildmon sent to Congress:

> I remember when
> Christ sucked my dick
> behind the pulpit
> I was 6 years old
> he made me promise
> not to tell no one.[9]

I will return to this poem, but first let me characterize the scandalous magazines that were the context for it. Frohnmayer describes *Queer City* accurately: "Although some of the pieces were sexual in tone and content, they were clearly meant to be artful rather than prurient."[10] *Queer City* is a collective work of local culture, positing New York as a vibrant site of global sexual identity, a multinational place where people come to traverse the streets, live the scene, have sex, write stories and poems about it, and take pictures of the people who live it with pleasure and impunity. It is an almost entirely apolitical book, except in the important sense that the title *Queer City* remaps New York by way of the spaces where queer sex takes place, so that sexual identities are generated in *public*, in a metropolitan public constituted by a culture of experience and a flourish of publicity.

In contrast, and although *Live Sex Acts* is also situated in New York City, a marked majority of its texts explain sex in terms of the national context and the political public sphere; indeed, many of the essays in *Live Sex Acts* are explicit responses to the right-wing cultural agenda of the Reagan revolution. They demonstrate that it is not sexual identity as such that threatens America, which is liberal as long as sex aspires to iconicity or deadness, but suggest rather that the threat to national culture derives from what we might call sex acts on the live margin, sex acts that threaten because they do not aspire to the privacy protection of national culture, nor to the narrative containment of sex into one of the conventional romantic forms of modern consumer heterosexuality. This assertion of a sexual public sphere is also striking because *Live Sex Acts* closes by moving beyond a sexual performance ethic and toward other live margins. Two final segments, Krzysztof Wodiczko's "Poliscar: A Homeless Vehicle" and a portfolio of poems by patients at Creedmoor Psychiatric Hospital, explicitly seek to redefine citizenship by naming who lives on the live margins, and how.[11] They show how the waste products of America must generate a national public sphere and a civic voice. To do this, the live margin must find its own media. A radically redefined category of live sex acts here becomes a mass medium for addressing and redressing the official national culture industry.

In any case, as Frohnmayer says, the scandal these two magazines created had nothing to do with what kinds of subversive effect their small circulation might conceivably have had or aspired to, with respect either to sexual convention or national identity. He describes the uproar as an effect of bad reading. Donald Wildmon has spent much time in the last decade policing sexual subcultures. He does this by attempting to humiliate state and federal arts councils that use taxpayer money to support transgressions of norms that a putative ordinary America holds sacred. To christen the national as a locale with discernible standards of propriety, he uses the logic of obscenity law, which since the 1970s has offered local zones the opportunity to specify local standards with respect to which federal law might determine the obscenity of a text.

Wildmon is unconcerned with the referential context of both the wild thing and the poem about it. This lack of concern is central to the story of the Central Park jogger: many have noted how a serious discussion of the wilding event—in terms of the politics of public spaces, of housing projects, of city parks as homes and public property, of gender, of race, of classes and underclasses, of sexuality, of mass media, and of the law—was deflected into a melodrama of the elite. Here, Wildmon seeks to make irrelevant any full exploration of the wilding poem by deploying the anti-live-sex terms of the "true" national culture he claims to represent. Already on record accusing the NEA of promoting "blasphemy" *and* "the homosexual lifestyle," Wildmon grasped the passage "Christ sucked my dick" and brought it to the attention of Jesse Helms, who shortly thereafter got Frohnmayer, whom Pat Robertson had nicknamed "Satan," fired.[12]

Frohnmayer claims to know nothing about homosexuality in the United States, and I believe he is right, though he knows something about homoeroticism: for example, in arguing against the Helms Amendment,[13] he suggests the difficulty of telling "whether homoeroticism differed from garden-variety eroticism, whether it applied to females as well as males, whether it would pass muster under the Fourteenth Amendment tests of rational classifications and equal protection, or whether it was illegal for two persons of the same gender to hold hands, kiss, or do something more in deep shadow."[14] Of course we know there is no deep shadow for gay sex in America: deep shadow is the protected zone of heterosexuality, or dead citizenship, and all that queers have is that closet. But if Frohnmayer does not know sex law, he knows what art is and also knows that when the NEA funds works of art it effectively protects them from obscenity prosecution.[15] Thus he legitimates this poem and *Queer City* in toto by reference to the standard of what art *attempts*. If the aspiration to art makes sexual representation protected by the national imprimatur, it is the content of "Wild Thing" that secures the success of its aspiration. Frohnmayer writes,

> These lines have been taken out of context and sensationalized. The poem, in its entirety, is emotional, intense and serious.... [It] deals with an actual event—the violent rape of a female jogger in Central Park—and must be read in its entirety in order to receive a fair appraisal. It's not meant to make us feel good. It's not meant as an apology for a violent act. And it's certainly not meant to be sacrilegious, unless pedophilia is part of religious dogma. The poem is meant to make us think and to reflect on an incredibly brutal act in an allegedly civilized society.[16]

Again, there is much to say about wilding, the wild thing, the poem about it, the song it refers to, and the wild incitement to govern expression that this unfinished event has generated, which result in the contest over national meaning and value. First of all, Wildmon reads the poem as a direct indictment of the church for its alleged implied support of homosexual child molestation. Frohnmayer contests this reading with one that focuses on the purported failure of the black family to guide youth toward disciplined obedience to patriarchal authority. In Frohnmayer's description, the fate of the white woman represents what will happen to America when undersocialized boys abused by life in the projects and failed by parents leave their degenerate natal locales. They will terrorize property, women, and the nation: they will be bad men.

Frohnmayer's version of the poem cuts out entirely the poet's image of the fun, the pleasure, indeed the death-driven *jouissance* of the wilding man, his relation to mass culture, to his own body, to his rage at white women and men, his pleasure in his mastery over language, and over the racist conventions he knows he inspires. Clearly that isn't the stuff of art or America. Most importantly, he also parentalizes the nation by locating the virtue of art in its disclosure that the source of sexual violence and social decay (the end of American civilization) is in absent fathers and failed mothers. He ventriloquizes the poet's ventriloquized poem about wayward youth to prophesy about the future of national culture, which is in danger of collective acts of wilding. This hybrid official image of the nation as a vicious youth, and as a formerly innocent youth betrayed by bad parenting, and as a child who might be saved by good official parents, is at the heart of contemporary citizenship policy. Here is a story about the attempt to construct a national culture that resists an aesthetic of live sex in the name of youth, heterosexuality, and the national future.

What "Adults" Do to "Little Girls": Minor Citizens in the Modern Nation

When Anthony Comstock made his pilgrimage to Washington in 1873 to show the Congress what kinds of literature, information, and advertisements about sex, contraception, and abortion were being distributed through the U.S. mails, he initiated a process of nationalizing the discipline of sexual representation in the United States in the name of protecting national culture. Comstock installed this regime of anxiety and textual terror by invoking the image of youth, and in particular, the stipulated standard of the little girl whose morals, mind, acts, body, and identity would certainly be corrupted by contact with adult immorality.[17] Until the 1957 *Roth v. United States* [354 U. S. 476; 1957] case and the 1964 rulings on the novel *The Tropic of Cancer* and the film *Les Amants,* the Comstockian standard of the seducible little girl reigned prominently in court decisions about the obscenity of texts; indeed, as Edward de Grazia describes in *Girls Lean Back Everywhere: The Law of Obscenity and the Assault on Genius,* this putative little girl who might come into harmful contact with unsafe sexual knowledge and thus be induced by reading into performing harmful live sex acts (at least of interpretation) has been central to defining minor and full citizenship in the United States. She has come to represent the standard from which the privileged "adult" culture of the nation has fallen. Protecting her, while privileging him, establishing therein the conditions of minor and full citizenship, has thus been a project of pornographic modernity in the United States.

To certify obscenity legally a three-pronged standard must be met. The material must appeal to a prurient interest in sex; must be patently offensive to contemporary community standards; and be "utterly without redeeming social value."[18] The Roth and Miller decisions nationalized obscenity law for the first time, thus defining the adult who consumes pornography as an American in the way that the fourteenth amendment enfranchised African-Americans as full citizens by locating primary citizenship in the nation and only secondarily in states. Speaking of pornography's consumers, Dworkin and MacKinnon put succinctly this conjuncture of what we might call pornographic personhood, an amalgam of nation, nurture, and sacred patriarchy: "Pornography is their Dr. Spock, their Bible, their Constitution."[19] De Grazia's history of obscenity in the United States, along with his anthology *Censorship Landmarks,* reveals how the pressure to define obscenity has all along involved a struggle to define the relative power of national, state, and local cultures to control the contact the public might have with prurient materials; for example, in *Jacobellis v. Ohio,* the Ohio case concerning *Les Amants,* Justice Brennan argued that "we recognize the legitimate and indeed exigent interest of States and localities throughout the Nation in preventing the dissemination of material deemed harmful to children. But that interest does not justify a total suppression of such material, the effect of which would be to reduce the adult population . . . to reading only what is fit for children."[20] This tendency to nationalize the obscene, the child, and the adult has been checked by the "community standards" doctrine embraced by Chief Justice Warren Burger in 1973. This doctrine empowers local police, judges, prosecutors, juries, and citizen interest groups to determine the standards of local morality from which the nation should protect them. The Burger court thus dissolved a major blockage to promoting a conservative cultural agenda, at least from the vantage point of Supreme Court precedent; the constitutional protection of free speech against the "chilling effect" of censorship, which sought to avert the terroristic effects of political repression on speech, could be avoided by localizing the relevant "context" according to the most local community standards. Central to establishing and maintaining these standards is the figure of the vulnerable little girl, a figure for minors-in-general. The situation of protected minor citizenship is thus a privilege for protection from adult heterosexual exploitation that national culture confers on its youth, its little girls and boys; paradoxically, the aura of the little girl provides a rationale for protecting the heterosexual privacy zones of "adult" national culture.

Sometimes, when the little girl, the child, or youth are invoked in discussions of pornography, obscenity, or the administration of morality in U.S. mass culture, actually endangered living beings are being imagined. Frequently, however, we should understand that these disturbing figures are fetishes, effigies that condense, displace, and stand in for arguments about who "the people" are, what they can bear, and when, if ever. The purpose of this excursus into the history of obscenity law has been to recast it within an assembly of parental gestures in which adult citizens are protected as children are protected from representations of violence and sex and violent sex, for fear that those representations are in effect understood as doctrine or as documentary fantasy. Even the most liberal obscenity law concedes that children must neither see nor hear immoral sex/text acts: they must neither know them nor see them, at least until they reach that ever more unlikely moment of majority when they can consent freely to reading with a kind of full competence they must first be protected from having.

Nowhere is this infantilizing confluence of media, citizenship, and sex more apparent and symptomatically American than in the work of Andrea Dworkin, Catharine MacKinnon, and the 1986 report on obscenity popularly called the Meese Commission Report. Much has been written on the paradoxical effects of this collaboration between these radical feminists and the conservative cultural activity of the Republican-dominated State: Carole Vance and Edward de Grazia give scathing, detailed accounts of the ideological excesses and incoherences of this collaboration, and MacKinnon and Dworkin write eloquently about why the sexual harms women experience must be mended by law.[21] I am not interested in adjudicating this debate here in its usual terms (civil rights/harmful speech/antipatriarchal versus first amendment/free speech/sex radical), but I mean to be entering it obliquely, by examining the logics of its citizenship politics. I am interested in how it has helped to consolidate an image of the citizen as a minor, female, youthful victim who requires civil protection by the state, whose adult citizens, especially adult men, seem mobilized by a sex- and capital-driven compulsion to foul their own national culture.

This story can be told in many ways. The first step of the argument by which pornography represents harmful speech that fundamentally compromises women's citizenship in the United States establishes that pornography is a live sex act. It is live partly because, as the Milwaukee ordinance avows, "Pornography is what pornography *does*." There is a sense here, shared by many textual critics (not just of pornography), that texts are muscular, active persons in some sense of the legal fiction that makes corporations into persons: texts can and do impose their will on consumers, innocent or consenting.[22] Second, this notion of textual activity, of the harm that pornographic texts perform as a desired, direct effect on their consumers, has become intensified and has been made more personal by the visual character of contemporary pornography.

The optical unconscious dominates the scene of citizenship and pornographic exploitation the Meese Commission conjures. I quote at length the opening to the chapter called "The Use of Performers in Commercial Pornography." This chapter opens with a passage from Andre Bazin's "The Ontology of the Photographic Image": "The objective nature of photography confers on it a quality of credibility absent from all other picture-making.... The photographic image is the object itself, the object freed from the conditions of time and space that govern it."[23] The text glosses this representation of the image:

> The leap from "picture making" to photography was...the single most important event in the history of pornography: images of the human body could be captured and preserved in exact, vivid detail. As with every other visible activity, sex could now, by the miraculous power of the camera, be "freed from the conditions of time and space." "Sex" in the abstract, of course, remains invisible to the camera; it is particular acts of sex between individual people which photographs, films, and video tapes can record.[24]

By equating the violence that photography performs on history and personhood with the citizenship harms of pornography, the Commission locates the solution to sexual violence in a return to the scene and the mode of production, and indeed, in her own work, MacKinnon sees herself as a materialist feminist for this reason. This powerful view has effected a fundamental shift in the focus of assessments of pornography's effects. While social scientists are still trying to measure whether seeing violence leads to violence, and how, this antipornography view also insists on engaging with the backstory of the porn, taking its effect on performers and on the businessmen who control the condition of the performers as an important measure of its meaning. Furthermore, as we shall see, the exploitation of the pornographic performer becomes the model for the exploitation of and violence against all women involved in the circuit of pornography's circulation:

> Unlike literature or drawing, sexually explicit photography cannot be made by one person....No study of filmed pornography can thus be complete without careful attention to the circumstances under which individual people decide to appear in it, and the effects of that appearance on their lives. Nor is this an academic or trivial exercise. The evidence before us suggests that a substantial minority of women will at some time in their lives be asked to pose for or perform in sexually explicit materials. It appears, too, that the proportion of women receiving

such requests has increased steadily over the past several decades. If our society's appetite for sexually explicit material continues to grow, or even if it remains at current levels, the decision whether to have sex in front of a camera will confront thousands of Americans.[25]

The ordinary woman and the pornographic model will experience second-class citizenship in U.S. society, the argument goes, because sexualization constructs every woman as a potential performer of live sex acts that get photographed. They support this by showing how even models in pornographic films insist that "acting" in pornography is a fiction: it is sex work euphemized as acting; it is public euphemized as private and personal; it is coerced and exploitative euphemized as consensual and part of a simple business exchange.

To find a precedent for protecting actors in pornography from experiencing in their jobs the unfreedom that U.S. women experience in everyday heterosexual life, the Meese Commission, MacKinnon, and Dworkin turn to the model of child pornography, both to psychologize the vulnerability of women and to justify the prosecution of all pornographers. "Perhaps the single most common feature of models is their relative, and in the vast majority of cases, absolute youth." By definition, pornographers are exploiting young girls when they pay women to perform sex acts in front of cameras. Exploiting women-as-young-girls, they are performing a class action against women's full citizenship in the U.S. public sphere:

Pornographers promote an image of free consent because it is good for business. But most women in pornography are poor, were sexually abused as children, and have reached the end of this society's options for them, options that were biased against them as women in the first place. This alone does not make them coerced for purposes of the Ordinance; but the fact that some women may "choose" pornography from a stacked deck of life pursuits (if you call a loaded choice a choice, like the "choice" of those with brown skin to pick cabbages or the "choice" of those with black skin to clean toilets) and the fact that some women in pornography say they made a free choice does not mean that women who are coerced into pornography are *not coerced*. Pimps roam bus stations to entrap young girls who left incestuous homes thinking nothing could be worse.... Young women are tricked or pressured into posing for boyfriends and told that the pictures are just "for us," only to find themselves in this month's *Hustler*.... Women in pornography are bound, battered, tortured, harassed, raped, and sometimes killed.... Children are presented as adult women; adult women are presented as children, fusing the vulnerability of a child with the sluttish eagerness to be fucked said to be natural to the female of every age.[26]

Leo Bersani has argued that the big secret about sex is that most people don't like it, but also that the fundamental transgressiveness and irrationality of sex makes its enactment a crucial opportunity to resist the dead identities of the social.[27] We see in the antipornographic polemic of MacKinnon and Dworkin a fundamental agreement with Bersani's position, although they reach antithetical conclusions: they would argue, more dramatically, that the little girl too sexualized to be a citizen has no privilege, no "adult" advantages, that would allow her to shuttle between legitimated sociality and a sexual resistance to it. Rather, she is the opposite of "someone who matters, someone with rights, a full human being, and a full citizen."[28] The sentimental logic of this antipornography argument thus links women and children to the nation in a variety of ways. In terms of the public sphere, where civil rights are experienced as a matter of everyday life, women are paradoxically both the bearers of the value of privacy and always exposed and available to be killed into identity, which is to say into photography, into a sexual optic, and into heterosexuality, but not the sacred kind. Thus the cycle of pornography: it makes men child abusers who sentimentalize and degrade their objects; meanwhile, because young girls and women need to survive both materially and psychically in a culture of abuse, they become addicted to the stereotypical structure of sexual value and exploitation, forced to become either subjects in or to pornography. In this way the child's, the young girl's vulnerability is the scene merely covered over and displaced by the older woman's pseudo-autonomy; the young girl's minority is the true scene of arrested development of all American women's second-class citizenship. For this reason, this logic of infantile second-class citizenship has become both a moral dominant in the public sphere and a precedent in court prosecution of pornography.

Court prosecution of pornography found its excuse to rescue adult women from pornographic performance by taking the image of the vulnerable child performer of sex acts as the auratic truth of the adult. The Supreme Court decision on *New York v. Ferber* in 1982 for the first time extended its analysis of such material to encompass the "privacy interests" of the performers, in this case children. Filming children in the midst of explicit sexual activity not only harmed them because of the sexual abuse involved, but also because "the materials produced are a permanent record of the children's participation and the harm to the child is exacerbated by their circulation." In addition, the continued existence of a market for such materials was bound to make it more likely that children would be abused in the future, thus justifying a ban on distribution.[29] We have seen this argument before—that child abuse begets itself, child porn begets both abuse and porn, and that these beget the damaged inner children of adult women, who therefore must be saved from the child pornography that is the truth of their submission to the sex apparatus that befouls the national culture whose privileges women have either no access to, or access to only by virtue of proximity to heterosexual genital intercourse. The stakes of this vision of juridical deliverance are therefore not just personal to some American women, but reveal fundamental conditions of national identity for all women in the United States.

Even more striking is how vital a horizon of fantasy national culture remains, even to some radicals, in its promise of corporeal safety and the privacy of deep shadow. When Dworkin asserts that women's everyday experience of sexual degradation in the United States is both a condition of their second-class citizenship, and the most fundamental betrayal of them all, she also seeks to occupy the most politically privileged privacy protections of the very national sexuality whose toxic violence defines the lives of American women. Here America's promise to release its citizens from having a body to humiliate trumps the feminist or materialist visionary politics Dworkin might have espoused, politics that would continue to imagine a female body as a citizen's body that remains vulnerable because public and alive, engaged in the ongoing struggles of making history.

How to Raise PG Kids in an X-Rated Nation

We have seen that in Washington the nationalist aspirations to iconicity of the high arts and the ars erotica play out a wish to dissolve the body. They reveal a desire for identity categories to be ontological, dead to history, not in any play or danger of representation, anxiety, improvisation, desire, or panic. This sentimentality suggests how fully the alarm generated around identity politics in the United States issues from a nostalgia or desire for a suprahistorical, nationally secured personhood that does not look to acts of history or the body for its identifications. Recently, the education of the American into these fantasy norms of citizenship has become an obsession about pedagogy. My third "inhibit" in this argument about how the moral domination of live sex works in contemporary U.S. culture takes the form of a book report on Tipper Gore's *Raising PG Kids in an X-Rated Society.*[30]

It would be very easy to cite passages from this book in order to humiliate it. It is full of bad mixed metaphors, pseudoscience, and rickety thinking. But I want to take seriously its images of the citizen as a minor: the mirror that Gore looks into shows a terrible national present and foretells a frightening future for what she calls our national character. Her representation of the inner child of national culture repeats precisely the icon of feminized infantile vulnerability I have described as the scene of national anxiety in the previous two sections of this essay; she assumes as well the absolute value of the implicit, private, sacred, heterofamilial fetish of national culture. But my main interest is to trace the logic and social theory of citizen action that emerges here, which has become dominant in the contemporary U.S. public sphere, for reasons I have tried to suggest. The book's very reference to "PG kids" in its title suggests a theory of national personhood in which each person is an undeveloped film whose encounters with traumatic images and narratives might well make him or her a traumatized person who repeats the trauma the way a film repeats scenes. It suggests that a rating system for such persons might reveal their identities to each other, and protect us all from the mere repetition of violence that is the social text of the United States, an X-rated place with X-rated adult citizens begetting a generation of monsters (someone might call it "Generation X").

Raising PG Kids in an X-Rated Society opens like a slasher film, with a scene of Tipper Gore fleeing New York City to the "familiarity, love, and comfort of home" in bucolic Washington, DC.[31] Yet she finds that the sin of the big city has invaded Washington through the infectious circuits of mass culture. At home Gore faces what she has purchased for her eleven-year-old daughter: a record, *Purple Rain,* that contains "Darling Nikki," a song that glamorizes masturbation. With MTV, Gore realizes, Prince and his ilk make sexual trouble for her daughters: "These images frightened my children; they frightened *me!*"[32] Gore then sets out on a pilgrimage from her living room, through Washington, to the nation, to defend youth from premature contact with sex. By "sex" she means the practice of violent liveness the antipornography activists above also employ, as portrayed here in lyrics, on album covers, in rock concerts, and on MTV. Meanwhile, what she means by youth is similarly elastic, as the vulnerable little girl citizen of American culture ranges in this book from age one to her early twenties, the time when, Gore admits, kids are finally competent to enter "sexual relationships."[33] However, she also uses the consumer bromide "youth of all ages" to describe the ongoing surprise, hurt, humiliation, and upset even adults experience when having unwonted encounters with all kinds of "excess," including sex, alcohol, drugs, suicide, and satanism.

Under the pressure of this youth crisis, which also generalizes to all ages and is therefore in her view a crisis of national character and national culture, Gore joined with other concerned wives of men powerful in the

U.S. state apparatus to engender a counterpublic sphere via the Parents Music Resource Center (PMRC), whose purpose is to make the profit-driven, sexually suffused popular music industry nationally accountable for terrorizing a generation of American youths through premature exposure to a world of live sex acts. Gore claims her arguments are antimarket but not anticapitalist, anti–sex explicitness but not pro-censorship, "pro-morality" but not antisex. She notes acutely that there seems to be a lyric/narrative hierarchy in obscenity law. Although children are indeed not permitted access to adult films, books, and magazines, they are permitted access to equally explicit record covers, live rock concerts and videos of songs, as well as lyrics that perform the same acts minors are not allowed to consume when they are not the market population designated by capitalists. "If no one under eighteen can buy *Penthouse* magazine," she writes, "why should children be subjected to...hard-core porn in the local record shop? A recent album from the Dead Kennedys band contained a graphic poster of multiple erect penises penetrating vaginas. Where's the difference? In the hands of a few warped artists, their brand of rock music has become a Trojan Horse, rolling explicit sex and violence into our homes."[34]

In addition to pointing out the intemperance of the record industry and the artists who produce what she calls "porn rock," and in addition to exposing the contradictions in the law's stated intention to protect children, two other issues dominate Gore's reading of the general crisis in national culture. They do not involve critiques of the immorality of capitalism and law. They involve the failure of American adults to be competent parents and a passionate argument to extend the model of infantile citizenship to nonminor U.S. citizens through an image of the adult citizen as social parent. In particular, Gore depicts the devastating effects of adults' general refusal to acknowledge the specifically limited capacities of children, such that proper boundaries between children and adults are no longer being drawn. She also testifies to the failure of the family to compensate for the escalating norms of sexual and corporeal violence in everyday life, mass culture, and the public sphere at large.

Gore turns to social scientists and psychologists to mourn the loss of childhood in America: not only for latchkey children whose mothers work, not in only broken families (that is, ones without fathers), but even in the 7 percent of families with intact, originary parents, stay-at-home mothers, and fully genetically related children, parents have begun to mistake the eloquence of children for "mature reasoning powers and critical skills."[35] However, she argues that "anyone who attempts to debate the porn rock issue as if young people are in the same intellectual and emotional category as adults does them a terrible injustice. We need to let children be children. Children think differently from adults, and process information according to their own stages of development."[36]

If the cognitive difference between children and adults were not enough to require special adult wisdom with respect to superintending the lives of children, Gore goes on to show that the dissolution of the "smiling nuclear family," increases in family violence, spouse abuse and child abuse, and most dramatically, the "violent world" of life in the United States have resulted simultaneously in the saturation of children's minds with scenes of terror and the desensitization of their minds toward terror, indeed through its transformation into pleasure and entertainment.[37] Gore argues that adults have ruined American society with their excesses, with their will to make public intimate and complicated relations, like sex, and with their negligent complacence about the violence, annihilation, exploitation, and neglect into which children are thrust daily. This sacrifice to the indulgences of U.S. adulthood is the distinguishing mark of the generation of children that currently exists. In contrast, Gore distinguishes (and, one must say, misremembers) her own generation, which we might call the generation of 1968, by its relation to two key texts: "Twist and Shout" and "I Love Lucy."[38]

Thus when Tipper Gore places the words "Explicit material—parental advisory" on the title page of her book, we are to understand that her project is to train incompetent American adults to be parents, as a matter of civic and nationalist pedagogy. Although all Americans are youths in her view—in other words, incompetent to encounter live sex acts or any sex in public—she also desperately tries to redefine "adult" into a category of social decay more negative than any national category since the "delinquent" of the 1950s. The new virtuous category of majority is "parent." The new activist citizenship Tipper Gore imagines to express the true morality of U.S. national culture refuses the contradictions of traditional patriarchal privilege that both moralizes against and promotes the erotic terrorizing of women and children. (No sympathetic mention is made of the sexually terrorized Others on the live margins of national heterosexuality.) Gore advises parents in every chapter to think of parenting as a public profession, like being a lawyer or a politician, and she encourages what she calls "parental solidarity" groups to take the private activity of nurturing children away from mass-media induced but home-circulated materials that promote sex and violence. She imagines a nation controlled by a local, public, community matrix of parental public spheres.[39] Above all, she characterizes this grassroots model of citizenship on behalf of the "rights" parents have to control what they and their children encounter as a model for national political agency itself. Here are the last words of the conclusion: "It's not easy being a parent these days. It's even tougher being a kid. Perhaps together we can help our society grow up."[40]

Wild Things

I was cruising, one early morning in 1993, the Sunday morning talk shows: *Meet the Press, This Week with David Brinkley, Face the Nation*. But along the way I ran across a couple of video events that I have not yet recovered from seeing. The first was a Jerry Falwell commercial, played during the *Old Time Gospel Hour*. In this minute-long segment he offers us the opportunity to spend four dollars engaging in citizenship acts. We might call 1-900-3422 in support of "the new homosexual rights agenda" soon, he said, to be signed into law by President Clinton. Or we might call 1-900-3401 to say that although we pray for the president, we do not support "the new homosexual rights agenda," we do not want our "children to grow up in an America where a new homosexual rights agenda" is law. He keeps repeating the phrase "new homosexual rights agenda," and posts the phone numbers on the TV screen, the background for which is a purple (not a lavender-tinted) American flag. Next I flipped to C-Span, which happened (I say, as though it were random) to be showing a tape of a speech given by Major Melissa Wells-Petry, sponsored by the Christian Action Network, a speech shown at least once later the same day, which I taped and watched compulsively. Major Wells-Petry, a U.S. military attorney, was giving a speech about why gays ought to be barred from the military. She described the vast incompatibility of the nation and the gay man; she knew the law, well, colloquially. Her reason for rejecting a gay presence in the military was that when someone says, "I am a homosexual," there is "data" to support the idea that he is "likely to engage in homosexual acts." There is no possibility that a homosexual has an identity that is not evidenced in acts. She says the courts have proven that to be homosexual is to behave as a homosexual, just as a pilot can be said to be a pilot because he flies airplanes. I have no idea as to whether she was secretly thinking about the "cruising" altitude of planes, or about the cliché that queers are light in the loafers. In any case, she also argues that gayness is only one of many behavioral identities the army bars from service, and she names two others: in an aside, she notes that fatness makes you unfit for service; more elaborately, she recounts a case where a Nazi walked into a recruiting station and asked to enlist, but was barred from enlisting because being a Nazi makes you unfit to serve in the U.S. military. I fell into a dream that day, about *Griswold v. Connecticut* and *Roe v. Wade*, two cases I was teaching the following week. These two cases are generally thought to be crucial to the struggle to gain sex equality in the United States. *Griswold v. Connecticut* made it possible for married couples to buy birth control; *Roe v. Wade* made it possible to abort some fetuses birth control didn't prevent from being conceived. But the language about heterosexuality and pregnancy promoted by these cases did nothing to shake up the normative relations of sex and nationality in modern America. In my dream, I tried to explain to someone in a supermarket how the zone of privacy established for married sex acts in Griswold even further enshrined heterosexual reproductive activity as the fundamental patriotic American fetish, so powerful that it was entirely private and was the only fixed sign in the national language; indeed, I insisted on telling her, with great, painful prolixity, of Justice Harlan's opinion that "the right of privacy is not an absolute. Thus, I would not suggest that adultery, homosexuality, fornication and incest are immune from criminal enquiry, however privately practiced. [But]...the intimacy of husband and wife is necessarily an essential and accepted feature of the institution of marriage, an institution which the State not only must allow, but which always and in every age it has fostered and protected."[41] Then, somehow bored in my own dream, I turned my back and looked out the window, where I saw a pregnant woman wandering naked in traffic. I watched her, transfixed, for the longest time. When I awoke, I asked myself, What is the wish of the dream? I didn't know, but what flashed up instead was a line from *Roe v. Wade:* "The pregnant woman cannot be isolated in her privacy."[42]

Let me review the argument. Insofar as an American thinks that the sex he or she is having is an intimate, private thing constructed within the lines of personal consent, intention, and will, he or she is having straight sex, straight sex authorized by national culture; he or she is practicing national heterosexuality, which makes the sex act dead in the sense I have described, using a kind of metaphor that foregrounds the ways heterofamilial American identity reigns as a sacred national fetish beyond the disturbances of history or representation, protected by a zone of privacy.

The privacy zone that projects national culture as a shadow effect of scandalous or potentially destabilizing acts of sexual alterity has a history, and I have tried to telegraph it here as a history of some live acts that counter an ideology of dead citizenship. Most important, until recently there has never been, in the United States, a public sphere organized around sex and sexuality, that is, a public sphere demarcated by what Geoff Eley has described as a political culture.[43] The prehistory of this moment must transform our accounts of the contemporary public sphere as well as of citizenship, nationality, acts, identities, sex, and so on. It might start with racial and gendered corporeal counterpolitics of the period after the Civil War, part of a general citizen reform movement, but also specifically organized around issues of property and reproduction, the two most sacrosanct areas the Constitution designates. Suffrage was meant to bring these nineteenth-century primativist categories into national modernity, and the history of national sentimentality this essay partly tells has to do with the public failure of suffrage to solve the relation between the body and the state in the United States, so that a tactical shuttling between assimilation and banishment remains central to the complicated histories of those sexed, racialized, female, underclassed subjects who can be seen animating the live margins of the U.S. scene. In any case, as the Queer Nation motto, "We Are Everywhere, We Want Everything," suggests, the scandal of sexual subculture in the contemporary American context derives in part from its assertion of a noninfantalized, political counterpublic that refuses to tie itself to a dead identity; that sees sexuality as a set of acts and world-building activities whose implications are always radically TBA; that aspires to undermine the patriotic ethics in which it is deemed virtuous to aspire to live in abstract America, a place where bodies do not live historically, complexly, or incoherently, guided by a putatively rational, civilized standard. The basic sex-radical tactic has been to countercorporealize at every moment, and so to de-elect the state and other social formations that have patriarchalized and parentalized national culture. This is not enough, as Michael Warner has argued.[44] But it is the beginning of a *movement,* and it's a live one.

This is to say that a radical social theory of sexual citizenship in the United States must not aspire to reoccupy the dead identities of privacy, or name the innocence of youth as the index of adult practice and knowledge, or nationalize sexuality or sex as the central mode of self-legitimation or public identity-making. In this way it can avoid repeating the utopian identification that infantile citizenship promises, which distracts everyone from turning to the nation form and thinking about its inexhaustible energy for harnessing capitalism to death through promises of eternal identity and images of life activity. It can then avoid repeating the struggle between crassness and sentimental sublimity that defines all of our bodies in the United States, all of our live sex if we're lucky enough to have it; our dead citizenship; and our potentially undead desires to form a live relation to power, nature, sensation, and history within or outside of the nation form as we know it. The risk is that peeling away the fantasies that both sustain and cover over the sexual bodies living the good life in the zone of privacy will also tear away some important protective coverings, like the fantasy of privacy itself, the way a Band-Aid covering an unhealed wound will take away part of the wound and its bit of healing with it. But such violence and failure, such an opening of the wound to air, is a foundational condition for the next steps, which, after all, remain to be taken, seen, and critiqued, though not rated with an X, a PG, or a thumbs up—unless the thumb is related to something else, like a fist.

Notes

Thanks to Roger Rouse, Kim Scheppele, Michael Warner, Jody Greene, and the great audiences at the University of Michigan, Rutgers, Harvard, and Brown for much-needed conversation and challenge.

1. Andrea Dworkin, quoted in Edward de Grazia, *Girls Lean Back Everywhere: The Law of Obscenity and the Assault on Genius* (New York: Random House, 1992), 581.

2. Michael Kammen describes the particularly intensified manipulations of national nostalgia and amnesia during the gestation and rise of the Reaganite right in *Mystic Chords of Memory: The Transformation of Tradition in Modern American Culture* (New York: Vintage, 1991), 618–88.

3. Michael Taussig names this saturation of the politics by the nation "state fetishism" in *The Nervous System* (New York: Routledge, 1992), 111–49, 223.

4. The original texts meant to be reviewed were Allison Assiter, *Pornography, Feminism, and the Individual* (London: Pluto Press, 1989); Gail Chester and Julienne Dickey, *Feminism and Censorship: The Current Debate* (Dorset: Prism Press, 1988); Andrea Dworkin, *Pornography: Men Possessing Women* (New York: E. P. Dutton, 1989); Susan Gubar and Joan Hoff-Wilson, *For Adult Users Only: The Dilemma of Violent Pornography* (Bloomington: Indiana University Press, 1989); Gordon Hawkins and Franklin E. Zimring, *Pornography in a Free Society* (New York: Cambridge University Press, 1988); Catherine Itzin, *Pornography: Women, Violence, and Civil Liberties* (New York: Oxford University Press, 1992). I have also read more widely in the literature pro and con, and assume the entire oeuvre of Catharine MacKinnon in this essay as well.

Of those listed above, the British feminist texts (Assiter, Itzin, Chester, and Dickey) share with the work of MacKinnon and Dworkin a sense that issues of sexual difference cannot be solved by U.S.–style liberal thinking about ontological selfhood, but must address the ways the state and the nation frame the conditions of sex, sexual identity, and gender value. Of the U.S. texts that do not take a clear pornography-is-patriarchy position, the most useful is *For Adult Users Only*, which rehearses and extends the feminist debate over the causes, effects, and possibilities pornography poses for American women.

But the discussion over sexuality and public life is stunted by the referential dullness or hyperelasticity of the category "pornography," along with the unstated heteronormative assumptions (about what "good" sexuality is, about the relation of the natural and the normal, about what "bad" representations do) that almost always accompany these discussions, and a scrupulous specificity is necessary for any discussion of politically rezoning the place where national culture meets intimacy forms like sex. This is why this chapter seeks to place this discussion of national sexuality in a context of thinking about the sexual politics of citizenship in the contemporary United States.

5. *New York Times,* Tuesday, 25 May 1993, A8.

6. I take this way of thinking about the processes of making an institution appear hegemonic from Chandra Mohanty, who takes it from Dorothy Smith. See Chandra Talpade Mohanty, "Cartographies of Struggle: Third World Women and the Politics of Feminism," in *Third World Women and the Politics of Feminism,* eds. Chandra Talpade Mohanty, Ann Russo, and Lourdes Torres (Bloomington: Indiana University Press, 1991), 15–16; Dorothy E. Smith, *The Everyday World as Problematic: A Feminist Sociology* (Boston: Northeastern University Press, 1987), 108.

7. John Frohnmayer, *Leaving Town Alive: Confessions of an Arts Warrior* (Boston: Houghton Mifflin, 1993), 3, 337.

8. Ibid., 314, 202.

9. Ibid., 324.

10. Ibid., 326.

11. Wodiczko's Homeless Vehicle has generated a number of consequential essays, the most important of which for thinking about subjectivity, capitalism, and citizenship is Neil Smith, "Contours of a Spatialized Politics: Homeless Vehicles and the Production of Geographical Scale," *Social Text* 33 (1992): 54–81.

12. Frohnmayer, *Leaving Town Alive,* 291, 324–25.

13. The "Helms amendment" was offered to the U.S. Senate on 7 October, 1989. It reads, "None of the funds authorized to be appropriated pursuant to this Act may be used to promote, discriminate, or produce materials that are obscene or that depict or describe, in a patently offensive way, sexual or excretory activities or organs, including but not limited to obscene depictions of sadomasochism, homo-eroticism, the sexual exploitation of children, or individuals engaged in sexual intercourse." See *Congressional Record,* 1st session, 1989, v. 135, no. 134, S12967.

14. Frohnmayer, *Leaving Town Alive,* 69.

15. De Grazia, *Girls Lean Back Everywhere,* 637.

16. Frohnmayer, *Leaving Town Alive,* 326, 328–29.

17. De Grazia, *Girls Lean Back Everywhere,* 4–5.

18. Ibid., 436–37. See also Edward de Grazia, *Censorship Landmarks* (New York: R. R. Bowker, 1969).

19. Andrea Dworkin and Catharine A. MacKinnon, *Pornography and Civil Rights: A New Day for Women's Equality* (Minneapolis: Organizing against Pornography, 1988), 48.

20. *Jacobellis v. Ohio* 378 U.S. 184–204 (1964); see also de Grazia, *Girls Lean Back Everywhere,* 423–33. The case from which Justice Brennan quotes is *Butler v. Michigan,* 352 U.S. 380, 383.

21. Carole S. Vance, "The Pleasures of Looking: The Attorney General's Commission on Pornography versus Visual Images," in *The Critical Image: Essays on Contemporary Photography,* ed. Carol Squiers (Seattle: Bay Press, 1990), 38–58.

22. See Robin West, "Pornography as a Legal Text," in *For Adult Users Only,* 108–30.

23. Attorney General's Commission on Pornography, *Final Report,* July 1986, v. 1, 839.

24. Ibid.

25. Ibid., 839–40.

26. Dworkin and MacKinnon, *A New Day,* 43, 45–46.

27. Leo Bersani, "Is the Rectum a Grave?" *October* 43 (winter 1987): 197–222.

28. Dworkin and MacKinnon, *A New Day,* 46.

29. Attorney General's Commission on Pornography, *Final Report,* v. 1, 849.

30. Tipper Gore, *Raising PG Kids in an X-Rated Society* (Nashville: Abingdon Press, 1987).

31. Ibid., 17.

32. Ibid., 18.

33. Ibid., 41.

34. Ibid., 28.

35. Ibid., 39.

36. Ibid., 42.

37. Ibid., 43–48.

38. Ibid., 11.

39. For all its greater liberalism and greater belief in the wisdom of a welfare state, Hillary Rodham Clinton's *It Takes a Village and Other Lessons* (New York: Simon and Schuster, 1996) fully joins Tipper Gore's *How to Raise PG Kids* in characterizing the ideal United States as a parental public sphere.

40. Ibid., 167.

41. *Griswold v. Connecticut,* 381 U.S. 499 (1965), 479–531.

42. *Roe v. Wade,* 410 U.S. 159 (1973), 113–78.

43. Geoffrey H. Eley, "Nations, Publics, and Political Cultures: Placing Habermas in the Nineteenth Century," in *Habermas and the Public Sphere,* ed. Craig Calhoun (Cambridge: MIT Press, 1992), 289–339.

44. Michael Warner, "The Mass Public and the Mass Subject," in *Habermas and the Public Sphere,* ed. Calhoun, 399–400.

9

Fat and Culture

Laura Kipnis

Fat. Few topics excite as much interest, emotion, or capital investment. With a multibillion dollar diet and fitness industry, tens of millions of joggers, bikers, and power walkers out any sunny weekend all trying to banish fat, work off fat, atone for fat, health ideologues who talk of little these days besides fat, research and development dollars working overtime to invent no-fat substitutes for fat, our intense wish for fat's absence is precisely what ensures its cultural omnipresence.

Fat is the theme of our new national literature; its drama never ceases to compel us and hold us in its thrall. A book on measuring fat spent over three years on the *New York Times* best-seller list: no other subject can so reliably incite Americans to actually read. The novel may be floundering, but the war on fat (like so many of our previous wars) is rich with literary possibilities: a heroic, epic, tragically doomed battle waged by a frontline of diet strategists and tacticians, armed with the latest physiological intelligence (monounsaturates, good cholesterol, high carbohydrates), and backed up by a phalanx of psychologists on the home front, bent on putting fat on the couch and interpreting its deeper meanings (it's your anger, your fear of sex, your hatred of your mother, your needy inner child).

Given the vast quantities of energy and resources devoted to annihilating it, and to making life miserable for those who are unfortunate enough to bear the humiliation of its exposure, fat could be considered, not just an obsessive focus, but even the crux of contemporary American culture. The mission of all this cultural energy? To insure fat's invisibility. To banish it from sight, exterminate it from public view.

So what accounts for the existence of a pornographic subgenre whose entire purpose is to *expose* fat, revel in fat, eroticize it? But there it is, an extensive array of magazines and videos featuring extremely large, naked women in sexual situations (by large I mean between maybe two hundred and five hundred pounds), with titles like *Plumpers and Big Women, Jumbo Jezebel, Life in the Fat Lane,* and *Love's Savage Cupcake,* or for gay male clientele, titles like *Bulk Male, Husky,* and *Bustin Apart at the Seams.* According to my informant at Frenchie's, a Chicago porn emporium, they can barely keep these items in stock: when a new one arrives it sells out instantly.

The brazen appearance of fat on the shelves of your local pornographer certainly does defy what many have come to think of—in large part due to the efforts of the feminist antiporn movement—as the typical in hard-core porn: a vast undifferentiated mass of sexualized violence. But the fact is that most pornographic subgenres do devote themselves to exploring precisely those themes most antithetical, if not hostile, to the central aesthetic preoccupations of their day. So long as pornography's guiding principle is one of *anti-aesthetics,* at least one aspect of its social function will be to provide a repository for those threatening, problematic materials and imagery banished from the culture at large. Pornography becomes something of an archive of the contemporary unaesthetic, and thus the fact that it offers such a cozy refuge for fat has a certain inevitability to it, at least in our own time. Too bad for the interests of *politesse* that these loathsome eyesores contemporary sensibilities try and try again to deport from sight don't seem content to be shunted off to their visual leper colonies, never to be heard from again. Instead they're continually circling the perimeter, waiting for the right moment to break back in. The aesthetic realm has to be forever vigilant against incursions from all these banished images, or worse, from the unsightly classes themselves, and forever vigilant against the profoundly unsettling effect they have on national sensibilities.

In pornography, fat does contain an erotic charge, despite (or is it because of?) a mainstream culture so maniacally devoted to achieving thinness that vomiting food is a national epidemic among college women. And what exactly does separate a sexual preference for fat bodies from those "normal" fetishes, like preferences for thin, in-shape anatomy? Or to put it another way, if the prevailing sexual aesthetic demands svelte, toned, bulgeless bodies to the degree that it currently does, will it immediately follow that everyone's sexual preferences fall obediently into line? When they don't, or when sexual desires fall outside the boundaries of bodily fashion, does this automatically qualify the aesthetic iconoclast in question for the damning label

Lingerie-clad woman from the pages of *Dimensions* magazine.

"fetishist?" (Even the porn industry labels fat porn "fetish material," although perhaps with less scorn, and less *medicalization,* then the culture-at-large).

Or is it that fat is somewhat pornographic anyway? Even a magazine like *Dimensions,* whose visuals are far tamer than those in *Playboy* or *Penthouse* (no nudity), is available only in hard-core porn stores or by mail. *Dimensions,* a magazine "where big is beautiful," is about fat admiration, but largely written in the idiom of social activism: its primary topic is discrimination against fat and fat admiration. Although there are numerous pictorials of huge, semiclad women, *Dimensions* is on the side of discretion (the lingeried body) and taste (no dirty jokes here). Yet it happens that its taste is for fat; thus, into the pornography racks it goes.

I

When writing about the pornography of the past, whether visual or literary, scholars and art historians routinely discover within it allegorical meaning, even political significance. The question of how its manifest content relates to its ulterior purposes, or to its historical context and operative social contradictions, displaces questions about whether it should or shouldn't have existed, or how best to protect its publics from offense to their sensibilities. Historically, it may be somewhat easier to see the ways that pornography engaged social issues and preoccupations. Historian Lynn Hunt points out that until around 1800, pornography was never seen as a distinct category, but always adjunct to something else: a vehicle for using the shock of sex to attack religious and political authorities, who responded with attempts to suppress it. Pornography was defined not so much by its content (although explicit depictions of sexual acts are certainly its medium) but by the efforts of religious and state authority to regulate it. It is fairly well recognized that pornography operated against political and religious authority as a form of social criticism. It had a social agenda.[1]

Yet when writing about the pornography of the present, its critics are overcome by a stultifying literalness: a breast is a breast, a penis is a penis, and pornography is simply about sex (although it's true that regarding an exposed crotch as an objectification of women and a penis as a lethal weapon are fairly *imaginative* interpretations). In fact, for many of our contemporary writers, pornography appears to wield almost magical powers of persuasion, able to transform men into rapists and women into objects in the flash of a camera lens. Feminist critics of pornography have viewed the social "expressing" that pornography does as expressing one thing alone: the misogynist project of controlling women's bodies. One of the guiding projects of the feminist antiporn movement has been to close down the range of pornography's symbolizing capability to this singular dimension. I'm not arguing that porn isn't sexist, but as anthropologist Mary Douglas tells us, the way the body is symbolically employed invariably "comes clothed in its local history and culture."[2] In other words, in a misogynist culture, bodily symbols will come so garbed. Sexism is certainly one "channel of meaning" in pornography, but I want to explore here the other more neglected planes of meaning and less frequently discussed motifs.

What is it about pornography that's so crucial at the current moment? Why all this hand-wringing, uproar, fervor? Whether you're terribly offended (antiporn feminists, the cultural right, the Church) or terribly interested (certainly a lot of porn *is* sold in this country), these must be flip sides of the same response: a deeply felt, deeply visceral engagement with pornography's motifs. Douglas proposes that the human body is always treated as an image of society. It's impossible to consider representations of the body and bodily symbols that don't simultaneously involve a social dimension. All cultures express social situations through bodily symbols, and this is particularly true for issues of social control, for which the body and its representations are privileged forms of symbolic expression.[3]

These campaigns to suppress porn are curiously contradictory though, an effort to remove from visibility precisely what the dominant culture has already exiled to the hinterlands of representation. To be relegated to the pornographic is a form of intracultural exile for contents that are entirely central and entirely marginal simultaneously. What might be called the pornographic response: the visceral, sexual, aesthetic disquietude porn produces (hardly dissimilar in its proponents and its adherents) demands an outlet, whether beating off or sounding off. The vast subjective disquietude produced in the collision between psyche and pornography does afford a glimpse of just how deeply embedded in the fabric of subjectivity these margins and borders lie and how very deeply aesthetics (and bodily aesthetics) are installed in the individual subject. There is no aesthetic response, no pornographic response, no visuality or vision, that is not already profoundly social. This indicates, I hope, that my local argument about fat pornography has larger ambitions in terms of cultural analysis and its practices, rather than being a crusade to promote pornography in the name of some quest for sexual liberation or to endorse a politics of sex radicalism for its own sake.

II

Fat is a site of deep social contradiction. Fat is something a significant percentage of the American public bears not only undisguised contempt for but also, in many cases, an intense, unexamined, visceral disgust (and although I'm writing about norms within white America here, minority cultures are hardly exempt from the bodily ideals peddled by the dominant culture). Here, a trained psychiatrist writes of the feelings of repugnance stirred in him by a fat woman patient he calls Betty:

> I have always been repelled by fat women. I find them disgusting: their absurd sidewise waddle, their absence of body contour — breasts, laps, buttocks, shoulders, jawlines, cheekbones, *everything*, everything I like to see in a woman, obscured in an avalanche of flesh. And I hate their clothes — the shapeless, baggy dresses or, worse, the stiff elephantine blue jeans with the barrel thighs. How dare they impose that body on the rest of us?

"The origins of these sorry feelings?" he wonders. The answer: "I had never thought to inquire," although the patient who scratches this nerve does provide the psychiatrist (also a professor at Stanford), the opportunity to work through what he calls "a great trial of counter-transference."[4] This fat-hating shrink is hardly alone in his undertheorized anxiety: according to fat activists, fat hatred is more or less demanded by the culture, not to mention the last remaining protectorate of safe bigotry.[5] A recent *New England Journal of Medicine* study claiming to be the first "to document the profound social and economic consequences of obesity," merely confirms what any fat person will tell you: that this culture treats the fat population with an unparalleled viciousness.[6]

What is remarkable is how little general cultural explanation there is for this national revulsion about fat. Anyone who has cruised the psychology section of any bookstore lately knows that an expanding body of literature is devoted to the devastating effects of the cult of thinness on women's lives, generally pointing a blaming finger at the media and fashion industries. An extensive literature—clinical, popular, literary—exists on anorexia and bulimia, and there is a corresponding expansion of metaphor around the vicious cycle of food deprivation and overconsumption. All the metaphors suggested by these titles point to a psychology of neediness: *The Famine Within; The Hungry Self, Starving for Attention, Feeding the Empty Heart, Feeding the Hungry Heart,* and so on. Most of us can knowledgeably speculate about why people, most often women, voluntarily starve themselves: at the level of individual psychology, any eating-disorder cognoscenti will tell you that it's about mothers and control issues. Turning to social psychology, we find feminist indictments of society's desire to diminish women, particularly now that women are achieving more social power and visibility. Intellectuals have provided us with sophisticated analyses of cultural ambivalence about the maternal body, and even geopolitical insights about what it might mean to refuse food in a society devoted to overconsumption. Even philosophers have speculated about what thinness means in our social cosmology: thinness speaks for the self, it embodies aspirations concerning the control of impulses and regulation of desires in a society that encourages us to lose control at the sight of desirable commodities: the slender body signals a well-managed self.[7] But surprisingly little attention is devoted to just what it is about fat as *fat* that's so very disturbing at this particular historical moment, and to what could account for the intense, visceral repulsion it provokes. It seems, actually, like a fairly stupid question.

One reason the question seems so stupid is the appearance of "nature" and common sense that attach themselves to this anxiety and repulsion about fat. Fat is simply unaesthetic. If pressed we resort to medical explanations. "It's not healthy to be fat," we proclaim knowledgeably as we reach for the little pink envelope of chemical compounds known to cause fatal diseases in lab rats, or as we ingest glutinous and ill-conceived oxymorons like non-fat desserts. And current medical ideology works overtime reinforcing this common sense. I say "medical ideology" to make a stab at stripping away some of its claims to scientific certainty. In fact, the visual taste for thinness — fairly hegemonic since the end of WWI — far preceded current medical notions about fat: medical ideology followed fashion rather than vice versa.[8] Recent studies in Scandinavia have indicated that fat women actually live longer than thin women,[9] and there's a preponderance of evidence that weight and distribution of body fat are for the most part genetically determined. A recent National Institute of Health study concluded, "There is increasing physiological, biochemical, and genetic evidence that overweight is not a simple disorder of will power, as is sometimes implied, but is a complex disorder of energy metabolism." But this has had little effect on the medical establishment's insistence on low ideal body weights or the guilt trips it imposes on the fat population. Neither has the genetic research had any impact on the larger culture's fat phobia, which according to anecdotal accounts by fat people, doctors equally share. The reliance on medical explanations for fat loathing hardly seems to account for the intensity of the experience, and is rather, I suspect, part of the symptomology rather than its source, particularly if you consider that smokers or drinkers are generally treated with mild disapproval at worst — certainly nothing near the full-fledged contempt reserved for the fat.

III

This cult of bodily thinness and obsession with banishing fat are historically recent and in sharp contrast to bodily aesthetics for the past four hundred years or so. Between roughly 1500 and 1900, a hefty body was a visually appealing body for both men and women. Paintings throughout the period portray both sexes as solid and even rotund. Nudes like those of Rubens shamelessly displayed thick, pink rolls of flesh. And clothes themselves were bulky and designed to add volume to the body rather than emphasize a svelte profile; if you were thin, you did your best to hide it under large, bunchy garments.

That body types have or had complicated social connotations is a fairly unproblematic insight when it comes to art history. In Rubens's time, for example, thinness had largely negative connotations of poverty and deprivation, along with the insinuation of disease and old age. Being thin implied something dark and suspicious about the person's inner being as well: a spiritual poverty or moral insufficiency. The thin lacked good fortune, not to mention will and zest: thinness connoted morbidity, a lack of life. Previously, in the Middle Ages, thinness had been considered aesthetically pleasing, given the way it echoed the Church's teaching on the unimportance of the flesh. But by the time Rubens came along, an emerging humanism, represented in the Renaissance faith in the limitless possibilities of the human mind and body, was expressed visually in depictions of bodies of weight and rotund sensuousness, with the full, solid body expressing a sense of social stability and order.[10]

What will the art historians of the next century have to say about late-twentieth-century bodily norms and fashions? What will they make of our particular mode of depicting bodies, including the photographic record? After all, there are a range of body types in the culture, and if only one type is typically represented in our advertisements, movies, and TV, this type, like the depictions of bodily largeness in Rubens's day, must certainly reveal something about our social preoccupations. What connections between socially sanctioned bodies and social ideologies will become obvious?

One link between the body and the social is the complex chain of association between body type and social class. Since the beginning of the century, thinness had begun to be affiliated with wealth and higher social standing, whereas fatness now tends to be associated both stereotypically and in terms of real, earned income with the lower classes. (And of course everyone knows the Duchess of York's adage, which inspired three generations of upwardly mobile anorexics with its assertion that you can never be too rich or too thin.)

There is, in fact, a higher concentration of body fat the lower down the income scale you go in this country. According to the National Center for Health Statistics, almost 30 percent of women with incomes below $10,000 a year are obese, as compared with 12.7 percent of those with incomes above $50,000 a year.[11] But all the cliches — that fat is more tolerated farther down the social rung, or that there's a greater consumption of pork rinds and doughnuts — are not so much the case as that fat is actually (and simply) a predictor of downward mobility: if you are fat, you have a lower chance of being hired, and if hired a lower chance of being promoted. And this is particularly true in jobs with a greater concentration of women — sales, secretarial, not to mention receptionists or flight attendants — jobs where appearance, whether acknowledged or not, is often part of the criteria in hiring and promotion. Heterosexual fat women are less likely to marry "up" socially or economically. And given that the tendency to fat is genetically inherited, fat children are more likely to be born into a lower social class and because of fat discrimination, to stay there.[12]

The association between fat and the lower classes is yet another twist in the twisted tale of current social responses to fat. On the one hand, fat clearly provokes a certain imaginary narrative on the part of its witnesses: an origins story about how the fat person got to be that way, which bypasses the genetics of fat, or even the pain of fat discrimination, relying instead on moralizing scenes of gluttony and overconsumption, to which the response will typically be varying degrees of disgust and condemnation. All this moralizing about gluttony is certainly something of a displacement in terms of class, as it assigns responsibility for gluttony to the social class by far least culpable of overconsuming (given the extent to which fat *is* concentrated in the lower classes). Researchers studying the psychology of body image report that fat is associated with a range of fears, from loss of control to a reversion to infantile desires, failure, self-loathing, sloth, and passivity.[13] Substitute "welfare class" for "fat" here and you start to see that the phobia of fat and the phobia of the poor are heavily cross-coded, and that perhaps the fear of an out-of-control body is not unrelated to the fear of out-of-control masses with their voracious demands and insatiable appetites, not just for food, but for social resources and entitlement programs.

In fact, linking the poor to fat is now an explicit tactic in Republican aspirations to cut welfare: as one-time Republican presidential hopeful Phil Gramm told an audience, referring to a Dallas newspaper's article about a family rationing food to avoid hunger, "Did you see the picture? Here are these people who are skimping to avoid hunger, and they are all fat!" Laughing, he continued, "Because of the impact of food stamps where we force people to buy food when, given a choice, they would choose to spend the aid we give them on other things, we're the only nation in the world where all our poor people are fat."[14] (Now it becomes clear that Clinton's New Democrat enthusiasm for slashing welfare can be read as something of a reaction-formation to his own weight-control problems.)

How could consumption issues *not* provoke the most anxious and ambivalent responses about the control of desire and appetite, given a society that on the one hand deeply wishes us to overconsume, yet savagely punishes all bodily evidence of overconsumption? Our society also, somewhat illogically, links such bodily testaments of consumption (namely, fat) to various forms of failure: to sexual failure (not being "attractive enough"), the failure to be a proper consumer (the connotations of lower-classness), and general all-round social failure (the fat pariah). Control of the body, desire, and appetite are qualities historically associated with the bourgeoisie and their social triumph: fat not only signifies loss of self-mastery, but also threatens loss of the class status for which bodily self-control is a prerequisite.

The fat are seen to be violating territorial limits: they take up too much room, too many resources (much like our nation, and extreme obesity is seen internationally as a peculiarly American disorder). But why is it that fat stands in so well for all forms of overconsuming; why is fat so mocked and ridiculed when other spectacles of overconsumption, like TV producer Aaron Spelling's ridiculously bloated, fifty-million-dollar, 52,503-square-foot, 123-room Beverly Hills mansion (with an entire room devoted to gift-wrapping packages for wife, Candy), earns him instead a layout in *Vanity Fair*? Fat is by far the only physical characteristic so deeply culturally connotative. Clearly the burden borne by the fat is not only of pounds, it's the sorry fate of being trapped in a body that conveys such an excess of meanings.

IV

One of the best accounts of the social experience of being fat and of living one's life as the bearer of such an array of signification is a book called *Such a Pretty Face.*[15] The title derives from what seems to be a universal experience of fat women: hearing this sanctimonious one-liner delivered by everyone from "well-meaning" relatives to (in startling violation of norms of social conduct) strangers on the street or in restaurants. What the line means, of course, is "if *only* you'd lose weight." But what puts the public on such terms of immediate intimacy with the fat? Fat people report that it's very common to have pig noises directed at them when they walk down the street. Other types of public ridicule are common. In one anecdote, a fat woman tells of attending a college lecture class with over a hundred people in it. The professor stops speaking in the middle of a sentence and says to her "When are you going to lose weight? You're really fat."[16] What makes the fat a kind of public property whose bodies invite the vocal speculations and ridicule of strangers? And why are these verbal assaults so often prescriptive, so dedicated to the project of inducing the fat to thinness? What imaginative investment does our citizenry have in putting the fat on diets?

The individual body in American culture is pretty much the sole locale for scenarios of transformation: you can aerobicize it, liposuction it, contract it through diet, or expand selected parts with collagen injections. A fat person seems to be regarded as a transformation waiting to happen, a vast, virgin, American frontier onto whose body can be projected the transformative fantasies of the culture at large. Maybe the scandal of fatness is its insult to those collective transformative fantasies, the affront of a body that dares to remain fat and untransformed. The real scandal, of course, is that this utopian investment in potential social transformation is, when displaced to the individual body, both fantasmatic and doomed to fail: the recidivism rate in weight loss is estimated at 98 percent. Although there must be some disavowed level of awareness on the part of the public that to be fat is largely beyond individual control, at the same time the culture's deeply held belief is that the fat could change but have *chosen* not to, whereas the experience of being fat is wanting to change but not being able to. This incapacity is the basis of the fabulous success of the diet industry, and what makes it a perfect investment opportunity.

The angry, contemptuous social reaction to the resistance of the fat to transforming themselves is a testament to the degree of our investment in the potential for change. The reaction toward this spectacle of stasis is, in many cases, actual violence: a quarter of fat men and 16 percent of fat women reported being hit or threatened with physical violence because of their weight, and emotional violence is nearly universal: 90 percent of fat people surveyed report derision, ridicule, contempt, and scorn.[17]

Fat also conjures up the terrifying specter of an insatiability that all we social citizens have all, to varying degrees, learned to suppress. Fat advertises "naked need," need that surpasses the ability of the available resources, whether edible, monetary, or emotional, to quell it. A fat person is a one-body smash-and-grab riot: like that anarchic, rebellious moment when social controls fail and you take what you want, when you want it, without regard for proprieties like ownership, or eat all you want, without regard for consequences like obesity. The spectacle of fat and the bedlam of free-form consumption that the nonfat imagine as its origin excite those same longings for plenitude (and equal distribution of it) that factor into our simultaneous fascination and hatred for the rich. Can it be coincidental that the best slogan for socialism is "Eat the rich," given that consumption is the everyday negotiation between need, desire, and resources, which always exists in combination with a wary, jealous watchfulness about who might be getting the "bigger portion of the pie?"

V

The issue of volition, of "choice," does seem central to the fat problematic. Fat activists have seized on evidence provided by recent genetic research indicating that the propensity for fat is genetic as conclusive evidence of fat oppression and social victimization. Their argument is that if fat is no more chosen than say, race, then bigotry toward the fat should be no more officially sanctioned than racism, and activists hope that these new findings will result in institutional recourse like their own Title 7 act (Only one state,

Michigan, currently has laws forbidding employment discrimination on the basis of size). Activists are now able to claim confidently that the fat glutton is a vicious stereotype and that the fat often actually eat less than the thin: being fat, they say, has nothing to do with food or caloric intake but is a metabolic disorder. Very little in fat activist literature goes so far as to endorse choosing to be fat: the fat person is generally cast in the role of the victim (although often an angry victim) rather than the role of the defiant. It's a condition that's been foisted upon you by your metabolism, rather than one for which you are culpable.

This ambivalence over personal responsibility for socially marginal or reviled traits resonates interestingly with the recent controversial and much-discussed findings by a researcher at the National Cancer Institute indicating a genetic basis for homosexuality: evidence that links male homosexuality to a particular region of the X-chromosome. This discovery led to speculation in the mainstream press that this would be the great leap forward for more widespread social acceptance of homosexuality: after all, the argument seemed to go, if you don't choose to be gay but are "born that way," then there really is little grounds for discrimination (which, of course, reveals remarkable amnesia about the experience of racial minorities in this country).

Coincidentally, the discovery of the "gay gene" came along just as one wing of the gay community has appropriated the formerly derogatory label "queer" as the badge for a new kind of political activism, and just as AIDS activists, too, are insisting that issues surrounding sexual object choice and the public health issues that overlap with sexuality are political. Proponents of queer politics make a distinction between being gay and being queer: to follow the genetic analogy, you might be born gay, but you choose to be queer: being queer is a political act.

Fat activist literature, on the other hand, to continue the analogy—has tended to take the genetic, "born-that-way" line, as opposed to the "choosing-to-be-queer" position. Until quite recently there's been little stomach for choosing to defy social bodily norms along the lines of a queer politics. The preference among an earlier generation of fat activists, perhaps in reaction to the general cultural insistence on individual blame for fatness, had been to regard fat as nonvolitional and to demand the majority's understanding, as opposed to an in-your-face defiance of social bodily controls. Recently younger, angrier fat women have spawned a number of fat "zines," small, homemade, cheaply and independently published magazines, that import a queer sensibility to the issue of fat. Zines like *Fat!So?* "for people who don't apologize for their size," and *Fat Girl,* "A Zine for Fat Dykes and the Women Who Want Them" take a more mutinous tone than the earlier generation's lamentations about social prejudice.

But still, while much of the political wing of the gay community reacted with suspicion to the news of the "gay gene," protesting that whenever a new "cause" for homosexuality is proposed, proposed "cures" shortly follow,[18] we do not see the same zeal to preserve fat against elimination. Certainly there are extensive protests against the dangers of specific fat cures, like surgery, which risks death for thinness, and against the insistence on diets, because diets don't work, but in general you would have to search long and hard to find anyone who, given a choice, would choose a fat body. There may currently be even greater discrimination against fat than against homosexuality, and with none of the same pleasures or rewards; there is no comparable fat subculture (no bars, no parades, no landmark events to rally around like Stonewall), although one organization, NAAFA (National Association to Advance Fat Acceptance) does have an annual convention and local social events. Instead of fat subculture, there's the diet industry, and the everpresent, inescapable conversational din about calories, grapefruits, fat grams and the five pounds you gained on vacation, which provides the aural backdrop of American culture at the end of the twentieth century, all of which means the death knell to fat. Regardless of who suffers the "most" discrimination, queers or fats, the experience of being fat in this culture is so devastating that a majority of those who have lost weight through surgery report that they would rather lose a limb, or for many, even eyesight, than be fat again, which is some testimony to the degree of paralyzing, devastating cultural hatred that fat citizens endure, although less and less silently.

VI

Fat pornography takes its audiences on another ride altogether. Affirming and celebrating the fat body against a universal chorus of fat-loathing, it's a safe haven for fat's defiance of social norms and proprieties, for its complaints against all the significations of the thinness. Fat pornography aligns itself against the thin body's chicken-hearted aspirations for order and control, opposing its conformist desire to simply take up an assigned place in the regime of the normal.

In fat pornography, no one is dieting. These bodies aren't undergoing transformation. Cascading mounds of flab, mattress-size buttocks, breasts like sagging, overfilled water balloons, meaty, puckered, elephantine thighs, and forty to fifty-inch waistlines are greeted with avid sexual enthusiasm. The more cellulite the better. Magazines like *Plumpers and Big Women* encourage respect toward their models and fat women everywhere; the features stories and bios detailing the likes and dislikes of a 350-pound pin-up are written with the same breathless awe of an *Esquire* feature on Cindy Crawford. Fat pornography has its own stars, and its canon of video classics with the requisite spinoffs and sequels. Teighlor, one of the biggest stars (in all senses of the word) even has her own fantasy love doll.

Gay male fat porn is focused less on soft fat than on bulk: bodies in the 250–300 pound range, or to use the vernacular, the "teddy bear." Teddy bears are beefy, barrel chested, pot-bellied, and most importantly, hairy: *Bulk Male* is like a full-body Hair Club for Men ad or a shower drain's worst nightmare: carpets of chest hair, back hair, full beards. Here the operative turn-on terms are *husky, bearlike,* and *grizzly,* although articles also swoon over big-bellied TV icons like John Goodman, Ed Asner, Carroll O'Connor, and Hoss Cartwright. "Daddy bear" Charles Kuralt is held in particular esteem.

Fat porn's mission is to bring fat out of the closet and deliver it up for public viewing. Here you have the unhindered flaunting of fat, and the assertion of the fat body's sexual existence. Where else can you find stretch marks, cellulite, weight-gain, and flabby thighs publicly represented? (And aren't these features closer to the bodily attributes of most of the population than the *Vogue* ideal?) Displaying fat at all is socially objectionable; to be fat in public is to be a problem, a subject for endless commentary and jokes. Consider Roseanne, Liz Taylor, Oprah, all of whose bodies have been sites for public melodramas of transformation. Ridiculed when fat, heaped with exaggerated acclaim and tributes when thin: the culture seems to have an insatiable interest in these transformations. When Oprah loses weight, even the *New York Times* reports it.

Some fat porn—both gay and straight, both videos and magazines—falls into the category of hard core, meaning that penetration takes place. Given that hard core is structured around a specific conclusion, that is, the act of penetration (generally with certain specified detours along the way, namely oral sex), its narrative structure has a certain inevitability, a sense of purpose and direction. But even within hard core there are formal variations, for example, whether the act of penetration is treated as a "scene" or as a "narrative"; that is, whether the act is simply portrayed, or whether it is described as having a temporal dimension that unfolds and develops. The distinction between the "scene" and the "narrative" is one of the ongoing debates in theories about how memories are encoded, one debate being whether different types of memories, say, traumatic memories, are encoded differently, perhaps as "flashbacks," or scenes. It's intriguing that pornography, a form of fantasy suspended somewhere between the dream, the wish,

Hirsute masturbator from the pages of *Bulk Male* magazine.

and the memory (and perhaps even invoking traumatic memory, i.e., the "primal scene"), should rely on the same aesthetic devices, and perambulate the same aesthetic ground.[19]

A hard-core video like *Life in the Fat Lane* simply presents a series of scenes of quite gigantic women having sex with various normal-sized men. (There is a structuring device here: a tuxedoed master of ceremonies introduces each segment and then, of course, has his own moment in the sun at the end.) *Bulk Male,* a magazine, is similarly non-narrative, simply offering up stills of hefty, hirsute men engaged in lumbering sex acts. But a magazine like *Jumbo Jezebel* is organized narratively, recounting, through a series of quite artful color stills, the courtship of a cheerful, curly-haired fat woman.

"Jezebel," dressed to the nines, from the pages of *Jumbo Jezebel* magazine.

We open with Jezebel, dressed to the nines in a ruffled print frock, black lace stockings, bejeweled, made up, and awaiting her gentleman suitor. He arrives, and the story moves from a kiss on the hand, to tentative fondling, to open-mouthed kisses, and as the evening progresses, from heavy petting, to oral sex, penetration, and the inevitable cum shot. All of this takes place in a quite beautiful antique- and art-filled room, with most of the action taking place on a lush, black leather couch; between the decor, which says "parvenu," and the bodies which say "wrong side of the tracks," all sorts of narrative potential beyond the penetration plot gets put into circulation.

Other examples of the genre exist simply to display the glories of fat without any pretext such as penetration. Since their only structuring principle is fat, these videos take on the formless, meandering quality of Absurdist theater. In *Mother Load I,* two very fat women in stretchy lingerie (with a combined weight of 790 pounds, the video's jacket copy helpfully informs us) spend an hour discussing whether or not they should go shopping. Asks one fat roommate confrontationally, "Should we go shopping?" "We don't need anything," replies the other. "I want to go shopping," says the first, plangently. This is a film with the timeless circularity of *Waiting for Godot:* you just know they will never go shopping. Instead, they don bright red boxing gloves (making quite a visually striking tableau against the bright blue walls of the bedroom set), and begin boxing each other as a way to work out these minor domestic differences. They batter away while the camera roves around, over and between mountains of soft, quivering blubber in extremely long, unedited takes, and the two "roommates" get progressively more out of breath. Finally they collapse on the bed and do some perfunctory fondling of each other. Eventually some of the lingerie comes off, and the frame fills with rolls and rolls of fat, and the camera gets as close as it can without causing injury. It seems to want to lodge itself in between those mounds of flesh and take up residence as these two huge bodies heave and crash together like some ancient race of flabby female Titans. Like Theater of the Absurd for the consumer age, it ends where it started: "We forgot to go shopping." "I almost forgot. I want to go shopping." Other than fat and its sustenance, the human situation seems quite devoid of purpose or meaning here, but still, we don our boxing gloves and go on.

VII

Dimensions is a magazine put out by and for "Fat Admirers," who feel like an oppressed and ridiculed minority for this alarming preference, which these days has certainly supplanted homosexuality as "the love that dare not speak its name." We will refer to these men (as they do themselves) as "FAs." *Dimensions* consists of photospreads of quite fat, lingeried models, along with articles and self-help columns about getting along as an FA in a culture that places this kind of preference somewhere on a spectrum between farcical and criminally perverse. Many of the articles are concerned with the social difficulties and complexities of dating fat women, whose self-esteem is often negligible, and whose self-hatred is high. What happens when you introduce your fat wife to your unsuspecting colleagues, or when your fat girlfriend goes on a diet? How do you deal with stares or, worse, rude comments on the street? And there are articles by fat women, for whom FAs are sometimes a mixed blessing, many of them Don Juans, say the articles, for whom fat women are interchangeable. Or they're looking for their mothers, or are untrustworthy, ambivalent, or just generally dogs. Really, it sounds pretty much like your standard single heterosexual woman's complaint list about men.

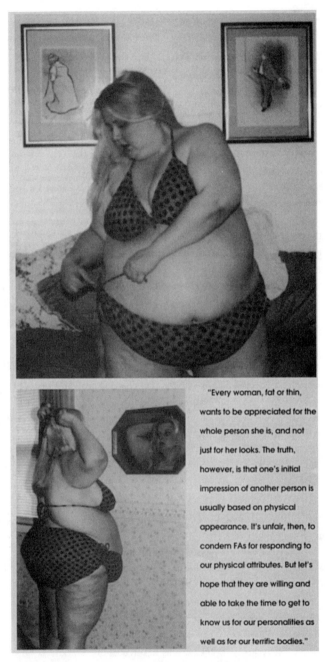

"Every woman, fat or thin, wants to be appreciated for the whole person she is, and not just for her looks. The truth, however, is that one's initial impression of another person is usually based on physical appearance. It's unfair, then, to condemn FAs for responding to our physical attributes. But let's hope that they are willing and able to take the time to get to know us for our personalities as well as for our terrific bodies."

Musing woman in bikini from the pages of *Dimensions* magazine.

Dimensions grew out of what is known as the "size-acceptance movement" and takes an activist position in relation to the indignities and physical dangers inflicted on the fat, which range from run-of-the-mill discrimination to stereotypical media portrayals and controversial, highly risky weight-loss surgeries (which is, according to *Dimensions,* a billion-dollar-a-year medical industry with an alarmingly high fatality rate). On the other hand, its articles can display an irritating tendency to whininess, frequently, for example, reproaching fat women themselves for the travails and oppressed minority status of male FAs, given that fat women can be just as uncomfortable with a man admiring their bodies as is the larger, fat-hating society. A lively dialogue is carried out between one faction, generally represented by fat women, whose hopeful position is that weight and size should not be acceptable criteria for judging worth ("love me for myself"), and a second faction of men who are positively turned on by fat women and have a strong preference for fat women. Some even have erotic, weight-gain fantasies about women (a group known to insiders as "feeders"). This subculture within the subculture struggles for acceptance of what many, even in this community, consider an unacceptable fantasy, with some women taking the feminist position that the weight-gain fantasy is another form of male control, merely the flip side of the insistence by men in the general culture that their partners lose weight, since both versions employ the same tactics of cajoling, coercing, bribery, and domination about food and poundage.

This debate will probably seem bizarre to the noninitiate, particularly if we neglect to consider how intensely issues of size so routinely enter into even mainstream dating and mating rituals. Personal ads, for example, whatever the publication in which they appear, are typically rigorous in their specifications about bodily preferences: "slim," "weight proportional to height," "no chubbies" are common requests for both gays and straights. These criteria obviously apply to every form of mate selection for much of the "nonperverse" population. To have a rigid sexual preference for a slim partner, even over, say, a fat Nobel Prize laureate, is a culturally acceptable and far from surprising sexual aim.

But then issues of size, in general, are recurring motifs in sexual attraction, from the routine issue of height preferences for both men and women, to male attention to female breast size, to women's emerging (although sometimes ironic and retaliatory) attention to penis size. Of course, size is a pivotal motif in the culture generally. An interest in issues of scale, particularly the gigantic, occupies much cultural attention across a range of sites, from children's literature, to sports "giants" (and the tacit acceptance of steroids to produce them), to cultural icons like Arnold Schwarzenegger, whose acting talents alone were perhaps not what propelled him so firmly into the cultural imagination. The gigantic has always been the subject of mythology. With the invention of officialdom and its institutions, church and state, the gigantic is appropriated from mythology for pragmatic ends: vastness, grandeur, and the massive scale of monuments and official architecture became ways of symbolizing the power of institutions and the insignificance of individuals; the hugeness of early cathedrals, for example, dwarfing the human with their immensity, was calculated to attract worshipful converts.[20]

Largeness also seems to invite cultural ambivalence. Note that fat comes packaged in two gendered varieties. Soft, fat largeness connotes the maternal, perhaps aggravating long-buried and tangled imaginative relations to issues of consumption, and by extension, to issues of resources, distribution, and equity. When large and solid (the gigantic), largeness connotes patriarchial masculinity: another symbolization of power and its abuses. Perhaps the systematic way the fat are stripped of social power symbolically stages the overthrow of sovereignty that symbolizes its authority through scale, of both maternal and paternal varieties, to the misfortune of those large humans whose lives are scarred by the hostile, and perhaps, to some degree, residual fascination with matters of scale and size.

VIII

The culture's anxiety about fat is endless, as is its hypocrisy. And certainly it's safe to say that any issue of physical appearance affects women far more disproportionately than men. Everywhere in pop culture you will find thoughtful, concerned articles on the social plagues of anorexia and bulimia side by side with diet tips and fashion photos of waif models. But liking fat in current American culture makes you a "fetishist," whose sexuality is by definition "pornographic." Perhaps this indicates just how thoroughly pornography and fetishism are shifting social categories whose relation to the larger culture is one of defiance, transgression, and even critique.

Pornography's celebration of fat, even its "objectification" of fat women, defies all societal norms and social controls. Its insistence on visibility for fat asserts the spectacle of fat *as* fat, rather than as an array of connotations. Fat is what our culture, for all of the reasons suggested above, does not want to look at. Pornography, in response, puts it on view. Fat pornography commemorates bodies that defy social norms. It solicits an erotic identification with bodies that are unresponsive to social control: voracious, demanding, improper, non–upwardly mobile, socially transgressive bodies. What this and other pornography provides, in the aesthetic realm, is a free-zone in which to defy the dictates and the homogeneity imposed on aesthetics, on sexuality, and on bodies.

For nonfat admirers, the disbelief and incredulity (or more likely I suspect, reflexive disgust and aversion) that enormously fat bodies can be in any nonperverse way beautiful, even a turn-on, shows just how deeply these social dictates are embedded in our psyches and construct our very mode of seeing the world. The pornographic idiom, including fat, at least currently, causes distress to those sensibilities, which have been cannily shaped by our culture to appear, falsely, as "natural." If you doubt it, think about the ruthlessness so frequently directed at the fat population, not in the pages of *Love's Savage Cupcake,* but in response to the mere appearance of a fat body walking down the street on a summer day. Fat's visibility risks provoking the most savage forms of bodily policing. It's an instant excuse for the citizenry to transform themselves into a sadistic public militia, dedicated to squelching whatever potential insurrection or threat that exposed fat augurs for the twentieth-century psyche.

For all of these reasons, instead of seeking to suppress the pornographic aesthetic, why not regard it as performing a social service? It exposes these cultural sore spots, reframing the connection between sex and the social in the idiom of lived experience. With one swift kick to the aesthetic, the inextricability of our desires, our "selves," and the casual everyday brutality of cultural conformity are bared as deeply visceral matters.

Notes

1. See Lynn Hunt, ed., *The Invention of Pornography: Obscenity and the Origins of Modernity, 1500–1800* (New York: Zone, 1993), especially Hunt's introduction, 9–45.

2. Mary Douglas, *Natural Symbols: Explorations in Cosmology* (London: Barrie & Rockliff, 1970).

3. Douglas, *Natural Symbols.*

4. Irvin Yalom, *Love's Executioner* (New York: Basic Books, 1989), 88.

5. See Lisa Schoenfielder and Barb Wieser, eds., *Shadow on a Tightrope: Writings by Women on Fat Oppression* (San Francisco: Spinster Press, 1983).

6. Gina Kolata, "Women Pay High Price for Being Overweight," *New York Times* (Oct. 30, 1993), A14.

7. Susan Bordo, *Unbearable Weight: Feminism, Western Culture, and the Body* (Berkeley: University of California Press, 1993), 185–212.

8. Anne Hollander, "When Fat Was in Fashion," *New York Times Magazine* (Oct. 23, 1977), 122. See also, Anne Hollander, *Seeing Through Clothes* (New York: Viking, 1978).

9. Reported in the 1992 Canadian documentary, "The Famine Within," produced by Katherine Gilday and broadcast on PBS.

10. Hollander, "When Fat Was in Fashion," 36.

11. Gina Kolata, "Burdens of Being Overweight," *New York Times* (Nov. 22, 1992), A14.

12. One study estimated that for every pound they are overweight, businessmen too lose a thousand dollars a year in salary. See Kolata, "Burdens of Being Overweight," A1.

13. Natalie Angier, "Why So Many Are Prejudiced against the Obese," *New York Times* (Nov. 22, 1992), A38.

14. Robert Sherrill, "Phil Gramm's Trail of Sleaze," *The Nation* (March 6, 1995), 301.

15. Marcia Millman, *Such a Pretty Face: Being Fat in America* (New York: Berkley, 1980).

16. Kolata, "Burdens of Being Overweight," 18.

17. Ibid., 18.

18. Lesbian historian Lillian Faderman, quoted in Natalie Angier, "Research on Sex Orientation Doesn't Neatly Fit the Mold," *New York Times* (July 18, 1993), A24.

19. Ian Hacking discusses these debates in *Rewriting the Soul: Multiple Personalities and the Science of Memory* (Princeton, NJ: Princeton University Press, 1995), 250–54.

20. Susan Stewart, *On Longing: Narratives of the Miniature, the Gigantic, the Souvenir, the Collection* (Durham, NC: Duke University Press), 1993.

10

Viscerality, Faith, and Skepticism: Another Theory of Magic

Michael Taussig

Underlying all our mystic states are corporeal techniques, biological methods of entering into communication with God.

— *Marcel Mauss,* Les
Techniques du Corps.[1]

The sorcerer generally learns his time-honoured profession in good faith, and retains his belief in it more or less from first to last; at once dupe and cheat, he combines the energy of a believer with the cunning of a hypocrite.

— *Edward Burnett Tylor,*
Primitive Culture[2]

My aim in this essay is as follows: to tackle the vexatious problem of faith, as in religious and magical faith, by means of (1) highlighting the fact that faith often seems to coexist with skepticism, suggesting that (2) such faith may even require skepticism, that (3) there is a deep-seated public secret as to the existence of a trick that allows this (perhaps necessary) coexistence to function, that (4) this usually involves some physical substance or object that exists in relation to the insides of the human body, and thus, finally, we may conclude that (5) there is a relation between faith and skepticism, no less than between faith and viscerality, that has escaped notice in some classic illustrations of magical healing made famous, indeed iconic, by an earlier anthropology, in that the success of such ritual lies not in concealing but in revealing trickery and that this is the peculiar mix of craft and *mysterium tremendum* that lies at the basis of magical efficacy, theories such as that of Claude Lévi-Strauss referring such efficacy to purported structuring, or of Evans-Pritchard's use of E. B. Tylor's idea as to some combination of statistical reasoning involving the category versus the particular, or theories of symbolic and metaphoric potency, notwithstanding.[3] The real skill of the practitioner lies not in skilled concealment but in the skilled revelation of skilled concealment. Magic is efficacious not despite the trick but on account of its exposure. The mystery is heightened, not dissipated, by unmasking, and in various ways, direct and oblique, ritual serves as a stage for so many unmaskings. Hence power flows not from masking but from an unmasking which masks more than masking does. Horkheimer and Adorno no less than Nietzsche were correct in discerning magic in Enlightenment, and this is reinforced when we consider the texts on shamanism and magical healing by Lévi-Strauss and Evans-Pritchard as themselves shot through and empowered by the magic they ostensibly transcend.[4] Let me now flesh this out, beginning with what for me stands as the ur-scene of conjuring and viscerality on the part of the sorcerer.

Uttermost Parts and Humbuggery

"Frequently the chief object of a raiding party, in the perpetual clan warfare of the Ona," wrote Lucas Bridges on the basis of decades of intimacy with these legendary people at the turn of the century in Tierra del Fuego, "was to kill the medicine man of an opposing group."[5] Raiding was a constant preoccupation, as therefore, was sorcery, so we can conclude that magic and sorcery were of considerable importance in this "uttermost part of the earth," as Bridges entitled his extraordinary memoir.[6] Indeed, he felt he had to decline the invitation of his Ona friends to become a medicine man, or *joon,* saying, "No! I would not become a *joon,* to be blamed, maybe, for a fatal heart attack a hundred miles away."[7]

Yet it was curious how the fear of magic coexisted with humbuggery. The first of the Ona superstitions, according to Bridges, was "fear of magic and of the power of magicians, even on the part of those who, professing that art, must have known that they themselves were humbugs. They had great fear of the power of others."[8]

"Some of these humbugs were excellent actors," noted Bridges, and it will be useful to follow him in his description of what he calls "acting" and observe the focus, if not obsession, with the object, the object as withdrawn from the interstices of the living, human, body:

> Standing or kneeling beside the patient, gazing intently at the spot where the pain was situated, the doctor would allow a look of horror to come over his face. Evidently he could see something invisible to the rest of

us.... With his hands he would try to gather the malign presence into one part of the patient's body — generally the chest — where he would then apply his mouth and suck violently. Sometimes this struggle went on for an hour, to be repeated later. At other times the *joon* would draw away from his patient with the pretense of holding something in his mouth with his hands. Then always facing away from the encampment, he would take his hands from his mouth gripping them tightly together, and, with a guttural shout difficult to describe and impossible to spell, fling this invisible object to the ground and stamp fiercely upon it. Occasionally a little mud, some flint or even a tiny, very young mouse might be produced as the cause of the patient's indisposition.[9]

Reading the state of the soul from the bodily exterior, insides from outsides in relation to the human body and especially in relation to the face, has a long history in Western and Middle Eastern traditions of physiognomy.[10] But here at the Uttermost Part some things are different; the practitioner seems not to read external signs so much as look through them into the body, and he uses objects, inert and alive, as proof of such discernment and the therapy entailed.

As an aside be it noted that a salient feature of physiognomy are the eyes, and those of the medicine man, perforce an expert in physiognomy, are no exception. Take those of the great medicine man, Houshken. He was over six feet tall, and his eyes were exceedingly dark, almost blue-black. "I had never seen eyes of such color," mused Lucas Bridges, and he wondered whether Houshken was nearsighted. Far from it; not only was the man a mighty hunter, but it was said that he could even look through mountains.

These are the sort of eyes that can look through the human body, as was brought out when Bridges allowed another famous medicine man, Tininisk (who some twenty years later became one of Father Martin Gusinde's most important informants), to begin inducting him into the ways of the medicine man. Half reclining, naked on guanaco skins by the fire sheltered by a windbreak, Bridges had his chest gone over by the medicine man's hands and mouth as intently, said Bridges, as any doctor with a stethoscope, "moving in the prescribed manner from place to place, pausing to listen here and there." Then come those eyes again, those eyes that can see through mountains, the mountain of the body: "He also gazed intently at my body, as though he saw through it like an X-ray manipulator."[11]

But it is not only the eyes that allow this. For might there not be a certain potential, at least, for transparency of the body, for a certain instability of flesh involved in bodily flowing and becoming animal?

The medicine man and his helper stripped naked. The medicine man's wife, one of the rare women healers, took off her outer garment, and the three of them huddled and produced something Bridges thought was of the lightest grey down, shaped like a puppy and about four inches long, with prick-ears. It had the semblance of life, perhaps due to their breathing and the trembling of their hands. There was a peculiar scent as the "puppy" was placed by the three pairs of hands to his chest where, without any sudden movement, it disappeared. Three times this was repeated, and then after a solemn pause Tininisk asked whether Bridges felt anything moving in his heart or if he could see something strange in his mind, as in a dream?

But Bridges felt nothing and eventually decided to abandon what he had found to be a fascinating course of studies because for one thing, he would frequently have to lie, "at which I was not very clever," and for another it would separate him from his Ona friends. "They feared the sorcerers; I did not wish them to fear me, too."[12] Although it waned, however, the desire to learn magic never completely left him.

When he later met up with the famous Houshken about whom he had heard so much, Bridges told him he had heard of his great powers and would like to see some of his magic. The moon was full that night. Reflected on the snow on the ground, it cast the scene like daylight. Returning from the river, Houshken began to chant, put his hands to his mouth and withdrew a strip of guanaco hide three times the thickness of a bootlace and about eighteen inches long. His hands shook and gradually drew apart, the strip stretching to about four feet. His companion took one end, and the four feet extended to eight, then suddenly disappeared back into Houshken's hands to become smaller and smaller; when his hands were almost together, he clapped them to his mouth, uttered a prolonged shriek, and then held out his hands, completely empty.

Even an ostrich, comments Bridges, could not have swallowed those eight feet of hide without a visible gulp. But where else could it have gone but back into the man's very body? He had no sleeves. He stood butt-naked in the snow with his robe on the ground. What's more, there were between twenty to thirty men present, but only a third of them were Houshken's people, and the rest were far from being friendly. "Had they detected some simple trick," writes Bridges, "the great medicine man would have lost his influence; they would no longer have believed any of his magic."[13]

Houshken put on his robe and seemed to go into a trance as he stepped toward Bridges, let his robe fall to the ground, put his hands to his mouth again, withdrew them, and when they were less than two feet from Bridges's face, slowly drew them apart to reveal a small, almost opaque object, about an inch in diameter, tapering into his hands. It could have been semitransparent elastic or dough, but whatever it was, it seemed to be alive, revolving at great speed.

The moon was bright enough to read by as he drew his hands apart, and Bridges realized suddenly the object was no longer there: "It did not break or burst like a bubble; it simply disappeared." There was a gasp from the onlookers. Houshken turned his hands over for inspection. They were clean and dry. Bridges looked down at the ground. Stoic as he was, Houshken could not resist a chuckle, for there was nothing to be seen. "Don't let it trouble you. I shall call it back to myself again."

By way of ethnographic explanation Bridges tells us that this curious object was believed to be "an incredibly malignant spirit belonging to, or possibly part of, the *joon* (medicine man) from whom it emanated." It could take physical form, or it could be invisible. It had the power to introduce insects, tiny mice, mud, sharp flints, or even a jellyfish or a baby octopus into the body of one's enemy. Bridges writes, "I have seen a strong man shudder involuntarily at the thought of this horror and its evil potentialities."[14] "It was a curious fact," he adds, "that, although every magician must have known himself to be a fraud and a trickster, he always believed in and greatly feared the supernatural abilities of other medicine-men."[15]

Viscerality and the Gay Science

At this juncture I want to draw your attention to several things that shall preoccupy me in this essay, as they may stimulate and even instruct us as to the sleight-of-hand demanded by powerful knowledges recruiting the inside-outness of the body in staring down fate. First there is the mirroring of what comes out and goes back into the healer's body by what is meant in other circumstances to occur with the patient's body or with the enemy's body, no less than in the preparation of a novice healer. In other words the feats displayed are among what we might allude to as the "primary mechanics" of the shamanism in question.[16]

Then there is the exceedingly curious object that is said to be a spirit belonging to or actually forming part of the body of the medicine man; it appears to be alive, yet it is an object all the same; it marks the exit from and reentry into the body; it has a remarkably indeterminate quality: the *fluffy puppy* of down, the *weird elasticity* of the guanaco strip, the *semitransparent dough* or elastic *revolving at high speed,* all in some way acting like extensions of the human body and thus capable of connecting with and entering into other bodies, human and nonhuman.

I also want to draw your attention to the sudden appearances and equally mysterious disappearances of these objects no less than to an emphasis on movement, most notably bodily movement, meaning not only the place of the body in space, nor simply rapid extension of limbs in what is almost a form of dance, but also very much a movement of egress and ingress, of insides into outsides and vice versa, combined with a movement of sheer becoming, transforming being and nonbeing into the beingness of transforming forms; to the metamorphosing capacity of curious, unnamable, animate objects to become more clearly recognizable but out-of-place things like baby octopi, or mud, or a flint in the body of the enemy, a capacity not only for change but for an implosive viscerality that would seem to hurl us beyond the world of the symbol and that penny-in-the-slot resolution called meaning.[17]

Above all at this point I want to draw attention to the skillful display of magical feats and tricks and to wonder about their relationship to the utterly serious business of killing and healing people, the very point of this essay. This combination of trickery, spectacle, and death must fill us with confusion, even anxiety, as to the notion of the trick and its relation to both theater and to science, let alone to truth and fraud. We therefore need to dwell upon this corrosive power creeping along the otherwise imperceptible fault lines in the sturdy structure of language and thought, splicing games and deceit to matters of life and death, theater to reality, this world to the spirit-world, and trickery to the illusion of a world without trickery—the most problematic trick of all. Here one can sympathize with Nietzsche in *The Birth of Tragedy,* where he writes that "all of life is based on semblance, art, deception, points of view and the necessity of perspectives and error,"[18] no less than with the attempt by Horkheimer and Adorno to position not Eve and the tree of the knowledge of good and evil but shamanism and its magic as the true Fall from grace onto the first faltering steps of Enlightenment and what has come to be called science, imitating nature so as by this "deception" to control nature, including human nature, transforming trick into technique and knowledge into power/knowledge.[19]

Following Nietzsche, I assume two somewhat separate points here, one being his often-repeated assertion regarding the long-term well-being provided by error and untruth in human and social life, and the second being the injunction for us not to labor under the illusion of eliminating trickery on the assumption that there is some other world out there beyond and bereft of trickery, beyond and bereft of what has come to be known as power/knowledge and the artistry associated therewith, but to practice instead our own form of "shamanism," if that is the word, as philosophy and as search for understanding, if that is the word, and come up with a set of tricks, simulations, deceptions, and art or appearances in a continuous movement of counterfeint and feint strangely contiguous with yet set against those weighing on us.[20] It is something like this nervous system, I believe, that Nietzsche had in mind with his Gay Science, a "mocking, light, divinely untroubled, divinely artificial art" built around the idea, if I may put it this way, that exposure of the trick is no less necessary to the magic of magic than is its concealment.[21]

"To Describe Any Considerable Number of Tricks Carried Out by the Shamans, Both Chuckchee and Eskimo, Would Require Too Much Space."

The word *shaman* is taken as the name for one of the several classes of healers amongst the Tungus of Siberia, and from its very inception, the naming and the figure of the shaman on the anthropological stage was profoundly insinuated in the vigorous display of trickery by means of startling revelations as to ventriloquism, imitations of animal spirit voices, curtained chambers, mysterious disappearances and reappearances, semisecret trapdoors, knife tricks, and so forth, including — if trick be the word here, and why not? — sex changes by men and women.[22] By the last quarter of the twentieth century so-called shamans came to be thought of by anthropologists no less than by laymen as existing everywhere throughout the world and throughout history as a universal type of magical and religious being, and the *trickery* tended to be downplayed as the *mystical* took center stage. The term *shaman* itself had become diffused early on throughout Western languages, thanks to the Siberian ethnography, the phenomenon thus joining an illustrious company of colonially derived native terms such as *totemism, taboo, mana,* and even *cannibalism.*[23]

Hearken to the wonderful tricks presented for Waldemar Bogoras by the Chukchee shaman of Siberia, Bogoras's 1904 monograph being one of the high points in the birth of shamanism as a Western object of study. Bogoras was fascinated for instance by the shamans' skill in ventriloquy and the creation by this means of soundscapes so complex and multilayered that it seemed like one was immersed in a spirit-world. He took pains to capture the trick of voice-throwing on a phonographic record and was surprised that he could do so, as if delighted by his own trickery. Another form of trick was performed by a shaman wringing her hands so as to make a large pebble reproduce a continuous row of small pebbles on top of her drum. Bogoras tried to trick her into revealing her trick, but was unable. Another of her tricks was to rip open the abdomen of her son to find and remove the cause of illness. "It certainly looked as if the flesh was really cut open," he wrote. On both sides, from under the fingers flowed little streams of blood trickling to the ground. "The boy lay motionless; but once or twice moaned feebly, and complained that the knife had touched his entrails." The shaman placed her mouth to the incision and spoke into it. After some moments she lifted her head, and the boy's body was quite sound. Other shamans made much of stabbing themselves with knives. Tricks were everywhere. As Bogoras concluded, "To describe any considerable number of tricks carried out by the shamans, both Chukchee and Eskimo, would require too much space."[24] Yet can we resist mentioning two more? "Upune, for instance, pretended to draw a cord through her body, passing it from one spot to another. Then suddenly she drew it out, and immediately afterward pretended to cut in two with it the bodies of several of their children, who sat in front of her. These and other tricks resemble to a surprising degree the feats of jugglers all over the world. Before each performance, Upune would even open her hands, in the graceful manner of a professor of magic, to show us she had nothing in them." The greatest trick of course was not that of being able to descend and walk in the underground, but to change one's sex, thanks to help from the spirits, a change that could well eventuate, at least in the case of a man, in his taking male lovers or becoming married to a man. Such "soft men," as they were called, were feared for their magic more than unchanged men or women.[25]

"A Peculiar State of Mind:"
"It Would Be Wonderful If a Man
Could Talk with Animals and Fishes."

"It is perfectly well-Known by all concerned," wrote the eminent anthropologist Franz Boas, toward the end of his career, "that a great part of the shamanistic procedure is based on fraud; still it is believed in by the shaman as well as by his patients and their friends. Exposures do not weaken the belief in the "true" power of shamanism. Owing to this peculiar state of mind, the shaman himself is doubtful in regard to his powers and is always ready to bolster them up by fraud."[26]

At the risk of being odiously pedantic, allow me to try to catch this slippery fish of Kwakiutl shamanism by itemizing its contradictory components as they come across here in Boas's rendering. I am aware that all I demonstrate is that the more you try to pin this fish down, the more it wriggles, and this is, I guess, my labored point, to watch the figure of logic emerge from the vengeful force of pins and points bent on restraint.

1. All concerned know that a great part of shamanistic practice is a fraud.
2. Yet shaman, patient, and friends, all believe in shamanism.
3. Moreover, exposure of its fraudulence does not weaken belief in shamanism.
4. Thus he resorts to (further) fraud.
5. Now start with item 1 again.

And after close study, Stanley Walens states that anthropologists "have often wondered why it is that the natives do not complain that the shamans are performing tricks and not real cures. They have found it difficult to explain the seeming paradox that while Kwakiutl shamans are admired for their abilities at legerdemain, if a shaman bungles one of these tricks, he is immediately killed."[27] "Unlike his more mystical and more spiritual counterparts," writes Irving Goldman, contrasting Kwakiutl with arctic shamanism, "the kwakiutl shaman relies heavily on elaborate tricks in his public demonstrations. He devises hidden trapdoors and partitions, and uses strings to cleverly manipulate artificial figures. He is in appearance the modern magician."[28]

At this point let us pause and cast an eye over the strategies one might pursue to understand the fraudulent as not only true but efficacious, the trick as technique. One could find relief in Boas's statement that not all but only a (great) part of the shamanistic procedure is based on fraud, and hope that the lesser part may turn out to be the more important. Or one could plunge into the heady waters of interrogating the meaning of "belief" as in "still it is *believed* in by the shaman as well as by his patients," thus forcing the issue of the difference between belief as a personal psychological state and belief as "tradition," as some sort of cultural "script" (the British "intellectualist" approach to magic versus the French approach of Durkheim and Levy-Bruhl), and so forth. One would also want to ask questions like, To what extent is belief ever an unflawed, totally confident, and uncontradictory thing anyway? How much does one have to "believe" for shamanism to work? and so on (a well-worn path, actually).

Or one could use the E. B. Tylor maneuver taken up by Evans-Pritchard that because what we might call "scientific" procedures of verification or falsification of the efficacy of magical healing are either not available, not practiced, or by definition inapplicable, *there is always a way of explaining failure away* (e.g., bad faith or ritual error on the part of the healer, a stronger sorcerer at work in the background, unstoppable malevolence on the part of a too-powerful spirit...). This argument is usually packaged with another: that this infamously "closed system," about which so much has been written with regard to Africa, is in some yet to be plausibly connected way associated with the yet to be explained belief that *although any particular shaman may be fraudulent, the institution of shamanism is nevertheless valid* (believed in, plausible, worth a shot?); like the modern police, it takes more than a few bad apples to spoil the barrel, as the New York Police Commissioner is fond of saying.

Or one could do something still more interesting, even fruitful and original, and substitute for the word *fraud* the word *simulation* or *mimesis*. This has remarkable fallout poetically no less than philosophically, and is uncannily resonant with the ethnographic record itself, as we shall later see. With this, perhaps, our fish would stop wiggling and start to swim, a manner of "resolving" contradiction I find preferable to that of pins and points.

Boas's intimate knowledge concerning this "peculiar state of mind" came from his four-decades-long relationship with his Kwakiutl informant George Hunt and the ten thousand pages of material they published, plus several thousand more existing in manuscript form.[29] Their weighty conversations about Hunt's shamanic experiences began in 1897 and reached a peak in the 1925 *auto*biographical text of Hunt's published in Kwakiutl and in English in 1930 as *I Desired to Learn the Ways of the Shaman,* a text delivered from obscurity by Claude Lévi-Strauss in a famous essay entitled "The Sorcerer and His Magic,"[30] which was an attempt to provide what must now seem more of an expression of faith, as in structuralism, than an explanation of faith, as in magic, the point being that Hunt, known at the beginning of the 1930 essay as Giving-Potlatches-in-the-World, becomes by his own admission a famous shaman not so much despite as because of his profoundly skeptical attitude.[31]

In fact, over the twenty-nine years from 1897 to 1925, *Hunt had given Boas no less than four accounts of his experience in becoming a shaman,* and it was remarkable for Boas how the last account — the one that became published as *I Desired to Learn the Ways of the Shaman* — eliminated what Boas called all the supernatural elements in the earlier versions in which Hunt vividly described his mysterious fainting fits as a child, finding himself naked in the graveyard at night, the visits by immensely powerful spirits such as the killer whale named Tilting-in-Mid-Ocean, who told him how to cure the chief's sick boy the following day, how the feather-down indicative of disease appears of its own accord in his mouth as he is sucking out the disease, how killer whales accompanied his canoe, how he ate of the corpse of the shaman Life-Maker, and so forth. Most of the time, it seems, in the early versions, he was falling unconscious, passing out, entering these other realms, while in the last version, that of 1925, Hunt takes the position, as Boas puts it, "that his only object was to discover the frauds perpetrated by shamans."[32] Small wonder then that, confronted with contradictions such as these and resolute to the facts at hand, Boas, unlike the fledgling British science of social anthropology in the pioneering hands of Malinowski with his simplistic formula relating part to whole, for instance, never came up with a general theory or picture of Kwakiutl society.

At one point Boas commonsensically noted that the skepticism displayed by Kwakiutl people as to magic should be seen as a political defense; Indians did not want to come across to whites as irrational and so would fake a critical attitude toward shamanism (how things have changed!). Hence at one stroke we could dismiss questions concerning the place of skepticism in faith and simply view such perplexity as mere artifact of another sort of fraud — or is it mimesis? — namely, that of Indian self-representation to whites at that time and place. But then of course another hypothesis intrudes: that if fraud is an essential part of (Kwakiutl) shamanism, or at least of its "greater part," as Boas elsewhere states with much vigor, and if skepticism exists alongside such fraud, then it probably would require little effort, if any at all, to "adopt" (as Boas puts it) a skeptical attitude toward shamanism when talking to whites for two connected reasons. First because skepticism is part of the "greater part," and the Indian is merely being honest and nonfraudulent, and is in fact giving "the native's point of view" in admitting to the fraud, and second because, insofar as one is being fraudulent vis-à-vis the white interlocutor, presumably one has had much practice with fraud and skepticism in discussing shamanism with fellow Indians anyway.

And what are we to make of the fact that Hunt's scathingly skeptical 1925 autobiographical account of shamanism comes not at the beginning but after forty years of friendship with Boas, and that it is the earlier versions, not the last, that are the credulously mystical ones? Given that their friendship would probably have become more intimate and trusting over the years, does this not tend to contradict Boas's attempt to interpret the veracity of his Indian informant, where he observes that the Indian is likely to stress skepticism with whites so as to appear rational? Wouldn't the later version be more likely to be more honest and less concerned with creating a good — that is, rational — impression?[33]

In any event, the colonial relationship, through which such epistemically sensitive and imaginative activity as shamanism is to be conveyed, inevitably becomes no less part of our object of study than the shamanic activity itself. To get to the truth of shamanism, we start to realize, means getting to the truth of an intercultural relationship objectified by means of autoethnographic, intercultural texts such as the fourth version over three decades of *I Wished to Discover the Ways of the Shaman.*[34] But this is most definitely not to say that the pervasive influence of colonialism accounts for skepticism with regard to the autoethnography of magic — on the contrary. The magic at stake here first and foremost concerns the way in which the colonial presence provides yet another figure to be caught in the legerdemain of revelation of concealment.

Perhaps an outline of George Hunt's meteoric shamanic career as he presents it in his final 1925 text will assist us here, although the comforting sense of a career does scant justice to the zigzagging through contradiction that is entailed. First let us dwell on the fact that from the very first line of his forty-one page account, he presents himself as the arch-doubter, *yet wants to learn* the ways of the shamans.

The tension here seems so crucial, so carefully highlighted, that it is surely fair to venture the hypothesis that *learning shamanism means doubting it at the same time,* and that the development of such a split consciousness involving belief and nonbelief is what this learning process is all about. "I desired to learn about the shaman," he starts off, "whether it is true or whether it is made up and whether they pretend to be shamans."[35] His doubting is all the more striking, given that the two shamans he is involved with are also, as he states, his "intimate friends."

His first step is to be the target of a shaman's vomited quartz crystal during a public healing ceremony. He himself, we might say, becomes a display object, a ritual within a ritual, a trick not unlike the trick with the concealed feather-down in the mouth that he later learns for healing. Next he appears as a powerful shaman in the dream of a sick boy, the son of a chief, whose dream acts as a detailed script full of technique for the subsequently effective cure he practices on the young dreamer, and with this his fame is ensured, his name changed, and a succession of shamanic competitions ensues as he travels the land in search of truth and technique, and exposes other shamans as fakes, or at the least puts the healing efficacy of their techniques in grave doubt, so that they are convinced that he possesses a secret more powerful than their own.[36]

From the outset he not only privately doubts shamanism but goes out of his way to publicize the fact. It seems culturally important to do this, making it clear that he is "the principal one who does not believe in all the ways of the shamans, for I had said so aloud to them."[37] And in case you assume he is unique in either his doubting or in giving voice to his doubting, he lets you know that one of the first persons he meets after the quartz was shot into him asks, "Have you not felt the quartz crystals of the liars, the shamans, the one that they referred to that was thrown into your stomach? ... You will never feel it, for these are just great lies what the shamans say."[38] And the head chief, Causing-to-Be-Well, the next person with whom he speaks, similarly disabuses him: "They are just lies what the shamans say."

Just about everyone, so it seems, revels in declaring shamans to be fakes and rarely lets an opportunity slip to insist on this elemental fact. Moreover, as if in keeping with what we might call this sadomasochistic attitude of loving skepticism toward truth and authenticity, each time Hunt, known here as Giving-Potlatches-in-the-World, serves as a target of opportunity for the revelation of this fakery, *his desire to learn the ways of the shamans redoubles*. One really has to admire his enthusiasm, no less than that which the accomplished shamans bring to the task of revealing their secrets.

Take the case of the famous Koskimo shaman, Aixagidalagilis, he who so proudly sang his sacred song:

> Nobody can see through the magic power.
> Nobody can see through my magic power.

But when Giving-Potlatches-in-the-World (i.e., George Hunt) cured the patient whom Aixagidalagilis was unable to cure, and did this through his *pretense* of trembling and through his *pretense* of sucking out the bloody worm of disease (I am merely emphasizing here what he says in his text), then Aixagidalagilis implores him not so much to reveal "the secret," although certainly that, too, but first and implied in this request, to reveal the ontological status, the reality, if you will, of the technique employed: "I pray you to have mercy and tell me what stuck on the palm of your hand last night. Was it the true sickness or was it only made up?"[39] It seems like a wrenching pathos here, an almost childish pleading, surfacing with a terrible anxiety as to whether or not the technique is a trick.

Giving-Potlatches-in-the-World responds, again striking the appropriate ontological concern but disturbing its gravity with what seems like a rather mischievous, rather nasty, bit of teasing, "Your saying to me is not quite good, for you said, 'is it the true sickness, or is it only made up?'" Note that this is the same Giving-Potlatches-in-the-World who has just finished singing his sacred song on completing his successful cure in front of the assembled throng, humiliating Aixagidalagilis:

> He tried to prevent me from succeeding, the one who does not succeed.
> Ah, I shall not try to fail to have no sacred secrets.[40]

(This string of double negatives must tell us something crucially important about the curious transparency of the secret in the shamanic cure, no less than in the sacred.)

And having been bettered, Aixagidalagilis then pours out his secrets: "Let me tell you the way of my head ring of red cedar bark," he says.[41] "Truly, it is made up what is thought by all the men it is done this way. Go on! Feel the thin sharp-pointed nail at the back of the head of this my cedar bark ring, for I tell a lie when I say that the alleged sickness which I pretend to suck out from the sick person.... All these fools believe it is truly biting the palm of my hand."[42]

Secrecy is infinitely mysterious here because it is allied with and creative of what we might call the sacredness of a hiddenness within the theatricality that mediates between the real and the really made up, no less than between trick and technique and therapeutic efficacy. What is equally crucial is that not only do the established shamans, once they lose out in competition, beseech him for the secret of the technique but, in doing so, they seem even more concerned to tell him their own secrets. In fact, their predisposition to confessing their secrets is amazing. The secret teaching of shamanism has thus a peculiar confessional, post-hoc, belatedly historicist turn to it: secrets revealed after they are no good, secrets discarded after they have failed to maintain the tension of reality as really made up.[43]

This curious excavating mechanism of confession proceeds in passionate and intricate detail to describe how deception was achieved. Nothing seems without pretense any more, other, of course, than this exposure itself (and the double-headed serpent with the head of a human in its middle; see below). "It would be wonderful," Aixagidalagilis says at one point, "if a man could talk with animals and fishes. And so the shamans are liars who say they catch the soul of the sick person, for I know we all own a soul."[44]

His daughter, Inviter-Woman, then tells us what happened to this cynical manipulator who is her shaman father, of the great unholiness that befell herself and him when, on account of his shame, they fled the haunts of men and in their wandering came across a creature lying crossways on a rock, which they recognized as the double-headed serpent with a head at each end and a large human head in the middle. Seeing this, they died, to be brought to life by a man who told them he would have brought them good fortune but because she was menstruating, they would have trouble till they died.[45] And from then on they were driven out of their minds. She was laughing as she told this, and then she would cry, pulling out her hair, and her father, the great pretender, died crazed within three winters. And the moral? "Now this the end of talk about Aixagidalagilis who was believed by all the tribes to be really a great shaman who had gone through [all the secrets]. Then I found out that he was just a great liar about everything that he did in his shamanism."[46]

Thus, we might say, shamans might be liars, but menstruation and double-headed serpents are not without a decidedly nasty potential. And surely this is one of those tales that not only belies the satisfaction of a moral or any other system but delights in exploiting the idea of one. This we might with truth call a "nervous system," in which shamanism not only thrives on a corrosive skepticism but in which skepticism and belief actively cannibalize one another, so that continuous injections of recruits like Giving-Potlatches-in-the-World, who are full of questioning, are required. They are required, so it would seem, so as to test and therewith brace the mix by serving not as raw material of doubt positioned so as to terminate as believers, nor yet as cynical manipulators, but as exposers — vehicles for confession for the next revelation of the secret contained in the trick that is both art and technique and therewith real and really made up.

Technique is thus revealed as trick, and it behooves us to inquire further into this momentous distinction, recalling how fundamental a role the passage from trick to technique is in Horkheimer and Adorno's argument regarding the role of mimesis in the extraordinarily pivotal role of (what they refer to as) shamanism in Enlightenment and modern technology.

Here we are indebted to Stanley Walen's reading of shamanic tricks as technique in the Boas-Hunt texts, because he points out the awesome magic of mimesis in which the practitioner sets up a performance that, through its perfection, spirits will copy. This follows from the fact that the Kwakiutl believe their world is mimetically doubled in several ways, that "animals and spirits lead lives exactly equivalent to those of humans. They live in winter villages, perform dances, wear masks, marry, pray, and perform all other acts that humans perform." When the shaman sucks disease from the human body, the spirits are there sucking too. In this way magic involves what Walens calls "the magnification and intensification of a human action to a greater level of power."[47] Hence he can claim that there is no real paradox involved in shamanism, because the tricks turn out to be models or scenes for the spirits to follow, and it is the spirits who ultimately supply the cure. It is as if the paradox is an artifact of the Enlightenment, of the way of looking at human and social phenomena that comes from a disenchantment with the world and that therefore, so the stream of thought goes, spirits are to be explained rather than providing the explanation. It is thus devastating, I think, to read Walens when he tells us that the shaman is at all times dependent on the spirits and that "the Kwakiutl pay no attention to the thoughts of the shaman while he is performing the act because the spirits effect the cure using the shaman as their instrument, and the shaman's thoughts are irrelevant to the efficacy of his cure."[48]

Nevertheless, how would this help us understand the continuous anxiety as to pretense and the continuous excavation of fraud through revelation of the (failed) secret? Could it be that the shaman is not only tricking the human but also the spirit world, on which he or she is dependent? And what sort of "dependency" is this?

Here something innately carnal takes center stage, something bodily tied to the mimetic faculty defined as "the nature that culture uses to create second nature," as when Walens points out that the "critical part of the cure is the fluidity, skill, and physical perfection with which the shaman performs his tricks, for it is the motions of the tricks (reinforced by their exact duplication by the spirits) that effect the cure."[49] Although at times he refers to the reciprocation of humans and spirits as responsible for this, note that it is mimesis that is at stake and not some form of instrumentally conceived mutual-aid contract. "The characteristics of the physical movement made by the ritualist are of the greatest importance," he says, "for the particular qualities of the movement he makes during the performance of the ritual will be repeated exactly in form, but with greatly increased power by the spirits."[50]

An immensely suggestive feature is left hanging here, along with perfection and skill, and that is *fluidity*. "As long as the shaman performs his actions with fluidity," insists Walens, "the spirits are conjoined by cosmic forces to use their power to cure."[51] And whatever fluidity is, it is the opposite of *bungling:* "The shaman who bungles his tricks," Walens goes on to say, "forces the spirits to perform actions that are as disjointed, undirected, and destructive as his." Not only does this bungling not result in a cure, but it actually kills people by unleashing what Walens refers to as "uncontrollable chaotic power on the world." For this reason, the bungler himself must be immediately killed before he can do greater damage.[52] This puts Giving-Potlatches-in-the-World's desire to learn the ways of the shaman in admirable perspective.

This reminder as to flow and its immense importance in building the simulacrum that is the trick that is technique has the merit of sensitizing us to the play of metonymy within and extending beyond metaphor, in other words to a certain play of bodiedness, contagion, and physical connection as the co-component of the mimetic alongside the idea, the symbol, the distanced visual or quasi-visual dimension of things. There are many terms and dichotomies for this, testimony (if any is to be required) to our studied and probably necessary incapacity to put the "language" of body into language per se: Jakobson's metaphor versus metonymy, Nietzsche's Apollonian versus Dionysian, Fraser's homeopathic versus contagious forms of sympathetic magic, Benjamin's aura versus tactility, Delueze and Guattari's rhizomic "logic" becoming animal, and so forth.

Whatever we might mean by sacredness and its attendant dangers and rites, it surely has a great deal to do with such dichotomies uniting yet dividing spirit from body, so that the *flow* in technique in Kwakiutl shamanism, be it noted, bears heavily on soul/body dislocatability (spirit-caused illness) or the implosion via mystical force of Otherness into the body of the victim (sorcery). Hence flow directly implicates not one but several bodies and energies flowing into and out of one another, across borders accessed by dream, surreality, and animal visitations such as the toad, or the wolves that come down the beach vomiting foam over the body while the others lie dying on account of the holocaust brought by the white society in the form of smallpox, reducing the Kwakiutl population by an unbelievable 80–90 percent from 1862 to 1929.[53]

The flow is between animals and humans, as it has been from the very beginning of Kwakiutl time when the original ancestors took off their animal masks and skins to present their human selves. The flow is also from the clothes, presumably of the white people, the flow of the pox. "After we had stepped from our canoe," recounts Fool, describing how he became a shaman, we found much clothing and flour. We took them and ten days later became sick with the great smallpox. We lay in bed in our tent. I was laying among them. Now I saw that all our bodies swelled and were dark red. Our skins burst open and I did not know that they were all dead and I was laying among them. Then I thought I also was dead." Wolves came down the beach, whining and howling, licking his body, he recounted, vomiting foam which they put into his body. They tried hard, he explains, to put foam all over my body, continuously licking him and turning him all over. When it was all licked off, they vomited over him again, licking off the scabs of smallpox in the process: "Now I saw I was lying among my dead past nephews."[54]

The flow may be no less interior than exterior, as in getting certain insides outside so that they may disappear again inside the healer's body, the first requisite being a type of diagnostic anatomy as in the searching of the chest, mighty theater of the unknown: "For a long time he felt of the middle of the chest. I heard Aixagidalagilis say that there was no sickness in the middle of the chest. Then he felt of the right hand side of the chest. Then he pointed with his first finger to the place where the heart of Wawengenol was beating. Then the shaman spoke and said, 'I have now found the place where the sickness is,' [and] he put his mouth to the place where was beating his heart. Four times he blew at it and then he sucked."[55] And then maybe the sickness is dispatched by being swallowed by the healer. Or else the intestines and not the chest shall be the focus, as with the woman shaman Helagolsela at Nimkish pressing down with both hands on the lower part of the ribs of the poor woman patient, pressing so strongly that she went to the backbone, passing over the navel as she groaned in the pain of it, coming down inside the crotch, repeating this over and over again so it sounded as if her intestines were boiling. She had now gotten the sickness to go downward to collect at the rectum from where it would be defecated, she said, blowing for a long time from the stomach to the inside of the crotch. This is done by these shamans for man or woman, for headache or for urinary obstruction—this sickness called "blocked up inside."[56]

As with the very concept of the mimetic and its magic, let alone the degree to which spirits themselves can be fooled, is there not a crucial secret here in that while the shaman pretends to suck out disease and demonstrate the success of this action with a fake worm or piece of down supposedly retrieved from the insides of the patient's body, the spirit actually does extract something, so that we might say that the trick "tricks" (calls, encourages, seduces?) first and foremost the spirit so as to become a fluidly efficacious technique? Is it here where imitation in being fraudulent ensures realness and works it wonderful magic? "We might say," says Walens elsewhere, "that the Kwakiutl play games as much with the spirits as with their human opponents."[57]

In this regard it is illuminating to read the vicissitudes of Boas's translation of the Kwakiutl name of the stupendously important Winter Ceremonial, when the spirits emerge in their fullness from November until well into the following year and take over the life of the villages, during which time humans impersonate the spirits, enact the myths pertaining to the origins of human acquisition of supernatural powers from some fifty-three human-animal doubles such as Wolf, Killer Whale, Eagle, Thunderbird and Man-Eater (Cannibal Dancer).[58]

The name of the Winter Ceremonial, *tsetseqa*, is curious; Boas says it means "fraudulent" or "to cheat" (as well as being synonymous with "to be good-minded" and "happy"). "For instance, when a person wants to find out whether a shaman has real power or whether his power is based on pretense, he uses the same term meaning *"pretended, fraudulent, made up* shaman. Even in the most serious presentations of the ceremonial, it is clearly and definitely stated that it is planned as a *fraud*."[59] In *The Mouth of Heaven,* Irving Goldman tries to mitigate this curiousness by arguing that Boas's translation is crude. It should, claims Goldman, using Boas's posthumous grammar, mean "imitated."[60]

Here, I think, fortuitous as it may be, we have located the core of the riddle, especially when one notes that Boas had, according to Goldman, "in an earlier stab at translation" suggested that the stem of the word for the Winter Ceremonial, *tseka,* meant *secrets.*

There is a certain anxiety, even pain and craziness, here, as Goldman heatedly insists that to imitate is not necessarily to secularize. Who said it was? What's the problem? All these words start to swim in multiple and multiply conflicting configurations of overlapping associations and streams of reversible meanings;

- fraud
- simulation
- exalted
- imitation
- secret
- happiness
- sacred

From here on, the philosophical ground becomes steep and slippery, and perhaps only Fool dares go further as the mysteries of representation and reality, within Western philosophy alone, not to mention Kwakiutl, emerge full force.

Yet if there is a moral, it might be this: that the real novice in this story, *I Wished to Discover the Ways of the Shaman,* was Boas and, beyond him, by implication, the science-of-man he came to spearhead and the momentous historical moment of modernity that spawned this science. Of course, this very much implicates us, too, and yet gives us the choice provided by this insight. For the point of the text as I read it (and as is amply confirmed by Boas's later commentary) is not that Boas as a neutral observer and recording angel somehow lucked out and found the one, unique, Enlightenment individual ready to challenge hocus-pocus and give the inside story to Our-Man-from-New York, nor even that there seems to be a ready supply of such skeptics, but that the text in itself, artifact of the fledgling science of anthropology, especially that given over to Giving-the-Natives'-Point-of-View, is an utterly perfect instance of the confession of the secret, being the very acme of the skilled revelation of skilled concealment. In other words this text is not so much about shamanism as it is shamanic in its conformity to the cannibalistic logic of needing ever-fresh recruits for ceaseless confession such that in its very skepticism lies its profound magic, and Lévi-Strauss can quite inappropriately conclude that, at the end, Giving-Potlatches-in-the-World seems to have lost sight of his fallacious technique and, by implication, has crossed the threshold from skepticism to faith, from science to magic. The problem arises in not having taken with enough seriousness the necessity for skepticism in magic as relayed through rituals of exposure and unmasking, and, second, in not having seen the text *I Desired to Learn the Ways of the Shaman,* as in itself just this very ritual transposed into textual form, readied by the anthropologist as science. Leaving this text as raw material in the mode of Boas's textual realism, or recruiting it as does Lévi-Strauss for purpose of validating structuralism, misses the point but also the invitation that such ritual offers: that it lives as magic and makes claims even on us in its request for a reciprocal response composed in equal measure of confessional responsibility and judicious and intricately moving medleys of skepticism and faith, continuously deferred through the opening and closing of the secret.

For we have our tricks to develop too, "the trick of the floating quartz crystal" we might call this, involving a heightened sensitivity to fluidity, mass, and movement no less than to ecstatic moments of appearance and disappearance of objects inside and between bodies as the liberated quartz crystal vomited out by the shaman Making-Alive enters into the body of our friend here, Giving-Potlatches-in-the-World. "Now this one will be a great shaman, said he."[61] This suggests a certain fluidity of performance with identities if not with the logic of becoming, itself, the song leaders beating fast time as Fool looks upward watching the quartz float around in the cedar beams while Making-Alive staggers like a drunk around the fire in the middle of the house in front of a great mass of onlookers.

For might we not say that the reality of shamanism hangs on the reality of this fragment of flickering-light-in-tumbling-stone passing between intestines through streams of vomit, lost for the moment in a graceful float up there in the cedar rafters? There are many issues here, but keep your eye on the quartz crystal floating free, for who knows for how short or long a time it will stay up in the air heavy with the tension of bodily interconnection. The quartz is a trick, and the trick is a figure, and the figure of the trick is one of continuous movement and metamorphosis in, through, and between bodies carrying power one jump ahead of its interpretation. The language of true or false seems not just peculiarly inept here, but deliberately so.

At one point struggling to understand the place of theater and spirit-impersonation in the Winter Ceremonial, Goldman seems to be stating that mimetic simulation is a way of keeping hidden things secret while displaying them. "The ceremonies deal with the secret matters that are always hidden and can be experienced, therefore, only in a simulated form."[62]

I can think of no deeper way of expressing my thesis regarding the skilled revelation of skilled concealment.

Dancing the Question

Indeed, scepticism is included in the pattern of belief in witch-doctors. Faith and scepticism are alike traditional.[63]

Witchcraft was ubiquitous in Zande life when Evans-Pritchard, fondly remembered in anthropological circles as E. P., did fieldwork there in the very south of the Sudan in the watersheds of the Nile and Congo rivers in the early 1930s, and it was witchcraft, oracles, and magic that were the focus of interest of his first publication about these people in a book that through the sheer brilliance of its writing and intellect came to define the field of the study of magic, and much else beside.[64] Yet at the outset I should emphasize how curiously unclear this ostensibly transparent book actually is when any particular point is examined, how certainties dissolve into ever more mystifying contradictions magically dispelled, momentarily as it were, by the author's self-assured explanations of the multifarious aspects of magical phenomena. I take this to be striking confirmation of how magic begs for and at the same time resists explanation most when appearing to be explained, and that therefore in its unmasking, magic is in fact made even more opaque, a point given a special twist here through the technique (or is it a trick?) of what Clifford Geertz has called E. P.'s "transparencies."[65] It is then to the issue of technique and trickery and the use of tricks to out-trick other tricks that we need to pay attention, not to further the mystifying effects of unmasking that the Enlightenment, transparency, project, seems to assume, but to lay foundations for something along the lines of that gay science Nietzsche proposed as its critical, masquerading alternative, or even what Walter Benjamin seems to have often had in mind as ploys of demystification *and* reenchantment in his Marxist-inspired search for a critical language of social forms and political power drawn from Jewish mysticism no less than from Christian theories of allegory in European, Baroque drama.

Now, witch-doctors are those persons, generally male, whose task it is to divine the presence and identity of a witch in this witch-infested Zande land and heal the sicknesses arising therefrom. They form corporations with group secrets, and initiation into the group is long and arduous. These secrets are the knowledge of medicines and what E. P. calls their "tricks of the trade," principal of which is the actual extraction by hand or mouth from the body of the victim of witchcraft-objects such as bits of charcoal, splinters, black beetles, or worms. There are plenty of other tricks too, such as vomiting blood, extracting worms from one's own person, resting heavy weights on one's chest, and shooting black beetles and bits of charcoal from one's leg into the body of somebody else, even over large distances, but no trick is as secretly guarded in E. P.'s narrative as that of extracting the witch-craft-object from the body of the sick. Whether we are to call these tricks or techniques I for the moment leave for you to decide. That is pretty much an E. P. sort of sentence, in both senses of the word.

The doctors would not divulge their secrets to E. P., who decided that entering into the corporation would be counterproductive, and so instead he paid for his Zande servant, Kamanga, a gullible man with profound faith in witch-doctors, to undergo initiation and "to learn all about the techniques of witch-doctors."[66] E. P. was able to learn even more by using the secrets elicited by Kamanga to play on rivalries between doctors, but he felt sure that certain things, especially the extraction of witchcraft-objects, would not be told Kamanga, since he had acted straightforwardly, as he puts it, in telling the doctors that Kamanga would pass on to him all that he learned. "In the long run, however," E. P. adds, striking a militant note, "an ethnographer is bound to triumph. Armed with preliminary knowledge nothing can prevent him from driving a deeper and deeper wedge if he is interested and persistent."[67]

But what would happen if it turned out that the secret lies in there being no secret, and that this is what will always resist the wedge of truth no matter how interested, or persistent, or, for that matter, white the wedge might be?

To the extent that the secret can be and is revealed, therefore, I would like to suggest that revelation is precisely what the secret intends; in other words, part of secrecy is secretion, and this is especially the case with what I call the "public secret," that which is known but not generally articulated. To put it another way, thus bringing out its quality of paradox, it is that which it is known not to know, and so this talk of wedges and driving deeper and deeper is beside the point, or it is the intended and labored drama of its make-believe which, in this case, E. P.'s remarkable text fulfills remarkably well. The play of the secret in the colonial relationship, itself often a highlighted version of Enlightenment staging, often functions this way, with the public secret being displaced by the notion of the secret, the penetration of which serves to demonstrate both the pugnacity and cleverness of the seeker after truth.[68]

We are a long way from Nietzsche's gay science, in which "We no longer believe that truth remains truth when the veils are withdrawn. . . . What is required for that is to stop courageously at the surface, the fold, the skin, to adore appearance."[69] But like most of us, E. P. just has to get to the bottom with his wedge driving deeper and deeper, it being precisely his aim to expose the exposure of the witchcraft extracted through the surface, the fold, the skin, as penetrated by surgical incision. What's more, his obsessive search for truth here is uncannily mimetic of that of the doctors whose secrets he is intent on uncovering: "It would, I believe, have been possible by using every artifice to have eventually wormed out all their secrets, but this would have meant bringing undue pressure on people to divulge what they wished to hide."[70] Yet in fact, as we shall see later, he has no scruple in applying such pressure and does so in a most devastating way.

And while the anthropologist dives deep, be it noted, the witch-doctor brings the secret to the surface, counterposed movements destined to meet in making the pages of the monograph, a triumphant conjunction of movements through which the anthropologist is drawn into a ritual scheme neither of his own choosing nor understanding — that in telling the witch-doctors that his servant is to reveal to him the secrets they tell to him, he is thereby fulfilling to the letter the need for unmasking that the secrets of their magic actually demand. In other words there is this oblique ritual of exposure of the secret within the ritual of the witch-doctors, which the presence of the anthropologist has here drawn from its otherwise obscure existence.

Such rituals of exposure amounting to meta-rites of secretion of the secret thus account for the ubiquitous "trickery" and also the skepticism alongside faith in witch-doctors and seem especially pronounced among the Azande at the time of E. P.'s stint there. It was not uncommon for young nobles to expose witch-doctors by tricking them, which E. P. refers to as "testing" and as "playing a joke." He also cites how a commoner friend of his, Mbira, once placed a knife in a covered pot and asked three doctors to divine what lay within. The three doctors danced in the fierce sun the better part of the day trying unsuccessfully to ascertain the contents and, grabbing the opportunity, one sought out Mbira in his hut and pleaded to be secretly told the answer and thus avoid humiliation, but Mbira refused, calling him a knave.[71] Only a people imbued with a measure of skepticism could indulge in such activities, E. P. points out (neglecting to wonder at the witch-doctors' motivation in agreeing to participate in such tests), and yet Mbira believed firmly in every kind of magic, was himself a magician of standing, and consulted witch-doctors when he had a problem. But I want to go further and ask why a sincere or even just your middling sort of skeptic would want to indulge in such sport, given such skepticism? And the answer, I submit, has a good deal to do with the need for rites of exposure built into rites of magic so as to strengthen magic itself.

There is in this book a dramatic moment of great poignancy concerning rites of exposure, and as an aside, I would like to note how postmodern this 1930s, straight-from-the-hip text is, how it has sneaked into the canon for other than what it is, you might say, with its powerful personal anecdotal form of analysis, its steady layering of exemplification, its studious, almost manic aversion to theory in place of storytelling, its constant swerving away from what is supposed to be the point, and, above all, the way its chaos does not merely pass for a seamless argument, regarding the explanation of witchcraft, for instance, but is indispensable to it.

Far be it from me to expose such exposure, no matter how close I may appear to be to E. P. that memorable day he out-tricked the tricker when his servant, Kamanga, under the tutelage of his instructor, Bogwozu, was about to wipe the body of a sick man (another servant of E. P.'s) with the poultice of grass prepared by Bogwozu. This, we are told, is standard medical practice. It is wiped over the abdomen of the patient with the aim of extracting an object of witchcraft which, if extracted, is shown to the patient who is then likely to recover. But it was this technique which, to E. P.'s chagrin, the witch-doctors stubbornly refused to impart to Kamanga because "they were naturally anxious that I should not know their trade secret."[72] It was a complicated state of affairs, made even more so by the fact that Kamanga himself stubbornly held to the belief that there was no trickery involved in this technique. Now I want you to concentrate on the complexity of this situation in its various shadings of gullibility and trickery, faith and skepticism.

First the anthropologist tricks the witch-doctor:

> When the teacher handed over the poultice to his pupil I took it from him to pass it to Kamanga, but in doing so I felt for the object which it contained and removed it between my finger and thumb while pretending to make a casual examination of the kind of stuff the poultice consisted of and commenting on the material....
>
> It was a disagreeable surprise for Kamanga when, after massaging his patient's abdomen through the poultice, in the usual manner of witch-doctors, and after then removing the poultice, he could not find any object of witchcraft in it.[73]

Then comes the exposure:

> I considered the time had now come to stop proceedings and I asked Kamanga and his teacher to come to my hut a few yards away, where I told them that I had removed the charcoal from the poultice, and asked Bogwozu to explain how it had got there. For a few minutes he pretended incredulity and asked to see the object, since he said that such a thing was impossible, but he was clever enough to see that further pretense would be useless, and, as we were in private, he made no further difficulty about admitting the imposture.[74]

There is something awesome in the anthropological authority exposed by this combined exposure of trickery and gullibility, the anthropologist giving away his tricks of the trade like this, interposing himself between the teacher and pupil, the disease and the patient, the event and the reader. We can interpret this with moralizing energy as yet another crass instance of colonial power flexing Enlightenment muscle against primitive magic, staging its own rites of scientific method right there in the heartland of magic, and we can at the same time marvel at the imagination and daring it might have taken to do this.

We could also read this in a quite different way, coinciding with the first reading, assuming that the anthropologist was doing little more than the culturally appropriate thing. For just as Mbira took delight in ridiculing witch-doctors as described above, so the anthropologist was following a well-worn path, although there are no instances described of Zande being as sneaky or as daring as E. P. in actually removing the key to the trick midway through the healing of a sick person. After all, it is one thing to *test* a doctor's powers. It is another thing to *trick* him.

In any case, whether staging Enlightenment triumph or Zande ridicule, the point to consider here is whether or not the anthropologist was himself part of a larger and more complex staging in which exposure of tricks is the name of the game, and that what we are witness to via the text is an imaginative, albeit unintended and serendipitous, rendition of the skilled revelation of the skilled concealment necessary to the mix of faith and skepticism necessary to magic.

Finally we have to consider the effect that the teacher's confession and the revelation of trickery had on the young pupil:

> The effects of these disclosures on Kamanga was devastating. When he had recovered from his astonishment he was in serious doubt whether he ought to continue his initiation. He could not at first believe his eyes and ears, but in a day or two he had completely recovered his poise and *developed a marked degree of self-assurance which, if I am not mistaken, he had not shown before this incident.*[75]

In short, unmasking adds to rather than eliminates the *mysterium tremendum* of magic's magic.

We see this also in what I can only call studied exercises in unmasking that hardly appear as such on account of the optic that, constantly on the lookout for "tricks," fails to see that this optic is instead party to the skilled revelation of skilled concealment. For example, Kisanga, "a man of unusual brilliance," told E. P. how a witch-doctor begins:

> When a man becomes sick they send for a witch-doctor. Before the witch-doctor comes to the sick man he scrapes down an animal's bone and hammers it till it is quite small and then drops it into the medicines in his horn. He later arrives at the homestead of the sick man and takes a mouthful of water and swills his mouth round with it and opens his mouth so that people can look into it. He also spreads out his hands to them so that every one can see them, and speaks thus to them: "Observe me well, I am not a cheat, since I have no desire to take anything from any one fraudulently."[76]

"Some training in trickery is essential," writes the anthropologist in that confidence-restoring tone that talking about other people's trickery seems to always instill:

> In the first place, the Zande has a broad streak of scepticism towards his leeches who have therefore to be careful that their sleight-of-hand is not observed.... If the treatment is carried out in a certain manner, as when the *bingba* grass is used as a poultice, he will be frankly suspicious. But if the witch-doctor sits down on a stool and calls upon a third person to cut *kpoyo* bast and make a poultice of it, rinses his mouth with water, and holds his hands for inspection, suspicions will be allayed.[77]

It is hard not to feel these ostentatiously demonstrative acts of denial are saying the very opposite and everyone knows (and enjoys) that. It is also hard to believe that the anthropologist is alone in detecting skilled concealment of trickery as when he writes, "If you accompany a witch-doctor on one of his visits you will be convinced, if not of the validity of his cures, at least of his skill. As far as you can observe, everything which he does appears to be above-board, and you will notice nothing which might help you to detect fraud."[78]

He is so busy looking for concealed trickery he doesn't realize that he might be a privileged witness of the skilled revelation of trickery and that the secret of the secret is that there is none or, rather, that the secret is a public secret, being that which is generally known but cannot generally be articulated. This is not a question of seeing more or seeing less or seeing behind the skin of appearance. Instead it turns on seeing how one is see-ing. Whatever magic is, it must also involve this turn within the known un-known and what this turn turns on, namely a new attitude to skin.

There are, however, by E. P.'s reckoning, two ways by which faith manages to live with and overcome skepticism concerning witch-doctors. One is what was noted by E. B. Tyler by way of *probabilities*, wherein one says even though most doctors are fake there are some who are not, and it is often the case, says E. P., that a Zande never knows whether any particular doctor is a cheat or not, and hence faith in any particular practitioner is tempered by skepticism. There is, in other words, a rock-steady ideal of the truly en-dowed witch-doctor who can divine and cure the evil effects of witches, and now and again the ideal is actualized despite the fact that many, prob-ably the great majority, of practitioners are faking it. Note that the probabil-ity of the ideal being actualized increases the further you go from home; the magic of the Other is more truly magical and faith lies in distance and therefore difference.

The second modality wherein faith inheres is by way of *substances*, of which there are two; herbal medicines and the human body, as with the body of the witch, inheritor of witchcraft substance, *mangu*, and as with the witch-doctor's medicine-laden body in motion, dancing the questions.[79]

It is *deferment* that these apparently dissimilar explanations for the co-existence of faith with skepticism have in common, continuous and relent-less deferral: a positing and flow of intellection that stands in marked con-trast to the driving of the wedge, a driving itself driven by the quest for the catharsis of the triumphant revelation of the secret and supposed "principles" hidden behind the facade of the social world. The explanation through prob-abilities and the logic of the particular versus the general in its very tautolo-gousness is by definition a deferral referring us back to where we started in the middle of the problem of magic's truth, which is a truth continuously questioning its own veracity of being. Circular reasoning and doublings back are the movements of intellection here, not the wedge. Deferral also lies here in the power of the "stranger-effect," meaning that truth lies in a never-attainable beyond, and cheating is merely the continuous and expected pre-lude to the mere possibility of authenticity, for behind this cheat stands the receding shadow of the real in all its perfection, but it is strange and never homely or destined for homeliness for all of that. Authenticity is that be-yond, permanently below the horizon of being.

As for medicines, in many ways the bedrock of the entire system of witch-doctoring and subject of careful instruction over years of training and to much secrecy as well, deferral could not be more obvious on account of the massive, world-consuming tautology on which the medicines rest; namely that not only do they serve as the basis for faith in witch-doctoring, as E. P.'s text tirelessly informs us, but the medicines are themselves the quintessence of magical power, and so we end up with no end in sight but that of tracing an endless circle in which magic explains magic. Medicine ensures magical power, as in accuracy of divination. "Thus my old friend Ongosi used to tell me," the anthropologist informs us, "that most of what the witch-doctors told their audiences was just *bera,* just 'supposition': they think out what is the most likely cause of any trouble, and put it forward, in the guise of an inspired oracle, as a likely guess, but it is not *sangba ngua,* the words of medicine, i.e. it is not derived from the medicines they have eaten."[80]

To become a witch-doctor one must learn the medicines and partake of the communal meal thereof with other doctors as well as be taken to the source stream in the watershed of the Nile and Congo rivers where, in caves, some of the more powerful plants are to be found. There are many magical things about medicine, beginning with the fact that medicine connects the interiority of the body with exterior substance; indeed it is with medicine that the very force of corporeality and metonymy, as opposed to metaphor, is best established, medicines being the fluid flow by which the exterior penetrates the interior to fundamentally empower the soul of the doctor-in-training.

The novice must hold his face in the steam of the cooking pot, but with his eyes open so that the medicines will eventually allow him to see witches and witchcraft. The medicines are served in a highly ritualistic way with the server offering the spoonful of medicine from the cooking pot to the mouth of one man, only to quickly remove it as he goes to swallow it by offering it to another. Incisions are made on the chest, above the shoulder-blades, and on the wrists and face, and medicine is rubbed in.[81] The medicines are spoken to as they are being cooked and as they are rubbed into the novice's body. As soon as a novice has eaten medicine, he begins to dance.

Medicine must be paid for; otherwise it may not work, and payment must be made in sight of the medicine. "Purchase is part of the ritual conditioning of the magic which gives it potency," we are told, and this seems to imply some almost humanlike mentation and capacity for retribution on the part of the medicine itself, as much as of a dissatisfied vendor. E. P. tells us of a witch-doctor placing money (an Egyptian piastre) of his own on the ground when treating a patient, explaining "that it would be a bad thing if the medicine did not observe a fee, for it might lose its potency."[82] At one point E. P. refers to this exchange as that of a gift.

If angered, a witch-doctor can use magic to remove the magic of the medicine he has sold to a novice by taking a forest creeper and attaching it to the top of a flexible stick stuck in the ground to form a sort of bow-string, to which he brings a few drops of the magic of thunder, so that the medicine will roar and sunder the creeper, the top half flying on high, the lower staying in the earth. As the top half flies, so the medicine flies out of the novice.[83] It is of some importance that this is one of the very few instances of Lévi-Straussian metaphoric or structuralist magic, or of Tambiah's analogic formuls, present in the magic of witch-doctoring. By far the bulk of the instances supplied in this long text referring to witch-doctors are, to the contrary, metonymic and what we might call visceral; they concern flows and interruptions to flows of physical connectedness.[84]

In any event it cannot be gainsaid that here we have anything but profoundly powerful instances of magic explaining magic in a circular, albeit staggered, manner and that this is the movement of deferral par excellence, in which the very idea of a secret behind a facade is not just plain silly but a sign of another sort of philosophic despair, even illness, that we have to associate with the will to knowledge.

Nowhere does this question of deferral intrinsic to the mix required of faith and skepticism find more dramatic epistemological expression that in the witch-doctors' seance of divination. "A witch-doctor does not only divine with his lips, but with his whole body. He dances the questions which are put to him," states the anthropologist in what must be the most exquisite description of dance in anthropological writing, comparable to that of Maya Deren.[85]

He dances the questions. His body moves back and forth in the semicircle bounded by the witch-doctors' upturned horns filled with medicines. He kicks up his leg if annoyed by the slackness of the chorus of young boys and may shoot black beetles into them. The spectators throw their questions about the witchcraft bothering them. Back and forth, question and answer, another circle is being traced as the doctor leaps and swirls through the heat of the day for hours on end as the answer is ever more refined through clever elimination of alternatives and leaps of intuition. Gongs and drums resound. Back and forth go the questions and the answers as the public secrets of envy and resentment are aired in this flurry and fury of intellect and bodies in motion.

The dancing is ecstatic and violent. The dancer slashes his body, and blood flows. Saliva froths around the lips. The medicines in the body are activated by the dance, just as the medicines in their turn activate dancing, these medicines of divination. When a question is put to a particular doctor, he responds by going up to the drummers to give a solo performance and when he can dance no more, as if intoxicated, he shakes his hand-bells to tell the drummers to cease and, his body doubled over, looks into the medicines contained in his upturned horns on the ground and he voices his oracular reply. He dances the question, and the dancing is spectacular. "The dance of the Zande witch-doctors," writes the anthropologist, "is one of the few performances I have witnessed in Africa which really comes up to the standards of sensational journalism. It is weird and intoxicating."[86]

Here trickery is deferred, transmuted into theater, where theater meets the magic—the weirdness and intoxication—of a ritual. The various dichotomies of trick and technique, intellect and intuition, secrecy and public secrecy, are deferred by a series of other epistemic efficacies given in a body dancing the question under an open sky. This is most definitely not a question of replacing mind by body nor sense by the senses but of giving to the skilled revelation of skilled concealment a density and fluidity almost sufficient to dispel the craving for certainty that secrecy inspires. It is this revelation of the already known, the public secret, that the witch-doctor dances in his dance of faith and skepticism.

And while the secret magnifies reality and creates a vivid sense of mysterious other worlds of magic and witchcraft, sorcery and religion, the public secret provides the reservoir of the secret's secretion, bound as that is to the skin of the secret announcing the existence of secrecy through marvelously ritualized permutations of concealment and revelation concerning the known unknown, a species of knowledge no less political than it is mysterious.

This is all the more impressive in the Boas and Hunt record of the Kwakiutl, wherein the shaman's performance of healing provides the model for the spirit helper and, so we are told, the success of this spiritual mimesis depends upon the fluidity and perfection of the shaman's movements. That these movements are tricks and fraudulent seems common knowledge and a most powerful instance not only of the public secret, but of that most elusive trick of all, the magic of mimesis itself—at heart a fraud, yet most necessary for that ceaseless surfacing of appearances we defer to as truth.

Turning Tricks

All along I have been asking myself, What, then, is a trick? I keep thinking of the way a trick highlights nature's mysteries as well as displaying them—the trick of an acrobat or a diver performing twists and somersaults and backward flips, or a cardsharp pulling aces. I think of these tricks as requiring inordinate skill, inordinate technique, inordinate empathy with reality. Would this put the trick on a par with technology? What then of magic? Would magic then mean cheating on technique, or instead a supreme level of technique, so rarified and skilled that it passes from "mere" technique to something else we might dignify as magic or even sacred — as with a musician, a brain surgeon, or a short-order cook, for example? Here magic and technique, as in scientific technique, flow into one another, magic, we might say, being the highest form of science.

What is not a trick? What for instance is the opposite of a trick? Is a technique the opposite of a trick? Is reality the opposite of a trick? And why do these pairings effectively eliminate the ethical issue in trickery, that it's somehow dishonest and amounts to a dishonest technique, a phony reality, reality in disguise, and so forth? The very notion of the trick, we might say, seems to sabotage binary logic, let alone reality, and does so most pointedly by making a clever mess of good and evil in relation to ontology and technology. Might it be that reality itself is one big trick, and the professional responsible for relating to this, such as the shaman, entertains such cosmic trickery while extracting a small profit in the form of healing power and sorcery? It makes a lot of sense, then, to think of magic as mimesis, imitating reality so as to deceive it.

Yet by the same token it would be an enormous mistake to restrict this to magic, and thus let reality off the hook. Indeed the whole point here, thanks to the opening made by a close reading of ethnography of so-called primitive societies, is to see reality as infused with trickery and that magic is a quality of Realism for dealing with the power of the ways of the world. Reality is no less magical than magic. Yet in the continuously broached end, the deception of reality by the mimetic trick will always be a temporary, albeit continuously renewed, drama. Infused with trickery, reality will always out-trick human trickery modeled on reality so as to deceive it, but the seduction provided by the attempt is awesome, whether it be a shaman extracting mice and octopi from the human body, or Oppenheimer and his buddies smashing atoms and Hiroshima and crying afterwards. Truly it is easier, as Fredric Jameson has said, to imagine the end of the planet, than the end of capitalism.[87]

Notes

1. Marcel Mauss is cited in Gibert Rouget, *Music and Trance,* translated by B. Biebuyck (Chicago: University of Chicago Press, 1980), 320.

2. Edward Burnett Tylor, *Primitive Culture,* vol. 1, *The Origins of Culture* (New York: Harper, 1958), 134.

3. Claude Lévi-Strauss, "The Sorcerer and His Magic," in *Structural Anthropology* (New York: Doubleday, 1967), 161–80; and E. E. Evans-Pritchard, *Azande Magic, Witchcraft, and Sorcery* (Oxford: Clarendon, 1937).

4. Max Horkheimer and Theodor W. W. Adorno, *Dialectic of Enlightenment* (New York: Continuum, 1969).

5. Lucas Bridges, *Uttermost Part of the Earth* (New York: Dover 1988), 264. First published in 1949. Note that Ona and Selk'nam are interchangeable names.

6. The epigraph to Bridges's book reads, "And ye shall be witnesses unto me both in Jerusalem . . . and unto the uttermost part of the earth" (Acts I, verse 8); not a bad epigraph for anthropology, either.

7. Ibid., 264.

8. Ibid., 406.

9. Ibid., 262. Bridges spoke the Ona language; when he describes speech as "guttural," he is not necessarily mistaking foreign speech.

10. The discipline of physiognomics was not invented by the Greeks, writes Tamsyn S. Barton. In Mesopotamia from the first half of the second millennium B.C. onward, fragments of manuals have been found dealing with the prophetic significance of aspects of individual human bodies. See her *Power and Knowledge: Astrology, Physiognomics, and Medicine under the Roman Empire* (Ann Arbor: University of Michigan Press, 1994), 100.

11. Bridges, *Uttermost Part of the Earth*, 263.

12. Ibid., 264.

13. Ibid., 285.

14. Ibid., 286.

15. Ibid.

16. It is with reluctance that I bend to linguistic convention and employ the all-too-universalizing term *shamanism*, as readers of my previous work will readily understand.

17. The phrase "penny-in-the-slot" or something like it comes from Walter Benjamin's essay on surrealism, referring to a universe of dislocating, unstable, and carnal meaning as opposed to the "penny-in-the-slot" variety of predictable, mechanistic, semiotic, and other related meanings of meaning.

18. Friedrich Nietzsche, *The Birth of Tragedy*, translated by Walter Kaufmann (New York: Vintage, 1967), 23.

19. Horkheimer and Adorno, *Dialectic of Enlightenment*, 3–43.

20. As regards the first point concerning error, "The falseness of judgment is for us not necessarily an objection to a judgment; in this respect our new language may sound strangest. The question is to what extent it is life-preserving, species-preserving, perhaps even species-cultivating. And we are fundamentally inclined to claim that the falsest judgments (which include Kant's synthetic judgments *a priori*) are the most indispensable for us. . . . To recognize untruth as a condition of life—that certainly means resisting accustomed value feelings in a dangerous way; and a philosophy that risks this would by that token alone place itself beyond good and evil." Friedrich Nietzsche, *Beyond Good and Evil*, translated by Walter Kauffman (New York: Vintage, 1989), 11–12; first published in 1886.

21. Friedrich Nietzsche, "Preface for the Second Edition," *The Gay Science* (New York: Vintage 1974), 37; first published in 1886.

22. Waldemar Bogoras, *The Chukchee, Parts I, II, and III,* Memoirs of the American Museum of Natural History, volume 11, edited by Franz Boas, 1904–09 (New York: Steehert, 1909; Leiden: E. J. Brill, 1909; reprint, New York: Johnson, 1969), 433–67.

23. "Totemism" of course came in for a curious attempt at dismantling in the hands of Claude Lévi-Strauss, whose object, however, was not to emphasize the strange curving back of the North American Indian concept to find a useful place in Western European sensibilities, but to elaborate "totemism" as a fictitious entity best understood as but part of special kinds of classificatory systems using metaphor and opposition.

24. Bogoras, *The Chukchee, Parts I, II, and III,* 447.

25. Ibid. The term *juggler* preceded the term *shaman* in the ethnographic literature.

26. Franz Boas, "Religion of the Kwakiutl Indians," in *Kwakiutl Ethnography,* edited by Helen Codere (Chicago: University of Chicago Press, 1966), 121.

27. Stanley Walens, *Feasting with Cannibals: An Essay on Kwakiutl Cosmology* (Princeton: Princeton University Press, 1981), 24–25.

28. Irving Goldman, *The Mouth of Heaven* (New York: John Wiley, 1975).

29. Boas's texts on Kwakiutl society have been described by Stanley Walens as "one of the monuments of American cultural anthropology," in *Feasting with Cannibals,* 7. Walens also points out in a footnote that the "degree to which the excellence of Boas' work is the result of the meticulousness and diligence of both men [Hunt as well as Boas] has never been amply discussed" (9). Irving Goldman describes these texts as "probably the greatest single ethnographic treasure [in existence]," in *Mouth of Heaven,* vii.

30. Claude Lévi-Strauss, "The Sorcerer and His Magic," in *Structural Anthropology* (Garden City, NY: Doubleday, 1967), 161–180.

31. On Kwakiutl names and naming, Goldman writes, "The name is the essential ingredient of religious worth" (*Mouth of Heaven,* 56).

32. Boas, 'Religion of the Kwakiutl Indians," 121.

33. This is hardly the place to make an extended analysis, the Boas/Hunt mode of ethnography contains enormous problems for the interpretation of Kwakiutl culture precisely because the character of the relationship between the two men is not opened to analysis. Why did Hunt write? How did he see his task? What instructions did Boas give him? What did Hunt think he was doing telling a white man about the secrets of shamanism? Later research may uncover much in this regard, but the point is that these issues must be confronted in the actual Boas/Hunt texts themselves if they are to be of real use.

34. I acquired this terminology from Mary Louise Pratt.

35. Franz Boas (and Hunt), *The Religion of the Kwakiutal Indians: Part 2* (New York: Columbia University Press, 1930), 1.

36. On a certain equivalence between secret and sacred, see Goldman, *Mouth of Heaven:* "In many places, however, the Hunt manuscript is more precise [than Boas's edited and published version] in rendering Kwakiutl meanings. For example, Boas characteristically converts Hunt's 'secret' to 'sacred' " (86–87).

37. Boas (and Hunt), *Religion of the Kwakiutal Indians,* 5.

38. Ibid., 5.

39. Ibid., 31.

40. Ibid., 30.

41. Again, see footnote 36 above concerning the equivalence between secret and sacred.

42. Boas (and Hunt), *Religion of the Kwakiutal Indians,* 31–32.

43. Note the implications of this for re-sorting Foucault's distinction, crucial to his later work, regarding transgression and confession, where he contrasts the transmission of bodily knowledges through a master-apprentice system ("ars erotica") versus through the confessional, as with modern Western sexuality as the secret that has to be spoken.

44. Boas (and Hunt), *Religion of the Kwakiutal Indians,* 32.

45. In his first major monograph (of 1895) Boas described this double-headed serpent, the Sisiul, as perhaps the most important of the fabulous monsters whose help was obtained by the ancestors and have therefore become the crest of a clan. To eat, touch, or see it is to have one's joints dislocated, one's head turned backwards, and eventually to die. But to those persons who have supernatural help, it may instead bring power. See Franz Boas, *The Social Organization and Secret Societies of the Kwakiutal Indians* (Washington, DC: United States National Museum Report, 1895), 371–72.

46. Boas (and Hunt), *Religion of the Kwakiutal Indians,* 35.

47. Walens, *Feasting with Cannibals,* 24.

48. Ibid., 25. Even with his focus on mythology and ideas, Claude Lévi-Strauss makes the mistake of omitting this from both of his famous essays on magic, "The Effectiveness of Symbols," concerned with Cuna shamanism in the San Blas islands off Panama, and "A Sorcerer and His Magic," most of which works through George Hunt's 1925 account of his shamanic experiences written down for Boas. In the Cuna case, Lévi-Strauss devotes his entire analysis to finding structuralist closure in his assumption that the sick person understands, both mentally and especially bodily, the curing song sung in a specialized shamanic language—a most dubious proposition, since the ethnography indicates that ordinary Cuna do not understand such language, and the song is intended not for the patient but for the spirits, providing through words much the same sort of simulacrum Walens describes for the tricks practiced by the Kwakiutl shamans. It is curious how this fundamental empirical error is made in both of Lévi-Strauss's essays, and the implications are immense, swinging the analysis away from metonymic, mimetic, and transgression considerations to "totemism" and a particular epistemology of "structure," series, and contradiction.

49. Walens, *Feasting with Cannibals,* 25. "The nature culture uses to create second nature," is a phrase I coined to define the mimetic faculty in my book *Mimesis and Alterity* (New York: Routledge, 1993).

50. Walens, *Feasting with Cannibals,* 24.

51. Ibid.

52. Ibid., 25. Compare this with Boas on the reaction of the seal society when they notice a mistake in the dancing or singing of the performer in the Winter Ceremonial; they jump from their seats and bite and scratch the person who made the mistake, who then pretends to faint, meaning that the spirit has taken the performer away. In fact, members of the seal society sit on the platform of the house or stand during the dances so as to be certain of discovering mistakes. If the cannibal dancer falls while dancing, it is said in former times he was killed by the other cannibal dancers, often at the insistence of the dancer's father; see Boas, *Social Organization and Secret Societies,* 433–34.

53. Joseph Masco, " 'It's a Strict Law which Bids Us Dance': Cosmologies, Colonialism, Death, and Ritual Authority in the Kwakwaka'wakw Potlatch, 1849 to 1922," *Comparative Studies in Society and History*, 1995, 55–56. He cites Robert Boyd's estimate of an almost 70 percent loss in the 1862 smallpox epidemic, from a population before then of 7,650 people. The precontact population is estimated as between 15,000–20,000 people.

54. Boas (and Hunt), *Religion of the Kwakiutal Indians*, 41–42.

55. Boas (and Hunt), *Religion of the Kwakiutal Indians*, 25.

56. Ibid.,35–37.

57. Walens, *Feasting with Cannibals*, 26.

58. Goldman gives a figure of fifty-three from Boas's report of 1895 in *The Mouth of Heaven*, and sixty-three from Edward S. Curtis, *The North American Indian*, vol. 10, 1915.

59. Boas, "Religion of the Kwakiutal Indians," 172.

60. Goldman, *Mouth of Heaven*, 102.

61. Boas (and Hunt), *Religion of the Kwakiutal Indians*, 4.

62. Goldman, *Mouth of Heaven*, 102.

63. E. E. Evans-Pritchard, *Witchcraft, Oracles, and Magic among the Azande* (Oxford: Clarendon Press, 1937), 193.

64. Ibid.

65. Clifford Geertz, "Slide Show: Evans-Pritchard's African Transparencies," *Raritan* 3, no. 2 (fall, 1983): 62–80.

66. E. P. was unlike Frank Hamilton Cushing, who through bluff and trickery more or less forced himself into the priesthood of the Bow Lodge of the Zuni; see his "My Adventures in Zuni," in *Zuni: Selected Writings of Frank Hamilton Cushing*, edited by Jesse Green (Lincoln: University of Nebraska Press, 1979), 99–101.

67. Evans-Pritchard, *Witchcraft, Oracles, and Magic*, 152.

68. The great geographical "discoveries" of European modernity, such as the discovery of the New World, or of Machu Picchu, have something of this too.

69. Nietzsche, *The Gay Science*, 38.

70. Evans-Pritchard, *Witchcraft, Oracles, and Magic*, 151.

71. Ibid., 186.

72. Ibid., 230.

73. Ibid., 231.

74. Ibid.

75. Ibid., emphasis added.

76. Ibid., 191–92.

77. Ibid., 232. The word *leech* is an archaic English term for a "folk" healer. Like other terms used by Evans-Pritchard, such as *ensorcell* and *knave*, this term creates its own mystique if not mystification combined with an implicit notion that African medicine is on a developmental line that British society superseded. This is unfortunate and probably far from the author's intention.

78. Ibid., 232–33.

79. I have not analyzed here the deceit wherein the witch-doctor is supposed to cut a deal with the witch who caused the disease so that both will share in the fee for curing (ibid., 191–93). Here the skepticism about the magical powers of the witch-doctor is balanced by faith in those of the witch to cause and withdraw misfortune

by mystical means, and that these means reside in *mangu* substance inherited at birth in the body of the witch. The question begged by this account is why would there be a need for the elaborate performance of the witch-doctor? Why can't the doctor act more like a lawyer or peace-maker? Why the art? In the healing practiced by the people indigenous to the New World (if I may be so bold as to generalize), the answer lies readily at hand: the art is essential as the mode of establishing a mimetic model with the spirits. I know too little about Africa to comment, but I suspect the New World notion is applicable here too, raising a totally different approach to the one of rationality and the philosophy of science that has dogged British commentary on magic.

80. Evans-Pritchard, *Witchcraft, Oracles, and Magic,* 184.

81. Ibid., 210–11.

82. Ibid., 209.

83. Ibid., 213–14.

84. See Claude Lévi-Strauss, *The Savage Mind* and *Totemism,* see also Stanley J. Tambiah, "Form and Meaning in Magical Acts: A Point of View," in *Modes of Thought,* edited by Robin Horton and Ruth Finnegan (London: Faber and Faber, 1973); and Giles Deleuze and Felix Guattari, *A Thousand Plateaus* (Minneapolis: University of Minnesota Press).

85. Evans-Pritchard, *Witchcraft, Oracles, and Magic,* 154–82; Maya Deren, *Divine Horsemen: The Living Gods of Haiti* (New York and London: Thames and Hudson, 1953).

86. Evans-Pritchard, *Witchcraft, Oracles, and Magic,* 162.

87. Fredric Jameson, *Seeds of Time* (New York: Columbia University Press, 1994), xii.

11

Posthumous Critique

Marjorie Levinson

Introductory Note

The following paper, written for delivery at the Culture Conference, is presented unrevised. I have not expanded the occasionally elliptical development of some logical sequences, nor have I standardized my sometimes colloquial usages. The most obvious sign of the rhetorical situation of this essay is its handling of citation. Many of the quoted statements have the status of commonplace within the discourse of critical thought, and I have left them unreferenced but for the author in order to indicate that currency. When I draw upon less familiar or more discipline-specific sources in criticism and theory, I provide author and title of the text in question, but I do not give page numbers—again observing the decorum of oral presentation. Finally, when mentioning arguments heard in lecture format and/or read in manuscript, I give my working information base only.

Readers of this essay will see that toward the end, I propose some experiments with critical genres. These experiments are driven by a wish to change the ways in which critical thought circulates in the academy and through it to other sites and circuits of information. My nonstandard and orally marked referencing style is one small way that I try to keep argument and discourse embedded and also to indicate the collectivity and/or dispersion of authorship accountable for the thinking here.

Preface

I am ambivalent about this paper, which is only fitting, since the essay is about ambivalence and uses a set of sharply incompatible procedures to perform that fact. I intend the term *ambivalence* in the strong sense, meaning a commitment to mutually exclusive positions and a refusal to strike a compromise, to engage the contraries in a dialectical action, or to propose a master-term that would contain and thus dissolve the conflict. My aim is to produce a hardworking, interesting, but overall (or, with respect to the intersection of institutional and intellectual economies) a nonprofit exercise.

As you will see, the ambivalence centers on what I describe as the dual commitment of materialist critique, understood as an interventional practice taking the general form of ideology critique. Such readings "intervene" in the explicit, ideational structures of the work in question (structures that reflect more widespread and compelling orders in the culture at large) by setting against these unified forms an array of particulars, generated through a sociohistorical rewriting of the text.

At the same time, however, *materialist* implies an attachment to effects that resist reinscription as social practice and perhaps even as semantic forms. We cannot bring them under a concept (except the concept of that elusiveness, as in Kant's sublime). Although effects such as these trace back to the work's conditions of origin and transmission, their functional character as irreducibly and thus unknowably "material" comes into being only against the interpretive horizons that spring up as we exercise our enlightenments. They do not exist prior to our critical labors. A more general way to cast this might be by way of a distinction between a historical and an iconic materialism, when *iconic* refers not just to the visual qualities of writing but to all the sensuously available modes of the medium. Internal to power, knowledge, and the normative codes of the present, these effects can be disruptive and even transfigurative. However, the effort to realize that potential through an act of critical translation seems fated to self-destruct, taking with it the arresting alterities that called it forth.

This essay dances on the horns of that dilemma, generating an example of a critique that wants to keep its value immanent in its textuality. It tries not to circulate easily within the marketplace of ideas; or, what amounts to the same thing, not to lend itself to an available style of consumption. It does this primarily by keeping the logical space between its two arguments disorganized. As I explain in the essay, Spinoza's nonlogical mix of ontological monism and epistemic dualism first provided me a philosophic framework for this kind of thinking and writing. Another model, brilliantly explained and explored by Arkady Plotnitsky (*Reconfigurations: Critical Theory and General Economy*), comes from Niels Bohr's theory of "complementarity," a notion I first encountered in David Bohm's *Causality and Chance in Modern Physics*. Here is Plotnitsky's lucid summary of the theory:

Quantum mechanical descriptions are . . . complete descriptions of whatever they describe, even though, and indeed because, in Bohr's own
phrase, "such kinds of information cannot be combined into a single picture by means of ordinary concepts." . . . As used by Bohr and in general,
the very word *complementarity* suggests both a degree of completeness
of description, and, at certain points, a necessary mutual exclusiveness
of the features involved. . . . Bohr's point is the radical incompleteness
of all possible descriptions. They cannot be complete in the classical
sense of causality, coordination, wholeness, coherence, logic, demanding
a rigorous suspension and redefinition—reconfiguration—of all these
concepts.[1]

I reference models (Spinoza's, Bohr's) rather than instances of this practice because the latter do not exist in any recognizable form in areas familiar to me or most of my readers. Neither do I offer this essay as itself embodying the possibilities I work to derive here. This is to say, I cannot "do"
the kind of critique (call it "incommensurable," "complementary") that drives
me. I can only propose it as a kind of thought-experiment, and to some extent simulate it through rhetorical means in this essay. For example, rather than
conclude my essay by explaining its import and application (the "value"
move that defines closure in critical writing), I name a set of exercises (some
in existence, some hypothetical) that might produce the enlightenments associated with a suspicion hermeneutics but that also cleaves to the heterological (I am tempted to call it, the "aesthetic") element in knowing. In place
of the conventionally generalizing move, I offer a list, the very form of
"particulars." From a formal perspective, one could say that the essay as a
whole thus emerges as a member of the set that it generates. It could be
that the logical effect of this part-whole, member-set, example-argument reversal is to implode the either-or structure of the essay, twisting that external relation into a recursive one. If that happened, the truth-claims of the
essay would retain their formal identity while undergoing a shift in rhetorical
status. Instead of projecting the truth of proposition and argument, these
claims would express the different truth of the performance, maybe even
the representation of truths. In other words, we might see a reversal of the
Romantic project of philosophizing poetry; here, aestheticizing critical thought.
    There is an affective side to the ambivalence that triggered this essay
and that colors my present response to it. I wrote this paper, the second of
three such experiments, in order to overcome a resistance to reading.[2] I
traced this effect to the unmistakable compliance of critical reading with
the identitarian economies of dominant culture. The usual safeguards—a
degree of reflexivity, an interventional posture, a strongly constructivist or
dialectical notion of culture—seemed if anything to facilitate the absorp-

tion. To cast this irony in the more general and philosophic idiom of deconstruction is to see it as another boring example of the "winner loses" logic of representation. I do not see it that way. For me, it is a concrete and situated irony occurring in my own history as a reader of Romantic poetry and in the history which that poetry both stages and suppresses. To submit that particular literature to a sociohistorical critique is to rehearse its own governing logic, for Romanticism, standardly defined, is a writing the organization of which is itself dialectical, and its cultural insertion, antithetical. Naturally, there are differences. Where the poets had set Nature as the realizing other to the human, historicist and materialist critics uncover culture and history, in the sense of practices, events, and tendencies either collective or transpersonal in their agencies, and, in their content, contradicting the ideologies of autonomy guiding aesthetic production. Nevertheless, the *form* of our critical exercise is coded in the poetry, and that is to say that the poems anticipate and even solicit assault on their closures.[3] Far more effectively than the older formalist readings, the new historicisms confirm and renew the values and workings of the poetry: its normative picture of the human.

The myth of Antaeus is one way, far too idealist, of framing this paradox. Another, more keyed to the overdetermination of the thing, and also its bathos, is the old joke about the masochist and the sadist: the masochist says, "Hit me," and the sadist says, "No." There's a new twist, though, when the subject is reading and resistance. There, the masochist *always* wins, since no means yes to persons whose pleasure is pain, and yes also means yes, because it brings the double pain of the refusal to refuse pain. Because critical reading thrives on resistance, it will always turn nonresistance into metaresistance.[4] Like the paradoxes of writing, the perversity of reading has a different character, however—is a different *thing*—in different contexts.

The particular hermeneutic circle that contains Romantic poetry and its readings turns on certain paradigms of value peculiar to the capitalist economies and endlessly reproduced in the critiques thereof. The connection hinges on the work model of activity, a definition of the human that is central to the ideology if not the mechanisms of capitalist formations as to the Marxist critique and the post-Marxist philosophies of praxis. A very clear and searching discussion of the oppositionality inscribed in that work model, a quality that binds idealist and materialist thought, is given by Seyla Benhabib, in her book *Critique, Norm, Utopia*.[5] It is explored in a more situated way by J. M. Coetzee. In an essay from his collection, *White Writing*, Coetzee reflects on the challenge of Hottentot indolence not just to the early ethnographers with their explicit Eurocentrism, but to the modern anthropologist, whose openmindedness, he says, insidiously betrays that idling state. It does so through its a priori that there is something at work where there is nothing. That hardworking and recuperative "something," he says, is culture.[6]

Romanticism worked hard to escape paradigms of productive opposition (you see the problem). Its efforts to redefine value so as to make it processual, participatory, sensuously embodied, and unique form a very large and complex subject. I introduce it only to suggest that critique of the literatures of modernity — which is to say, the literatures that *themselves* resist and critique modernity — may well be helpless to escape the rhetorics of Romanticism. I am thinking, to give one example, of the way in which an important goal of materialist critique, namely, the production of historical and cultural difference, becomes problematic in economies organized around the commodity form: economies that proliferate *formal* differences, the content or material value of which is their interchangeability, their *in*difference.

The substantive repetitions binding capitalism and its critiques are disturbing, but because the historical parallel also releases historical differences, it opens a space for technological innovation: room for maneuver, if not for contestation. What saps my confidence in the paper I present here is my awareness of absorption at the level of style and procedure: the failure of techne, or tactics. The carefully suspended rhetoric of my essay, its delicate withdrawal from the marketplace of ideas, its refusal to conceptualize and thus recuperate the values it releases, its nonopportunistic stance toward its textual objects: in this impeccably postmodern niceness, I do no more than rehearse the Romantic critique of utility and of instrumental reason. That is to say, I reinvent the aesthetic in its first, most ideal, and also formalist incarnation, the standard slogan for which is Kant's "purposiveness without purpose." Compare that to my own expression for the novel contribution of this paper: a hardworking but cumulatively nonproductive, nonprofit exercise.

It gets worse. You will see that I produce this suspended critique by setting one kind of procedure against another, running two arguments in parallel. On the one hand, an old-fashioned theory-passion, anguished and severe, and on the other, a cool pragmatism, knowing-as-doing in a postfoundational world. The difference between those procedures is illusory, in a most specific, a most Romantic way. Grave and gay, agony and anarchy, reflection and creation, the authority of the past and that of the future, add up in short to a very wet and a very dry Romanticism. On the wet side, a habit of pushing my terms to logical extremes unmet within ordinary life; and beyond that, this paper's sublime of a desire *finally* to know ("sublime," because possessed by the wish to know *that* and *why* we *cannot* finally know); its drive to say things so clearly and classify so crisply as to open a space for perfectly self-accounting acts of knowing. Underwriting this method is the premise that analytic questions (e.g., What's the problem with cultural critique?) are at bottom hermeneutic questions, and that these are answered by genetic and deep-structural accounts. Also assumed is that the genealogical account, if sufficiently rigorous and penetrating, will deliver up answers to the *practical* question: What is to be done? Or, knowledge precedes practice; knowledge will set you free; the revolution must take its poetry from the past. Idealist abominations for a materialist critic.

My turn midway through the essay to a brief for tactical, nontheorized practices of knowing, yielding something like knowledge effects rather than knowledge proper is meant to mark a departure from the theory-passion of the first part. My proposal for what I call in the essay a "restorative mimesis" (following a usage of Michael Taussig), looks to me now like an anemic repetition of Romanticism's Nietzschean strain, mirror-image of the Hegelian model inscribed in the first part.[7] Byron, the poet who contains all things, stood on both sides of that glass: on the one hand, the Promethean hand, "Manfred" and *Childe Harold's Pilgrimage,* and on the other, "Beppo" and *Don Juan,* the performance-art of a poet who has not only said goodbye to all that but who has passed beyond valedictories and their tragic or pathetic tones, crossing over (in more ways than one) into the gay science. Students of Romanticism have always known that the disenchantment of disenchantment is the most Romantic position of all. What always surfaces from the wreckage is a belief in unmediated act: the pure, absolute, death-dealing act of Dada; the diffident, nonsemiotic, single-speak of Gertrude Stein. Both are returns to the heartland of the Romantic ideology: literally, to Blake's vales of Innocence.

Why present an argument, the failures of which I have just outlined? Because the essay is an answer, and a good one, to a question many people are asking these days: namely, what happens when cultural critique becomes a growth industry? One, small thing that happens is this essay, which I offer up as a symptomatic discourse. That is not, I would insist, the same as a sacrificial lamb. I do not see the errors of my thinking as the effect of a disease that could be cured, an ignorance awaiting enlightenment, a repression to be lifted. "Symptomatic" is the same as saying "a Romantic critique of Romanticism."

The reason why persons with no interest in the period and its literatures should care about this is that Romanticism was the enacted insight on the part of a segment of the bourgeoisie, that it was and would always be historically dedicated to contesting and *thereby preserving* that class. In other words, if you belong to the group whom Coleridge named "the clerisy" — in today's idiom, professional intellectuals or academics — then you are, as the movie *Freaks* says and as Altman's *The Player* repeats, "one of us." Romanticism was the recognition on the part of what was then a new class that its critical function was to negate from within, enabling a dialectical process that went nowhere: that is to say, it went everywhere, penetrating global and psychic space, but it did not go *temporal*, linear, or progressive. Romanticism was the moment when history came to consciousness of its driving contradictions. It was the moment when the law of capitalism, its ceaseless self-revolutionizing, was grasped as the law of the aesthetic and of critical knowing. Maybe this is why the Romantics lost their belief in the possibility of an end to history: of a moment when, for example, the state, the monadic individual, the paradoxes and treachery of representation would wither away. At the very moment when the old millenarian hopes seemed for the first time capable of material realization, Romanticism guessed at the fabulous resourcefulness of capital.

So, when I say this is a "symptomatic discourse," you can see that I'm calling up Althusser's definition. It is easy to forget how pondered a definition that is. For Althusser, the work comes into being inside a social, historical, and epistemic field. The work cannot name or think its relation to that field precisely because that field provides the work its means and methods of naming and thinking: its practicing identity. However, the work *betrays* that relationship through its lapses and oversights: its symptoms, which are also, by this argument, our access to the processes that are the work's deepest truth.

What happens in this paper of mine in an exaggerated way should illuminate tendencies in more muted and balanced work. In other words, I do not think cultural critique has escaped the shadow of Romanticism. For all the real differences between then and now, the problematic, as they say, is still in place.

That may not be disastrous. To indicate why and also to close this preface, I quote two sentences written by the most Romantic of today's Romanticists. Jerome McGann was the first to imagine a materialist reading of that ideal poetry, and he remains at once the most scrupulous of textual historians and the most transfigurative of readers. I say that I quote "sentences" rather than "statements" because they are given as part of a dialogue between invented personae of the author. That is how Romantics write.

"As I recall, Trotsky quoted liberally from the tsar and tsarina's papers and from government police reports, when he constructed his *History of the Russian Revolution.* Every word uttered makes a commitment to the truth, even if mistaken or duplicitous, even if self-deceived."[8]

I

> *"Difficult" writing, writing that "resists" consumption, is almost a definition of art, or of the arts that distinguish themselves from mass culture — that is, the arts of the early 19th century through the present. This is not to say that all kinds of difficulty are equally negotiable, only that in recognizing a work as difficult, we bring to bear a set of codes that raises all particular obstacles to reading to the level of [interchangeable] examples of difficulty. The slide from difficulty to metatextuality to literature-of-resistance (from form to content) is irresistible. But even if the work is not actually read [much less critically read], circulation absorbs it— consumes it— in its economy of cultural reproduction. Perhaps the only writing that is inaccessible is that which is literally so— meaning, work that never enters circulation.*
> *— Paul Mann*[9]

I start with a well-known quotation from Wittgenstein's *Philosophical Investigations* (115): "A *picture* held us captive. And we could not get outside it, for it lay in our language and language seemed to repeat it to us inexorably." This little fable about the treachery of representation puts the captivity in a particular picture, in the past, and outside the reflective consciousness of the narrator. This is to say, it is a trap. It is also something of a disciplinary in-joke and update, scripted for an audience that reads "Wittgenstein" as a synonym for posthermeneutics and that is wise to the ways of Cretans who say that all Cretans are liars. It was Wittgenstein who made the argument that beyond, beneath, behind the pictures there are more pictures: pictures and stories all the way down. The claim was not that reality is nothing but words and word-practice, only that the experience of a reality unmediated by the codes that define human societies cannot be considered any kind of experience, not even the experience of nothingness or of nonsense, much less of the gap between the real and our knowledge of it. Phenomena that are not presented in our languages are not susceptible to our sense-making practices. These practices—irreducibly perspectival and also public events, or, language games—*are* experience, by another, more analytic name. And, at once closing the language loop and opening onto grammatology, the *Investigations* carry us back to the root of the word *phenomenon*: from the Greek *phanein,* "to show." Phenomena that are not constructed in representation are not even phenomena: by definition, observable facts or events susceptible to description and explanation.

Derrida's famous pronouncement, "Il n'ya pas de hors-texte," makes the point more economically. What Wittgenstein gains through the excess of his anecdote is a wickedly reflexive twist. "A *picture* held us captive." One can see (even without Wittgenstein's italics) that the sentence is itself a picture, an image of or metaphor for knowledge production. It is also, as it happens, a picture of that kind of knowledge we call mimesis, which casts mind as the mirror-image, the picture, of nature. The technical name for this sort of piggyback or exponential metaphor is catachresis. Once launched, it unravels reference and multiplies intertextuality until nothing but language is left and of language, nothing but swerves and substitutes. In its form, the sentence embeds an ineluctable narrative of captivation. Like all anecdotes, it is a little story standing in for a bigger one.

The long version might take the following form. In order to recognize the picture you inhabit, to see it *as* a picture and yourself as its captive, you must have entered another picture and become captive again, which is to say, blind to its constructedness and horizons, and illiterate in the languages of other pictures, including the one whose frame you now perceive. The recognition is not, therefore, the reflexive thing it imagines itself to be, namely, a knowledge of the conditions of one's own picture. It is instead (and this is a best-case scenario) a sort of boundary perception of some other picture: the inferential intuition of a place one cannot enter. Nor does this awareness have available to it a language that could name it or even sensualize it without in the same stroke dissolving it into the codes that make up the new picture.

It would seem that knowledge of any particular world (which is also agency within it, beginning with the act of making sense), occurs only so long as the bounding outline and internal grammars of that world remain invisible. Once you see them, you know that you are no longer in that world and that your critical understanding of it is factitious. Or, knowledge of a world, restricted to its citizens, can never produce a consciousness of itself and its conditions that is anything but another kind of language game belonging to the set of games composing that world.

If these are the paradoxes attending the pursuit of reflexive knowledge, without which empirical knowing cannot achieve certainty about itself and its object-relations (and therefore its objects), then the possibility of *underived* knowledge — knowledge of otherwise worded and pictured worlds, or of realities that are not metaphysically transcendental but that are also not always already "for us" — is literally out of the question. To posit a possible awareness just of the *existence* of other worlds is to propose something like an epiphenomenal byproduct of a limit-case perception of one's own world. But again, the linguistic argument could readily deconstruct that Kantian (and also aesthetic) postulate.

This paper is about what happens to critique, defined as a hermeneutic practice descending from Kant and Hegel (one could also say, Enlightenment and Romanticism), when the sort of thinking represented by Wittgenstein's allegory becomes axiomatic for scholarship in the humanities, the social sciences, and even the physical sciences. The names Kant and Hegel mark the moment in our intellectual histories when the primacy of metaphysics and ontology is displaced by epistemology and its immanent critique: or, Hegel doing to Kant what Kant did to everyone else (that is, calling the question in a critical and empirically situated way on the self-determination, transparency, or givenness of the foundational terms for that particular discipline of knowing, that science; establishing the conditions of possibility of the experience on which that critical exercise operates). In Kant and Hegel, first philosophy's privileged and inscrutable questions of being and its transcendental conditions are referred to the study of experience and consciousness, and of the worldly conditions of those events. Both experience and consciousness are conceived as active and constitutive processes, or what we would call today practices of knowing. In this very important respect, Wittgenstein is heir to the Kant-Hegel legacy.

At the same time, and this is where Wittgenstein parts company, both of the critical philosophies struggle at some logical cost to maintain the objective, dogmatic, or unconstructed element in knowing and to make it internal to the process, not a feature of the object. In Kant, that role is played by the regulative categories that deliver intuition in the form of experience and by the "in itself" presupposed by those categories. In Hegel, this underived otherness resides in the origin and endpoint of his system (respectively, plenitude and totality), and in that initial fracture that entails the movement from one to the other, the movement of externalization and reappropriation that is history. Something of this primordial otherness spills over into the nonidentity term within each dialectical moment. I refer to the fact that for Hegel, what determines any positive existent, any form, is the self-differing or negation within it. This reflects the original antinomy of an infinite Geist that realizes itself through its ceaseless overcoming of the finite conditions it posits.

These openings to otherness, positioned by both philosophies at the logical and genetic core of things and our experience of them, remain outside of language. In Kant, this is for structural reasons (as it were, ontological reasons), and in Hegel, for phenomenological and temporal reasons: reasons of history. This contradictory belonging-together-in-opposition of identity and difference, intuitions and concepts, representation and the sublime, culture and nature, history and something else, is claimed as the inner structure of experience, which is claimed as the reality of "what is," for all practical purposes. Philosophy's mission, henceforth, is to advance the understanding of this paradox, which generates the form and content of the domains of the knowable. (Maybe at this point in the narrative, we should say "theory" rather than "philosophy" out of respect for the troubled and topically central reflexivity of the enterprise.) The mark of enlightened reason is a consciousness that reflects on the intractable paradoxes of knowing even as it knows itself and those very reflections caught up in those paradoxes. The freedom and the torment of this awareness are directly proportional.

By contrast, agony and aporia have no place in the Wittgensteinian universe. There, any claim about an otherness or externality that constitutes experience is incoherent. Such claims describe an artifact of our grammars: a metaphysical origin. And, as against Hegel's postulate of the identity of identity and difference, the linguistic argument holds that any difference one can articulate within a code has already been assimilated to it. If the difference is *in* the identity, then it has lost the salient, the externality, that made it a difference.

Both critical projects, Kant's and Hegel's, posit an unknowable element that founds the very materials, methods, and motives of knowing. Rather than kick it upstairs, both try to factor this puzzle, this horizonal effect, into their practical, critical labors. Both, along with the Marxian and Freudian critiques that derive from them, are logocentric in form but heterological in their content, and they stand behind many of the premises that drove our decade's suspicion hermeneutics.

The new historicisms, to the extent that they incorporated the Marxian or Freudian paradigms, or insofar as they retained some equivalent to nature or the unconscious, can be conceived as the last of the confidently hermeneutic engagements with the literatures of other worlds — in this case, past worlds. This is, possibly, the last critical practice to figure the relation between the text and its reading as objectively determined, the reading solicited by the structures and provenance of the object itself. The new historicisms that fit this description can be taken to represent the constructively skeptical phase of the Kant-Hegel project: inquiry into the logical and/or dialectical contradictions that generate the seeming immediacy of experience. The goal of analysis is to reread the object in such a way as to trace its achieved cultural identity to its historically conflictual conditions. The picture of a finished or final world is replaced by a narrative of that world's coming into being and of its coming to assume the look of a picture.

I use that characterization only as a reasonably solid platform from which to launch some thoughts about the opportunities for critical work today, now that the field of cultural studies has grown so crowded and complex, and the new histories are neither so new as they once were nor, in a way, so historical. For example, the chiasmic thinking so marked in cultural and historicist studies (e.g., the subject in history/the history in the subject) points toward a reciprocity, balance, and symmetry that would seem to dissolve the tension and resistance that are integral to a dialectically materialist and dynamic understanding of history. This paper is not about the life and death of academic movements. It is a practical effort to review the options, such as they are, for persons who share the kind and degree of awareness embodied in the Wittgenstein parable, *and* whose stake in reading—whose intellectual, political, and libidinal attachment—has been and remains in some way materialist. My inquiry will not hold much interest for those who consider themselves pragmatists, relativists, or Rortian hermeneuts. Nor will those who equate facts with information and information with knowledge (as is sometimes the case in textual studies, literary history, and canon revision) be alive to the themes I will be considering.

That phrase, "in some way materialist," means in one way or another (1) committed to the picture of texts and readings as products of and participants in the forces and relations that bring about the ceaseless reproduction of physical and social life. (Before proceeding, let me say that these features do not add up to an all-purpose or prescriptive definition of materialism. I merely spell out the meanings of the word as I use it in this paper.)

Materialist, by this working definition, also entails (2) a critical practice that repositions the text in any of the force fields that concretely defined it at any given moment in the past, and (and this is crucial) in the present, one field that a materialist critique cannot afford to ignore. That caveat harks back to the Kantian theme I mentioned. Even as you accept the explanatory status of certain categories and the validity of the moves that bind them to the problem at hand (that is, even as you accept the content and form of the materialism specific to your time and place), you also stick to the Kantian program of trying to establish the conditions of those categories and procedures. This is the reflexive dimension of the exercise. It is always incomplete and deluded, and it knows and tries to signify that fact.

In addition (and here is the Hegelian strain), (3) materialist critique associates meaning with determinate negation, a prolific incursion on the seeming immediacy and sufficiency of the object, an object mistaken for the

Real. The *re*-production of that negatively produced meaning in the form of *knowledge* entails a second, more deliberated rupture of the object's self-presentation at the point of inquiry. This occurs for some technical reasons having to do with the machinery of semiotics, but more important, on account of a view of textual production as determined by a multitude of factors, many of them drawn from domains defined by that culture as incompatible or mutually exclusive. The introduction of those domains into the critical field thus assumes the character of an assault upon the formal integrity of the work. Moreover, because the otherness of those domains is often a function of causal or determinative relations that the text cannot acknowledge — for example, the relation between the economic and the aesthetic — those orders may occupy the discourse as a kind of unconscious, what we call a political unconscious. Again, the raising up of this material and these relations will challenge the work's self-representation.

There is a fourth element, a wildcard, in my definition of materialism, and that is (for want of a better word) heterology: the study of what exists at some sort of tangent to the identity principles of the culture in question. This is the element deriving from Kant and Hegel by way of Marx, Freud, and among others, Althusser, Lacan, Bataille, Lévinas, Deleuze, de Certeau, and Lyotard, all of whom posit a dimension beyond representation but somehow implicated in it: what Lyotard calls "an immanent sublime." In Marx, for example, it is "the fixed framework within which the subject forms a substance that it encounters."[10] In Freud, it would be the preeconomic, prestructural workings of repression and also the negativity that drives through and beyond the pleasure principle. In Althusser, it is the magic of structural causality, the (nonmechanical, nonexpressive) effectivity of the whole in its parts: a whole that is "neither an unknowable thing-in-itself, nor . . . a string of events or set of facts . . . [but] rather an asymptotic phenomenon, an outer limit, which the subject approaches in the anxiety of the moment of truth."[11] For Lacan, it is the gaze "to which I am subjected in an *original* way," that is, in such a way as to originate me, the subject, as lack, or the inability to see myself seeing, to grasp my conditions of being.[12] When the citing of this dimension is coupled with a discourse or stylistic performance of its ineffability, it is the marker of critique as such. It locates the point where, historically, critical theory split off from first philosophy, and also where aesthetic modernity came into being. By that I mean first the Romantic and then the avant-garde project of representing the unpresentable (or, borrowing once again from Lyotard, presenting that there *is* something unrepresentable): namely, the medium and the frame of the particular artwork, of the category of the aesthetic, and of the subject and origin effects engendered by both.[13]

Unlike metaphysics, heterology treats this unspeakable otherness as a special feature of the social-historical made-ness of things, not as their transcendental ground. Through some peculiar position or embodiment within the dominant codes, this otherness resists symbolization absolutely. It thus assumes an effective or what might be called a *virtual* materiality, taking on under certain conditions or in certain contexts an irreducibly thing-like character. The materialist reading tries, with completely conscious illogic and knowing bad faith, to display, preserve, and even to share in that quality.

Material, in this context, means unreadable. It means a text or some part of a text that is either transparent or opaque and thus not exactly or not completely a text at all. Because of its effective closure and self-presence (that is to say, its success in realizing those effects), the material object does not absorb. It fascinates. It is the effect or the reading some poets hope for: not the one that exclaims, "Heavens, I recognize the place, I know it!" but the reading that says, "Hell, I don't recognize the place, or the time, or the 'I' in this sentence. I don't know it."[14] The meaning of this object will not take shape as a narrative or history (both are forms of intention), no matter how troubled, repressed, or dispersed. Instead, meaning here amounts to something like action potentials or adhesive surfaces, and because these intensities cannot break free and assume some form of equivalence, the object cannot circulate. To that extent, *which is far from total,* it generates no value. The economy to which it relates is not the "restricted economy of accumulation but the general economy of meaning as unusable flow and unrecompensed loss."[15] Or, for a tougher expression, one that sidesteps the romance of Bataille's general economy, one could say that the object releases a meaning that *has* no meaning. It is just something else in the world. A something else that differs from the rest, however, by neither reflecting nor yielding to a human interest. Except of course (a very big exception), the interest in otherness as such once it gets objectified through the critical or aesthetic discourses. Heterology would *like* to avert this interest (nothing would make it happier), but it never can.

Baudrillard has written of the dream of the status of the object and consumption beyond exchange and use, beyond value and equivalence. *Dream* is the operative word here, but just as crucial is the fact that dreams are socially made and coded and thus both real and shared experience with real consequences. This particular dream, which classically comes under the heading of the aesthetic (and also, within related discourses, under the rubric of nature), is capitalism's special and perhaps even its sustaining fantasy. Unlike the commodity, which is paradigmatically readable due to the sharpness of its form-content contradiction, the object enjoys an effective self-identity that opens no space for intervention. Thus, we are told, it never completely gives up its secret, which is, of course, that it has none (probably: one can never really know). The *object,* a word one must bracket so as to keep foregrounding its character as a social (in the manner of *anti*social) Imaginary and as the effect of particular histories of cultural production, affords nothing to do. It offers no contradictions to resolve, no interior to penetrate, no gaps to outline and then, by way of a metadiscourse, to suture — in short, no resistance to reading and therefore no payoff. To this extent, it challenges the work model of activity grounding those philosophies of the subject that engendered the aesthetic as such, that is, as a *critique* of that work model, in the late eighteenth and early nineteenth centuries. And because the object (so-called) does not mount its challenge as a project, oppositional or otherwise, it undermines that aesthetic from the other side, exposing its negativity for another value-form. As against the *an*-aesthetic signature of the object, the autotelic hedonism of the aesthetic starts to look very like a distracted shopper. Or the object highlights the complicity between, on the one hand, art and interpretation as forms of value- and subject-production, and on the other, the particular model of humanness specified by the capitalist modes of production.

Then again, one cannot help noticing that the mysterious self-possession of the object and the passivity of its reception are also the *effects* of the commodity, that elementary unit of capitalist production and exchange, when it is working most efficiently, or when it most thoroughly erases its social and its labor content. In other words, the object's thwarting of a productive, semiotic consumption can offer itself as a critique of those processes of abstraction, instrumentality, and equivalence that rule the world of exchange. By calling the question on that particular system of value, however, no matter how artlessly, the object generates another discourse of value, one that comes to be synonymous with ideology itself or its inverting and obscuring of actual social processes. Over and above its material dividends, the object produces an illusion of escape from the political economy of the sign, an illusion essential to the healthy functioning of that economy.

But then again (what I am tracking by these turns is the dialecticity of this would-be postdialectical object), the rational, skeptical conquest of such illusions, as outlined in the paragraph above, is the very telos of economic reason. It is realized when thought is so thoroughly formalized as to be "robbed of that for the sake of which men [and women] think."[16] That phrase is Adorno's, as is the general approach to these paradoxes of progress.

From this dialectical tangle, familiar to students of Romanticism, the Frankfurt School, and the avant-garde, we may conclude that to read the myth of the object, to expose its founding material and social conditions, is not to exhaust the reality of that myth. It is, rather, to release the myth from the unreality of its reified form. Possibly, it is to change its sign from a cultural practice that is on balance affirmative to one that exerts more critical force. *What we do next*, however, to keep that reality (in philosophical terms, that posit; in a Marxist idiom, that second nature) from getting reified all over again is the question that drives heterology. It is a question to ask *now*, now that through the work of the past ten years the dead are awakened.

Michael Taussig proposes a mode of analysis that works its way free of various notions of contradiction in order to capture the "decided undecidability that could so clearly, so mistily, be seen in Marx's statement regarding the fetish quality of commodities"—the "flip-flop from spirit to thing and back again."[17] Throughout his collection, *The Nervous System*, Taussig juxtaposes what Paul Ricoeur identified in Freud as, on the one hand, a suspicion hermeneutics, and on the other, a restorative mimesis. Taussig calls this a critical practice that both "demystifies and reenchants." It reenchants because it knows that alongside the mystery of why, when, and how—questions of motive, manner, and meaning—there remains the nagging and deeply disquieting question of *what*, aimed at the webs of contingency, mere combination, and excess that render the disenchanted world (Vico's well-lit theater of history and culture) such a twilight zone. Those epistemic boundary paradoxes I traced at the beginning of this essay help to explain this phenomenon. A more concrete explanation, the kind Taussig favors, would look to the always ironic and punctually horrific history of the advanced capitalist societies, many of whose crises foreground the internal limits of Enlightenment and its practices of knowing and ordering, its domination of nature.[18]

Oppositional critique might at this point take its bearings from Taussig's observation that "context as explanation is the fixed screen" onto which many of our histories from below are projected. It is this screen, Taussig argues, "that poses the greatest resistance to change, [and all] the forgotten and oppressed voices we cast upon it," he says, do not alter that surface. He cites our "profound and self-constituting entanglement" in that screen of interpretation as "the great arena where world history . . . folds into rules of customary sense." Heterology reminds us that once that fold between history and custom disappears, once a paradigm of knowing starts feeling like the form of the real, once the screen becomes a transparent medium—the wall of the cave— we must "work harder *not* to understand,"[19] knowing all the while we will never reach that place of intelligent indifference and that if we did, we would not recognize ourselves.[20] That is because we would not *be* ourselves.

The older heterologies project a place beyond economic reason and by the same token, anti-Oedipus. They describe a state of loss that is not the prelude to possession, a silence that is not speech under erasure. They imagine a representational practice that withdraws from the no-win language game of supplements (Derrida's semiotic elaboration of the commodity and the money forms). They suggest a Deleuzian or Nietzschean dream of affirmation without negation, or production without consumption at *either* end, an escape from what Coleridge called the laws of grammar and psychology. Alongside "investment, desire, passion, seduction . . . expression and competition—the hot universe," they set "ecstasy, obscenity, fascination, . . . hazard, chance and vertigo—the cold universe."[21]

A more recent heterology takes incorporation as its model of embodiment that is not paid for by the domination of both internal and external otherness.[22] In place of recuperative self-alienation as well as identity and praxis politics, this incorporative model proposes aleatory combination, machinic assemblage, and transcategorical affinity as its formal principles. One can discern in this most recent, postmodern, but still Marxist critique of the subject an extension of Adorno's great and tragic campaign against the triumphalism of the emancipatory materialisms of the nineteenth century. What is new and radical about the effort to rethink cultural critique by reference to a technologically and sociohistorically reinvented nature is its drive beyond the state-approved playground of the aesthetic: its work on the productivist paradigm itself, something that Adorno in the 1940s through the 1960s, a period of multi- but not transnational or information-based capitalism, could not begin to accomplish. In place of the mastery models of materialization and individuation, and their productive consumption of nature, these social critics propose a model of embodiment "understood as a complex, labile, overtone structure, neither dependent upon nor reducible to, an organic substrate or historical object."[23]

This sort of thinking, like the older, hotter heterologies, is genuine only when it comes about through contextual rewriting and ideology critique. Lacking that, heterology is indistinguishable from phenomenology or ontology, pragmatism, pluralism, or any other jargon of authenticity. Heterology begins only after the apparent self-identity and givenness of the object has been negated, replaced by a narrative of its participation in the historical and social formations and projects of its own time and that of the critic: once, that is, the work's objective character, consisting in its functional relations within the social whole or wholes, has been established.

Since, however, neither the social whole nor, therefore, the objective character of the discourse can ever be definitively established (particularly since they involve the everchanging variable of the critic's position), one must ask what it is that curtails this exercise and initiates heterology (and also a question I consider below: What happens to the oppositional and cognitive force of sociohistorical reinscription if heterology is refused). In large part, the answer to the question of what prompts a heterological phase will turn on the current conditions of knowledge production for the field and object at issue, conditions in one way or another organized by the economic and social whole. One wonders, however, whether the two actions, critique of textual production and heterology, might enjoy a more integral relation. I want to venture an imagination of the way those two critical actions, both of them materialist, but one in an anthropocentric or sociocentric way and the other in a way that verges on metaphysics, might summon each other.

First, though, I have to say why I belabor a point that must remain speculative (and in passing, explain what I meant when I said that the new historicisms are somehow not as historical as they once were). It seems to me that a present-day materialism wanting to hold onto the tension between the Wittgensteinian or constructivist picture and the hermeneutic, heterological, critically reflected strain will have a hard time of it, for reasons that concern the recent history of literary studies in our country and on account of larger, more determinant tendencies in the culture. In the academy, there is the fact of the long-awaited and much-deserved prestige of the sociohistorical rewriting of literature and other cultural icons. By that I mean the work of restoring the artifacts that make up our cultural canons to their condition as social practice, conceived as irreducibly historical and as both driven and mediated by specific and conflicting interests. These interests are shown to be underwritten by more compelling, pervasive, and obscure, but no less constructed pressures. The work of disclosing these dynamic patterns has come to be synonymous with critique as such and also with a liberationist as opposed to a liberal set of values. It is grouped with the resistance literatures it often studies, and with the antihegemonic strains it discerns within many of the high cultural discourses and many more of the popular ones.

Ranked on the other side, the reactionary side, are resources associated with both the formalist movement, prominent here in the 1940s and 1950s, and the historical scholarship that preceded it, the paradigm of literary study before the war. Both were rejected for their objectivism, or for their way of masking their own political investments as well as the politics (cultural and topical) embedded in the "data," the aesthetic or the historical record on which they worked. Also on that losing side were the ontological and linguistic preoccupations of "theory," or of the Continental traditions revived in this country in the 1960s. What was rejected there was the general argument that being and language, and also their aporetic or antinomial relation to each other, have an objective and fixed reality independent of cultural practice. The essentialist and universalizing form of the proposition — again, its false objectivity — marked it as an idealism.

I offer this overview so as to highlight the institutional problems faced by a materialism that has not withdrawn its investment in objectivity or, to use a less burdened and binary word, Adorno's word, "nonidentity." It conceives this order of things as a thoroughly mediated phenomenon that may at certain points exceed the causalities that brought it into being. Nor does a materialism of this kind repudiate theory — borrowing again from Adorno, a striving by the concept to transcend the concept, or (and this is Jonathan Culler's recent definition of theory) a critique of the natural through investigation of the mode of study in which you have some experience. When it sees that critique of the natural has become the natural, it takes *that* as its problem, along with the matter of finding a mode of study that is not wholly, or rather, not *evenly* enmeshed in that problem. The element of theory is, among other things, a line of defense against the tendency of stories, however dialogic or dialectical, to become facts, and of facts, however constructed and contingent, to become fetishes. Theory interferes with the self-witnessing authenticity of narrative and factual presentment (of everything, one might hazard, but poetic presentment, and that too, eventually). It counters, if only by foregrounding, the tendency of all knowledge practices, including itself, to remake the other into a version of the self, and of all such versions to recapitulate the self-aggrandizing but also ultimately self-defeating philosophy of the subject, as built up by the four great critiques of the modern period, those of Kant, Hegel, Marx, and Freud. A materialist critique maintains these commitments because it is alive to the fact that knowledge, no matter how antinomial, has no defenses against the form of the system, and that the system, "the form of presenting a totality to which nothing is extraneous, absolutizes the thought against each of its contents and evaporates the content in thoughts. It proceeds idealistically before advancing any arguments for idealism."[24]

As little as five years ago, it seemed that a postproductivist but still Marxist materialism could satisfy these dual commitments. It could puncture the constructivist paradigm by positing some version of both nonidentity and the whole — nature and history — the two poles of a dialectical objectivism. At the same time, it could make a problem of the status of labor, production, and the economic, the textbook mediations between those poles (by status, I pinpoint the conception of these practices as singular or unified functions within a systematic account of social practice). While it challenged the primacy of those moments and elements, along with the ontological centrality of the working class, the notion of prehistory, and the postulate of antagonism between the human and the natural, Marxism's epistemic field was still ordered by the figure of contradiction. The content of objectivity might have been abandoned, but the differential structure that produced it as a scientific form remained. The mechanism of dialectics in history and its workings in the relation between critique and its object and critique and the dominant subject forms of its own moment commanded belief in a way that seems no longer the case. By contrast, the work that has been done on the politics of identity as opposed to class, work in gender, race, and post-coloniality, has redrawn our pictures of the relation between material conditions and labor on the one hand, and consciousness, ideology, and agency on the other, with the general effect of making such two-handed formulations and even the more dynamic and recursive versions thereof obsolete. The very notion of structures, relations, and forces that exist in some sort of generative and scientifically explanatory tension with one another is no longer standard even for Marxist analysis. Contamination, hybridity, subalternity: these are not the handsomely structured and dynamic differences-in-identity that support the Freudian and Marxian hermeneutics. In fact, these shape-shifting and semipermeable formations are more like a usurpation of that function, just as transgression tends to squeeze out the classical forms of negation and opposition.

The more general and also technical obstacles to a materialism that is curious to entertain hypertextual or countertextual worlds—worlds that are, for different reasons, incommensurable with the given codes—come into play at the point of reception, where our critical studies enter the larger cultural marketplace. Here they are subjected to the routine defensive mechanisms of late capital, where cultural recognition, approving *or* critical, does the work of absorption. (This is not to say that the processing begins at this point; the setting of goals and the availability of methods are also determined.) This is what Adorno meant, or anticipated, by his phrase "the form of the system" in the passage quoted above. The attacks on the academy's revisionist pictures turn out to be yet another way to reproduce and circulate those pictures, a way in short to commoditize and thus neutralize opposition. Attack at this level proceeds mechanically and therefore inexorably.

As many have noted, the once disturbing exposures of the historically determined and (more disturbing) *over*determined particulars that generate the reality of cultural appearances at given moments have lost their edge. More precisely, they have lost their immanence, the quality that distinguishes critique from criticism, or historical from criteriological analysis.[25] Through no fault of their own, our stories of cultural production have become episodes in capitalism's masterplot: the transformation of matter into value, suffering into meaning, givenness into necessity, nature into culture. It is as if the gap in the phrase "historical materialism" (at best a negotiated coupling) has closed over. A redemptive logic has come to embrace the initially estranging, counterintuitive, and for those reasons materially realizing rewritings of the closures that made up our canons, and those of us who do this work are the hapless agents of that redemption. Naturally, the subject we celebrate is no longer the autonomous individual, nor is it the autotelic text. Instead, we have groups, genders, and races (the elements of an identity politics) as well as disciplines, discourses, and practices of consumption (a more impersonal but no less coherent and creative set of agencies). The new subject's labors of self-making are constrained, opposed, and even thwarted, but the heroic story of bourgeois reproduction remains. That story is objectified in our critical performances, through which history's contingencies are woven into a pattern of conflicting, unselfconscious, but individually coherent intentions. At the same time, the effrontery of these patterns (often a function of the dissonance that organizes them) establishes the reader who reveals them as a bold and original producer, clearing a space in a crowded market. One is reminded of the competitive subject of capital, who takes real risks that cannot help but ensure the stability of the system they appear to threaten. In addition, in waging these warfares against the inertias that govern our present and our uses of the past, we realize ourselves as virtuous citizens of an enlightened society, acting out that great theme from the repertoire of bourgeois liberalism: free speech, internal opposition, consensus by way of dissensus.

There is, in other words, a certain truth to the perception of a tyranny of the politically correct. Institutional and therefore coercive approval — correctness — *is* what happens to difference and more emphatically, dissidence, in a society like ours. The particular founding impulses of the critical action are erased, its techniques abstracted, standardized, and taught, its productivity harnessed and enhanced, and the affront made over into a normative position.

There's no going back, nor should there be. But, when self and other are fused or chiasmically entwined, when history becomes nothing but the creative living of ideology, and ideology becomes the productive base, then we lose our capacity to recognize history as "what hurts," to borrow Jameson's famous epithet. If in our stories we weave the past's excess and contingency into patterns of conflicting, unwitting, but socially coherent intentions, making it all come out even, making it all come out *"meaning,"* then history is everything and thus nothing, and we might as well be doing phenomenology. In theory, everyone knows that critique of the natural is always becoming the natural. We will never find a mode of study that is not enmeshed in that problem, but then again, not all modes of study are evenly and everywhere possessed. The most unlikely candidates may become at particular moments a line of defense against the tendency of stories, however dialogic or dialectical, to become facts and of facts, however constructed, to become fetishes.

I want to be very explicit about the fact that a turn toward heterology is not an attempt to revive either a metaphysically referenced picture or an infrastructurally reflective one, nor is it a return to the predialectical materialisms. *It is only to try to embody in a way that produces some sort of distance effect qualities that do not add up to the human as currently constituted (that is, something that punctures the reality effect) without at the same time dissolving those qualities into a mystique of otherness, another orientalism. It is to do this, acknowledging in both the form and substance of one's practice the futility of the thing but the value of the effort.* Ideally, one performs this impossible practice without romanticizing it. You try *not* to imagine that the wish or capacity to sustain these contradictions springs you from the trap of normal science or, returning to Wittgenstein's model, releases you from your picture.

Still, a heterology that arises from and remains in a cranky and fitful way within a sociohistorical practice may well be a different *kind* of normal science, a different way of occupying the picture. Very few of our knowledge models try to justify their aims and methods by reference to external criteria, but most want to project some sort of logical consistency, or validity within their own terms. Heterology, by contrast, declares itself internally inconsistent without going on to devise a metalogic to rationalize its practice. The justification occurs concretely, performatively, within each exercise and cannot be generalized from one to the next. If it takes the form of a concept, its relation to the practice is *figured* as a relation, constructed for the purposes of the exercise. Nonetheless, a more regulative and objective notion of validity in interpretation survives in the very postulate of an outside or other to representation, albeit a historically constructed and changing outside.[26] It seems possible that heterology, just by materializing the longing for effects that are empirically unavailable, may conjure the bounding line of those interests and practices that make up the writer's human nature, at this time, in this place. To take an interest in these effects is also to maintain a critical and a utopian attitude toward the conditions of contemporary life. It is to hold faith with Enlightenment ideas about knowledge as social transformation and with Romanticism's insistence on that but refusal to pay the price of short-circuiting something more radical, like change in the economies of desire. Let me add that the technical, conceptual, and political problems facing a heterological critique are insurmountable. Still, for persons possessed of certain values, the staging of these problems seems a good thing—at certain times, the best thing—to do.

I return to the question of how the two strains of the materialism I have been constructing might be related. Sociohistorical rewriting of the work will, if it is effective, do violence to the self-understanding and professed values of the work. This will persist until such time as the community's concept of textual and cultural nature expands to absorb the antithetical element (in a formalist idiom, until such time as the work manages to intentionalize the orders of difference visited upon it). Up to that point, however, critical reconstruction of the work in its social habitats will take apart its given integrity (some reasons for this are given above, in reference to the relation between a critical negativity and the political unconscious of the text in question). If we narrow the field to texts that descend to us under the sign of literature, or the aesthetic, or even just "culture," high or low, then the violence of a materialist reading is explained by the fact that whatever those discourses do or did in the way of affirming or denying their material conditions of being, whatever their idealizing intentions or effects, their reproduction as literature or art, or their social ontology as symbols of the cultural whole in one way or another effaces the material facts of their life. This may not be the case for cultural production in the present, but it does seem to apply to works produced from the Enlightenment through the high modern period. And it is also true for works that have been or currently are *re*produced by methods invented during that span. This has to do with distinctions between the aesthetic and the practical (broken down, the cognitive, ethical, and juridical), a diacritics hammered out in the late eighteenth century. The breach of that decorum must involve a rupture at the level of self-representation.

At the same time, the self-representations involved in the critical act are also put at risk. One violence breeds another. In mounting an antithetical but immanent critique of the identity principles of the past, our words enter into an altered relation to present-day discourses of dominance, inevitably engaged during the process of writing. The work of articulating the blindness-insight ratios that link the discourse to its moment may outline the traces of a similarly implicated relation between our own technologies of knowing and the identity principles of our time and place. This chain reaction may be a function of the highly contained field in which the demystifying exercise takes place. And it may happen only in cases where the study-text emerged from the conditions, however uneven, of capitalist production and ideology, where the aesthetic is granted its own self-regulating domain. The text's discovered bondage to the conditions of its time and place, juxtaposed with our own critical autonomy, may put that freedom of ours in question. (Remember that critique is classically figured as the most liberated and citizen-defining action available to members of enlightened, democratic societies.)

Or the ideological distancing whereby we come to perceive the constructedness of our forms of knowing may have to do with more technical matters. I am thinking of the relative speed and intimacy that characterize the circulation of academic discourse today within what has been called the information society. In very short order, we see our language cited, framed, used, abused, and so forth. The reproduction of our arguments happens so fast and so close at hand that its reality *as* reproduction rather than response or commentary emerges. The individual producer-critic is positioned to see how little she controls the meanings she writes. She sees how public and also unpredictable an event her argument is, or how her argument *includes* its effects, its readings and misreadings. She sees what is typically concealed by capitalist relations: the social production of meaning. (This is a good thing.)

There may also be something like a dialectical logic that helps explain the punctual availability of heterology as a materialist operation. In rewriting the myths of the past, we cast them in the new body of present-day enlightenment discourse. By the same token, thus do we mingle our own distinctive error, *our* myths, with an alien body, that of the texts upon which we enact our enlightenments. One possible result of this miscegenation is a sensuous excess at the level of textuality, an order, or rather a disorder, that highlights the dissonance within our own practices of knowing: something like the ideological distantiation Althusser attributes exclusively to art. I associate these effects with the violent juxtaposition of two different social formations in the confined space of a textual exercise, a reading, performed upon any sort of discourse. The aesthetic then becomes a name for the results of this clash, not for the work or category that enables it. I call these results excess because while they will not submit to totalization or translation, they owe their occurrence to those actions, to which they are related as a by-product and horizon.

This excess exerts an oppositional force, but its style of resistance is peculiar. Dispersed, disorderly, noncumulative, it prevents the formation of an equal and opposite subject or identity form. The style of attack is more like terrorism than orchestrated warfare. Like Kant's sublime, these uncoordinated points of reference bring us up against the inadequacy of our cognitive codes, and in so doing, they make us feel the presence of those codes. They crystallize the medusan tangle of knowledge and falsehood, freedom and confinement, that structures our subjectivity but whose contents must remain a blank to us. Then we know that we cannot know the conditions of our knowledge, but only, and this is a best-case scenario, its aporetic form.

It would seem that the obvious thing to do with these effects that resist the hermeneutic that released them is to conceive them as a site of encounter with a cultural repressed. What then? The effort to search out whatever it is that we cannot know precisely because that particular ignorance is the condition of our knowing is, naturally, pointless. Only if the search proceeds in some extravagant and unseemly way, a way that falls outside our logical practices, can it perhaps trick us into "other" awareness. Consider the optical illusion (a deep truth, as it turns out) used by Freud to instance the uncanny. The mirrored door suddenly swings open, giving the good doctor a reflection of himself *not* absorbing his gaze and therefore not abridging the self-alienation of personhood in the way one's mirror image comes to do. All at once, the objective conditions of his usual gaze, his subjectivity, materialize. For a moment, he is othered, but with a sense of return to an identity that preceded the coherence of his ego-self. (Or consider what it means for a subject, conceived as nothing but the effects of a repression, to conduct an inquiry into that process. The transferential method, a restorative mimesis, is Freud's solution to this logical dilemma.)

To reject these visions of excess as a reactionary fantasy of transcendental or reflexive origins is also to betray what should be elementary for materialist critique: namely, that it is only materialist so long as it remains historical, and that means willing to reinvent its form and its content as its own conditions of production change. Lacking that, it is idealism by another name. To persist in a certain kind of cultural critique once it has become second-nature within the age's practices of knowing is to comply with the absorptive tendencies of capital. Or, since there can be no such thing as a uniformly, universally, or ultimately effective noncompliance, one should say that it is to stop producing the wish to interfere with the machinery that profitably incorporates difference into the mainstream.

More than thirty years ago, Roland Barthes pondered the unbridgeable gap between what he called "speaking the object" and penetrating it: the latter an act of rendering it, in his words, "permeable to history," a move Barthes rejects. He refers to that, the historicizing operation, as mythology and ideologism, while he terms the other labor poetry: "the search for the inalienable meaning of things."[27] The binary setup is dated and even at the time, it had to be disingenuous, but the conclusion Barthes draws from this sterile opposition would not be rejected today: namely, that the idea of a critical discourse bound as a subject to an object-text is bankrupt. In its place, Barthes proposes an implosion of the art-versus-knowledge, speaking-versus-penetrating binary. The writing he imagines would enact a subject-predicate relation in the world, a practical as opposed to a power relation, chiming with Kenneth Burke's proposal of a hyphenated rather than hierarchical relation. This is a view in keeping with the aesthetic turn, so called, taken by some critical work today. That phrase describes a knowledge discourse imitative of collage or montage in its efforts to incorporate but not absorb the material object or effect, nor erase its categorial difference from the host discourse. What is rejected is the logocentrism (and circularity) of the argument-and-example approach.

And yet the big, old questions remain. How does the subject-predicate relation, the sentence that is writing, aesthetic or critical, relate to the more dominant or coercive sentences inscribed in the literatures we study? Can it relate to a world of sentences outside our culture, or at its breeding center, interstices, or peripheries? To call this new sentence postmodernism (and it certainly conforms to the profile), is to read it as a declaration that cultural modernity in the sense of a simultaneously oppositional relation to the state and a reflexive relation to its own medium has run its course. What kind of writing can develop under these constraints that will still satisfy the conditions of a materialist critique as I have defined it?

To answer that question and to do it without inviting the absorptions I have been tracking, I will first make some general observations based on the preceding analysis of the problem. Then I will give some examples of work that embraces rather than denies the contradictions that arise for a critique that is both historically and reflexively materialist.

First, a general reorientation. We could make a shift from a practice of knowing conceived along the lines of individual intellectual production to a critical writing that in one way or another disclaims that control. I do not mean, although I also do not exclude, collaborative writing, nor am I thinking primarily of coteries or schools. The gesture the writing makes is not toward recognized others, as in partners, opponents, or potential converts. Instead, it finds ways to bring out what is in fact the case, that is, the social production of meaning, and to make that fact work not to annihilate difference but to multiply it. The trick is to understand the social not as a monolithic, coherent, or even knowable body, nor as a constituency waiting to be fashioned. Rather, the social could serve as a name for the unforeseeable otherness that comes to occupy our writing as it makes its way in a time-frame that is always more uneven than it seems, including slices of the future, not just the past. "Making its way" can mean an open-ended set of encounters between the many agencies and intentions that our critical writing embodies and the many that reembody it. It can mean the mercy of misreading, a providence it is easy to concede when we are the ones misreading, and doing it upon what would otherwise be the abstract and unreal literatures of the past. It is a harder thing to apply the logic not just to one's own critical work but to present-day reception, where there are no historical differentials to sanctify the violence. It seems worth doing because, from the perspective of the individual knowledge producer, it must be, following Wittgenstein, pictures and stories all the way down. Some people will find that fact depressing because they will understand that it is always "our" stories and pictures, no matter how wide we cast the content net. From the standpoint of a transindividual discourse production, however — neither the standpoint of the whole nor of the part, but rather of the series — "a surplus of the Real over every symbolization that functions as an object-cause" may materialize.[28] This standpoint can never be seized. (One could also say the series cannot be totalized.) That is why Hegel called the series a "bad infinity." For me, that may be its goodness: the virtue of a standpoint that can only be recognized after the fact or extrapolated from textual encounters. It is always all before us or behind. It resembles what Homi Bhabha has called "a space of 'translation,'" where we may construct "a political object that is new, *neither the one nor the Other*" (he means by that phrase neither the Master nor the Slave).[29] As Barthes said, "I am always powerless to render the wholeness of the object." But part of that may have to do with the way that the very establishment of a knowing, rendering "I," as against a world of unconsecrated otherness, recapitulates the subject-object divide that "knowing" presumably wants to close. Perhaps the felt gap between poetry and science, speaking the object and penetrating it, would narrow if the writerly "I" could set aside the closures of self-definition. It could, for example, reinvent its concept each time it puts its identity into practice. Instead of purposes and projects, this sort of knowing would have ways of proceeding, different ways and means for each occasion.

Perhaps the one fairly restricted thing that more than any other makes critique so pliable to the regimes of the marketplace is its management of its concepts. The relation between the idea, methods, and materials of any particular critique is always problematic, for reasons no more profound than the fact that the combinations making up the histories we study are always in flux, that the decision as to where a story begins and ends is just that, a decision, and that the act of deciding the outlines of the story is also an episode in that story, one that can never fully account for itself there. But these particulars get buried as the work takes its place in an institutional economy. If a writing could keep its concept, which is for writing what self-consciousness is for persons, sealed in its practice, it might perform the symbolic act of instancing a subjectivity that is not given in advance and that is more permeable to its textual and social environments than is customary in our critical language games. The embodiment of these possibilities may be the most powerful thing critique can accomplish today. It may clear a space in which the otherness of our language and objects can materialize, and alongside it, not above, some understanding of those mysteries.

No kind of writing escapes the loop of recuperative expenditure. But it can circulate in odd and disturbing ways that make it harder to reproduce than the other commodities. It can define orbits that are larger and less predictable than those laid out by capital. As Paul Mann has argued in his book *The Theory-Death of the Avant-Garde,* every cultural gesture, no matter how anarchic, ascetic, or densely coded, becomes a value-form: the form of equivalence between unlike things and qualities.[30] In intellectual currency, this equivalence takes the form of the concept. We cannot prevent the concept from emerging alongside the practice, nor should we try, because the concept is also, for dialectical reasons, deliverance from the spurious transparencies projected by practice. The wish that drives heterology, however, is to control the possession and use of this value-form. Again, there is nothing like a foolproof or final way to do this. But by making a problem of the relation between theory and practice, a writer can restrict the possession of her language to those who will do the work of reinventing it in the special circumstances that define their own work. The original will then relate to its reinvention as a version, losing its privileged status as first and definitive. In the play of these determinate but interactively unstable languages, the object of heterology may take shape. What to do with it is another question, but just to ask it is already to have breached (a little) the economy of white writing.

The impulse is to bring even this thought of a conceptually problematic practice under a concept. For example, de Certeau's distinction between strategy and tactics would seem to explain the disjunctive, decentered, and noncumulative character of a postcritical practice. Strategy is "the calculation... of power relationships that becomes possible as soon as a subject with will and power... can be isolated. It postulates a *place*... delimited as its *own* and serv[ing] as the base from which relations to an *exteriority* can proceed." Tactics, conversely, are defined as "calculated action[s] determined by the absence of a proper locus.... The space of a tactic is the space of the other.... It does not have the means to *keep to itself*.... It operates in isolated actions, blow by blow. It takes advantage of 'opportunities'... being without any base where it could stockpile its winnings, build up its own position.... What it wins it cannot keep."[31]

Tactics punch holes in the fabric of ideology. They do not negate, an action that always seems to affirm somewhere else, if only by lending itself to narratives of progress, purification, or simply change (that is, the value of the new). Since negation has been, for capitalist formations, an important maintenance technique — legitimation by opposition, staying in place by moving forward — materialist critique must perhaps find ways to become oblique, interstitial, disorganizing, incorporative, or proliferative rather than oppositional.[32] Once attack on the institution of art becomes art, or attack on the institutions of culture and capitalism becomes those things, critique must find different ways to embody its drive toward difference. And then too, there is the proverbial bottom line: tactics are what we use when we come up against the radical impossibility of a thing that still seems the best thing to do. That is a good definition of the state of affairs for materialist critique as I have read it in this paper.

Still, tempting as it is to block out the field into tactics and strategy, who would submit to another decorum, especially one so comfortably binary as that? One could, however, imagine collapsing the binary into an irregular oscillation between those mutually exclusive practices of resistance. One would have strategies interrupted by tactics, purposes interrupted by methods, and vice versa, so that which is the law and which the exception, which one dominant and which transgressive, which the theory and which the practice, could not be programmatically determined.

To conceive of critique as practice that makes a problem of its concept is to imagine a critical aferlife that is not just the new, more inclusive, insidious version of the same dull round. Not necessarily the dying into life accomplished by our discourses of crises and ends. Not the recuperation of critique by a narrative of its failure. It is more like Charles Bernstein's imagination of the different life that is lived after the narrative has reached conclusion. "They all lived happily ever after." End of narrative. The story, however, continues. What Bernstein means is that life goes on, happily, providing examples that never quite clinch the claim because you never know which is the last unit in the series, so you never know when the potential for the *un*happiness that would disprove the claim has been banished. This is critique imagined as more of the same, but because critique was always, by definition, a dismantling of "the same," an action carried out in unlike terms, so that the difference could not be added to the identity, could not make "more" of it, continuation proves to be, in this case, a different kind of difference. One could think of critique carried out under this anti-rule as examples awaiting the law that will reveal them as examples *of something.* Until that time, they are and are not examples, for what exactly is the status of an instance for which one cannot find the principle? Perhaps it becomes an example of anything and possibly everything—everything except nothing, that is. That was modernism's rule. Now I would like to give some examples.

1. Impenetrable writing, as in some work by the L-A-N-G-U-A-G-E poets and critics, where the effort is to make language a syntactic or a lexical chaos: a shutout. This writing composes an antigrammar minus the organized presentation of that anarchy, for that would turn it into antithesis. It wants to avoid generating another standard deviation, as in what Bruce Andrews calls the "old chest-busting negativism of the avant-garde."[33] The social signature of this work is that of the coterie or restricted language game, signifying withdrawal from the public sphere.

At the same time, one could observe (by way of radicalizing that L-A-N-G-U-A-G-E gesture) that the action of publishing these silent forms in places that, no matter how marginal, can become part of the loop, deprives that rejection of its categorial fixity. Is it a posture or a policy? Is it a means or an end? Is it the postmodern as commercial conservatism or radical resistance? In Fredric Jameson's terms, is it the Bonaventure Hotel or the Gehry House?

This is a technical response to the challenge of writing from the periphery or the interstices. How to do it without at the same time projecting an image of yourself doing it on the screen of interpretation that dissolves difference by representing it, letting the medium do the old, crude work of polemic? How to construct an apartness within a culture where making is automatically making visible, and visibility is entry into simulation? The special sort of productivism that characterizes our age easily digests the difference that was alienation.

My opinion is that there is no deep, logically grounded way to contain the thriving life of the afterlife of the philosophy of the subject, because depth, seriousness, and logical rigor are part and parcel of that discipline. Nor, however, should we rush to abandon that discipline with its commitment to rational autonomy and logical fulfillment as opposed to utopian transfiguration. The double gesture of silence and speech, hide and seek—the impure genre approach—*is* a technical and superficial response, but it also preserves, albeit in an ironic form, the logocentrism that it resists.

2. A related way for a critical practice to confound rather than contest the metalogic of our sign economies is by proliferating its presentments, themes, and references. By overcrowding the field of meaning, you effectively put all the meanings and the very meaning *of* meaning in question. Interpret anything and everything so that the act and its products lose their traditional cultural authority. What you want to avoid is the minimalism or blankness that characterized the negative way of modernist critique. That is a language game everyone knows how to win (and in this case, winning is losing). So, instead of that, use *over*production as a way of deflating the currency of meaning. The resurgence of interest in Joyce and Byron, the prolifics of their ages—or Blake, "Enough! or too much!"—is something to consider.

3. A book by Malcolm Ashmore, *The Reflexive Thesis: Wrighting Sociology of Scientific Knowledge.*[34] (I thank Barbara Herrnstein Smith for alerting me to this work.) "Wrighting" in the sense of (a) crafting, (b) inscribing, (c) steadying or correcting, meanings that both mesh and collide. The "thesis" of the title refers both to the fact that the text of the book is indeed, as signaled throughout, the author's doctoral thesis, and also that its thesis in the sense of argument is the reflexivity it exemplifies. (A sociohistorical critique would usefully observe that at one time the two meanings had an integral, practical unity: before, that is, the publication of the dissertation, that thoroughly situated and process-oriented exercise, became instrumental in the obtaining of tenure and had to be mystified accordingly, reframed as a singular "thought" or thesis: a spontaneous and self-justifying contribution to the march of ideas.) This is a book constructed in the manner of the Escher drawing that illustrates its cover: circuits of self-reflection, so rigorously pursued that the point of reflective departure (the subject-position) and the objectness of the topic dissolve. Once these two poles vanish, the discreteness of the procedures and performance, and the ratio of means to end melt away. Ashmore succeeds in avoiding the alternative positivity of the deconstructive method (the "counter" rationality it engenders) by anchoring his method to its highly particular, even unique institutional circumstances. This embeddedness is accomplished by arguments that are fashioned as scholarly and casual correspondence, as examination questions, as transcripts of lectures and the question-answer exchanges that follow. Does the book *present* (thematize, fictionalize, stylize) certain social acts, or is it just doing what comes naturally in certain academic circles but doing it onstage, which makes it unnatural. Various deformations of the logic of expository presentation (such as a section entitled "Final Entry" on page 85 of a 250-page book, and also on page 85 a section heading, "The Next Entry") help establish an

interesting but not really a valorized reflexivity. It is not as if they are the practice that illustrates the theory; you cannot tell which is which, and so you don't know what to do with the effects. Your attention as you read is increased, but to no obvious end, and thus the extra- or counter-disciplinary potential of that increased energy is kept alive. Somewhere, Wittgenstein speaks of value never belonging to the set of things that are valued. In Ashmore's book, value is put exactly there, inside the set, which means that it is and is not value. It withholds the expected dividend of metaconsciousness, of reflexivity as an intellectual and ethical value. It enacts a strictly hedonistic narcissism: not looking at yourself so as to realize, improve, extend, or empower yourself (and not to abstract the imago for symbolic and exchange purposes), but just looking for the pleasure of feeling yourself betwixt and between self and other, the body of sensation and the mirror-image: what used to be called "the pleasures of imagination."

4. Write the problem of representation and resistance as it informed a particular historical context and its culturally defining practices: Paul Mann in the moment of the avant-garde and the postmodern; T. J. Clark in the moment of Impressionism; Henry Louis Gates in the violently juxtaposed moments of Edmund Burke's prosecution of Governor Hastings (a major campaign in Burke's war against the ethos of Enlightenment); and Richard Wright's (surprising) brief for an Africa enlightened by European notions of progressive nationalism.[35] Each of these studies develops the historical and logical paradoxes so richly and clearly that the local emerges as a thoroughly reflected and legible field. However, the reading of that field as such—a zone delimited by reference to other zones and to the system that embraces them—is held in abeyance. Not dismissed, devalued, or declared impracticable: just not done. As a result, the particulars do not rise (or sink) to illustrate, instance, or even index the general. This is cognitive and even causal mapping but with the effect of destabilizing the categories of explanation. The authorial perspective is internal and external. (A visual analogy: the famous street and house map of Paris, where the graphic detail, indicating features far more ephemeral and contingent than the natural formations designated by ordinary maps, as well as the iconicity of the actual figures and designs fights against the indexical and abstract conventions of modern maps—a scalar dissonance.)

Another version of this thoroughgoing mediational practice: Houston Baker's work on rap, rape, and the nondialectical enfoldedness of urban planning and urban wildness, Wall Street and Harlem, monopolization of the entertainment industry and the figure of the black independent music producer.[36] Here the aesthetic and the economic, resistance and repression are situational artifacts, called forth by the critical act, which displays itself as part of that cultural reality.

5. The land-mine: plant the critique with user-triggered anomalies, similar to Stanley Fish's model of affective stylistics, where reader response is written into the script and manipulated so as to ironize the intentional structures of the work, creating parallel or differently coded texts within the same discourse. In the surprised-by-sin model, the ironies add up to a heresy. That counterinstruction is the safety net: the stable relation between well-defined and internally coherent positions. In the example I am imagining, one would have dissonance or inconsistency rather than contradiction or opposition. The integrity of both texts would suffer or change. Overall, the effect might resemble the deterritorialized writing that Deleuze constructs from the example of Kafka's fiction: an example of critique seeming to undergo a process of "becoming minor," perhaps becoming fiction, or more probably dissolving the distinction.[37] The effect is of pleasure, the pleasure of *coming* to know, as opposed to the finality of knowledge.

6. Cultivate artifice and extremity: an obsessional practice. Impose on the study-text so steadily that you call up a reaction from it and from the reader. Stretch a layer of thought over the surface and pull it so tight that the minute defects in the surface will show through, like the designs children make by chalk-rubbing any mildly uneven surface ("frottage").

7. The exercise: a hands-off, nonnarrative, informational display. Collect facts, beliefs, loosely revolving around an event or problem. Let the material "speak for itself": that is, allow the orders that speak through the materials and combinations to come through with less static than usual. Or let the arrangement speak with all the puzzling arbitrariness and intimation of pure design. The invented archive, reproduced, not indexed or narrativized: catalogue *irr*aisonné.

8. Assemble symmetrically incompatible facts, beliefs, accounts, and receptions, as in Jerome McGann's reading of the contested chapter arrangement in *The Ambassadors*.[38] McGann advances mutually exclusive but equally justified narratives of textual production, and with them, incommensurable hermeneutic possibilities.

A related practice: Louis Renza's paratactic method in *"A White Heron": The Question of Minor Literature*.[39] Renza offers the full transcript of the Sarah

Orne Jewett story and then, *specimens* of readings, no one of which can speak as a truth discourse because all are put forth as "kinds" rather than cases. The method engages attention without enthralling it. It imitates, or perhaps replicates, the canonical, formal, and rhetorical "minority" of the story it addresses — its thwarting of the *Voluptas* of literary production.

9. Critique on the model of self-consuming performance-art. Cornel West, for one: performing political theology.

10. Circulation of documents, characterized by time-lags, crossed messages, parallelism, divergence. The model here is definitely *not* dialogue, which evokes the Eden of orality, presence, the consensus of common language users. Instead, a writing exchange, where you edit and intervene in one another's work, breaching the boundaries of the scriptural and authorial entities but not blurring them into a composite text. E-mail criticism.

11. Framing: build a context that carries with it fairly determinate hermeneutic norms, or that codes certain affective responses. Present the focal text, the one that should serve to demonstrate the inscribed principles. Read in that text, read around it. Don't, however, *do* the reading or even coherently intimate it. Show it genuinely outflanking the semiotic apparatus. Show yourself not getting all you could out of the opportunity and not making a virtue (i.e., renunciation) from the restraint: E. Val Daniel, "Crushed Glass: A Counterpoint to Culture."[40]

12. Lateral critique, as against the verticality of hermeneutics, the tease of hidden depths, the privileging of a textual inwardness that tropes the writer's interiority and suggests an identical subject-object. This is critique as textual commentary in no way subordinate to the self-presence of the work. One might use the devices of marginalia, gloss, scholia, parallel texts, facing-page translations: the technical inventions of editors turned to cognitive use: Donald Ault's *Narrative Unbound*,[41] Alexander Kojève's *Hegel,* or antiquated and highly stylized representational formats: Spinoza's geometrical theorems; Talmudic commentary, Mishnah.

To close, I quote again from Michael Taussig:

> Yet I do not think, just as Hegel in his parable of the Master and the Slave did not think, that such scrutiny can be undertaken alone. To assume it could, would be to fly in the face of . . . the dependence of being on the other. . . . In invoking the presence of images of constructed Others, I have not tried to speak for them . . . [n]or have I made it my goal to contextualiz[e] and thereby "explain" them, whatever that might

mean. What I tried to allow is for their voices to create in the context of our hearing contradictory images, dialectical images . . . in which their attempts to redress the use of themselves as mnemonics for the vast project of building other selves . . . bring our own expectations and understandings to a momentary standstill.[42]

I believe that the moment of dialectical images, when they were pregnant with redemption, is past. And I believe that Taussig, despite the language of the passage above, would say the same. Taussig's phrase, "momentary standstill," is meant to invoke Benjamin's *Jetztzeit,* that shocking and liberating punctum in the bland continuum of history. What we have today, and I use Taussig's own metaphor, is a screen. On it are projected fantastic images, images of (for example) a map of the universe showing the holes where the different eras were imperfectly stitched together. These openings are Benjamin's momentary standstills, Gadamer's horizon warps, Wordsworth's spots of time, and the innumerable ideas of otherness that haunt our writing. In the movie I am invoking, Terry Gilliam's *The Time Bandits,* these openings permit whatever is human (and therefore dwarfed) to recover the riches created by other human agents and to steal those riches back from the master-thieves controlling the environment. We can see, however, that the openings open onto the movie screen, a solid surface, and behind that, the surface of the entertainment industry, and so on.

The regression may be infinite and/or circular, but it need not be perfect. I remind myself that it is a mistake, an idealism encouraged by the workings of ideology, to impute to the orders of things a seamless operation. A pragmatic materialism, Kenneth Burke's, cites the virtues of inefficiency, some of which I have explored in this paper. That would appear to be one avenue untried by the great critiques of reason that have guided the heterological and nondominative side of our practice. Not Benjamin's destructive character; not Bataille's radical Other to reason and consciousness; not the monstrous and inverted anti-body of Bakhtinian carnival; not the negativity of a nontriumphalist and micrological dialectics; not the Freudian or the political unconscious. Instead, the inevitable, but with respect to time, place, manner, and effects, unimaginable breakdowns in the machinery of representation.

And yet one wants to do more in the way of a materialist practice than just recognize these interruptions of our plans and masteries when they come. Further, there seems to me a difference between soliciting effects and logics that interfere with the tendential idealism of every philosophy of the subject, and that means every hermeneutic, no matter how radical its materialism, and suffering them. I cannot say just what this difference is.

Notes

1. Arkady Plotnitsky, *Reconfigurations: Critical Theory and General Economy* (Gainesville: University of Florida Press, 1993); David Bohm, *Causality and Chance in Modern Physics* (University Park: University of Pennsylvania Press, 1957).

2. Marjorie Levinson, "Romantic Poetry: The State of the Art," *MLQ* 54, no. 2 (June 1993): 183–214; "Pre- and Post-Dialectical Materialisms: Modeling Praxis without Subjects and Objects," *Cultural Critique* no. 31 (fall 1995): 111–28; "Object Loss and Object Bondage: Economies of Representation in Hardy's Poetry," Lecture, Johns Hopkins, 1996.

3. Philippe Lacoue-Labarthe, Jean-Luc Nancy, *The Literary Absolute: The Theory of Literature in German Romanticism*, trans. P. Barnard and C. Lester (Albany: SUNY Press, 1988).

4. Paul Mann, *Masocriticism*, forthcoming (Albany: SUNY Press, 1998).

5. Seyla Benhabib, *Critique, Norm, Utopia: A Study of the Foundations of Critical Theory* (New York: Columbia University Press, 1986).

6. J. M. Coetzee, *White Writing: On the Culture of Letters in South Africa* (New Haven: Yale University Press, 1988).

7. Michael Taussig, *The Nervous System* (New York: Routledge, 1992); *Mimesis and Alterity: A Particular History of the Senses* (New York: Routledge, 1993).

8. Anne Mack, J. J. Rome, and Georg Mannejc, "Literary History, Romanticism, and Felicia Hemans," *MLQ* 54, no. 2 (June 1993): 215–36 (Jerome McGann).

9. Paul Mann, *The Theory-Death of the Avant-Garde* (Bloomington: Indiana University Press, 1991), *Masocriticism*.

10. Alfred Schmidt, *The Concept of Nature in Marx*, trans. Ben Fowkes (London: New Left Books, 1971).

11. Fredric Jameson, *Fables of Aggression: Wyndham Lewis, the Modernist as Fascist* (Berkeley: University of California Press, 1979).

12. Jacques Lacan, *The Four Fundamental Concepts of Psycho-Analysis*, ed. Jacques Alain Miller, trans. Alan Sheridan (New York: Norton, 1981).

13. Jean-Francois Lyotard, "The Sublime and the Avant-Garde," trans. Lisa Liebmann, *Artforum* 22, part 8 (April 1984): 36–43; and *The Lyotard Reader*, ed. Andrew Benjamin (New York: Basil Blackwell, 1989).

14. Charles Bernstein, *A Poetics* (Cambridge: Harvard University Press, 1992); Bernstein quotes from Helen Vendler, who in turn borrows from Elizabeth Bishop's poem, "Poem" (*Geography* 3, 1976).

15. Bernstein, *A Poetics*; quoting from Steve McCaffery, "Writing as a General Economy" in *North of Intention: Critical Writings, 1973–1986* (Roof Books, 1986).

16. Theodor Adorno, *Negative Dialectics*, trans. E. B. Ashton (New York: Continuum, 1973); *Aesthetic Theory*, trans. C. Lenhardt, ed. Gretel Adorno and Rolf Tiedemann (Boston: Routledge and K. Paul, 1984).

17. Taussig, *Nervous System*.

18. I refer very schematically first to the decisive and ideologically marked shifts from absolutist to bourgeois regimes in the early nineteenth century. As we know, this emancipation entailed the reification and essentialization (i.e., mystification) of class, race, and gender, without which the exploitation of particular groups and the self-representation of the bourgeoisie as the universal and consummate class could

not have proceeded. A second flashpoint in that history: the demonization of those essentialized Others to the Western male bourgeois norm, peaking with the military-industrial nation-states of the mid-thirties through the sixties and their genocidal and quasi-colonial wars of attrition.

The special and highly visible compact between the advanced theoretical, technological, industrial, and social sciences of these eras and their peculiarly atavistic excesses led many students of the human sciences to search out the mystifying potentials of intellectual practices that had seemed in some absolute sense emancipatory. The reflexive turn was unavoidable; the critique of analytic reason (regarded as a subset of instrumental reason) entailed a more skeptical, more locally, topically, and politically attentive appraisal of the techniques and even the objectives of such classically liberatory and post- or even anti-Enlightenment exercises as ideology critique, social-historical reconstruction, and canonical intervention. What survives as a methodological point of departure is the question of immanence: Is the method immanent to its object when the object is understood to be the actuality of its social history up through the present of its interrogation?

19. James Kincaid, "Who Gets to Tell Their Stories?" May 3, 1992, *New York Times Book Review*, vol. 97, p. 1.

20. That is, a sort of cognitive and also recursive parallelism to our objects of study; *not* intersubjectivity, to be sure, and not mimesis; something rather on the order of Spinoza's double-aspect model of materialist explanation. See Levinson, "Pre- and Post-Dialectical Materialisms."

21. Bernstein, *A Poetics*.

22. Jonathan Crary and Sanford Kwinter, *Incorporation* (New York: Zone, 1992).

23. Ibid.

24. Adorno, *Negative Dialectics*.

25. Benhabib, *Critique, Norm, Utopia*.

26. Louis Althusser and Etienne Balibar, *Reading Capital*, trans. Ben Brewster (London: New Left Books, 1970); *Lenin and Philosophy and Other Essays*, trans. Ben Brewster (London: New Left Books, 1971). Althusser's discussion of the necessity for symptomatic reading may illuminate this paradox. He explains the existence of certain lapses and inconsistencies, a certain hollowness within particular discourses of knowledge as signs of a concept unable to be produced within the discourse that it founds and, in its present-absent or nonnormative way, *occupies*; see *Lenin and Philosophy*, 20–30.

27. Roland Barthes, *Mythologies*, trans. Annette Lavers (New York: Noonday Press, 1972).

28. Althusser and Balibar, *Reading Capital*.

29. Homi Bhabha, "Commitment to Theory," *New Formations* 5: 5–23.

30. Paul Mann, *The Theory-Death of the Avant-Garde*.

31. Michel de Certeau, *Heterologies: Discourse on the Other*, trans. Brian Massumi (Minneapolis: University of Minnesota Press, 1986); Julian Pefanis, *Heterology and the Postmodern: Bataille, Baudrillard, and Lyotard* (Durham: Duke University Press, 1991).

32. Donna Haraway, *Simians, Cyborgs, and Women: The Re-Invention of Nature* (London: Free Association Press, 1991); Peter Sloterdijk, *Critique of Cynical Reason*, trans. Michael Eldred (Minneapolis: University of Minnesota Press, 1987).

33. Bruce Andrews, "Text and Context," in *The L-A-N-G-U-A-G-E Book*, ed. Bruce Andrews and Charles Bernstein (Carbondale: Southern Illinois University Press, 1984).

34. Malcolm Ashmore, *The Reflexive Thesis: Wrighting Sociology of Scientific Knowledge* (Chicago: University of Chicago Press, 1989).

35. Mann, *Theory-Death*; T. J. Clark, *The Painting of Modern Life: Paris in the Art of Manet and his Followers* (Princeton: Princeton University Press, 1986); Henry Louis Gates, Richard Wright Lectures, University of Pennsylvania, spring 1990.

36. Houston Baker, "The Black Urban Beat: Rap and the Law," Public lecture; University of Michigan, spring 1991.

37. Gilles Deleuze, *Kafka: Toward a Minor Literature,* trans. Dana Polan (Minneapolis: University of Minnesota Press, 1986).

38. Jerome McGann, Textual Studies Conference, University of Michigan, spring 1991.

39. Louis Renza, *"A White Heron" and the Question of Minor Literature* (Madison: University of Wisconsin Press, 1984).

40. E. Valentine Daniel, "Crushed Glass: A Counterpoint to Culture," in *Charred Lullabies* (Princeton: Princeton University Press, 1996), and E. Valentine Daniel, "The Limits of Culture" in this volume.

41. Donald Ault, *Narrative Unbound: Re-Visioning William Blake's The Four Zoas* (Barrytown, NY: Station Hill Press, 1987).

42. Taussig, *Nervous System.*

Contributors

Lauren Berlant teaches English at the University of Chicago. She is the author of *The Anatomy of National Fantasy: Hawthorne, Utopia, and Everyday Life* and *The Queen of America Goes to Washington City: Essays on Sex and Citizenship*, as well as the editor of "Intimacy," a special issue of *Critical Inquiry*.

E. Valentine Daniel is professor of anthropology and director of the Southern Asian Institute at Columbia University. He is the author of *Fluid Signs: Being a Person the Tamil Way* and *Charred Lullabies: Chapters in an Anthropography of Violence*.

Nicholas B. Dirks is professor of anthropology and history at Columbia University. He is the author of *The Hollow Crown: Ethnohistory of an Indian Kingdom*, editor of *Colonialism and Culture*, coeditor of *Culture/Power/History: A Reader in Contemporary Cultural Theory*, and is completing a manuscript entitled "Castes of Mind: Anthropology, the Archive, and the Colonial History of India."

Marilyn Ivy is associate professor of anthropology at Columbia University. She is the author of *Discourses of the Vanishing: Modernity, Phantasm, Japan*. Her interests currently focus on criminality, bourgeois sensibility, and technologies of inscription in postwar Japan.

Robin D. G. Kelley is professor of history and African studies at New York University. He is the author of several books, most recently *Race Rebels:*

Culture, Politics, and the Black Working Class and *Yo' Mama's Disfunktional! Fighting the Culture Wars in Urban America.* He is currently writing a book on composer/pianist Thelonious Monk.

Laura Kipnis teaches in the Department of Radio-Television-Film at Northwestern University. Her most recent book is *Bound and Gagged: Pornography and the Politics of Fantasy in America.* She is also the author of *Ecstasy Unlimited: On Sex, Capital, Gender, and Aesthetics* (Minnesota, 1993).

Marjorie Levinson, F. L. Huetwell Professor of English, University of Michigan, is the author of several books on British Romantic-period poetry. Her recent writing has been more broadly based on problems in representation and resistance. Her current project is a study of poetic and critical materialisms, from Hardy through Elizabeth Bishop.

Gyanendra Pandey is professor of history at the University of Delhi. He is the author of *Ascendancy of the Congress in Uttar Pradesh* and *The Construction of Communalism in Colonial North India,* and is a member of the Subaltern Studies editorial collective.

John Pemberton is associate professor of anthropology at Columbia University, with interests in Indonesian studies, colonial historiography, cultural politics, and performance. He is the author of *On the Subject of "Java."* His current work concerns exorcism, temporality, and narrative speculations on the end of the Soeharto regime.

Adela Pinch is associate professor of English and women's studies at the University of Michigan. She is the author of *Strange Fits of Passion: Epistemologies of Emotion, Hume to Austen* and other articles on eighteenth- and nineteenth-century English culture.

Michael Taussig teaches anthropology at Columbia University and previously taught performance studies at New York University. His books include *The Magic of the State, Mimesis and Alterity, The Nervous System,* and *Shamanism, Colonialism, and the Wild Man: A Study in Terror and Healing.*

Index

Compiled by Pamila Gupta

297